T0251192

CONNECTIONIST-SYMBOLIC INTEGRATION

From Unified to Hybrid Approaches

CONNECTIONIST-SYMBOLIC INTEGRATION

From Unified to Hybrid Approaches

EDITED BY

Ron Sun
The University of Alabama
Tuscaloosa, AL, USA

Frederic Alexandre
CRIN-CNRS/Inria-Lorraine
Vandoeuvre-les-Nancy, France

Psychology Press
Taylor & Francis Group

New York London

First Published by
Lawrence Erlbaum Associates, Inc., Publishers
10 Industrial Avenue
Mahwah, New Jersey 07430

Transferred to Digital Printing 2009 by Psychology Press
270 Madison Ave, New York NY 10016
27 Church Road, Hove, East Sussex, BN3 2FA

Copyright © 1997 by Lawrence Erlbaum Associates, Inc.
All rights reserved. No part of this book may be reproduced
in any form, by photostat, microform, retrieval system, or any
other means, without the prior written permission of
the publisher.

Library of Congress Cataloging-in-Publication Data

Connectionist-symbolic integration : from unified to hybrid approaches
/ edited by Ron Sun, Frederic Alexandre.
  p. cm.
Includes bibliographical references and index.
ISBN 0-8058-2348-4 (cloth : alk. paper). -- ISBN 0-8058-2349-2
(pbk. : alk. paper)
  1. Hybrid computers. 2. Systems engineering. 3. Neural networks
(Computer science) I. Sun, Ron, 1960-   . II. Alexandre,
Frederic.
QA76.38.C66   1997
006.3--dc21   97-30217
                                                        CIP

Publisher's Note
The publisher has gone to great lengths to ensure the quality of this reprint
but points out that some imperfections in the original may be apparent.

CONTENTS

PREFACE

This book is concerned with the development, analysis, and application of hybrid connectionist-symbolic models in artificial intelligence and cognitive science, drawing contributions from an international group of leading experts. It describes and compares a variety of models in this area. The types of models described in this book cover a wide range of the evolving spectrum of hybrid models. Thus, it serves as a well-balanced progress report on the state of the art in this area. We hope that it will also stimulate its future development.

This book is the outgrowth of *The IJCAI Workshop on Connectionist-Symbolic Integration: From Unified to Hybrid Approaches*, which was held for two days during August 19-20 in Montreal, Canada, in conjunction with the Fourteenth International Joint Conference on Artificial Intelligence (IJCAI'95). The workshop was co-chaired by Ron Sun and Frederic Alexandre. It featured 23 presentations, including two invited talks, and two panel discussions. During the two days of the workshop, various presentations and discussions brought to light many new ideas, controversies, and syntheses, which lead to the present volume.

We hereby wish to thank all the participants of the workshop for their contributions that lead to the present book. We expecially would like to thank the members of the program and organization committees who reviewed papers or in other ways helped the organization of the workshop: John Barnden, Steve Gallant, Larry Medsker, Christian Pellegrini, Noel Sharkey, Lawrence Bookman, Michael Dyer, Wolfgang Ertel, LiMin Fu, Jose Gonzalez-Cristobal, Ruben Gonzalez-Rubio, Jean-Paul Haton, Melanie Hilario, Abderrahim Labbi, and Ronald Yager. We thank the two invited speakers at the workshop: Jim Hendler and Noel Sharkey, as well as each of the panelists. We also thank the editors at Lawrence Erlbaum Associates for their part in producing this book.

CONTRIBUTORS

Frederic Alexandre
Crin-Cnrs/Inria-Lorraine
BP 239
54500 Vandoeuvre-les-Nancy, France
falex@loria.fr

Bernard Amy
LEIBNIZ
46 ave Felix Viallet
38031 Grenoble
France

Jim Austin
Dept. of CS
University of York
York, YO1 5 DD, UK
austin@minster.york.ac.uk

Haihong Dai
Department of Computer Science
Queen's University of Belfast
Belfast BT7 1NN, UK
h.dai@qub.ac.uk

Jose C. Gonzalez
Dep. Ingenieria de Sistemas Telematicos
E.T.S.I. Telecomunicacion
Universidad Politecnica de Madrid
E-28040 Madrid, Spain
jcg@gsi.dit.upm.es

Melanie Hilario
Centre Universitaire d'Informatique
University of Geneva
24, rue du General Dufour
CH-1211 Geneva 4, Switzerland
hilario@cui.unige.ch

Carlos A. Iglesias
Dep. Teoria de la Senal, Comunicaciones e Ing. Telematica
E.T.S.I. Telecomunicacion
Universidad de Valladolid
E–47011 Valladolid, Spain
cif@tel.uva.es

Todd Johnson
Ohio State Univ.
Medical Informatics
Columbus, OH 43210
tj@medinfo.ohio-state.edu

Rajiv Khosla
Expert and Intelligent Systems Laboratory
Department of Computer Science and Computer Engineering
La Trobe University
Melbourne, Victoria 3083, Australia
khosla@latcs1.lat.oz.au

Boicho Kokinov
Institute of Mathematics
Bulgarian Academy of Sciences
Bl.8, Acad. G. Bonchev Str.
Sofia 1113, Bulgaria
kokinov@bgearn.bitnet

Ramon Krosley
Dept. MCS
Colarado School of Mines
Golden, CO 80401
rkrosley@mines.colorado.edu

Abderrahim Labbi
Department of Computer Science
University of Geneva
24, Rue du General Dufour CH-1211
Geneve 4
Switzerland
labbi@cui.unige.ch

Yannick Lallement
Crin-Cnrs/Inria-Lorraine
BP 239
54500 Vandoeuvre-les-Nancy, France
lallement@loria.fr

Luis Magdalena
Dep. Matematica Aplicada
E.T.S.I. Telecomunicacion
Universidad Politecnica de Madrid
E-28040 Madrid, Spain
llayos@mat.upm.es

Maria Malek
LEIBNIZ
46, ave Felix Viallet
38031 Grenoble
France
maria.malek@imag.fr

Michael McTear
School of Information & Software Engineering
University of Ulster at Jordanstown
Newtownabbey
County Antrim BT37 0QB, UK
m.mctear@ulster.ac.uk

Manavendra Misra
Dept of Mathematical and Computer
Sciences
Colorado School of Mines
Golden, CO 80401
mmisra@mines.edu

Eric Mjolsness
Machine Learning Systems Group
Jet Propulsion Laboratory, Caltech
4800 Oak Grove Drive
Pasadena, CA 91109

Piyush Ojha
School of Information & Software Engineering
University of Ulster at Jordanstown
Newtownabbey
County Antrim BT37 0QB, UK
p.ojha@ulster.ac.uk

Bruno Orsier
Lab for Artificial Brain Systems
The Institute for Physical and Chemical Research (RIKEN)
Hirosawa 2-1, Wako-shi, Saitama 351-01,
Japan
orsier@zoo.riken.go.jp

Nam Seog Park
Department of Artificial Intelligence
University of Edinburgh
80 South Bridge
Edinburgh, EH1 1HN UK.
namseog@aisb.ed.ac.uk

Todd Peterson
Department of Computer Science
The University of Alabama
Tuscaloosa, AL 35487
todd@cs.ua.edu

Tony Plate
School of Mathematical and Computing Sciences
Victoria University of Wellington
PO Box 600, Wellington, New Zealand
TonyPlate@vuw.ac.nz

Dave Robertson
Department of Artificial Intelligence
University of Edinburgh
80 South Bridge
Edinburgh, EH1 1HN UK.
dr@dai.ed.ac.uk

Jose C. Gonzalez
Universidad Politecnica de Madrid
Dept Ingenieria de Sistemas Telematicos
ETSI Telecomunicacion
Cuidad Universitaria
E-28040 Madrid, Spain
jgonzalez@dit.upm.es

Alessandro Sperduti
University of Pisa
Dipartimento di Informatica
Corso Italia 40
56125 Pisa, Italy
perso@di.unipi.it

Antonio Starita
University of Pisa
Dipartimento di Informatica
Corso Italia 40
56125 Pisa, Italy
starita@di.unipi.it

Suzanne Stevenson
Department of Computer Science
Center for Cognitive Science
CORE Bldg, Busch Campus
Rutgers University
New Brunswick, NJ 08903
suzanne@cs.rutgers.edu

Ron Sun
Department of Computer Science
Department of Psychology
The University of Alabama
Tuscaloosa, AL 35487
rsun@cs.ua.edu

Juan R. Velasco
Dep. Ingenieria de Sistemas Telematicos
E.T.S.I. Telecomunicacion
Universidad Politecnica de Madrid
E-28040 Madrid, Spain
juanra@gsi.dit.upm.es

Xinyu Wu
School of Information & Software Engineering
University of Ulster at Jordanstown
Newtownabbey
County Antrim BT37 0QB, UK
w.xinyu@ulster.ac.uk

Jiajie Zhang
Ohio State University
Dept of Psychology
Columbus, Ohio 43210
zhang@canyon.psy.ohio-state.edu

1

AN INTRODUCTION TO HYBRID CONNECTIONIST-SYMBOLIC MODELS

Ron Sun

Department of Computer Science
The University of Alabama

1 MOTIVATIONS

There has been a considerable amount of research in integrating connectionist and symbolic processing. While such an approach has clear advantages, it also encounters serious difficulties and challenges. Consequently, various ideas and models have been proposed to address different problems and different aspects in this integration. The need for such models has been slowly but steadily growing over the past five years, from many segments of the artificial intelligence and cognitive science communities, ranging from expert systems to cognitive modeling and to logical reasoning. Some interesting and important approaches have been developed. There has been a general consensus that hybrid connectionist-symbolic models constitute a promising avenue toward developing more robust, more powerful, and more versatile architectures, both for cognitive modeling and for intelligent systems. It is definitely worthwhile pursuing research in this area further still, which might generate important new ideas and significant new applications.

The basic motivations for research in hybrid connectionist-symbolic models can be briefly summarized as follows:

- Cognitive processes are not homogeneous; a wide variety of representations and mechanisms are employed. Some parts of cognitive processes are best captured by symbolic models, while others by connectionist models (Smolensky 1988, Sun 1995). Therefore, a need for "pluralism" exists in cognitive modeling, which leads to the development of hybrid models as tools and frameworks.

1

■   The development of intelligent systems for practical applications can benefit greatly from a proper combination of different techniques, since no one single technique can do everything, as is the case in many application domains, ranging from bank loan approval to industrial process control (Medsker 1994). By combining different techniques, intelligent systems can explore the synergy of these techniques.

■   To develop a full range of capabilities in autonomous agents, an autonomous agent architecture needs to incorporate both symbolic and subsymbolic processing for handling declarative and procedural knowledge, respectively, in order to effectively deal with a variety of environments in which an agent finds itself (Sun and Peterson 1995). Such an agent architecture, incorporating both conceptual and subconceptual processes, leads naturally to a combination of symbolic models (which capture conceptual processes) and connectionist models (which capture subconceptual processes).

The book tries to bring to light many new ideas, controversies, and syntheses in this broad area. The focus is on learning and architectures that feature hybrid representations and support hybrid learning.

2   IMPORTANT ISSUES

There have been many important and/or crucial issues that have been raised with regard to hybrid connectionist-symbolic models. These issues concern architectures of these models, learning in these models, and various other aspects.

Hybrid models involve a variety of different types of processes and representations, in both learning and performance. Therefore, multiple mechanisms interact in complex ways in most of these models. We need to consider seriously ways of structuring these different components; in other words, we need to consider *architectures*, which thus occupy a clearly more prominent place in this area of research compared with other areas in AI. Some architecture-related issues are as follows:

■   What type of architecture facilitates what type of process?

■   Should hybrid architectures be modular or monolithic?

- For modular architectures, should we use different representations in different modules of an architecture or should we use the same representation throughout?

- How do we decide if a particular part of an architecture should be symbolic, localist, or distributed in its representation?

- How do we structure different representations in different parts to achieve optimal results?

- How do we incorporate prior knowledge into hybrid architectures?

Although purely connectionist models, which constitute a part of any hybrid model, are known to excel in their learning abilities, hybridization makes it more difficult to do learning. Most symbolic models and architectures are not specifically designed to perform learning, especially not in a fully autonomous and bottom-up fashion, and most of them have difficulties with learning in some ways. Therefore, the hybridization of connectionist and symbolic models inherits the difficulty of learning from the symbolic side and mitigates to some large extent the advantage that the purely connectionist models have in their learning abilities. Considering the importance of learning in both modeling cognition and building intelligent systems, it is crucial for researchers in this area to pay more attention to ways of enhancing hybrid models in this regard and to putting learning back into hybrid models. Some of the learning-related issues that need to be addressed include:

- How can learning be incorporated and utilized in each type of architecture?

- What kinds of learning can be done in each type of architecture, respectively?

- How do learning and representation interact along the developmental line?

- What is the relationship between symbolic machine learning methods, knowledge acquisition methods, and connectionist (neural network) learning algorithms, especially in the context of hybrid models?

- How can each type of architecture be developed with various combinations of the above-mentioned methods?

- How can learning algorithms be developed for (usually knowledge-based) localist connectionist networks?

1. single-module	
* representation	symbolic, localist, distributed
* mapping	direct translational, transformational
2. heterogeneous multi-module	
* components	localist+distributed, symbolic+connectionist
* coupling	loosely coupled, tightly coupled
* granularity	coarse-grained, fine-grained
3. homogeneous multi-module	
* granularity	coarse-grained, fine-grained

Figure 1   Classifications of Hybrid Models

- How can rules be extracted from, and refined by, (hybrid) connectionist models?

- How can complex symbolic structures besides rules, such as frames and semantic networks, be learned in hybrid connectionist models?

3 ARCHITECTURES

In terms of architectures of hybrid models, various distinctions, divisions, and classifications have been proposed and discussed. (see chapter 2). As a first cut, we can divide these models up into two broad categories: *single-module* architectures and *multi-module* architectures (including both homogeneous and heterogeneous multi-module architectures). See Figure 1.

For single-module architectures, along the *representation* dimension, there can be the following types of representations (see Sun and Bookman 1994): symbolic (as in conventional symbolic models, in which case, the model is no longer a hybrid model), localist (with one distinct node for representing each concept; for example, Lange and Dyer 1989, Sun 1992, Shastri and Ajjanagadde 1993, Barnden 1994), and distributed (with a set of non-exclusive, overlapping nodes for representing each concept; for example, Pollack 1990, Sharkey 1991). Usually, it is easier to incorporate prior knowledge into localist models since their structures can be made to directly correspond to that of symbolic knowledge (Fu 1991). On the other hand, connectionist learning usually leads to distributed representation, such as in the case of backpropagation learning. Along a different dimension, in terms of *mappings* between symbolic and connectionist structures (Hilario 1995, Medsker 1994), we see that there are the direct translational approach, which creates a network structure that directly corresponds to the symbolic structure to be implemented (usually in a localist network), such as in the implementation of rules in a backpropagation network by Fu (1991) and Towell and Shavlik (1993), and the transformational approach, which creates the equivalent of symbolic structures in connectionist networks without actually embedding the structures directly in networks, such as the encoding of trees in RAAM (Pollack 1990). The relative advantage of each is a still unsettled issue (which is related to the compositionality issue as being debated in the theoretical community). Another possible dimension is in terms of the *dynamics* of the models, rather than in terms of the static topology (i.e., the static mapping) of the networks used; that is, we can classsify models based on whether their internal dynamics is translational or transformational, which can be highly correlated with but not necessarily identical to the static topology of networks.

For multi-module models, we can distinguish between *homogeneous* models and *heterogeneous* models. Homogeneous models may be very much like a single-module model discussed above, except they contain several replicated copies of the same underlying structure, each of which can be used for processing the same set of inputs, to provide redundancy for various reasons. For example, we can have competing experts (of the same domain), each of which may vote for a particular solution. Or, each module (of the same makeup) can be specialized (content-wise) for processing a particular type of input or another; for example, we can have different experts with the same structure and representation but different content/knowledge for dealing with different situations.

For heterogeneous multi-module models, a variety of distinctions can be made. First of all, a distinction can be made in terms of *representations* of constituent modules. In multi-module models, there can be different combinations of different types of constituent modules: for example, a model can be a combination of localist and distributed modules (for example, CONSYDERR as described in Sun 1995, for cognitive modeling of commonsense reasoning and decision making), or it can be a combination of symbolic modules and connectionist modules (either localist or distributed; for example, SCRUFFY as described in Hendler 1991, mainly for practical applications).

Another distinction that can be made is in terms of the *coupling* of modules: a set of modules can be either loosely coupled or tightly coupled (Medsker 1994). In loosely coupled situations, modules communicate with each other, primarily through some interfaces as in, for example, SCRUFFY (Hendler 1991). Such loose coupling enables some loose forms of cooperation among modules. One form of cooperation is in terms of pre/postprocessing vs. main processing: while one or more modules take care of pre/postprocessing, such as transforming input data or rectifying output data, a main module focuses on the main part of the processing task. This is probably the simplest and earliest form for hybrid systems, in which, commonly, pre/post processing is done using a connectionist network and the main task is accomplished through the use of symbolic methods (as in conventional expert systems). Another form of cooperation is through master-slave relationships: while one module maintains control of the task at hand, it can call upon other modules to handle some specific aspects of the task. For example, a symbolic expert system, as part of a rule, may invoke a neural network to perform a specific classification or decision making or some other processing. A variation of this form is the processor-monitor (meta-processor) combination, in which a processing module does the work while a monitor module waits for certain events to occur in which case the monitor will inform and/or alter the working of the processing module. Yet another form of cooperation is the equal partnership of multiple modules. In this form, the modules (the equal partners) can consist of (1) complementary processes, such as in the SOAR/ECHO combination (see chapter 6), or (2) multiple functionally equivalent but representationally different processes, such as in the CLARION architecture (chapter 7), or (3) they may consist of multiple differentially specialized and heterogeneously represented experts each of which constitutes an equal partner in accomplishing the task. [1]

In tightly coupled systems, on the other hand, the constituent modules interact through multiple channels or may even have node-to-node connections across two modules, such as CONSYDERR (Sun 1995) in which each node in one module is connected to a corresponding node in the other module. For tightly coupled multi-module systems, there are also a variety of different forms of cooperation among modules, in ways quite similar to loosely coupled systems. Such forms include master-slave, processor-monitor, and equal partnership, each of which is basically the same as in loosely coupled systems, except in this case a larger number of connections exist and a lot more interactions are occuring among modules. However, another possibility in loosely coupled systems, i.e., pre/post-processing, is not one of the possibilities with tightly coupled systems, since it entails loose connections between the pre/post-processing module and the main processing modules.

---

[1] These forms have been referred to as *subprocessing, metaprocessing,* and *coprocessing* in chapter 2.

Another distinction that can be made of all multi-module systems is with regard to the *granularity* of modules in such systems: they can be coarse-grained or fine-grained. On one end of the spectrum, a multi-module system can be very coarse-grained so that it contains only two or three modules. On the other end of the spectrum, a system can be so fine-grained that it can contain numerous modules, such as the case in DUAL (see Kokinov 1995; see also chapters 11 and 12). Sometimes, in an extremely fine-grained system, each tiny module may contain both a (simple and tiny) symbolic component and a (simple and tiny) connectionist component. Such a form is termed "micro-level" integration of symbolic and connectionist models (by Kokinov 1995), as opposed to "macro-level" integration in which each module is much more powerful and complete and contains one type of model only. The advantage of such "micro-level" integration, computationally speaking, is that we can have a vast number of simple "processors" (i.e., fine-grained integrated modules) that constitute a uniform and massively parallel system that combines the power of connectionist as well as symbolic models. Such a system, in a way, is a homogeneous system in the sense discussed earlier.

4 LEARNING

One fundamental issue that clearly requires more attention from researchers in this area has been highlighted in this book: the issue of learning, which includes both learning the content/knowledge of an architecture as well as learning and developing the architectures themselves. Learning is necessary, both because it is a fundamental process of intelligence/cognition, and because it is practically indispensable in scaling up to large-scale systems.

Looking back to the proceedings of earlier meetings, earlier collections of papers, and/or earlier special issues of journals dealing with hybrid models, such as Hinton (1991), Sun et al. (1992), and Sun and Bookman (1994), the treatment of learning has been sparse. Many models were presented as simply representational ones: that is, a framework in which both symbolic and connectionist knowledge can coexist and can be represented in some ways, but not necessarily acquired automatically. The earlier workshop on this topic, as reported in Sun et al. (1992), was almost exclusively focused on representational issues. Such a focus might be justified at the early stage of development of this research area, since before we can learn complex symbolic representation in connectionist and hybrid connectionist models, we need to figure out ways of representing complex symbolic structures in the first place.

In Sun and Bookman (1994), the following question was raised:

> How can more powerful learning algorithms be developed that can
> acquire complex symbolic representation in connectionist systems, in-
> cluding localist systems? This is a difficult issue, in that simple learn-
> ing algorithms that build up functional mappings in typical neural
> network models are insufficient for symbolic processing connectionist
> networks, because of the discrete and discontinuous nature of symbolic
> processes and because of the systematicity of such processes. Newer
> and more powerful learning algorithms are needed that can extract
> symbolic structures from data and/or through interaction with envi-
> ronments. ...... Such algorithms should somehow incorporate some
> symbolic methods, as more powerful learning algorithms will result
> from such incorporation. (see p.9, Sun and Bookman 1994.)

Now, after a number of years of maturation, the hybrid model area is ready to
take on the real challenge of learning: not only of simple procedural skills, but
also of complex symbolic structures, and even of architectures themselves. Such
learned representations should be linked closely to the context of their use, not
as a stand-alone showcase of the "power" of a particular learning method.

A number of chapters in this book deal with the issue of learning, each to a different extent. Chapter 6 presents a model for abductive reasoning that learns
its internal representation through a combination of symbolic and connectionist
methods, aimed at cognitive modeling. Chapter 18 shows how RAAM (Pollack
1990) can be extended to deal with the learning of logical term classification in
symbolic reasoning. Chapter 7 (also Sun and Peterson 1995) presents a model
for learning sequential decision making in which symbolic declarative knowledge is extracted online from a reinforcement learning connectionist network
and is used in turn to speed up learning and to facilitate transfer. Thus, it
demonstrates not only the synergy between connectionist and symbolic learning but also the point that symbolic knowledge can be learned autonomously
in a bottom-up fashion, which is very useful in developing autonomous agents.

The future advance in this area is dependent on the progress in the development
of new learning methods in hybrid systems and the integration of learning
with complex symbolic representations. As was suggested in some chapters
here, symbolic representation and reasoning may well emerge from subsymbolic
processes, and a synergistic combination of symbolic and subsymbolic processes
is thus possible (see chapter 7 and also Giles et al. 1995).

5 SUMMARY

In summary, a variety of ideas, approaches, and techniques exist, in terms of both architectures and learning, and this abundance seems to lead to many exciting possibilities in theoretical advances (for example, in learning and knowledge acquisition) and in application potentials. We need to extend more effort to exploit the possibilities and opportunities in this area.

Despite the apparant diversity, there is clearly an underlying unifying theme: architectures that bring together symbolic and connectionist models to achieve a synthesis and the synergy of the two different paradigms (and the learning and knowledge acquisition methods for developing such architectures). With this book, we hope to provide an information clearinghouse for various proposed approaches and models that share the common belief that connectionist and symbolic models can be usefully combined and integrated, and such integration may lead to significant advances in our understanding of intelligence.

REFERENCES

[1] J. Barnden, (1994). Complex symboli-processing in CONPOSIT. In: R. Sun and L.Bookman, (eds.) *Computational Architectures Integrating Neural and Symbolic Processes.* Kluwer. Boston, MA.

[2] L.M. Fu, (1991). Rule learning by searching on adapted nets, *Proc. of AAAI'91*, pp. 590-595.

[3] C.L. Giles, B.G. Horne, and T. Lin, (1995). Learning a class of large finite state machines with a recurrent neural network. *Neural Networks*, vol.8, no.9, pp. 1359-1365.

[4] J. Hendler, (1991). Developing hybrid symbolic/connectionist models. In: J. Barnden and J. Pollack (eds.), *Advances in Connectionist and Neural Computation Theory*, pp. 165–179. Lawrence Erlbaum Assocciates. Hillsdale, NJ.

[5] M. Hilario, (1995). An overview of strategies for neurosymbolic integration. In: R. Sun and F. Alexandre, (eds.) *Connectionist-Symbolic Integration: From Unified to Hybrid Approaches.* IJCAI, Montreal, Canada.

[6] J. Hinton, (1991). *Connectionist Symbolic Processing: A Special Issue Of Artificial Intelligence.* MIT Press. Cambridge, MA.

[7] T. Johnson and J. Zhang, (1995). A hybrid learning model of abductive reasoning. In: R. Sun and F. Alexandre, (eds.) *Connectionist-Symbolic Integration: From Unified to Hybrid Approaches.* IJCAI, Montreal, Canada.

[8] B. Kokinov, (1995). Micro-level hybridization in DUAL. In: R. Sun and F. Alexandre, (eds.) *Connectionist-Symbolic Integration: From Unified to Hybrid Approaches.* IJCAI, Montreal, Canada.

[9] T. Lange and M. Dyer, (1989). High-level inferencing in a connectionist network. *Connection Science,* 1, pp. 181–217.

[10] L. Medsker, (1994). *Hybrid Neural Networks and Expert Systems.* Kluwer. Boston, MA.

[11] J. Pollack, (1990). Recursive distributed representation. *Artificial Intelligence.* 46 (1-2). pp. 77-106.

[12] N. Sharkey, (1991). Connectionist representation techniques. *AI Review,* 5. pp. 142-167.

[13] L. Shastri and V. Ajjanagadde, (1993). From simple associations to systematic reasoning: A connectionist representation of rules, variables and dynamic bindings. *Behavioral and Brain Sciences,* 16(3). pp. 417-494.

[14] P. Smolensky, (1988). On the proper treatment of connectionism. *Behavorial and Brain Sciences,* 11(1). pp. 1-74.

[15] R. Sun, (1992). On Variable Binding in Connectionist Networks, *Connection Science,* Vol.4, No.2, pp. 93-124.

[16] R. Sun, (1995). Robust reasoning: integrating rule-based and similarity-based reasoning. *Artificial Intelligence.* 75. pp. 241-295.

[17] R. Sun and T. Peterson, (1995). A hybrid learning model for sequential decision making. *The IJCAI Workshop on Connectionist-Symbolic Integration: From Unified to Hybrid Approaches.* IJCAI, Montreal, Canada.

[18] R. Sun and L. Bookman, (eds.) (1994). *Computational Architectures Integrating Neural and Symbolic Processes.* Kluwer Academic Publishers. Boston, MA.

[19] R. Sun, L Bookman, and S. Shekhar, (1992). *The Working Notes of the AAAI Workshop on Integrating Neural and Symbolic Processes: The Cognitive Dimension.* San Jose, CA.

[20] G. Towell and J. Shavlik, (1993). Extracting Refined Rules from Knowledge-Based Neural Networks, *Machine Learning.*

PART I

REVIEWS AND OVERVIEWS

2

AN OVERVIEW OF STRATEGIES FOR NEUROSYMBOLIC INTEGRATION

Mélanie Hilario

Computer Science Center
University of Geneva

1 INTRODUCTION

Throughout its brief history, the field of artificial intelligence (AI) has been the arena of jousts between two *frères ennemis*, symbolicism and connectionism. No sooner had connectionism recovered from Minsky and Papert's (1988) devastating blows than Fodor and Pylyshyn (1988) charged to the fore in the name of symbolic AI. They argued that connectionism cannot be a valid theory of cognition since it fails to account for the combinatorial syntactic and semantic structure of mental representations; at best, connectionism is just another implementation technology, an alternative means of implementing classical symbolic structures and processes. This implementationalist viewpoint has since been the traditional defense of symbolic AI against connectionism's cognitive claims. At the other extreme, according to Pinker and Prince's (1988) classification, eliminativism rejects the symbol level as a valid level of description of cognitive phenomena; symbolic theories are no more than crude approximations of what really takes place in the brain and must give way to connectionist or neural theories.

Between these two radical stances, a number of more subtle philosophies have emerged at the interface of connectionist and symbolic AI. Their origins have been inextricably linked with the proliferation of attempts at integrating neural and symbolic processing. This paper will give an overview of the various approaches to neurosymbolic integration. Roughly, these can be divided into two strategies: *unified* strategies aim at attaining neural and symbolic capabilities using neural networks alone, while *hybrid* strategies combine neural networks with symbolic models such as expert systems, case-based reasoning systems,

13

and decision trees. These two approaches form the main subtrees of the classification hierarchy depicted in Figure 1.

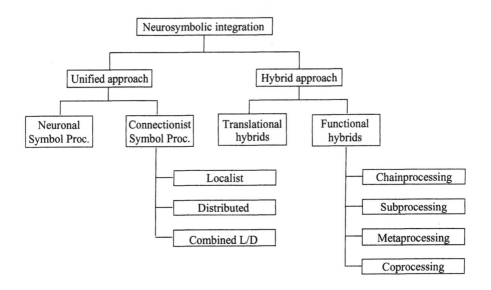

Figure 1   Classification of integrated neurosymbolic systems.

This chapter is organized as follows. Sections 2 and 3 discuss unified and hybrid strategies respectively; [1]. Section 4 relates these strategies to the various philosophical stances that have been observed in the literature vis-a-vis the relationship between connectionist and symbolic processing. Section 5 explores the major computational issues involved in neurosymbolic integration and Section 6 concludes.

2   UNIFIED STRATEGIES

Unified strategies are premised on the claim that there is no need for symbolic structures and processes as such; full symbol processing functionalities emerge from neural structures and processes alone. They can be subdivided into two distinct trends: neuronal symbol processing and connectionist (or neural) symbol processing. This distinction is based on Reeke and Edelman's (1988) ter-

---

[1] This overview does not include fuzzy-neural integration strategies, which are discussed in chapter 5 of this volume

minological convention, according to which the term *neuronal* denotes a close identification with the properties of actual (biological) neurons whereas *neural* implies only a general similarity to actual neurons.

2.1   Neuronal Symbol Processing

The neuronal approach aims at grounding all cognitive processes in biological reality. One particular case of this approach is neuronal symbol processing (NSP), whose specific objective is to model the brain's high-level functions. The neuronal approach is a bottom-up approach: its mandatory starting point is the biological neuron. Perhaps the most brilliant example of the neuronal approach is the theory of neuronal group selection (TNGS), better known as neural Darwinism (Edelman 1987). Built on three fundamental tenets—developmental selection, experiential selection and reentrant mapping—this theory attempts to provide a biological account of the full range of cognitive phenomena, from sensorimotor responses all the way up to concept formation, language, and higher order consciousness. The consistency of the TNGS has been demonstrated in a series of automata which avoid the preestablished categories and programming of standard AI. Constructed as networks of neuronlike units undergoing a process of natural selection, these automata carry out categorization and association tasks in a dynamic environment. In Darwin III (Edelman 1992), for example, recognition and categorization networks are combined with motor circuits and effectors that act on the environment. Objects are categorized on the basis of internal values like "light is better than no light"; the result of the automaton's neuronal activity becomes apparent as motor responses to categorized objects. The processes demonstrated in these automata—perceptual categorization, memory and learning—are precisely the fundamental triad of higher order brain functions, according to the TNGS. However, effective emergence of these higher level functions remains to be demonstrated in the Darwin or its descendant series. Neuronal symbol processing may yet be the ultimate proof-of-concept of the neuronal approach; however, the field is as immature as its ambitions are high, and it may take some time before real-world applications can even be envisaged.

2.2   Connectionist Symbol Processing

Connectionist symbol processing (CSP) or neural symbol processing lays no claim to neurobiological plausibility; the neuron in question here is generally a formal neuron. Artificial neural networks are used as building blocks to create a cognitive architecture capable of complex symbol processing. Typically, model construction starts with an idea of some high-level symbolic function to be performed and proceeds with the design of the appropriate connectionist infrastructure. In this sense, the neural approach can be thought of as a top-down strategy, despite the opposite thrust of its claim that complex symbolic functions emerge from neural structures and processes. However, CSP is not inherently top-down: in principle, nothing precludes it from actually starting out with neural networks from which non-predetermined symbolic structures and processes can emerge in unforeseen ways.

Historically, Fodor and Pylyshyn's (1988) critique has been a significant if negative driving force behind CSP: one of its persistent motivations has been to show that neural networks exhibit a combinatorial constituent structure—precisely what Fodor and Pylyshyn declared wanting in connectionist architectures. For instance, BoltzCONS is a connectionist model that dynamically creates and manipulates linked lists; according to its author, its aim is not just to implement complex symbol structures using neural networks, but rather to show how neural networks can exhibit compositionality and distal access, two distinguishing properties of high-level symbol processing (Touretzky 1990).

Work in connectionist symbol processing can be classified along two dimensions. From the point of view of the underlying representation scheme, CSP architectures can be localist, distributed, or combined localist/distributed. Localist architectures use a one-to-one mapping between individual units and symbolic structures. Each node in a neural network represents a concept or a combination of concepts, e.g., a two-place predicate, a relation, a rule (Shastri 1988, Ajjanagadde and Shastri 1991, Sohn and Gaudiot 1991, Lange 1992, Feldman and Ballard 1992). The principal disadvantage of localist architectures is that they quickly succumb to combinatorial explosion as the number of individual concepts increases. This has motivated the development of distributed architectures, where the most elementary concepts emerge from the interaction of several different nodes. Each knowledge item (e.g., concept, fact or rule) is represented using a combination of several units, and each unit can be used in the representation of several items. DCPS (Touretzky and Hinton, 1988), for example, is a distributed connectionist production system that uses coarse coding to store all entities manipulated by the rule interpreter. Each unit has a receptive field that is the cross-product of the six symbols in each of its three colums, given 216 triples per field. As a result, this distributed coding scheme can be used to construct a working memory that requires far fewer units than the number of facts that can potentially be stored. Coarse coding is also used in BoltzCONS (Touretzky 1990) to represent symbolic structures such as lists and stacks, whereas recursive distributed representations introduced in

Pollack's (1990) RAAM have been used to implement tree-matching (Stolcke and Wu, 1992). Finally, local/distributed architectures combine systems using these two representations as separate modules. The main justification of these systems is that they combine the efficiency of distributed representations with the power of localist representations. For instance, whereas DCPS is a highly constrained system that can represent only two triples in a rule's left-hand side, RUBICON (Samad 1992), a connectionist rule-based system that uses a combined localist/distributed rule-based system, allows for a variable number of expressions in the left and right hand sides of each rule. It also supports chain inferencing as well as addition and deletion of working memory elements.

From the point of view of system tasks, the CSP approach has been actively investigated in a variety of task domains, particularly in automated reasoning and natural language understanding. CONSYDERR (Sun 1991) implements commonsense reasoning using a localist network which performs rule-based reasoning and a distributed network which encodes feature similarities. The CHCL system (Hölldobler and Kurfess 1991) embodies a connectionist inference mechanism which uses W. Bibel's well-known connection method (Bibel 1987) to perform inferencing on Horn clauses using a matrix representation. An important subarea of work on logic and reasoning concerns variable binding (Sun 1992, Ajjanagadde and Shastri 1991, Touretzky and Hinton 1988, Chen 1992, Smolensky 1990, Pinkas 1994, Park and Robertson 1995). Indeed, this crucial problem needs to be solved if neural networks are to equal the expressive power of symbolic systems, which perform first-order predicate logic tasks as a matter of routine. Techniques experimented in the field of automated reasoning have been applied in connectionist expert systems such as MACIE (Gallant 1988, Gallant 1993), TheoNet (Bradshaw et al. 1989) and others (Saito and Nakano 1988, Hayashi 1991). Examples of studies in natural language processing via connectionist symbol processing can be found in (Bookman 1987, Dyer 1991, McClelland and Kawamoto 1986, Gasser 1988).

3 HYBRID STRATEGIES

The hybrid approach rests on the assumption that only the synergistic combination of neural and symbolic models can attain the full range of cognitive and computational powers. Hybrid neurosymbolic models can be either translational or functional hybrids.

3.1 Translational Hybrids

Translational hybrids—also called transformational models (Medsker 1994)—can be viewed as an intermediate class between unified models and functional hybrids. Like unified models, they rely only on neural networks as processors, but they can start from or end with symbolic structures. Typically, their objective is to translate or transform symbolic structures into neural networks before processing, or extract symbolic structures from neural networks after processing. Most often, the symbolic structures used are rules—classical propositional rules (Towell and Shavlik 1994, Dillon et al. 1994), fuzzy rules (Romaniuk and Hall 1991, Hayashi 1991, Magrez and Rousseau 1992), rules with certainty factors or probability ratings (Lacher et al. 1992, Fu 1989, Fu and Fu 1990, Mahoney and Mooney 1994, Tresp et al. 1993). Attempts have also been made to compile differential equations (Cozzio 1995) or deterministic finite state automata (Giles and Omlin 1993) into neural networks, and to extract hierarchies of concepts or schemata from them (Crucianu and Memmi 1992, Dillon et al. 1994). However, the key point is that symbolic structures are not processed as such in translational systems; for instance, rules are not applied by an inference engine within the system but only serve as source or target representations of knowledge built into neural nets. The implicit assumption seems to be that, whether purely connectionist systems are capable of full symbol processing or not, interaction with other (human or symbolic) systems imposes the need for a two-way transformation between neural network structures and high-level symbolic representations.

3.2 Functional Hybrids

Functional hybrids incorporate *complete* symbolic and connectionist components: in addition to neural networks, they comprise both symbolic structures and their corresponding processors—e.g., rule interpreters, parsers, case-based reasoners and theorem provers. Functional hybrids are so-called because, contrary to translational hybrids, they achieve effective functional interaction and synergy among the combined components. In a sense, translational hybrids are a degenerate case of functional hybrids; in the rest of this chapter, we shall therefore use the term *hybrid* to designate complete or functional hybrids, unless indicated otherwise.

Hybrid systems can be distinguished along different dimensions such as their target problem or task domain, the symbolic (e.g., rule-based reasoning, case-based reasoning) and neural (e.g., multilayer perceptrons, Kohonen networks) models used, or the role played by the neural (N) and symbolic (S) components in relation to each other and to the overall system. Although such dimensions allow for more or less clear distinctions between individual systems, they have little bearing on the central issues of neurosymbolic integration. We therefore propose a taxonomy of hybrid systems based on the degree and the mode of integration of the N and S components.

The **degree of integration** is a quantitative criterion: one can imagine a spectrum going from the simple juxtaposition of symbolic and neural components under a common supervisor to systems characterized by strong and repeated, if not continuous, interaction between the two components. Although this spectrum can be graded numerically to represent progression from one extreme to another, we shall simplify by distinguishing two main degrees of integration— loose and tight coupling. In *loosely coupled* systems, interaction between the two components is clearly localized in space and time: control and data can be transferred directly between N and S components (e.g., by function or procedure calls), or via some intermediate structure (e.g., domain or control blackboards accessible to both components) or agent (e.g. a supervisor), but interaction is always explicitly initiated by one of the components or by an external agent. In *tightly coupled* systems, knowledge and data are not only transferred, they can be shared by the N and S components via common *internal* structures. Thus a change in one of the components which affects these common internal structures has immediate repercussions on the other component without need for explicit interaction initiatives. Within this category, too, coupling is not uniformly tight from one system to another: whereas the shared structures are often simple links or pointers between the N and S components as in SYN-HESYS (Giacometti 1992), they can be significantly more important in number and function, e.g., nodes shared by a semantic marker-passing network and a distributed neural network, as in (Hendler 1989).

Along the qualitative dimension, the **integration mode** or scheme refers to the way in which the neural and symbolic components are configured in relation to each other and to the overall system. Four integration schemes have been identified: chainprocessing, subprocessing, metaprocessing and coprocessing (Figure 2). To define them, we suppose a system comprising one neural and one symbolic module, with the understanding that for more complex systems, there can be as many integration schemes as pairs of neural and symbolic components. In chainprocessing mode, one of the (N or S) modules is the main processor whereas the other takes charge of pre and/or postprocessing tasks. In subprocessing mode, one of the two modules is embedded in and subordinated to the other, which acts as the main problem solver. In metaprocessing mode, one module is the base-level problem solver and the other plays a metalevel role (such as monitoring, control, or performance improvement) vis-à-vis the first. In coprocessing, the N and the S modules are equal partners in the problem solving process: each can interact directly with the environment, each can transmit information to and receive information from the other. The two modules can compete under the supervision of a metaprocessor, or they can cooperate in various ways, e.g., by performing different subtasks or by doing the same task in different ways and/or under different conditions. These four integration modes are described in detail below.

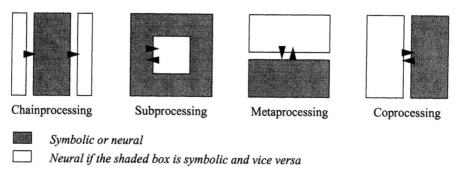

| Chainprocessing | Subprocessing | Metaprocessing | Coprocessing |

▦ *Symbolic or neural*

☐ *Neural if the shaded box is symbolic and vice versa*

Figure 2   Hybrid neurosymbolic integration modes.

Chainprocessing

Two main configurations can be distinguished in chainprocessing mode: (1) the symbolic module acts as the main problem solver and is assisted by a neural preprocessor and/or postprocessor; (2) the neural module is the main processor and is assisted by a symbolic preprocessor and/or postprocessor.

The first configuration is illustrated by a respiratory monitoring system where a rule-based expert system is assisted by a connectionist preprocessor (Ciesielski et al. 1992, Hayes et al. 1992). The system receives data from a ventilator which records a patient's airway pressure and lung pressure every 15 seconds. At the outset, the system consisted of a simple PC-Expert rulebase whose task was to recommend actions to be taken to avoid breathing complications. Top-level rules were typically: "If *qualitative-state* then *action*," where *qualitative-state* is a symbolic representation of a change in a pressure parameter over time, e.g., "pressure is constant," "pressure is rising gradually," or "pressure is rising rapidly." Determination of these qualitative states on the basis of ventilator output turned out to be the knowledge acquisition bottleneck: while domain experts found it relatively straightforward to express top-level rules recommending actions on the basis of qualitative states, they had a hard time formulating criteria to determine these qualitative states. Hence the idea of using a neural preprocessor to accomplish this task (see Figure 3).

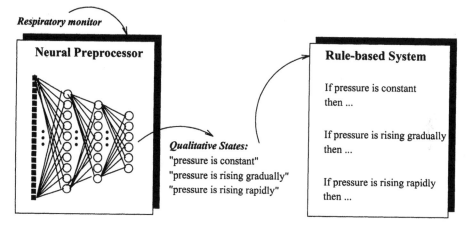

Figure 3 An example of neural preprocessing.

A feedforward neural network was trained using backpropagation. It had 20 inputs (patient data produced by the ventilator), two hidden layers with 10 and 8 units respectively, and 6 output units, each representing a specific interpretation of pressure variations. Its result, the qualitative state corresponding to the output unit with the highest activation, was then stored in the working memory of the expert system for use in the firing of action rules. After training on a set of 54 examples, the accuracy of the systems was measured on a test set of 78 cases. With neural preprocessing, development time was cut down from 3 to 2 months. Moreover, the hybrid system was considerably more accurate (97.5 %) than the rule-only version (74.5 %). It also turned out to be more sensitive, i.e., it detected a respiratory problem after examining fewer data samples than the rule-only system. Understandably, execution time was slightly higher for the hybrid system (1.7 vs 0.5 seconds), though it remained well within the 15-second realtime constraint.

The reverse setup is that of a symbolic preprocessor assisting a connectionist main processor. An example is the combination of ITRULE and neural networks (Goodman 1989, Greenspan et al. 1992). The preprocessor (ITRULE) is a rule induction algorithm which automatically generates probabilistic rules from databases. Learned rules are 0-order rules of the form *If attribute-1 value-1 then attribute-2 value-2 with probability p*. All attributes are binary-valued so they can be mapped directly to binary units. These rules are then compiled into a neural net: attributes of rule conditions are mapped onto input units, attributes of rule conclusions onto output units, and information metrics (such as p) onto connection weights. The result can then be loaded into the main processor, a neural network simulator. The originality of this approach lies in the fact that contrary to the vast majority of hybrid neurosymbolic systems, learning is done in the symbolic preprocessing phase; the neural network is used for inferential, not for generalization purposes.

Symbolic preprocessing may also be used as a means of alleviating well-known problems related to neural processing. One such problem is the learning time taken by feedforward networks before achieving acceptable error rates. Among the factors that slow down the generalization process is the presence of noise, not only in the feature values, but in the features themselves; more precisely, certain features have no significant effect on the network output and their elimination should result in faster convergence. To limit the number of input nodes in feedforward neural networks, Piramuthu and Shaw (1994) thought of using decision trees as feature selectors. The decision tree algorithm C4.5 (Quinlan 1993) uses information-theoretic measures to select the most important features from a given dataset. The selected features are used as input to a feedforward network which is then trained by backpropagation. The impact of this symbolic preprocessing method on training time was tested on the PROMOTER database, which consists of 106 examples belonging to either class 1 or 0. Each example consisted of 57 attributes and had no missing values. Without preprocessing, a 57–29–1 feedforward network took 84 seconds to converge (total sum of squares of error $= 2$); its average rate of accuracy over 10 trials was 77.7% on the training set and 55% on the test set. With symbolic preprocessing, the C4.5 algorithm generated a decision tree in 2 seconds and reduced the number of relevant attributes from 57 to 3. The resulting 3–2–1 network converged in 22 seconds, attaining a rate of accuracy of 96.4% for the training set and 66% for the test set. In short, 2 seconds of symbolic preprocessing accelerated convergence of the backpropagation learning process by a factor of 4 while improving accuracy on both the training and the test sets.

Whereas the preceding system reduces training time, WATTS (Wastewater Treatment System) (Krovvidy and Wee 1992) attempts to reduce the problem-solving time taken by a Hopfield network to converge to an optimal solution. WATTS' application task is to determine a treatment train, i.e., a sequence of processes aimed at eliminating wastewater contaminants before discharge to the environment. Since each contaminant can be eliminated by a variety of treatment processes and technologies, selection of the optimal treatment train requires combinatorial search. One approach adopted in WATTS is the use of a Hopfield network whose outputs can be decoded into a solution (a treatment train). The network uses an energy function which was derived taking into account expert knowledge about interactions among these different treatment processes. In the simple NN approach, a random initial solution was generated and used to search for an optimal solution. In the hybrid CBR/NN approach, a case-based reasoner maintains a base of previous solutions and retrieves a relevant solution given a new problem. This solution is then used to initialize the Hopfield network in lieu of a random initial state. In general, the CBR/NN approach was found to improve performance both in terms of convergence time and—in a few cases—the quality of the solution.

Subprocessing

In subprocessing, one of the two components is embedded in and subordinated to the other, which acts as the main problem solver. Typically, the S component is the main processor and the N component the subprocessor. It is an open question whether the reverse setup is at all possible.

Neural subprocessing is used in two distinct conditions. In the first case, the symbolic main processor delegates to neural networks certain phases or subtasks of the application task that it presumably cannot do or does less well than NNs. This is illustrated in INNATE/QUALMS: the main processor, an expert system for fault diagnosis, calls on a set of multilayered perceptrons to generate a candidate fault, then either confirms their diagnosis or offers an alternative solution (Becraft et al. 1991). Another example is LAM™, a system for window glazing design (Medsker 1994). Its principal role is to serve as a design assistant: relying mainly on rule-based modules, it classifies glass types, checks for errors or improbable glass designs, and helps a user take design decisions such as choosing the glass type and then determining such properties as glass strength, solar specifications or sound control class. Design rules for properties such as structural strength of glass were easily constructed from architectural manufacturer specifications; however, two design tasks—selecting solar control and sound control properties of glass—are difficult to express in the form of situation/action rules since they involve estimating complex correlations between input and output parameters. At the same time, there exists a sizeable set of training/test data which accurately correlates known inputs with output predictions. Two three-layer feedforward networks were therefore trained to determine the appropriate solar and sound properties on the basis of other glass properties; during an interactive consultation, these two specific tasks are subcontracted to the neural network modules while a knowledge base of 578 *if-then* rules takes charge of all the other design phases.

The second case is where the symbolic processor calls on neural networks to perform specific internal functions, independently of the application task at hand. In Giambasi et al.'s (1989) system, for example, the connectionist component is not called explicitly by domain-level rules; it comes into action as an automatic subroutine of rule interpretation. When a rule is selected for execution, its associated neural net is activated to compute uncertainty factors for each of the facts added by the rule. Neural nets play a similar role in a hybrid system built on the SETHEO (Letz 1992) theorem prover. The system's default depth-first search strategy can be inefficient due to combinatorial explosion, thus the need for a heuristic means of detecting the most promising direction at each choice point. The prover therefore calls on a backpropagation neural network to estimate the probability that a candidate branch will lead to a proof. The input of the network is a set of features concerning the current formula (e.g., the number of literals or variables) as well as current state of the proof (e.g., current inference depth). Training data are pairs of feature vectors and desired estimations obtained from theorems proven by SETHEO using exhaustive search. The theorem prover selects the branch to follow on the basis of estimation results returned by the connectionist component. Tests have shown that the learned evaluation function can decrease search time by an order of magnitude in certain cases (Suttner and Ertel 1990).

Metaprocessing

Contrary to the widespread belief that metalevel capabilities are a prerogative of symbolic systems, both symbolic and connectionist modules can assume a metalevel role in hybrid systems. As in pure symbolic systems, a metalevel architecture is said to exist only if metaknowledge is explicitly represented (i.e., expressed in the representation language of the symbolic or neural component and not in their underlying implementation languages). According to this definition, a neural network can be considered a metaprocessor if it represents both domain and metaknowledge and if its output plays a metalevel role in the combined system. We thus distinguish between symbolic and neural metaprocessing systems, depending on whether the metaprocessor is symbolic or connectionist.

Symbolic metaprocessing is illustrated in ALVINN, Carnegie-Mellon's system for guiding autonomous vehicles (Pomerleau et al. 1991). Multiple networks are trained to become experts in specialized aspects of the autonomous vehicle control task (e.g., single-lane road driving, highway driving, collision avoidance). Once these networks are trained, their exploitation in real-world situations requires the ability to integrate their responses in order to ensure effective control in a variety of circumstances. Furthermore, a truly autonomous system needs to be capable of planning its itinerary to reach a goal. ALVINN uses a rule-based arbitrator for this task: the decisions of the driving neural nets are sent to the arbitrator, which decides which network to follow and therefore how to steer. To take a decision, the arbitrator relies on an annotated map which stores geometric information such as the location of roads and landmarks, what type of road the vehicle is in, whether there is a dangerous permanent obstacle ahead, and so on. The map also contains control information relevant to the current driving situation; for instance, a point where a road changes from one lane to two is indicated on the map so the arbitrator knows when to start following the decision of the two-lane driving neural network.

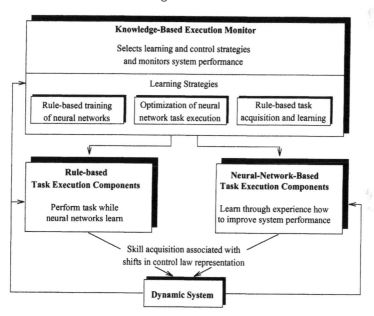

Figure 4   Symbolic metaprocessing for Robotic Skill Acquisition.

In the Robotic Skill Acquisition Architecture (RSA²) (Handelman et al. 1989, Handelman et al. 1992), the symbolic metaprocessor supervises both symbolic and neural baselevel components. The system's goal is to develop robots which perform complex tasks using designer-supplied instructions and self-induced practice. The approach is patterned after human motor learning, which shifts from an explicit to an implicit representation and from controlled, verbally oriented to automatic, reflexive execution. At the base level, a rule-based system provides a declarative representation of human expert knowledge, whereas neural networks embody reflexive procedural knowledge that comes with practice. The symbolic metaprocessor is a rule-based execution monitor which supervises the training of the neural network and controls the operation of the system during the learning process.

Robotic skill acquisition can be divided into three distinct phases (Figure 4). During the declarative phase, the system executes a given task using explicit instructions stored in the knowledge base. During the hybrid phase, neural network components observe and try to duplicate rule-based maneuver commands, thus learning by example. Since initial net performance is poor, the knowledge base continues to ensure task execution; however, as the networks develop robust patterns of learned behavior, task execution is increasingly shared by the symbolic and connectionist components. Finally, during the reflexive phase, network-based control is optimized via reinforcement learning. Transitions between these three phases are managed by rules of the execution monitor.

In instances of *neural metaprocessing* that we are aware of, the connectionist component enforces search control over the symbolic baselevel processor. One example is a system which solves high school physics problems (Gutknecht and Pfeifer 1990). Here, object-level rules encode kinematics equations: for instance, $v = v0 + at$ is mapped roughly into the rule: "If the goal variable is v (final-velocity) and the known variables are $v0$ (initial velocity), a (acceleration) and t (time), then the final velocity is known." However, if several of the needed variables are unknown, the rules say nothing about a crucial control problem: which subgoal variable to solve for next. This is the task of the metalevel connectionist module. A neural network, previously trained by backpropagation, receives as input the goal variable and the known variables at a given stage; it outputs the next variable to solve for in view of finding the value of the goal variable. The sequence of subgoal variables selected successively by the network in effect serves as a control plan for the problem-solving process.

Another example of neural metaprocessing is Kwasny and Faisal's (1992) natural language parser. Classical parsing systems map an input sentence into a parse tree by maintaining a lookahead buffer and an internal stack. Tree-building actions (e.g., creation of a new node) are taken by a set of rules after examining both buffer and stack. The main drawback of these systems is that they can only parse sentences whose form has been anticipated in the ruleset; but natural language is too rich to be encoded in such a set. In the proposed hybrid parser, symbolic parsing rules are replaced by a feedforward network which has been trained on a set of sentences generated by a deterministic grammar. The symbolic module manages the buffer and stack and codes their state as inputs for the network, which determines the action to be taken on a best-match basis. With this neural control component, the hybrid system is able to recognize grammatical as well as non-grammatical sentences, whether encountered previously or not.

Coprocessing

In coprocessing, the N and S components are equal partners in the problem-solving process: each can interact directly with environment, each can transmit information to and receive information from the other. They can compete under the supervision of a metaprocessor, or they can cooperate in various ways, e.g., by performing different subtasks, or by doing the same task in different ways and/or under different conditions. In SYNHESYS (Giacometti 1992), the same diagnostic task is executed by a rule-based system and a prototype-based neural network that learns incrementally. The neural component is tried first; if it comes up with a diagnostic, this output is validated by the rulebase in backward chaining mode; otherwise, the rulebase is activated in forward chaining mode and its diagnostic is used to train the neural network.

An example of the alternative setup—cooperative coprocessing by distribution of specialized subtasks—is a system where a neural network and a decision tree work together to detect arrythmia in heart patients (Jabri et al. 1992). Intra-cardial defibrillators (ICDs) are devices implanted in people with heart disorders: they sense the electrical activity of the heart and identify abnormal rhythms or "arrhythmias." These dysfunctions can be clustered into three main groups depending on the type of action they call for: continue monitoring, pace the heart, or apply high-voltage electric shock. Classification accuracy is, of course, crucial in this application. For so-called dual chamber classification (based on ventricular and atrial sensing), three architectures were tested: a single large multilayer perceptron (MLP), a multmodule NN consisting of three MLPs and two gates, and a hybrid decision tree/MLP model. In the hybrid model, the input data—sample signals sent by the ventricular and atrial probes—are sent to a decision tree which acts as a timing classifier and to a multilayer perceptron which performs morphology-based classification. The outputs of both modules are fed into an arbitrator which determines the class of the arrhythmia; this classification is then smoothed out by an "X out of Y" classifier to yield an "averaged" final classification. The decision tree/MLP hybrid attained an accuracy rate of 99% on a multi-patient database, whereas the best performance of the multimodule neural net was 96.2% and that of the simple MLP 89.3%.

Table 1 summarizes the above discussion by situating representative hybrid systems along the two classification dimensions—degree of coupling and integration scheme.

	Loose coupling	Tight coupling
Chainprocessing	Hayes et al. (1992) ITRULE (Goodman et al. 1989) Piramuthu and Shaw (1994) WATTS (Krovvidy and Wee 1992)	
Subprocessing	INNATE/QUALMS (Becraft et al. 1991) Giambasi et al. (1989) LAM (Medsker 1992) SETHEO (Suttner and Ertel 1990)	Hendler (1989)
Metaprocessing	ALVINN (Pomerleau et al. 1991) RSA[2] (Handelman et al. 1989) Gutknecht and Pfeifer (1990) Kwasny and Faisal (1992)	
Coprocessing	Jabri et al. (1992)	SYNHESYS (Giacometti 1992)

Table 1   Classification dimensions and instances of of hybrid NS systems.

4   PHILOSOPHICAL STANCES

In this section, we will relate the different computational strategies to philsophical stances in the symbolic/connectionist debate (see Table 2). First of all, an extreme philosophical assumption of the unified approach is eliminativism, i.e., the claim that the symbolic level can by no means provide a valid account of cognition.

Just as the unified approach to NSI can be divided into neuronal and connectionist symbol processing, Smolensky (1988) distinguishes between neuronal[2] and connectionist eliminativism. *Neuronal eliminativism*—the assumption underlying neuronal symbol processing—sees in neuronal models the only scien-

---

[2] We systematically translate Smolenksy's use of the term *neural* into *neuronal* for consistency with the terminology borrowed from Reeke and Edelman (1988).

CONNECTIONISM	NEUROSYMBOLIC INTEGRATION				SYMBOLICISM
	Unified		Hybrid		
	Neuronal Symbol Proc.	Connectionist Symbol Proc.	Funct. hybrids	Transl. hybrids	
Segregation	*Neuronal eliminativism*	*Connectionist eliminativism* *Limitivism* *Revisionism*	*Hybridization or cohabitation*		*Segregation* (*Implemen-tationalism*)

Table 2   Synoptic view of neural, symbolic and neurosymbolic approaches and their philosophical assumptions.

tifically valid cognitive models, while *connectionist eliminativism* also recognizes the validity of connectionist models. The latter, however, is just one of several positions that can be taken by exponents of the connectionist symbol processing approach; the others are limitivism and revisionism. Smolenksy's *limitivism* recognizes the validity of neuronal, subsymbolic and symbolic theories, while observing that symbolic models can only provide restricted and approximate descriptions (they cannot, for instance, provide complete and precise accounts of intuitive processing). *Revisionist connectionism* acknowledges the scientific validity of symbolic models *after* revision by connectionist theory; however, the precise nature of this revision varies. In Pinker and Prince's (1988) definition, this revision does not consist in simply adding connectionist models alongside symbolic models; rather, connectionist models will implement symbol-processing schemes in ways that have important emergent properties. Revisionist connectionism thus defined is the stand taken explicitly by a number of CSP researchers like Touretzky (1990) .

The revisionist position as interpreted by Smolensky seems to correspond more closely to the hybrid approach. In this view, the revision called for in symbolic models is a kind of division of labor: perception, memory, pattern matching and other "low-level" operations are relegated to connectionist networks while symbolic models retain control of hard, rational symbol processing. This brand of revisionism, which Smolensky calls by the French term *cohabitation*, is no other than *hybridization*, according to which only the synergy of symbolic and connectionist models can account for the diversity and power of human cognition. Finally, resistance to all integration efforts can be grouped under what Memmi (1992) calls segregationism—the claim that symbolicism and connectionism apply to different, non-overlapping domains and can pursue their respective tasks in peaceful coexistence, if not in mutual indifference.

5   BEYOND ELIMINATIVISM

The battle of philosophical (some would say 'ideological') stances reached its peak toward the end of the 1980s and gently subsided thereafter—to the greater profit of AI. Extremist views like eliminativism and implementationalism (which is no other than symbolic eliminativism) have been shown to rest on brittle assumptions. For instance, they are based on the premise that symbolic and connectionist processing are competing and irreconcilable models. As Honavar (1995) rightly points out, this dichotomy is more perceived than real. First, symbolic AI and NNs share the same assumption—they both characterize intelligence in terms of functional capabilities, independently of the physical substrates that support these functions. Second, both symbolic and connectionist processing have been shown to be Turing equivalent and can therefore effect any computation. Thus, if we abstract away cognitive/philosophical considerations and focus on computational issues, symbolic and connectionist AI appear clearly as complementary paths towards the reproduction of intelligent behavior, thereby giving neurosymbolic integration a vital role to play in the future of AI.

Similarly, once eliminativist tendencies of the unified approach are dissipated, there is no denying that connectionist symbol processing and hybridization are complementary strategies for neurosymbolic integration; either can exploit research results of the other in pursuing its own objectives. For instance, a common problem of both approaches is the representation and processing of structured knowledge in neural networks. Breakthroughs on this subject on either side will certainly be of use to both. Another important issue is that of reasoning power: neural networks have yet to demonstrate reasoning capabilities equal to that of first-order predicate logic. On this point, the hybrid position is certainly more comfortable. In certain cases, it can be said that the composite system is as powerful as its strongest component, since the latter can always be used whenever weaker components fall short of the required skill (which is stronger or weaker depends, of course, on the particular skill required). For instance, in functional hybrids where there is a division of labor between neural and symbolic components, the symbolic component can systematically be assigned tasks which require first-order deduction. On the other hand, there are cases when a system is only as strong as its weakest component:

for instance, despite the fact that rule-based systems routinely use first-order predicate logic, translational hybrids which compile rules into neural nets are all restricted to propositional logic for the moment. Such systems will certainly profit from intense research on variable binding which is being conducted in the CSP community. To sum up, we can say that just as NSI aims at combining symbolic and connectionist processing in order to get the best of both paradigms, there might be some way of integrating the unifed and the hybrid approaches to NSI in order to attain their common computational objectives, stripped of their conflicting philosophical assumptions.

6   SUMMARY

At the crossroads of symbolic and neural processing, researchers have been actively investigating the synergies that might be obtained from combining the strengths of these two paradigms. Neurosymbolic integration comes in two flavors: unifed and hybrid. Unified approaches strive to attain full symbol-processing functionalities using neural techniques alone while hybrid approaches blend symbolic reasoning and representational models with neural networks. This chapter attempted to clarify and compare the objectives, mechanisms, variants and underlying assumptions of these major integration strategies.

REFERENCES

[1] V. Ajjanagadde and L. Shastri, (1991). Rules and variables in neural nets. *Neural Computation*, (3):121–134.

[2] W. R. Becraft, P. L. Lee, and R. B. Newell, (1991). Integration of neural networks and expert systems. In *Proc. of the 12th International Joint Conference on Artificial Intelligence*, pages 832–837, Sydney, Australia. Morgan Kaufmann.

[3] W. Bibel, (1987). *Automated Theorem Proving*. Vieweg Verlag, Braunschweig, Germany.

[4] L. A. Bookman, (1987). A microfeature based scheme for modelling semantics. In *Proc. of the 10th International Joint Conference on Artificial Intelligence*, Milan, Italy. Morgan Kaufmann.

[5] G. Bradshaw, R. Fozzard, and L. Ceci, (1989). A connectionist expert system that actually works. In D. S. Touretzky, editor, *Advances in Neural Information Processing, 1*, pages 248–255. Morgan Kaufmann, San Mateo, CA.

[6] J. R. Chen, (1992). A connectionist composition of formula, variable binding and learning. In R. Sun, L. Bookman, and S. Shekar, editors. *AAAI-92 Workshop on Integrating Neural and Symbolic Processes: The Cognitive Dimension*, July.

[7] V. Ciesielski, Steven H., and B. Kelly, (1992). Comparison of an expert system and a hybrid neural network/expert system for a respiratory monitoring problem. In R. Sun, L. Bookman, and S. Shekar, editors. *AAAI-92 Workshop on Integrating Neural and Symbolic Processes: The Cognitive Dimension*, July. pages 141–143.

[8] R. Cozzio, (1995). *The Design of Neural Networks Using A Priori Knowledge*. PhD thesis, ETHZ, Zurich.

[9] M. Crucianu and D. Memmi, (1992). Extraction de la structure implicite dans un réseau connexionniste. In *Neuro-Nîmes 92. Neural Networks and their Applications*, pages 491–502. EC2, Nanterre, France.

[10] T. S. Dillon, S. Sestito, M. Witten, and M. Suing, (1994). Symbolic knowledge from unsupervised learning. In *International Symposium on Integrating Knowledge and Neural Heuristics*, pages 47–56, Pensacola, Florida, May.

[11] M. G. Dyer, (1991). Symbolic neuroengineering for natural language processing: A multilevel research approach. In J. A. Barnden and J. B. Pollack, editors, *Advances in Connectionist and Neural Computation Theory. Vol.1: High-Level Connectionist Models*, pages 32–86. Ablex Publishing.

[12] G. Edelman, (1987). *Neural Darwinism: The Theory of Neural Group Selection*. Basic Books, New York.

[13] G. Edelman, (1992). *Bright Air, Brilliant Fire. On the Matter of the Mind*. Basic Books, New York.

[14] J. Feldman and D. Ballard, (1992). Connectionist models and their properties. *Cognitive Science*, 6:205–254.

[15] J. A. Fodor and Z. W. Pylyshyn, (1988). Connectionism and cognitive architecture: a critical analysis. *Cognition*, 28:2–71.

[16] L. M. Fu, (1989). Integration of neural heuristics into knowledge-based inference. *Connection Science*, 1:325–340.

[17] L. M. Fu, editor, (1994). *International Symposium on Integrating Knowledge and Neural Heuristics*, Pensacola, FL, May.

[18] L. M. Fu and L. C. Fu, (1990). Mapping rule-based systems into neural architecture. *Knowledge-Based Systems*, 3(1):48–56, March.

[19] S. I. Gallant, (1988). Connectionist expert systems. *Communications of the ACM*, 31(2):152–169, February.

[20] S. I. Gallant, (1993). *Neural Network Learning and Expert Systems*. Bradford/MIT, Cambridge, MA.

[21] M. E. Gasser, (1988). A connectionist model of sentence generation in a first and second language. Technical Report Report UCLA-AI-88-13, University of California, Los Angeles, CA.

[22] A. Giacometti, (1992). *Modèles hybrides de l'expertise*. PhD thesis, ENST, Paris, November.

[23] N. Giambiasi, R. Lbath, and C. Touzet, (1989). Une approche connexionniste pour calculer l'implication floue dans les systèmes à base de connaissances. In *Proc. of the 2nd International Conference on Neural Networks and their Applications*, Nîmes, France. EC2.

[24] C. L. Giles and C. W. Omlin, (1993). Extraction, insertion and refinement of symbolic rules in dynamicallly driven recurrent neural networks. *Connection Science*, 5(3-4):307–337.

[25] R. M. Goodman, J. W. Miller, and P. Smyth, (1989). An information theoretic approach to rule-based connectionist expert systems. In D. S. Touretzky, editor. *Advances in Neural Information Processing, 1*, pages 256–263. Morgan Kaufmann, San Mateo, CA.

[26] H. K. Greenspan, R. Goodman, and R. Chellappa, (1992). Combined neural network and rule-based framework for probabilistic pattern recognition and discovery. In J. E. Moody, S. Hanson, and R. P. Lippman, editors. *Advances in Neural Information Processing, 4*, pages 444–451. Morgan-Kaufmann, San Mateo, CA.

[27] M. Gutknecht and R. Pfeifer, (1990). An approach to integrating expert systems with connectionist networks. *AICOM*, 3(3):116–127.

[28] D. A. Handelman, S. H. Lane, and J. J. Gelfand, (1989). Integrating knowledge-based system and neural network techniques for robotic skill acquisition. In *Proc. of the 11th International Joint Conference on Artificial Intelligence*, pages 193–198, Detroit, MI. Morgan Kaufmann, San Mateo, CA.

[29] D. A. Handelman, S. H. Lane, and Gelfand J. J, (1992). Robotic skill acquisition based on biological principles. In A. Kandel and G. Langholz, editors. *Hybrid Architectures for Intelligent Systems*, chapter 14, pages 301–327. CRC Press, Boca Raton, FL.

[30] Y. Hayashi, (1991). A neural expert system with automated extraction of fuzzy if-then rules and its application to medical diagnosis. In R. P. Lippman, J. E. Moody, and D. S. Touretzky, editors, *Advances in Neural Information Processing, 3*, pages 578–584. Morgan-Kaufmann, San Mateo, CA.

[31] S. Hayes, V. B. Ciesielski, and W. Kelly, (1992). A comparison of an expert system and a neural network for respiratory system monitoring. Technical Report TR #92/1, Royal Melbourne Institute of Technology, March.

[32] J. A. Hendler, (1989). Problem solving and reasoning: A connectionist perspective. In R. Pfeifer, Z. Schreter, and F. Fogelman-Soulié, editors, *Connectionism in Perspective*, pages 229–243. Elsevier.

[33] S. Hölldobler and F. Kurfess, (1991). CHCL—A connectionist inference system. In B. Fronhoefer and G. Wrightson, editors, *Parallelization in Inference Systems*. Springer-Verlag, New York.

[34] V. Honavar, (1995). Symbolic artificial intelligence and numeric artificial numeral networks: towards a resolution of the dichotomy. In R. Sun and L.A. Bookman, editors, *Computational Architectures Integrating Neural and Symbolic Processes*, chapter 11, pages 351–388. Kluwer.

[35] M. Jabri, S. Pickard, P. Leong, Z. Chi, B. Flower, and Y. Xie, (1992). Ann based classification for heart difibrillators. In J. E. Moody, S. Hanson, and R. P. Lippman, editors. *Advances in Neural Information Processing, 4*, pages 637–644. Morgan-Kaufmann, San Mateo, CA.

[36] S. Krovvidy and W. G. Wee, (1992). An intelligent hybrid system for wastewater treatment. In A. Kandel and G. Langholz, editors. *Hybrid Architectures for Intelligent Systems*, chapter 17, pages 358–377. CRC Press, Boca Raton, FL.

[37] S. C. Kwasny and K. A. Faisal, (1992). Symbolic parsing via subsymbolic rules. In J. Dinsmore, editor, *The Symbolic and Connectionist Paradigms: Closing the Gap*, pages 209–235. Lawrence Erlbaum Associates Inc., Northvale, NJ.

[38] R. C. Lacher, S. I. Hruska, and D. C. Kuncicky, (1992). Backpropagatin learning in expert networks. *IEEE Transactions on Neural Networks*, 3:63–72.

[39] T. E. Lange, (1992). Issues in controlling activation and inferencing for natural language understanding in structured connectionist networks. In R. Sun, L. Bookman, and S. Shekar, editors. *AAAI-92 Workshop on Integrating Neural and Symbolic Processes: The Cognitive Dimension*, July. pages 31–38.

[40] R. Letz, S. Bayerl, and W. Bibel, (1992). Setheo: A high-performance theorem prover. *Journal of Automated Reasoning*, 8(2):183–212.

[41] P. Magrez and A. Rousseau, (1992). A symbolic interpretation for back-propagation networks. *International Journal of Intelligent Systems*, 7:339–360.

[42] J. J. Mahoney and R. J. Mooney, (1994). Modifying network architectures for certainty-factor rule-base revision. In L. M. Fu, editor. *International Symposium on Integrating Knowledge and Neural Heuristics*, pages 75–84. Pensacola, FL, May.

[43] J. L. McClelland and A. H. Kawamoto, (1986). Parallel distributed processing. explorations in the microstructure of cognition. In J. L. McClelland, D. E. Rumelhart, and the PDP Research Group, editors, *Parallel Distributed Processing. Explorations in the Microstructure of Cognition*, volume 2, chapter 19, pages 272–325. MIT Press, Cambridge, MA.

[44] L. R. Medsker, (1994). *Hybrid Neural Network and Expert Systems*. Kluwer Academic Publishers, Boston.

[45] D. Memmi, (1992). Connectionism and artificial intelligence as cognitive models. In A. Clark and R. Lutz, editors, *Connectionism in Context*, pages 145–165. Springer-Verlag.

[46] M. Minsky and S. Papert, (1969). *Perceptrons*. MIT Press, Cambridge, MA.

[47] N. S. Park and D. Robertson, (1995). A localist network architecture for logical inference based on temporal asynchrony approach to dynamic variable binding. In R. Sun and F. Alexandre, editors, *IJCAI-95 Workshop on Connectionist-Symbolic Integration: From Unified to Hybrid Approaches*, pages 63–68, Montreal, CN, August.

[48] G. Pinkas, (1994). Propositional logic, nonmonotonic reasoning and symmetric networks—On bridging the gap between symbolic and connectionist knowledge representation. In D. S. Levine and M. Aparicio IV, editors, *Neural Networks for Knowledge Representation and Inference*, chapter 7, pages 175–203. Lawrence Erlbaum Associates Inc., Hillsdale, NJ.

[49] S. Pinker and A. Prince, (1988). On language and connectionism: Analysis of a parallel distributed processing model of language acquisition. *Cognition*, 28:73–193.

[50] S. Piramuthu and M. I. Shaw, (1994). On using decision tree as feature selector for feed-forward neural networks. In L. M. Fu, editor. *International Symposium on Integrating Knowledge and Neural Heuristics*, pages 67–74, Pensacola, FL, May.

[51] J. B. Pollack, (1990). Recursive distributed representations. *Artificial Intelligence*, 46:77–105.

[52] D. A. Pomerleau, J. Gowdy, and C. E. Thorpe, (1991). Combining artificial neural networks and symbolic processing for autonomous robot guidance. *Engineering Applications of Artificial Intelligence*, 4(4):279–285.

[53] J. R. Quinlan, (1993). *C4.5: Programs for Machine Learning*. Morgan Kaufmann, San Mateo, CA.

[54] G. N. Reeke and G. M. Edelman, (1988). Real brains and artificial intelligence. In S. Graubard, editor, *The Artificial Intelligence Debate. False Starts, Real Foundations*, pages 144–173. MIT Press.

[55] S. G. Romaniuk and L. O. Hall, (1991). Injecting symbol processing into a connectionist model. In B. Soucek and the IRIS Group, editors, *Neural and Intelligent Systems Integration*, chapter 15, pages 383–405. John Wiley and Sons, New York.

[56] K. Saito and R. Nakano, (1988). Medical diagnostic expert system based on pdp model. In *Proc. IEEE International Conference on Neural Networks*, pages 255–262, San Diego, CA.

[57] T. Samad, (1992). Hybrid distributed/local connectionist architectures. In A. Kandel and G. Langholz, editors. *Hybrid Architectures for Intelligent Systems*, chapter 10, pages 200–219. CRC Press, Boca Raton, FL.

[58] L. Shastri, (1988). A connectionist approach to knowledge representation and limited inference. *Cognitive Science*, 12:331–392.

[59] P. Smolensky, (1988). On the proper treatment of connectionism. *Behavioral and Brain Sciences*, 11:1–74.

[60] P. Smolensky, (1990). Tensor product variable binding and the representation of symbolic structures in connectionist systems. *Artificial Intelligence*, (46):159–216.

[61] A. Sohn and J.L. Gaudiot, (1991). Connectionist production systems in local and hierarchical representation. In N.G. Bourbakis, editor, *Applications of Learning and Planning Methods*, pages 165–180. World Scientific Publishing, Singapore.

[62] A. Stolcke and D. Wu, (1992). Tree matching with recursive distributed representations. In R. Sun, L. Bookman, and S. Shekar, editors. *AAAI-92 Workshop on Integrating Neural and Symbolic Processes: The Cognitive Dimension*, July.

[63] R. Sun, (1991). *Integrating Rules and Connectionism for Robust Reasoning. A Connectionist Architecture with Dual Representation*. PhD thesis, Brandeis University, Waltham, MA 02254. Technical Report CS-91-160.

[64] R. Sun, (1992). On variable binding in connectionist networks. *Connection Science*, 4(2).

[65] Ch. Suttner and W. Ertel, (1990). Automatic acquisition of search guiding heuristics. In *10th Int. Conf. on Automated Deduction*, pages 470–484. Springer-Verlag, LNAI 449.

[66] D. S. Touretzky, (1990) Boltzcons : Dynamic symbol structures in a connectionist network. *Artificial Intelligence*, 46(1-2).

[67] D. S. Touretzky and G. E. Hinton, (1988). A distributed connectionist production system. *Cognitive Science*, 12:423–466.

[68] G. G. Towell and J. W. Shavlik, (1994). Knowledge-based artificial neural networks. *Artificial Intelligence*, 70:119–165.

[69] V. Tresp, J. Hollatz, and S. Ahmed, (1993). Network structuring and training using rule-based knowledge. In S. Hanson, J. D. Cowan, and C. Lee Giles, editors, *Advances in Neural Information Processing, 5*. Morgan-Kaufmann, San Mateo, CA.

3

TASK STRUCTURE LEVEL SYMBOLIC-CONNECTIONIST ARCHITECTURE

Rajiv Khosla   Tharam Dillon

School of Computer Science and Computer Engg.,
La Trobe University, Melbourne, Australia

1   INTRODUCTION

Tasks and methods can be considered mediating concepts in problem solving (Chandrasekaran, Johnson and Smith 1992). The symbolic and connectionist methods because of their different philosophical, cognitive and computational underpinnings impose their own constraints on the quality (e.g. time, resources, user intelligibility, no. of levels of abstraction/solution hierarchy, reliability, etc.) of task accomplishment. Further these constraints can lead to task generation depending upon which constraints have been violated by a certain method, and the degree of tolerance of the violated constraints. A proper integration of symbolic and connectionist methods for task accomplishment can thus improve the quality of task accomplishment and restrict task generation. Besides such an integration has important implications in terms of overall understanding of the human information processing system. A proper integration of the symbolic and connectionist methods can be achieved by explicitly outlining integration at the task structure level, computational level, and the program level (see Figure 1).

In this direction, this chapter looks at the development of a task structure level symbolic-connectionist architecture for complex data/knowledge intensive domains. For that matter, this chapter is organized in the following sections

- Section 2 describes the perspectives for integration of symbolic and connectionist theories. These perspectives establish the constraints based on which the task structure level architecture is constructed.

TASK STRUCTURE LEVEL

OUTLINES THE GENERIC STRUCTURE IN TERMS OF TASKS AND
METHODS USED TO ACCOMPLISH THE TASKS IN VARIOUS DOMAINS
E.G. , DIAGNOSIS, PLANNING, MONITORING, CONTROL.

COMPUTATIONAL LEVEL

OUTLINES THE KNOWLEDGE CONTENT REQUIRED TO REALIZE
THE TASK STRUCTURE LEVEL ARCHITECTURE.
IT INCLUDES IDENTIFICATION OF KNOWLEDGE REPRESENTATION,
COMMUNICATION AND OTHER ONTOLOGICAL CONSTRUCTS.

PROGRAM LEVEL

OUTLINES THE DETAILS OF THE PROGRAMS, SUB-ROUTINES, DATA
STRUCTURES TO BE USED FOR IMPLEMENTING THE COMPUTATIONAL
ARCHITECTURE.

Figure 1: Three Levels of Symbolic-Connectionist Architecture

■ Section 3 describes the task structure level symbolic-connectionist architecture.

■ Section 4 makes some observations on the task structure level architecture,
   and

■ Section 5 summarizes the chapter.

2 PERSPECTIVES FOR INTEGRATION

The need for neurosymbolic integration has emerged from a number of perspectives given below. These perspectives provide an insight in terms of the
constraints that need to be taken into account while developing symbolic-
connectionist architectural theory of problem solving.

■ Philosophical Perspective

■ Neurobiological Perspective

■ Cognitive Science Perspective

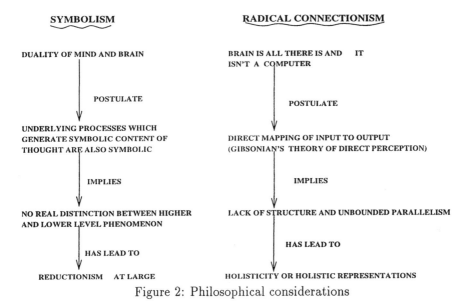

Figure 2: Philosophical considerations

- Computational and Artificial Intelligence Perspective

- Physical Systems Perspective

- Forms of Knowledge Perspective

- Learning Perspective

- User Perspective

2.1 Philosophical Perspective

Some of the philosophical underpinnings of symbolic and connectionist systems are shown in Figure 2. The parallel and distributed properties of the connectionist models and their apparent proximity to our neural structure have encouraged some of the proponents of connectionism (Churchland 1990; McClelland and Rumelhart 1986a; McClelland and Rumelhart 1986b) to claim that human memory has a holistic character. The simultaneous consideration of multiple constraints in Parallel Distributed Processing (PDP) (McClelland and Rumelhart 1986a) models imply a holistic proposition for solving a problem at hand. According to its proponents connectionism is said to perform direct recognition while symbolic AI performs recognition by sequentially computing intermediate representations.

On the other hand, determination of goals, sub-goals, sub-sub-goals and creation of structured problem sub-spaces as proposed by (Newell 1972) is indicative of the reductionist philosophy at work. The proponents of the discrete symbol systems propose logical chunking as a method of problem solving (Laird, et al. 1987; Newell 1980; Newell, 1981a; Newell 1981b).

The above philosophical comparison represents an inflexible and fundamentally opposing nature of the two problem solving philosophies. On the one hand, the symbolic systems, by pursuing a reductionist philosophy of logic and provability have become rigid and inflexible. Also, today using symbolic systems we can cope with highly specialized problems solved by human experts, but these very systems have problems coping with the easiest of problems which children can solve like walking, recognizing objects, etc. (Minsky 1991). The proponents of the reductionist view have implicitly assumed that the underlying processes at the micro level which generate the symbolic content of thought are also necessarily symbolic. This implicit assumption has been established as incorrect with the development of connectionist architectures (Chandrasekaran 1990; McClelland and Rumelhart 1986a; Smolensky 1990). On the other hand, the all embracing holistic philosophy has not delivered the goods as was initially expected when scaled up to complex tasks. While not undermining the success of these models in domains like character recognition, financial forecasting, etc., there are not as many real world applications around as was initially expected. Furthermore, the connectionist models are more concerned with modeling the dynamic rather than the structural characteristics of a system which can contribute to intelligent behavior.

The reductionist and holistic views thus have in a sense restricted the search for more generic information processing architecture which is composed of abstraction, structure and logic embodied in symbolism (Fodor, et al. 1988) and the underlying parallel and distributed processes.

2.2 Cognitive Science Perspective

One of the benefits of the symbolic-connectionist debate from a cognitive science viewpoint (Chandrasekaran 1990; Churchland 1990; Fieldman 1988; Fodor 1983; Fodor et al. 1988; Newell 1990; Shepard 1988; Smolensky 1990) has been that it has addressed a number of issues related to information processing, learning and knowledge representation. The aspects which emerge from an information processing viewpoint are the granularity of the processes (Chandrasekaran 1990; Fodor 1983; Lallement, Hilario and Alexandre, 1995; Lallement and Alexandre 1995b), notion of time (Newell 1990), and the levels of information processing (Fodor 1983; Fodor et al. 1988; Newell 1990). The macro and micro level granularity of the processes associated with human cognition have lead researchers to think that the symbolic and connectionist theories on their own are likely to be inadequate to cover the range of phenomena in cognition. Furthermore, the notion of time associated with these processes (which varies from 100ms to a few seconds/minutes (Chandrasekaran 1990; Newell 1990) further establishes that one has to account for sequential as well as automated form of reasoning mechanisms in an information processing architecture. Besides, according to Newell (Newell 1990), *the fact that human beings are grounded in the world implies additional constraints that must be taken into account in constructing our theories.* That is, it is essential that the information processes theories which emerge from such studies need to be grounded in the real world in which human beings interact with the physical systems surrounding them.

2.3   Neurobiological Perspective

The investigations into the visual nervous system of mammals reveals that the visual system works at different levels of abstraction (Rao 1995). The model designed by (Rao 1995) posits a role for the hierarchical structure of the visual cortex and its reciprocal connections between adjoining visual areas in determining the response properties of visual cortical neurons. Besides, the past studies (Beale and Jackson 1990) have shown that the complex cells in the visual cortex perform higher level functions whereas the simple cells and the ganglion cells perform lower level functions. The hierarchical arrangement of the complex cells, simple cells and the ganglion cells allows the visual system to extract more and more abstract information from the initial electric signals. Secondly, research into the functional principles of the brain shows that it exercises central and hierarchical control at different levels (sensory, motor, etc.) to provide both stability and adaptability (Beale and Jackson 1990). Finally, the highly connected and parallel design of the brain allows it to work on many different things at once (e.g. vision and speech). The brain, with its parallel design, is able to represent a host of different external stimuli/items of information in a distributed form and is able to process these items of information in a parallel manner.

2.4 Physical Systems Perspective

The underlying principles of abstraction and hierarchical control described in the previous section undoubtedly form an intrinsic part of man made systems like power systems, organizational systems, telecommunication systems, process control systems, etc. For example, in power systems, the power network is hierarchically decomposed into transmission, sub-transmission and distribution levels. The structure of these systems influences their behavior. Humans, while reasoning with these systems likewise engage in structural and/or behavioral decomposition of the problem and perceive the solution at different levels of abstraction.

Thus it can be said from the neurobiological and physical systems perspectives that the principles of abstraction and hierarchical control not only form a part of our neural hardware but also form a structural and behavioral part of our information processing strategy.

2.5 Levels of Intelligence Perspective

In (Bezdek 1994) a model outlining three levels of intelligent activity namely, computational, artificial, and biological is described. The computational level (or the lowest level), according to the model deals with numeric data and involves pattern recognition, whereas the artificial intelligence level augments the computational level by adding small pieces of knowledge to the computational processes. The biological intelligence level (the highest level) processes sensory inputs and, through associate memory, links many subdomains of biological neural networks to recall knowledge (Bezdek 1994; Medskar 1995). The computational and the artificial levels according to (Bezdek 1994) lead to the biological level. An integration of the computational and artificial intelligence levels can thus be considered as a way of modeling biological intelligence.

2.6 Learning Perspective

Learning forms an important ingredient of any intelligent system. Based on the cognitive science studies various types of learning techniques have been identified including learning of procedures, concept learning, reinforcement learning and others. One of the motivations for surge in interest in the connectionist models has been their ability to learn and adapt. However, most of the connectionist models are known to adopt the "Learning from scratch," philosophy.

This is probably not adequate for complex domains, a point already made by some prominent researchers in this area. To quote from (Arbib 1987, page 70).

Humans are intelligent because evolution has equipped them with a richly structured brain. This structure, while serving a variety of functions, in particular enables them to learn. A certain critical degree of structural complexity is required of a network before it can become self-modifying – no matter how sophisticated its reinforcement rules – in a way that we could consider intelligent.

Furthermore, to quote from (Malsburg 1988, page 26)

However, some fundamental problems remain to be solved before flexible robots can be realized. One of these problems is scalability to realistic size. Learning strategy based on exhaustive search of full combinatorial phase spaces blow up too quickly. The solution to this problem will very likely have to be based on the introduction of a clever a priori structure to restrict the relevant phase spaces.

2.7 Forms of Knowledge Perspective

Symbolic and connectionist research communities have developed a rich set of representational mechanisms which have enabled cognitive scientists to characterize human cognition. Broadly, the knowledge representation mechanisms can be categorized into three forms:

- sub-symbolic knowledge

- symbolic and non-formal, and

- symbolic and formal

Sub-symbolic knowledge can be seen as sub-conceptual, intuitive or tacit knowledge in a particular domain which necessarily cannot be articulated in terms of rules (Smolensky 1990). For example, a five-year old child learning to play baseball or cricket finds it difficult to express in natural language the patterns of response learned by him in hitting a ball thrown at him in different patterns. These types of problems are best expressed with sub-symbolic knowledge and may involve parallel processing for inference. Symbolic and non-formal knowledge can be seen as conceptual knowledge represented by frames and objects. It can also be represented by macro level heuristics/rules which are an outcome of experience of the human expert and generally cannot be formalized in a rigorous fashion (e.g., heuristics taught by a coach to a baseball or cricket player). Symbolic and formal knowledge can be seen as knowledge represented by a more rigorous formalism (e.g., physics, applied mathematics, etc.) such as a mathematical/structural/behavioral model or formal logic representation.

The different forms of knowledge also represent knowledge of varying granularity. The sub-symbolic knowledge layer has fine granularity. The fine granularity is based on the highly distributed nature of knowledge at the sub-symbolic or micro level. The granularity becomes coarser as one moves from the sub-symbolic knowledge level to the symbolic and formal knowledge levels.

2.8   User Perspective

Humans form an important part of solution to most real world problems. Thus it is imperative that any architecture which is derived out of using the two methodologies should result in reducing the cognitive barriers between the human experts and the computer. This is vital for the following reasons:

- **Acceptability.** - without cognitive compatibility, the system's behavior can appear surprising and unnatural to the user. In other words, architectures with low cognitive compatibility will lead to low acceptability

- **Effectiveness.** - without cognitive compatibility, effective interpretation of the user's or expert's problem solving behavior is at risk, which may result in unsatisfactory performance.

Thus user intelligibility should form an important aspect of system architecture because it will not only facilitate higher acceptability and better performance but will also facilitate a high level of user interaction.

Further issues like scalability and cost effectiveness (reduced development time, reduced memory requirements, fast execution, etc.) are equally important to enable use of integrated architectures on large-scale problems. Scalability requires that an architecture should permit an open-ended approach for system development. That is, any incremental changes in the systems can easily flow through the architecture with minimal damage to reliability, speed of operation, etc. of the whole system. The existing symbolic systems for complex large-scale problems invariably have deep solution hierarchies, whereas connectionist systems for such problems have to cope with issues related to precision and reliability.

3 TASK STRUCTURE LEVEL ARCHITECTURE

The task structure level architecture as shown in Figures 3a, 3b, and 3c respectively has been derived from the perspectives described in the preceding sections and the constraints imposed by them.

The task structure level architecture is defined in terms of the

- information processing phases
- tasks to be accomplished in each phase
- methods used to accomplish the tasks in different phases, and
- constraints which need to be satisfied for accomplishing a task.

Five information phases have been identified. These are the Global Preprocessing Phase, Decomposition Phase, Control Phase, Decision Phase, and the Postprocessing Phase. The information processing phases have been derived from the neurobiological, cognitive science and other perspectives which impose constraints like structure, control, granularity of processes, notion of time, conscious and automated behavior and others. The tasks, symbolic and connectionist methods and the constraints applicable in different phases are shown in Figure 3a, 3b, and 3c.

3.1 Global Preprocessing Phase

The global preprocessing phase involves two tasks:

- input conditioning, and
- noise filtering.

Global Preprocessing is done at the topmost level using symbolic methods for filtering out noise which is peculiar to the domain as a whole or common to many classes. However, prior to noise filtering some kind of input conditioning may be required for making the inputs from the external environment fit for processing. Symbolic methods or other mathematical methods may be used for this purpose.

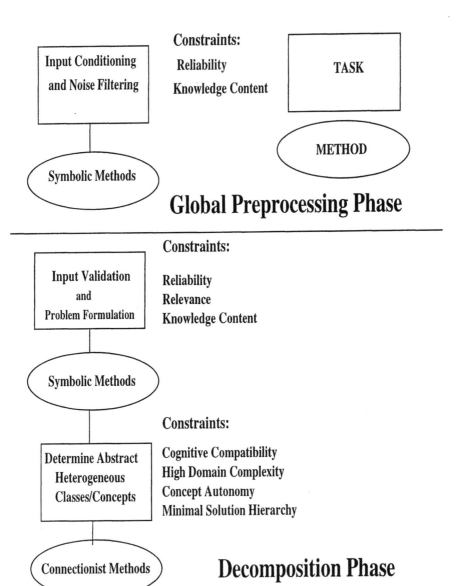

Figure 3a Task structure level architecture

3.2   Decomposition Phase

The different levels of abstraction used in information processing represent aggregations or generalizations of varying granularity. The goal of the decomposition phase is to decompose the problem under study into a set of abstract concepts/classes. Two distinct tasks are performed in the decomposition phase:

- input validation and problem formulation
- determination of abstract classes

The input validation can involve time and context validation of the input data, whereas problem formulation can involve something as simple as conversion of input data into a state which facilitates its use by a particular method and/or as complex as imposing constraints of time on the solution and nature of communication with its environment given a particular context. Input validation and problem formulation tasks need to be accomplished reliably as the quality of the solution impinges on it. The knowledge content of this task is invariably symbolic and thus symbolic methods are used to accomplish this task.

The second distinct task in the decomposition phase is determination of abstract concepts/classes which are not directly related to the problem to be solved and are not explicitly used or do not explicitly exist in the domain/problem space being addressed. They are abstractions of the existing domain classes and are used to reduce the complexity of problem in hand. These abstract concepts elementarily classify a domain and at the same time reduce the complexity of the problem in hand. From a cognitive viewpoint, humans are very quick and accurate in elementary classification in various domains. In other words, elementary classification or decomposition generally forms a part of our unconscious or automated behavior which is best reflected by neural networks. More so, constraints like concept autonomy (independent subsystems (Fodor 1983)), minimal solution hierarchy require consideration of multiple number of features simultaneously. Thus connectionist methods under the constraints of cognitive compatibility, concept autonomy, high domain complexity, and minimal solution hierarchy are used to accomplish this task.

3.3   Control Phase

Control Phase operates within each abstract heterogeneous class. In the control phase the following tasks are accomplished:

- local noise filtering

- input validation and problem formulation

- determination of decision level classes

- resolution of conflicts between decision-level classes

The local noise filtering, input validation, and problem formulation tasks are similar to those done in the global preprocessing phase and decomposition phase except that instead of doing these tasks at the global level, they are now done at the local level within each abstract class. The third task is to determine the decision-level classes within each abstract heterogeneous class. Decision-level classes are those classes inference on which is of importance to a problem solver. These decision-level classes generally explicitly exist in the problem being addressed. Thus the control phase captures the underlying domain structure of the problem under study. The granularity of a decision-level class can vary between coarse and fine. The coarsity and the fineness of a decision-level class depends on the context in which the problem is being solved and the context priority (or solution priority in a given context). That is, if the context priority of a particular decision-level class is low, then its granularity is coarse. In other words the problem solver is satisfied with a coarse decision on that class. If the context priority is high then the decision-level class has fine granularity and problem solver wants a fine set of decisions to be made on the decision-level class which would involve a number of microfeatures in the domain space. Thus in a given context if the decision-level class has coarse granularity the symbolic methods can do the [1]job. However, if the the decision-level class has fine granularity then connectionist methods will fit the bill. From a cognitive viewpoint, connectionist methods can be seen as learning the decision-level classes from the microfeatures and determine which decision-level classes in the next phase (i.e. decision phase) need to be activated. Besides the granularity/context priority constraint, other constraints like need for adaptation/incremental learning, incorrect/incomplete data will also determine the selection of symbolic/connectionist methods. Thus the division of responsibility between symbolic and connectionist methods is based on the satisfaction of various constraints in the control phase.

In the control phase, besides determining the decision-level classes another task is to resolve conflicts between the decision-level classes in the decision

---

[1] In fact in such circumstances a distinct control and decision phase may not be required and can be merged into one.

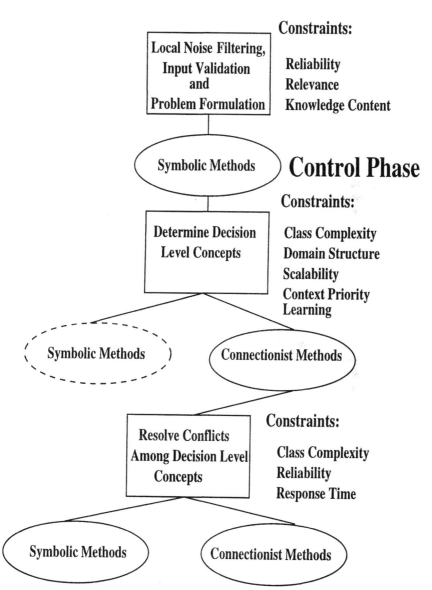

Figure 3b Task structure level architecture contd.

phase. Here again, for reasons similar to those given in the previous paragraph connectionist or symbolic methods can be used for resolving the conflicts.

Further, because of the difference in the nature of tasks involved in the control phase and decomposition phase, the nature of communication between the decomposition phase and control phase is different from the nature of communication between the control phase and decision phase.

3.4   Decision Phase

In the decision phase the goal is to determine the specific classifications within each decision-level class or instances of a decision-level class. Cognitively, it is in the decision phase that humans engage in generalization. For example, in a power system control center, the operator is accurate and quick in detecting whether a set of alarms are circuit breaker (CB) alarms or communication alarms, or whether they are 220kv CB alarms or 66kv CB alarms. However, the operator generalizes on whether these set of alarms depict a bus fault or multiple line fault. That is, if a bus fault occurs as a result of eight CB alarms in a bus section, the operator is likely to generalize the same fault for six CB alarms in real time. This is largely due to fine granularity and the distributed nature of microfeatures in this phase. Besides constraints like response time and others as shown in Figure 3c also need to be considered in this phase. Thus connectionist methods which have generalization capabilities can be used in this phase in order to determine specific classifications. These generalizations, however, need to validated. This is done in the postprocessing phase.

Some practical considerations and pragmatic constraints can also enforce use of numerical methods/mathematical algorithms in this phase.

3.5   Postprocessing Phase

Logic and provability which are the hallmarks of our conscious behavior explains our underlying unconscious behavior. Thus in the postprocessing phase symbolic methods are used to explain and validate decisions made by the connectionist methods in the decision phase. This is done by using symbolic-cross checking modules. These symbolic cross-checking modules can be fault propagation model/s or other application-dependent cross-checking modules.

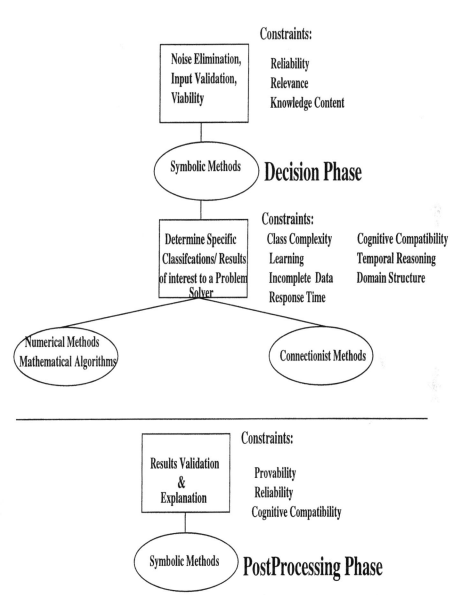

Figure 3c Task Structure Level Architecture Contd.

4   SOME OBSERVATIONS

The task structure level architecture described in the preceding section has outlined the information processing phases at different levels of abstraction, the tasks in each phase, the constraints on accomplishment of the tasks, and the symbolic and connectionist methods which can be used to satisfy the constraints. The information processing in the task structure structure level architecture can be seen to represent deliberative reasoning structure, where each phase consists of a mixture (with varying granularity) of analytical and automated reasoning. Further, the task structure level architecture described in the preceding section is independent of the type of connectionist/symbolic methods to be used or the type of learning techniques/algorithms to be employed.

It has not been determined at the task structure level what are the different knowledge constructs to be employed by the symbolic and connectionist methods in order to accomplish the tasks in different phases. Given the task structure level architecture it needs to be determined now what kind of learning knowledge is to be employed in different phases of the architecture, what kind of communication mechanisms are to be employed between different phases, etc.. All in all, symbolic knowledge representation constructs, belief knowledge, learning knowledge, communication knowledge constructs, and other ontological constructs need to be outlined. Besides this, some constraints like knowledge sharing and maintenance from a user's perspective also need to be addressed. This is done at the computational level, some aspects of which can be seen in (Khosla and Dillon 1994a; Khosla and Dillon 1995).

5   SUMMARY

In this chapter the task structure level symbolic-connectionist architecture has been outlined for complex data/knowledge intensive domains. The task structure level architecture is defined in terms of the information processing phases, tasks to be accomplished in each phase, constraints which need to be satisfied for accomplishing a task, and methods used to accomplish the tasks in different phases. The different aspects of the task structure level architecture have been derived from various perspectives including neurobiological, cognitive science, levels of intelligence, physical systems, learning, forms of knowledge, user, and others. The task structure level architecture is independent of the implementation details of the methods and the learning techniques employed. The ontological constructs to be employed by the symbolic and connectionist methods in order to accomplish the tasks form a part of the computational level architecture (Khosla and Dillon 1995). The architecture has been successfully used for developing a real-time distributed, object-oriented alarm processing application in a power system control center with encouraging performance results (Khosla and Dillon 1994b).

REFERENCES

[1] Arbib, M. A., *Brains, Machines and Mathematics*, Springer Verlag, New York, 19tex law87.

[2] Beale, R. and Jackson, T., *Neural Computing: An Introduction*, Bristol: Hilger, 1990.

[3] Bezdek, J.C., "What is Computational Intelligence?," in *Computational Intelligence Imitating Life*, IEEE Press, New York, 1994.

[4] Chandrasekaran, B., "What kind of information processing is intelligence," in *Foundations of Artificial Intelligence*, Cambridge University Press, pp. 14-45, 1990.

[5] Chandrasekaran, B, Johnson, T. R. and Smith, J. W., "Task-Structure Analysis for Knowledge Modeling," in *Communications of the ACM*, September, Vol 35, No. 9., pp. 124-137, 1992.

[6] Churchland, P.M., "Representation and High-Speed Computation in Neural Networks," in *Foundations of Artificial Intelligence*, Cambridge University Press, USA, 1990.

[7] Fieldman, J., "Neural Representation of Conceptual Knowledge," in *Neural Connections, Mental Computation*, MIT Press, pp. 69-103, 1988.

[8] Fodor, J. A., *The Modularity of Mind*, MIT Press, 1983.

[9] Fodor, J.A., and Plyshyn, Z. W., "Connectionism and Cognitive Architecture: A Critical Analysis," in *Cognition*, vol 28, no 1, pp. 2-71, 1988.

[10] Khosla, R. and Dillon, T. "Learning Knowledge and Strategy of a Generic Neuro-Expert System Model," in *International Symposium on Integrating Knowledge and Neural Heuristics*, FL, USA, pp. 103-112, 1994a.

[11] Khosla, R. and Dillon, T. "Task Structure and Computational Level: Architectural Issues in Symbolic-Connectionist Integration," in *Working*

Notes of IJCAI95 Workshop on Connectionist-Symbolic Integration: From Unified to Hybrid Approaches, Montreal, Canada, pp. 119-125, 1995.

[12] Khosla, R. and Dillon, T., "A Distributed Real-Time Alarm Processing System with Symbolic-Connectionist Computation," in *Proceedings of IEEE Workshop in Real Time Systems*, July, Washington D.C., USA, 104-109, 1994b.

[13] Laird, J., Rosenbloom, P. and Newell, A., "SOAR: An Architecture for General Intelligence," in *Artificial Intelligence*, Vol. 33, pp. 1-64, 1987.

[14] Lallement, Y., Hilario, M., and Alexandre, F., "Neurosymbolic Integration: Cognitive Grounds and Computational Strategies," in *World Conference on the Fundamentals of Artificial Intelligence*, Paris, pp. 107-115, 1995.

[15] Lallement, Y., and Alexandre, F., "Cognitive Aspects of Neurosymbolic Integration," in *Working notes of the Workshop on Connectionist-Symbolic Integration: From Unified to Hybrid Approaches*, Montreal, Canada, pp. 7-11, 1995.

[16] Malsburg, V. D., "Goal and Architecture of Neural Computers," in *Neural Computers*, Springer Verlag, Berlin, West Germany, pp. 24-28, 1988.

[17] McClelland, J. L., Rumelhart, D. E. and Hinton, G.E., "The Appeal of Parallel Distributed Processing," *Parallel Distributed Processing*, vol 1, Cambridge, MA: The MIT Press, pp. 3-40, 1986a.

[18] McClelland, J. L., Rumelhart, D. E. and Hinton, G.E., *Parallel Distributed Processing: Explorations in the Microstructure of Cognition*, vol 2, Cambridge, MA: The MIT Press, 1986b.

[19] Medskar, L. A., "Hybrid Intelligent Systems," Kluwer Academic Publishers, Boston, Massachusetts, USA, 1995.

[20] Minsky, M., "Logical Versus Analogical or Symbolic Versus Connectionist or Neat Versus Scruffy," *AI Magazine*, vol 12, no 2, pp. 34-51, 1991.

[21] Newell, A., and Simon, H. A., "The Theory of Human Problem Solving," in *Human Problem Solving*, Englewood Cliffs, NJ: Prentice Hall, 1972.

[22] Newell, A., "Physical symbol Systems," *Cognitive Science*, vol 4, pp. 135-183, 1980.

[23] Newell, A. and Rosenbloom, P. S., "Mechanisms of Skill Acquisition and the Lae in Practice," in *Cognitive Skills and Their Acquisition*, J. R. Anderson (Ed.), Hillsdale, NJ: Erlbaum, 1981a

[24] Newell, A., "The Knowledge Level," in *AI*, pp. 1-19, 1981b.

[25] Newell, A., 1990, *Unified Theories of Cognition*, Harvard University Press, Cambridge, Massachusetts, USA

[26] Rao, R.P.N. and Ballard, D.,(1995) 'Dynamic Model of Visual Memory Predicts Neural Response Properties In The Visual Cortex', *Technical Report 95.4, National Resource Laboratory for the study of Brain and Behavior*, Department of Computer Science, University of Rochester, Rochester, USA.

[27] Shepard, R.N., 1988, "Internal Representations of Universal Regularities: A Challenge for Connectionism," in *Neural Connections, Mental Computation*, MIT Press, pp. 104-135.

[28] Somolensky, P., (1990) "Connectionism and Foundations of AI," *Foundations of Artificial Intelligence*, Cambridge University Press, pp. 306- 327.

4

COGNITIVE ASPECTS OF NEUROSYMBOLIC INTEGRATION

Yannick Lallement
Frédéric Alexandre

CRIN CNRS INRIA Lorraine
BP 239 – Campus scientifique
54506 Vandœuvre-lès-Nancy Cedex
France

1 INTRODUCTION

The ultimate goal of AI is to emulate the human cognitive processes. During the brief history of AI, two main schools have competed with each other in this endeavor, namely the symbolic and the connectionist schools. Hubert and Stuart Dreyfus (1988, p. 15) have summarized this division by their famous phrase: *making a mind* vs *modeling the brain* . So far, neither of these schools has achieved the final goal. A new research field is growing more and more important at present, one which aims at combining the two schools into *neurosymbolic* models with the capacities of both the symbolic and connectionist models.

In this chapter, we present some representations to analyze different trends of research in artificial intelligence today. We propose to define two spectra: the AI spectrum representing a variety of AI models and the cognitive spectrum representing a variety of human cognitive operations. We show how the relationship between these two spectra can be interpreted as a strong argument for the necessity of neurosymbolic models, integrating connectionist and symbolic capabilities. We identify two major possibilities for the construction of neurosymbolic models: the unified approach and the hybrid approach.

2   COGNITIVE ASPECTS OF AI

In this section, we define two representations which will be useful to draw a link between AI and human cognitive processes: the AI spectrum and the cognitive spectrum.

2.1   The AI Spectrum

Two different schools are often distinguished in AI research: the symbolic and the connectionist ones. The two schools were born approximately at the same time, in the early 1950s (Crevier, 1993).

The symbolic approach, *making a mind*, starts at the higher cognitive level: symbol manipulation and language. The fundamental hypothesis of this approach is that the brain is not the only physical substrate able to produce thought processes. Its typical realizations are expert systems, and such famous natural language handling programs as Shrdlu or Eliza (Winston, 1977).

Contrasting with this, the connectionist approach, *modeling the brain*, starts at the lowest cognitive level: the neurons and the connections between them. The fundamental hypothesis of this approach is that the architecture of the brain has an influence on the thought processes. Its typical realizations are concerned with pattern matching systems (speech or image processing) (McLelland and Rumelhart, 1986).

It is widely admitted that these two main schools have different and complementary capabilities. Connectionist models often offer good performance in pattern recognition and generalization and offer features such as natural learning ability, noise tolerance and graceful degradation. They use a non-propositional, distributed, and, thus not easily understandable knowledge representation. In contrast, symbolic models often present a complementary profile: they offer good performance in reasoning and deduction and present such features as natural symbolic manipulation and explanation ability. They use a propositional, localized, explicit knowledge representation. The complementarity between the two paradigms is often discussed in great detail, see for example (Gallant, 1988; Hawthorne, 1989; Gutknecht, 1992). Table 1 gives a brief list of the capabilities usually attributed to connectionist and symbolic models.

However, this is only a superficial view of the field of AI, and things are in fact more complicated. Actually, when we look more closely at various AI

	Conn. AI	Symbolic AI
Learning	Easy	Difficult
Explanation	None	Good
Performance degrad.	Slow	Fast
Algorithmics	Parallel	Sequential
Noise resistance	Good	Weak
Generalization	Easy	Difficult
Data str. representation	Difficult	Easy

Table 1 Some features of typical connectionist and symbolic models

Connectionist   Symbolic

Figure 1 The AI spectrum

models, it often seems difficult to classify them as either connectionist or symbolic: most models will present some typically symbolic features *and* some typically connectionist features. As AI research progresses and new models appear, the symbolic – connectionist duality seems less valid. Moreover, it is not easy to clearly distinguish even between symbolic and connectionist features themselves: some features traditionally attributed to connectionism, such as learning capabilities, are sometimes present in symbolic models, whereas some features traditionally attributed to symbolic models, such as data structure representation, are sometimes present in connectionist models too (Honavar, 1994). Thus, there is not anymore a simple dichotomy between symbolic AI and connectionist AI, and it may be hard to classify a given model as either symbolic or connectionist. A particular model will be *mostly* connectionist or *mostly* symbolic, rather than purely connectionist or purely symbolic. To represent this "continuous dichotomy", we propose to draw a continuum leading from a purely connectionist side to a purely symbolic side. According to its respective shares of symbolic and connectionist parts, each AI model can be positioned somewhere on that continuum. We call this continuum the *AI spectrum* (see Figure 1).

For example (see Figure 2), a multi-layer perceptron is clearly on the very connectionist side (a kind of pure connectionist model), and a first-order logic-based expert system on the very symbolic side (a kind of pure symbolic model). Some models like cortical columns (Alexandre et al., 1991) or fuzzy-logic-based

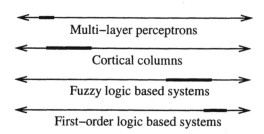

Figure 2   Some AI models

expert systems are neither purely connectionist nor purely symbolic, and thus are located somewhere in-between, according to their respective shares of numeric and symbolic parts.

2.2   The Cognitive Spectrum

From a cognitive point of view, we can notice that several types of mental processes exist and each of them plays a role in human intelligence (Newell, 1990; Richard, 1990; Cornu, 1992). In particular, consider the following two contrasting kinds of operations: *synthetic operations* versus *analytical operations* (Table 2).

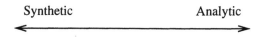

Figure 3   The cognitive spectrum

Synthetic operations are mostly concerned with low-level, non decomposable, unconscious, perceptual tasks. Some typical examples are vision and speech recognition: given a low-level input, the goal is to extract some higher-level information, such as objects present in the image or pronounced words. The knowledge involved in these operations is non-propositional, that is hard to express in words, but rather pictorial for example.

In contrast, analytical operations are mostly concerned with high-level, conscious, decomposable, reasoning tasks. Some typical examples are problem solving, decision making, or game playing: in each case, there is a conscious thought process and some conscious decisions made from explicit high-level in-

Synthetic	Analytic
Perception	Reasoning
Implicit	Explicit
Non decomposable	Decomposable
Automatic	Controlled
Unconscious	Conscious
Fast	Slow

Table 2 Some features of typical synthetic and analytical operations

formation. The knowledge involved in these operations is symbolic and propositional, that is, related to language. Allen Newell (1990) has classified these operations according to their duration.

In the case of this supposed dichotomy, it is once again clear that some operations can be mostly synthetic or mostly analytical rather than purely synthetic or purely analytical. A typical case is mental calculus: if the computation of 4×3 is clearly synthetic, the computation of 34×13 clearly analytical, what about the computation of 12×7 or 5×15? Certainly somewhere in-between. Another interesting case is musical practice: a beginner at guitar or piano needs to think of what he has to do; his knowledge about the chords and the piece to play is explicit, etc. A more experienced player is less explicitly conscious of his acts, and his playing improves. The playing of a professional musician is fully automatic.

Some complex cognitive operations can use synthetic operations as well as analytical operations. For example, driving a car uses synthetic operations (perception of the environment, of the motor noise...) as well as analytical operations (decision between turning left or right to reach the destination as soon as possible). Therefore we propose to draw a new mental continuum leading from synthetic to analytical operations, namely the *cognitive spectrum* (see Figure 3) on which we can situate simple and complex cognitive operations. The complex ones will be located on a wider segment of the spectrum, indicating that they imply several types of processes (see examples on Figure 4).

Our two spectra propose a simplified, but accurate view of the two domains. In the AI spectrum, we take into account only the dichotomy between symbolic

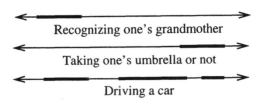

Figure 4   Some cognitive operations

and connectionist models, ignoring other models such as statistical pattern recognition or genetic learning. But between the two extremities of our spectrum lies the vast majority of the various AI models—which do not belong at either pole. Thus our spectrum covers a wide portion of the field of AI today. In the cognitive spectrum, we do the same kind of simplification, taking into account only one dimension to classify the different kinds of cognitive operations. In this case again, it appears that a single axis covers the variations of several important characteristics (more or less conscious, more or less decomposable, etc.) and thus is not an over-simplification.

3   THE CASE FOR NEUROSYMBOLIC INTEGRATION

The cognitive spectrum and the AI spectrum can be quite easily related to one another: the connectionist side of the AI spectrum mirrors the synthetic side of the cognitive spectrum, and the same is true for the symbolic and analytical sides. The same kind of vocabulary is used to define the synthetic and connectionist extremities on the one hand and the analytical and symbolic extremities on the other hand. Connectionist models and synthetic operations share many characteristics (e.g, parallelism, non-decomposability, non-propositional knowledge). This, together with the pattern matching and classification abilities of connectionist models, enables them to perform synthetic perceptual operations.

At the other ends of the spectra, symbolic models and analytical operations also share many features (e.g., sequentiality, decomposability, propositional knowledge). This, together with the symbol manipulation abilities of symbolic models enables them to perform analytical reasoning operations. Moreover, knowledge representation along the AI spectrum is akin to knowledge representation along the cognitive spectrum: from implicit, pictorial to explicit, symbolic. To summarize, connectionist models are best suited to perform synthetic operations, whereas symbolic models are best suited to perform analytical operations.

Thus, a cognitive operation, as defined above, can be situated on the cognitive spectrum, but also on the AI spectrum, according to the kind of model that will best simulate it. For example, a purely perceptual, discrimination operation will be placed on the connectionist side of the AI spectrum. In the same way, an AI model, according to the kind of operation it simulates, can be situated on the cognitive spectrum too. Typically, a pure symbolic model will be placed on the analytical side of the cognitive spectrum.

The isomorphism between our two spectra shows that current AI models are most often able to perform a kind of cognitive operation or another, but rarely both. It also shows that each kind of cognitive operation is related to some AI model which will best simulate it.

AI models striving to achieve the ultimate goal of AI must cover the full gamut of human cognitive processes. This can be easily illustrated in terms of our two spectra: such models have to cover the full cognitive spectrum and thus the full AI spectrum. This implies realizing neurosymbolic models, cumulating connectionist and symbolic capabilities. In the next section, we examine two ways of developing such models.

4 NEUROSYMBOLIC MODELS: UNIFIED *VS* HYBRID APPROACHES

In order to cover the full AI spectrum, two methods can be identified: adding several segments from various places on the spectrum or starting the coverage at one of the extremities and leading to the other one. We call the first method *hybrid*, and the second one *unified*: see Figures 5 and 6.

Numeric   Symbolic

Figure 5   Hybrid approach

Figure 6   Unified approaches

4.1   The Hybrid Approach

The hybrid approach tries to combine several models from different origins. Its basic assumption is that covering the AI spectrum is beyond the reach of a single paradigm. The research in hybrid models is currently very varied, and applications include natural language processing (Kwasny and Faisal, 1992), diagnosis (Hudson et al., 1992), industrial application (Madey et al, 1994)... A brief overview of several hybrid models can be found in (Lallement et al., 1995). This approach has the benefit of a psychological plausibility: the faculty psychology (Fodor, 1983) argues that human cognition consists of of several specialized subsystems. Each of these subsystems could be implemented by a particular kind of model. Of course, the synthetic subsystems will be naturally implemented by connectionist models, and the analytical subsystems will be naturally implemented by symbolic models.

4.2   The Unified Approaches

In contrast, the unified approaches start with a single paradigm and attempt to enhance it to get both the connectionist and symbolic capabilities. The two original paradigms can be seen as special cases of unified approaches, since, at the beginning, both of them claimed to be able to reach the final goal of AI. However, the current research in unified models is mostly concerned with neural networks. The starting point of a unified model can be either on the connectionist or on the symbolic side of the spectrum. In the first case, the approach is bottom-up, neuron-to-symbol oriented. The point is to make symbols emerge from neural networks. Such models are often inspired by neurobiology: see for example (Alexandre et al., 1991; Nenov and Dyer, 1993; Nenov and Dyer, 1994). In the latter case, the approach is top-down, symbol-to-neuron oriented. The point is to build connectionist architectures for symbol processing and thus to ground symbols in a connectionist substrate. This approach is widely known as *connectionist symbol processing*: see for example (Ajjanagadde, 1994; Hinton, 1990; Sun, 1992). In (Lallement et al., 1995) can be found a brief overview of several unified models.

5 DISCUSSION

Given our definitions—mono- or multi-paradigms—the two approaches seem to exhaust the current research in neurosymbolic integration. It is worth noting that hybrid models may include models which stem from the unified approach, but, even in that case, they remain hybrid since they are made up of several kinds of models.

A question naturally comes to mind: which is the most promising approach? Our definitions say nothing about this: there is no reason why one way to cover the cognitive spectrum would be better than the other. The hybrid approach is sometimes viewed as a short-term engineering expedient, whereas, in the long run, the unified approach would be the key to human cognition. Indeed, the hybrid approach has so far given more convincing results than the unified approach: for example, some models are already used in industrial applications. However, the two approaches are still in their infancy and have to solve a number of research issues before any real assessment can be made.

The research issues concerning the hybrid approach are mainly those of communication and task sharing between different tools. In the case of the unified approach, the main issue is to continue the bottom-up or top-down strategies that have just begun, to date, to reach the *sub-symbolic* level that seems to be the most relevant in human cognition (Hofstadter, 1985). It is definitely not clear at the moment which approach will turn out to be the most successful.

6 SUMMARY

In this paper, we defined some representations (the AI and the cognitive spectra) that we used to underline the necessity for neurosymbolic integration and to show how this integration can be achieved: through a hybrid or a unified approach. We suggest that these two approaches have a significant role to play in the future of AI, and that both of them are complementary rather than exclusive. The complexity and the diversity of human cognition and the human brain leads us to think that a single unified model may not be sufficient to achieve the final goal of AI: as Marvin Minsky (1991, p. 38) writes:

> *To solve really hard problems, we'll have to use several different representations.*

And indeed, considering the variety of problems yet to be solved, a single type of representation seems to be very far away. An interesting next step in the domain of neurosymbolic integration would certainly be to integrate classical models (connectionist or symbolic) together with unified models into new multi-hybrid models. This approach may well lead to some fundamental breakthroughs in AI: such models would present both biological and psychological plausibility, which is not the case in the current AI models.

ACKNOWLEDGEMENTS

The authors wish to thank Mélanie Hilario and Bruno Orsier for numerous discussions which contributed to the propositions developed in this paper in a noteworthy way. They also wish to thank Mark Walmsley for his helpful comments.

REFERENCES

[1] V. Ajjanagadde. Unclear distinctions lead to unnecessary shortcomings: Examining the rule vs fact, role vs filler, and type vs predicate distinctions from a connectionist representation and reasoning perspective. In *American Association Artificial Intelligence*, 1994.

[2] F. Alexandre, Y. Burnod, F. Guyot, and J-P. Haton. The cortical column: a new processing unit for multilayered networks. *Neural Networks*, 4(1), 1991.

[3] T. Cornu. *Machine Cellulaire Virtuelle: Définition, Implantation et Exploitation*. PhD thesis, Université de Nancy I and Supélec Metz, 1992.

[4] D. Crevier. *AI: The tumultuous history of the search for artificial intelligence*. Basic Books, New York, 1993.

[5] H. Dreyfus and S. Dreyfus. Making a mind versus modeling the brain: Artificial intelligence at a branchpoint. *Daedalus*, Winter, 1988.

[6] J. A. Fodor. *The Modularity of Mind: An essay on faculty psychology*. MIT Press, 1983.

[7] S. I. Gallant. Connectionist expert systems. *Communications of the ACM*, 31(2), February 1988.

[8] M. Gutknecht. The postmodern mind: Hybrid models of cognition. *Connection Science*, 4(3 & 4), 1992.

[9] J. Hawthorne. On the compatibility of connectionist and classical models. *Philosophical Psychology*, 2(1), 1989.

[10] G. E. Hinton, editor. *Artificial Intelligence, Special issue on connectionist symbol processing*, volume 46. Elsevier, Amsterdam, November 1990.

[11] D. Hofstadter. *Metamagical themas: Questing for the essence of mind and pattern.* Basic Books, 1985.

[12] V. Honavar and L. Uhr, editors. *Artificial intelligence and neural networks: steps toward principled integration.* Academic Press, New York, 1994.

[13] D. L. Hudson, M. E. Cohen, P. W. Banda, and M. S. Blois. Medical diagnosis and treatment plans derived from a hybrid expert system. CRC Press, 1992.

[14] S. C. Kwasny and K. A. Faisal. Symbolic parsing via subsymbolic rules. Lawrence Erlbaum, 1992.

[15] Y. Lallement, M. Hilario, and F. Alexandre. Neurosymbolic integration: Cognitive grounds and computational strategies. In M. DeGlas and Z. Pawlak, editors, *World Conference on the Fundamentals of Artificial Intelligence*, Paris, July 1995.

[16] G. R. Madey, J. Weinroth, and V. Shah. Hybrid intelligent systems: Tools for decision making in intelligent manufacturing. In C. H. Dagli, editor, *Artificial neural networks for intelligent manufacturing.* Chapman & Hall, London, UK, 1994.

[17] J. L. McClelland, D. E. Rumelhart, and the PDP Research Group. *Parallel Distributed Processing*, volumes 1 and 2. MIT press, Cambridge, Mass., 1986.

[18] M. Minsky. Logical versus analogical or symbolic versus connectionist or neat versus scruffy. *AI Magazine*, Summer 1991.

[19] V. Nenov and M. Dyer. Perceptually grounded language learning: Part 1 - a neural network architecture for robust sequence association. *Connection Science*, 5(2), 1993.

[20] V. Nenov and M. Dyer. Perceptually grounded language learning: Part 2 - Dete: A neural/procedural model. *Connection Science*, 6(1), 1994.

[21] A. Newell. *Unified theories of cognition.* Harvard University press, Cambridge, Mass., 1990.

[22] J.-F. Richard. *Les activités mentales.* Armand Colin, Paris, 1990.

[23] R. Sun. On variable binding in connectionist networks. *Connection Science*, 4(2), 1992.

[24] P. H. Winston. *Artificial Intelligence.* Addison Wesley, 1977.

5

A FIRST APPROACH
TO A TAXONOMY
OF FUZZY-NEURAL SYSTEMS

Luis Magdalena

Universidad Politécnica de Madrid

1   INTRODUCTION

The concept of *fuzzy-neural networks* was created two decades ago by Lee and Lee (1975) but the recent resurgence of fuzzy-neural systems with a great amount of published works may be motivated by the increasing recognition of the potential of fuzzy logic and neural networks in different areas of theoretical and applied research. At this moment, many researchers are investigating ways to build up fuzzy-neural systems by incorporating fuzziness or fuzzy rules in a neural network, or by applying the computational and learning potentials of neural networks to fuzzy systems. This chapter introduces a first approach to a taxonomy of fuzzy-neural systems. Two different classifications are proposed, the first one based on the symbolic and connectionist elements included in the fuzzy-neural system (Section 2), and the second one based on the application of the system (Section 3). Each class includes bibliographical references, pointing to papers describing fuzzy-neural systems belonging to the class. A brief analysis of the applicability of each kind of fuzzy-neural system is presented in Section 4.

2   SYMBOLIC AND CONNECTIONIST COMPONENTS OF FUZZY-NEURAL SYSTEMS

Fuzzy systems and neural networks have other features than their symbolic or their connectionist character. Fuzzy systems have functional and computational properties proceeding from fuzzy sets and logical operators that may be incorporated to a neural network without including symbolic ideas. Neural networks have analytical properties that may be applied to fuzzy systems without connectionism. This section introduces a classification of fuzzy-neural systems. based on the properties or characteristics that they incorporate from both approaches. This classification produces classes that are *fuzzy sets* of fuzzy-neural systems. where the systems might be members of more than one class with different degrees of membership. On the other hand, the classification may not be complete, and some ideas present on fuzzy-neural systems may take no place in any of the described categories. Seven categories are proposed in later subsections: Connectionist systems with fuzziness, Symbolic systems with analytical learning, Logic connectionist systems. Connectionist inference systems. Rule-like connectionist systems, Connectionist systems with symbolic acquisition of knowledge and Connectionist systems with symbolic description of knowledge.

2.1   Connectionist Systems With Fuzziness

A first approach to a symbiosis between neural systems and fuzzy sets arose when the notion of imprecision, described by the concept of fuzzy set, was applied to pattern recognition neural techniques as a meaningful way to reflect imprecisely defined categories. Frequently. the imprecision on definitions is related to the complexity of the categories, and at this level fuzziness is a tool for coping with the problem of complexity. The kind of knowledge applied in this case is not symbolic, but imprecise knowledge defined by a set of relaxed conditions and expressed through fuzzy sets. In this sense, this kind of fuzzy-neural systems could be viewed as connectionist systems categorizing by means of relaxed conditions.

Most of the described clustering systems (Bezdek et al. 1992; Dave and Bhaswan 1992; Huntsberger and Ajjimarangsee 1990; Krishnapuram et al. 1992; Newton et al. 1992; Simpson 1993), and others like (Carpenter et al. 1992; Keller and Hunt 1985; Kuo et al. 1993; Simpson 1992; Zhang et al. 1994). are connectionist systems applying fuzziness to produce outputs or work with inputs or internal states that include relaxed expressions of properties, conditions or restrictions, defining the problem to be solved.

2.2   Symbolic Systems With Analytical Learning

A major drawback of fuzzy inference systems is their unsuitability for learning and adaptation, one of the major qualities of neural networks. Some decisions. like the choice of the particular membership functions describing the fuzzy sets of

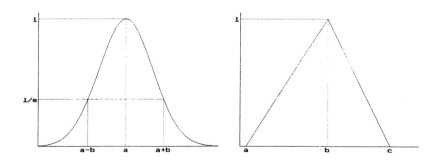

Figure 1 Parameterized fuzzy sets.

the system, are almost arbitrary decisions. The achievement of a method to fine tune these membership functions after their definition will be a major success on designing fuzzy systems. The analytical expressions of the learning methods used on neural networks are applicable to a fuzzy inference system considered as a composition of parameterized functions (membership functions, aggregation operators, fuzzy connectives, defuzzification method . . .). The chain rule or any other analytical method may be applied to obtain the influence of a certain parameter of one of those functions on the evolution of an evaluation function (as has been previously done in neural networks).

The learning process is applied to the analytical expressions of the knowledge and the processing mechanism that are involved in the symbolic system. Several fuzzy systems working with parameterized fuzzy sets in their antecedents and numerical consequents (or parameterized fuzzy sets) have adopted this tuning technique. Systems applying this concept are those propossed by Ichihashi and Tokunaga (1993) working with Gaussian membership functions, Nomura et al. (1992) using triangular fuzzy sets or Yamakawa et al. (1992) adjusting only the numerical consequents, all of them based on gradient descent method. Orthogonal least squares learning is used by Wang and Mendel (1992) working with Gaussian membership functions. Examples of parameterized Gaussian and triangular fuzzy sets are shown on Figure 1. These systems make no use of connectionism, even in the case of Yamakawa et al. (1992) which defines a neuron but uses a system composed of a single one. Learning is achieved working with the analytical expressions of parameterized fuzzy sets, fuzzy operators, connectives, or inference and defuzzification methods. Parameter

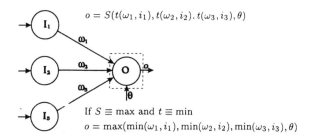

$$o = S(t(\omega_1, i_1), t(\omega_2, i_2). t(\omega_3, i_3), \theta)$$

If $S \equiv \max$ and $t \equiv \min$

$$o = \max(\min(\omega_1, i_1), \min(\omega_2, i_2), \min(\omega_3, i_3), \theta)$$

Figure 2   A possible neuron of a logic connectionist system.

tuning is based on a training data set and on the definition of some initial rules and membership functions.

2.3   Logic Connectionist Systems

Neural networks are usually arithmetic connectionist systems: their nodes of computation use arithmetic operators and functions. Logical operators as well as arithmetical may be applied to obtain the transference function of a computation node. Some of the fuzzy-neural systems proposed are connectionist systems implementing logical operators on their nodes. Such a system may incorporate the ability for working with symbolic information (being qualified as a certain type of symbolic connectionist system) or only use logical operators from a functional point of view. The idea of an extension of neural networks applying fuzzy operations is analyzed by Gupta (1992).

The terms *Fuzzy Neurons* or *Logic Neurons* are used by different authors to name the nodes of a neural net in which any kind of logical operation is performed. Some multi-layer networks containing Fuzzy Neurons or Logic Neurons but taking no profit from symbolical aspects have been proposed (Pedrycz 1992; Kwan and Cai 1994). Figure 2 shows a logic neuron (O) that performs logical operations. As defined on the figure, a possible expression of the output value (or the activation function) of the neuron is the maximum (or any other S-norm[1]) of the input values (including the bias), where input values are weighted using a minimum (or any other T-norm) operator. The use of learning methods as gradient descent may

---

[1]S-norms and T-norms are binary operators satisfying monotonicity, commutativity and associativity requirements, and the boundary conditions $S(0, a) = a$ and $T(1, a) = a$. These operators are used to implement the union and intersection of fuzzy sets (Lee 1990).

cause convergence problems as a consequence of the discontinuous derivatives of some logical functions, this problem is analyzed by Pedrycz (1991).

2.4 Connectionist Inference Systems

Neural networks, containing or not logical neurons, have been applied as fuzzy inference systems in two different ways: working with fuzzy inputs and generating fuzzy outputs, or including the descriptions of the fuzzy sets or the possibility distributions and working with numerical inputs and outputs.

Those systems that work with fuzzy inputs and outputs have analyzed the inference from different points of view: as a question of aggregation of evidence (Keller et al. 1992), in a purely functional way to obtain a neural version of a fuzzy simulator (Bulsari et al. 1992), as a way for coping with the problem of errors on fuzzification and defuzzification processes (Lee et al. 1994), or analyzing the problem from the view point of fuzzy sets representation (Ishibuchi et al. 1994).

Those systems that work with numerical inputs and outputs focus the inference in a functional sense (Keller and Tahani 1992), applying mathematical programming techniques (Narazaki and Ralescu 1992), or considering the relational structure of fuzzy systems (Pedrycz 1991).

2.5 Rule-Like Connectionist Systems

Some fuzzy-neural systems are neural networks that topologically or conceptually are structured as a rule-based system with IF-THEN clauses. These systems are generally obtained throughout a two steps (at least) process.

The first step when defining a Rule-like connectionist system is related to the definition of the number of rules and to the definition of the domain of each rule. This phase may be analyzed as a problem of unsupervised learning and solved by a clustering or a classification method. Once the number of input and output variables is defined and the number of rules is selected (there is no unique solution) the topology of the neural network is fixed. If the clustering method produces any kind of self organizing structure, this first step directly produces the IF parts of the rules (Yager 1994). Other systems use the resulting clusters to tune the elements of the net that represent the IF part by applying a supervised learning method (Takagi and Hayashi 1991; Takagi et al. 1992).

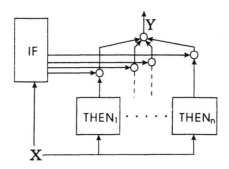

Figure 3   Rule-like connectionist system.

The second step produces the THEN parts of the rules through a process of supervised learning based on an input-output data and an optimization function. The consequents (THEN parts) may have a fuzzy structure or a numerical structure (Mamdani or TSK types, (Lee 1990)), both cases are analyzed by Horikawa et al. (1992).

In a rule-like connectionist system, a part of the connectionist structure (which plays the role of IF part) generates an activation value or a truth value for each THEN part. This value represents the membership function of a certain input value to the domain of each rule. Different parts of the connectionist system play the role of THEN structures, generating the output related to the corresponding rule. The output of the whole system is obtained by evaluating the outputs from each THEN element jointly with the truth value of the corresponding rule (IF part). This structure is represented on Figure 3.

Takagi et al. (1992) define a system that is able of adding new rules by splitting the existing ones. Other approaches need a complete learning process when a new rule is added to refine the system, but in this case the division of a rule is achieved by a cascade structure that allows the rest of the system remaining unchanged. This sort of modularity is a really important property usually not present in neural systems. A different but related approach is proposed by Mills et al. (1994), working with sub-models instead of rules, and applying an incremental process.

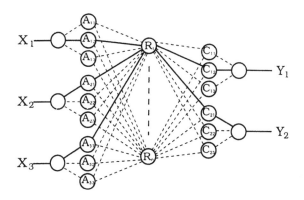

Figure 4 A rule in a connectionist system.

2.6 Connectionist Systems With Symbolic Acquisition of Knowledge

In some cases, the symbolic system is applied as an interface between an expert that possesses the knowledge to solve a certain problem and a neural network that is the processing unit for using that knowledge. Acquisition of knowledge from the expert is done by means of a fuzzy system. This knowledge is then implanted in a logic connectionist system, or used to train a neural net that may contain logical, arithmetical or both kinds of computational nodes. This approach to fuzzy-neural systems may be considered as a sort of symbolic connectionist hybridization, where knowledge is extracted by a symbolic system and applied by a connectionist one.

Different systems have the ability to directly incorporate the knowledge described by a rule base containing TSK-type fuzzy rules (Jang 1992) or Mamdani-type fuzzy rules (Narazaki and Ralescu 1993a; Narazaki and Ralescu 1993b; Nauck and Kruse 1992; Nauck and Kruse 1993). A method to perform this task is illustrated on Figure 4, where solid lines represent weights that initialized to 1, express the rule:

R_1 : if x_1 is A_{12} and x_2 is A_{21} and x_3 is A_{31} then y_1 is C_{12} and y_2 is C_{21}.

These systems can refine the resulting rules from experts by applying learning to the neural network. Experts' knowledge is usually viewed as the preliminary knowledge, and learning through the net as a fine tuning process (Figure 5). Other systems that apply the same methodology use predefined rule bases (Bouslama and Ichikawa 1993).

Figure 5   Acquiring knowledge through a fuzzy system.

Figure 6   Representing knowledge through a fuzzy system.

2.7   Connectionist Systems With Symbolic Description of Knowledge

On the other side of the connectionist systems with symbolic acquisition of knowledge are the connectionist systems with symbolic description of knowledge. In this case, the symbolic system is employed as an interface between the neural system that processes the knowledge and the expert or the operator that uses the system (Figure 6). Description of knowledge by means of fuzzy rules is done by backtracking in the neural net. Backtracking is more or less difficult depending on the functions implemented by the neurons. This is another type of symbolic connectionist hybridization, where knowledge included in and applied by a connectionist system is described and presented through a symbolic system (Mitra and Pal 1994). A part of the *logic connectionist systems* possesses a topology and a functionality that allow obtaining the fuzzy rules that generate a certain output.

2.8   Other Concepts

As has been said at the beginning of the section, some fuzzy-neural systems take no place in any of the previously defined categories. Some of these systems are discussed below.

The ARIC (Berenji 1992) and the GARIC (Berenji and Khedkar 1992) architectures are examples of this idea. As defined by Nauck et al. (1992), these are special architectures out of standard feed-forward nets, which can be interpreted as fuzzy controllers learning by updating its prediction of the physical system behavior. If comparing with the categories defined in previous paragraphs, these systems are composed of multiple elements that in some cases may match with predefined categories. Systems like ARIC or GARIC that do not match on any of the classes of the taxonomy, may be probably defined as systems with meta-processing. While a connectionist system plays a meta-processing role, a second connectionist structure representing a fuzzy system works as controller.

FUN (Sulzberger et al. 1993) is a second example of an uncategorized system, having a neural structure that is merely incidental, with binary weights in its connections and using stochastic search as one of its learning methods. Other example is FAMOUS (Ushida et al. 1994), with a more structured knowledge and containing heterogeneous neural systems.

3 APPLICATION ORIENTED CLASSIFICATION

A possible classification of fuzzy-neural (hybrid) systems is based on their application. When selecting a certain approach to mix fuzzy and neural techniques, the application may be a question to be considered. Comparing classes defined in the preceding section with those that are defined in this one, some connections may be found, as in *Connectionist systems with fuzziness*, which are tightly coupled with clustering and classification applications. Other groups like the *Symbolic systems with analytical learning* or the *Rule-like connectionist systems* are mainly directed to identification problems (identification of models or identification of controllers). This review focuses on a set of particular applications: Clustering, Classification, Modeling and Control.

3.1 Clustering

Given any finite data set of objects (X), the problem of clustering in X is to assign object labels that identify natural subgroups in the set. Because the data are unlabeled, this problem is often called *unsupervised learning*. The objective is to partition X in a certain number (c) of natural and homogeneous subsets, where the elements of each set are as similar as possible to each other and, simultaneously, as different from those of the other sets as possible. Most clustering methods are related to a certain distance from the point to be clustered to the center or prototype of the cluster.

Fuzzy systems have been applied to clustering since the very first years of fuzzy sets. Different approaches to clustering with fuzzy concepts have been proposed. The most popular set of algorithms is the fuzzy ISODATA or *Fuzzy c-means* (FCM) algorithm, extensively described by Bezdek (1981). Neural nets like the *Kohonen's-self organizing feature maps* or the Carpenter/Grossberg's *Adaptive Resonance Theory* have been widely applied to clustering. A taxonomy of neural nets applied to clustering and classification is defined by Lippmann (1987).

Most of the fuzzy-neural systems applied to clustering and classification are versions of previously existing neural systems which have adopted the concept of fuzzy membership functions. These systems have been described as Connectionist systems with fuzziness.

Based on or related to the main ideas of Kohonen's self-organizing feature maps, several approaches including the concept of membership function are proposed. In (Huntsberger and Ajjimarangsee 1990), a third layer is added to a Kohonen's self-organizing feature map to generate membership values of the input data to each cluster, returning membership values that are close to those of the standard Fuzzy c-means clustering algorithm. The integration of Fuzzy c-means and Kohonen Clustering Networks is proposed by Bezdek et al. (1992) defining a Fuzzy Kohonen Clustering Network. Other approaches to Fuzzy c-means algorithm, allowing clustering based on different prototypes (spherical, ellipsoidal ...) have been proposed and analyzed (Dave and Bhaswan 1992; Krishnapuram et al. 1992) defining the Fuzzy c-shells clustering algorithm.

Another area where hybrid systems have been proposed is clustering with a *follows the leader* approach, having some relations with the Adaptive Resonance Theory. Newton et al. (1992) defines the Adaptive Fuzzy Leader Clustering method by adding a procedure, based on the Fuzzy c-means algorithm, to update the clusters into a modified version of the Adaptive Resonance Theory. Simpson (1993) defines the clusters through the aggregation of fuzzy sets (with an hyperbox as the prototype) that are coded in the weights of a three-layer neural network.

3.2   Classification

The difference between clustering and classification is that clustering algorithms label given data sets $X \in R^p$, whereas a classifier is capable, once defined, of labeling every point in the entire space R^p. Classifiers are usually designed with labeled data, in which case they are referred to as supervised learning problems. The first approach to supervised pattern recognition using the framework of fuzzy sets is proposed by Bellman et al. (1969) analizing the problem in terms of abstraction and generalization. In the field of Neural Networks the single layer *Perceptron* and the *Multi-layer Perceptron* are classifiers producing different decision regions.

As in clustering systems, some fuzzy-neural classifiers are neural classifiers that simply add the concept of fuzzy membership function. In other cases logical operators are implemented in the nodes of multi-layer neural networks. A perceptron incorporating the concept of membership function is defined by (Keller and Hunt 1985). This fuzzy approach ameliorates the convergence problem when data are not linearly separable.

Zhang et al. (1994) add a fuzzification layer (with sigmoidal based membership functions) to a multi-layer perceptron modifying the back propagation algorithm to adjust the membership functions. A fuzzy-neural network model based on the multi-layer perceptron that uses the back propagation algorithm and capable of fuzzy classification of patterns is described by Mitra and Pal (1994). The nodes of the net incorporate logical operators in place of weighted sum and sigmoid functions (Logic connectionist system). Kwan and Cai (1994) describe a four-layer feed-forward fuzzy-neural net based in fuzzy neurons. The system applies a self-organizing learning algorithm to pattern recognition. Pedrycz (1992) defines and applies two different logic neurons in a three-layer network. The system works by learning and aggregating regions in which patterns are distributed.

Simpson (1992) defines the classes through the aggregation of fuzzy sets that are coded in the weights of a three-layer neural network. Carpenter et al. (1992) define a fuzzy version of ART classifier. Kuo et al. (1993) define a connectionist fuzzy classifier applying fuzzy membership functions to a four-layer neural network working with concepts of probabilistic neural networks.

3.3 Modeling

A model of a system is a description of some of its properties, suitable for a certain purpose. Modeling is the subject of constructing or selecting models. In fuzzy, neural or hybrid modeling, the model building is generally based on a set of input-output data or a sequence of input output data, and the objective is obtaining a system that (given the set or sequence of input-output data) minimizes the distance between its output and the corresponding data output. Generally speaking, model building is characterized by two questions: the selection of a mathematical tool to express a system model and the selection of an identification method. Here, the mathematical tool is the fuzzy implication or the neuron model, and the identification method is a parameter estimation method.

Probably Takagi and Sugeno (1985) produced the most significant work in the first years of fuzzy modeling, modeling based on fuzzy implications and reasoning. Multi-layer neural networks are applied to the identification of dynamical systems (Narendra and Parthasarathy 1990) employing a dynamic back-propagation method for the adjustment of model parameters.

In modeling and control some hybrid systems are multi-layer neural representations of fuzzy inference systems (Connectionist inference systems). These fuzzy-neural systems usually contain some kind of fuzzy or logic neuron. Bulsari et al. (1992) use a multi-layer neural network working as a fuzzy model of a process. Inputs and outputs of the neural system are fuzzy sets. Lee et al. (1994) define an identifier with a cascade structure composed of a fuzzification element, a multi-layer neural network and a defuzzification element.

Other multi-layer neural networks containing fuzzy or logic neurons and learning through an adapted back propagation method have been used by different authors as model identifiers. These systems have the fuzzy rules embedded in their structure, the extraction of these rules from the structure would be attainable but usually it is not treated on the papers. The fuzzy operators and connectives underlying the fuzzy system are contained in the logic neurons of the net. In some cases the system learns directly from a set of input-output data using a predefined topology of the net. The structure of the net may be selected according to the available input-output data using clustering techniques, rule-like connectionist systems (Yager 1994; Horikawa et al. 1992), training then the selected net by back propagation. The system proposed by Takagi and Hayashi (1991) may be viewed as the neural version of the TSK fuzzy system, applying the IF-THEN structure of fuzzy rules. A modified version of the previous work (Takagi et al. 1992) includes a sub-clustering method that produces a sort of cascade of multi-layer neural networks. The fuzzy rules may be directly translated to a neural network, connectionist systems with symbolic acquisition of knowledge (Narazaki and Ralescu 1993a; Narazaki and Ralescu 1993b), using the learning capabilities of the net to fine tune the predefined rules.

A particular case is described by Nomura et al. (1992), tuning a fuzzy system by a gradient descent method according to a data set. Wang and Mendel (1992) use Fuzzy Basis Functions and add tuning by using orthogonal least-squares learning. Yamakawa et al. (1992) use a neuron that is a particular type of TSK fuzzy system where each implication contains a single fuzzy input and a numerical output. This technique is applied to prediction of nonlinear dynamical systems. An Associative Memory Network working with fuzzy sets and logical operators is applied by Mills et al. (1994).

3.4   Control

The objective of a control system is to make the output of a controlled system behave in a desired fashion by properly selecting its input or its input sequence. Mamdani (1974) first applied fuzzy techniques to process control. From this starting point countless related applications, papers and books come out. A comprehensive review of Fuzzy Logic Controllers is made by Lee (1990).

Several works included in the previous subsection (Modeling Applications) have been or may be applied to control by using their identification characteristics to identify a controller of a system (Nomura et al. 1992; Lee et al. 1994; Takagi et al. 1992; Mills et al. 1994).

As in modeling, multi-layer neural networks containing fuzzy or logic neurons and learning through an adapted back propagation method have been applied in control. Having the advantages of fuzzy systems for linguistic knowledge acquisition, connectionist systems with symbolic acquisition of knowledge, this kind of system is faster in response than the equivalent fuzzy controller because it uses the computational power of neural systems. Nauck and Kruse (1992 and 1993) code the rule base of a fuzzy controller in the connections of a three-layer neural net, representing the fuzzy sets by the shared weights associated with the connections. The ANFIS architecture (Jang 1992) is functionally equivalent to a TSK inference system and is applied to control dynamic systems by incorporating and tuning predefined rules, or by learning its own rules. Bouslama and Ichikawa (1993) apply a multi-layer neural network, modeling a predefined fuzzy controller, to control an inverted pendulum.

Ichihashi and Tokunaga (1993) obtain the rules of a fuzzy controller by applying gradient descent method to a cost functional of integral form. Suh and Kim (1994) proposse a different approach related to radial basis functions networks and employing fuzzy membership functions as basis functions. In this case a fuzzy-neural interpolating network is added to the system.

The FUN architecture (Sulzberger et al. 1993) replaces weighted connections by binary (existing or not) connections and improve the performance of a predefined rule base. An architecture composed of a multi-layer representation of a fuzzy controller, a multi-layer network that evaluates actions proposed by the controller,

and an element that modifies the actions according to the evaluation, is proposed in
(Berenji 1992; Berenji and Khedkar 1992). The FAMOUS architecture (Ushida et al.
1994) uses two different associative memories to represent two kinds of knowledge:
static knowledge (for steady state) and dynamic knowledge (for state transitions).
Cho and Lee (1994) add a multi-layer perceptron, as a predictor of error, to a control
system based on a fuzzy controller. The output of the net modifies the input of the
fuzzy controller through an adaptation unit.

3.5   Other Applications

Not included in previous subsections, inference processing is not a particular but
a general concept appearing in different applications. A set of works devoted to
inference are grouped in this subsection. It is important to notice that the existing interest is not only directed to the practical application but to the theoretical
aspects related to applications too. In this sense, efforts have been done to analyze the problem of fuzzy logic inference as the key of fuzzy systems, producing
different ideas to apply connectionism to the inference process, and generating the
group of Connectionist inference systems. Narazaki and Ralescu (1992) employ a
neural network containing some logical neurons as a connectionist mechanism for
the inference on a fuzzy rule base and translate the inference problem to a mathematical programming problem. Keller and Tahani (1992), performe the inference
with conjunctive clause and disjunctive clause rules by a three or four-layer neural
network respectively. Keller et al. (1992) investigate inference as a question of
aggregation of evidence implemented in a net with logical neurons. Ishibuchi et al.
(1994) examine the use of α-cut representations of fuzzy sets and its influence on
inference and interpolation of sparse fuzzy if-then rules.

Eklund and Klawonn (1992) transform fuzzy logic programs to neural networks
including the ability to adapt the uncertainties of implications by using backpropagation learning. Rocha et al. (1992) apply a neural net whit logic neurons to
knowledge extraction from natural language data bases.

4   APPLICABILITY ANALYSIS

Different generic approaches have been described, but an important question is to
draw some guidelines for choosing a specific approach for a certain application. This
section describes different situations selecting the applicable fuzzy-neural systems.
Some questions to have in mind during this selection are: the amount and type of

available knowledge (if any) at the beginning of the learning or training process, the type of information to be used to drive the learning process, and the information to be sent to and required from the system when in the real application.

- If there is no initial information and the output variables are discrete and with a reduced number of possible values (some clustering and classification problems), a Connectionist system with fuzziness or a Logic connectionist system can be used.

- If there is no initial information but the system will have continuous output variables (modeling and control problems), a Rule-like connectionist system or a Logic connectionist system can be used.

- When a set of predefined fuzzy membership functions is available, a Connectionist inference system with fuzzy inputs and outputs can be used.

- When some previous knowledge allowing to split the working area of the system into different working regions is available (a short of clusters), a Rule-like connectionist system can be used.

- When a predefined fuzzy controller or a complete Knowledge Base is available, a Connectionist system with symbolic acquisition of knowledge can be used. A Symbolic system with analytical learning, obtained by adding learning capabilities to the predefined controller, is a second choice, but in this kind of system is more difficult to modify the rule base when using rules with fuzzy antecedent and consequent.

- When output explanation is needed the only choice is a Connectionist system with symbolic description of knowledge.

These selections are related to specific situations but cover a certain range of systems. The comparison with these specific situations, in addition to the information contained in sections 2 and 3, gives some hints when choosing a certain kind of fuzzy-neural system for a concrete application.

5 SUMMARY

Fuzzy logic and neural networks are two disciplines applied on information processing. Both techniques have their advantages and their weaknesses. The interest on synthesizing the most promising features of both approaches has produced multiple and diverse works in recent years. An approach to a taxonomy of fuzzy-neural system has been presented considering that these systems incorporate properties from fuzzy logic and from neural networks. Fuzzy-neural systems have been classified according to their symbolic and connectionist components, and their application. Some ideas on how to select a type of fuzzy-neural system for a specific application have been presented.

ACKNOWLEDGMENTS

This research is funded in part by the Commission of the European Communities under the ESPRIT Basic Research Project *MIX: Modular Integration of Connectionist and Symbolic Processing in Knowledge Based Systems*, ESPRIT-9119.

REFERENCES

R. Bellman, R. Kalaba, and L. Zadeh (1969). Abstraction and pattern classification. *Journal of Mathematical Analysis Applications 13*, 1–7.

H. Berenji (1992). A reinforcement learning-based architecture for fuzzy logic control. *International Journal of Approximate Reasoning 6*(2), 267–292.

H. Berenji and P. Khedkar (1992). Learning and tuning fuzzy logic controllers through reinforcements. *IEEE Transactions on Neural Networks 3*(5), 724–740.

J. Bezdek (1981). *Pattern Recognition with Fuzzy Objective Function Algorithms*. Advanced Applications in Pattern Recognition. Plenum Press.

J. Bezdek, E. Tsao, and N. Pal (1992). Fuzzy Kohonen clustering networks. In *Proc. 1992 IEEE International Conference on Fuzzy Systems*, San Diego, USA, pp. 1035–1043.

F. Bouslama and A. Ichikawa (1993). Application of neural networks to fuzzy control. *Neural Networks 6*, 791–799.

A. Bulsari, H. Saxen, and A. Kraslawski (1992). Fuzzy simulation by an artificial neural network. *Engineering Applications of Artificial Intelligence 5*(5), 401–406.

G. Carpenter, S. Grossberg, N. Markuzon, J. Reynolds, and D. Rosen (1992). Fuzzy ARTMAP: A neural network architecture for incremental supervised learning of analog multidimensional maps. *IEEE Transactions on Neural Networks* 3(5), 698–713.

K. Cho and K. Lee (1994). An adaptive fuzzy current controller with neural network for a field-oriented controller induction machine. *International Journal of Approximate Reasoning* 10(1), 45–61.

R. Dave and K. Bhaswan (1992). Adaptive fuzzy c-shells clustering and detection of ellipses. *IEEE Transactions on Neural Networks* 3(5), 643–662.

P. Eklund and F. Klawonn (1992). Neural fuzzy logic programming. *IEEE Transactions on Neural Networks* 3(5), 815–818.

M. Gupta (1992). Fuzzy logic and neural networks. In *Proc. Tenth International Conference on Multiple Criteria Decision Making*, Taipei, Japan, pp. 281–294.

S. Horikawa, T. Furuhashi, and Y. Uchikawa (1992). On fuzzy modeling using fuzzy neural networks with the back-propagation algorithm. *IEEE Transactions on Neural Networks* 3(5), 801–806.

T. Huntsberger and P. Ajjimarangsee (1990). Parallel self-organizing feature maps for unsupervised pattern recognition. *International Journal of General Systems* 16(4), 357–372.

H. Ichihashi and M. Tokunaga (1993). Neuro-fuzzy optimal control of backing up a trailer truck. In *Proc. 1993 IEEE International Conference on Neural Networks*, San Francisco, USA, pp. 306–311.

H. Ishibuchi, H. Tanaka, and H. Okada (1994). Interpolation of fuzzy if-then rules by neural networks. *International Journal of Approximate Reasoning* 10(1), 3–27.

J. Jang (1992). Self-learning fuzzy controllers based on temporal back propagation. *IEEE Transactions on Neural Networks* 3(5), 714–723.

J. Keller and D. Hunt (1985). Incorporating fuzzy membership functions into the perceptron algorithm. *IEEE Transactions on Pattern Analysis and Machine Intelligence* 7(6), 693–699.

J. Keller, R. Krishnapuram, and F. Rhee (1992). Evidence aggregation networks for fuzzy logic inference. *IEEE Transactions on Neural Networks* 3(5), 761–769.

J. Keller and H. Tahani (1992). Implementation of conjunctive and disjunctive fuzzy logic rules with neural networks. *International Journal of Approximate Reasoning* 6(2), 221–240.

R. Krishnapuram, O. Nasraoui, and H. Frigui (1992). The fuzzy c spherical shells algorithm: A new approach. *IEEE Transactions on Neural Networks* *3*(5), 663–671.

Y. Kuo, C. Kao. and J. Chen (1993). A fuzzy neural network model and its hardware implementation. *IEEE Transactions on Fuzzy Systems* *1*(3), 171–183.

H. Kwan and Y. Cai (1994). A fuzzy neural network and its application to pattern recognition. *IEEE Transactions on Fuzzy Systems* *2*(3), 185–193.

C. Lee (1990). Fuzzy logic in control systems: Fuzzy logic controller - part I-II. *IEEE Transactions on Systems, Man and Cybernetics* *20*(2), 404–435.

M. Lee, S. Lee, and C. Park (1994). A new neuro-fuzzy identification model of nonlinear dynamic systems. *International Journal of Approximate Reasoning* *10*(1), 29–44.

S. Lee and E. Lee (1975). Fuzzy neural networks. *Mathematical Biosciences 23*, 151–177.

R. Lippmann (1987). An introduction to computing with neural nets. *IEEE ASSP Magazine 4*, 4–22.

E. Mamdani (1974). Application of fuzzy algorithms for simple dynamic plant. *Proceedings IEE, Part D 121*, 1585–1588.

D. Mills, M. Brown, and C. Harris (1994). Training neurofuzzy systems. In *Proc. AIRTC'94, IFAC Artificial Intelligence in Real-Time Control*, Valencia, Spain, pp. 213–218.

S. Mitra and S. Pal (1994). Logical operation based fuzzy MLP for classification and rule generation. *Neural Networks 7*(2), 353–373.

H. Narazaki and A. Ralescu (1992). A connectionist approach for rule-based inference using an improved relaxation method. *IEEE Transactions on Neural Networks 3*(5), 741–751.

H. Narazaki and A. Ralescu (1993a). Implementation of fuzzy systems using multi-layered neural network. In *Proc. 1993 IEEE International Conference on Neural Networks*, San Francisco. USA, pp. 317–322.

H. Narazaki and A. Ralescu (1993b). An improved synthesis method for multilayered neural networks using qualitative knowledge. *IEEE Transactions on Fuzzy Systems 1*(2), 125–137.

K. Narendra and K. Parthasarathy (1990). Identification and control of dynamical systems using neural networks. *IEEE Transactions on Neural Networks 1*(1), 4–27.

D. Nauck, F. Klawonn, and R. Kruse (1992). Fuzzy sets, fuzzy controllers, and neural networks. *Scientific Journal of the Humboldt-University of Berlin. Series Medicine 41*(4), 99–120.

D. Nauck and R. Kruse (1992). A neural fuzzy controller learning by fuzzy error backpropagation. In *Proc. NAFIPS'92*, Puerto Vallarta, Mexico, pp. 388–397.

D. Nauck and R. Kruse (1993). A fuzzy neural network learning fuzzy control rules and membership functions by fuzzy error backpropagation. In *Proc. 1993 IEEE International Conference on Neural Networks*, San Francisco, USA, pp. 1022–1027.

S. Newton, S. Pemmaraju, and S. Mitra (1992). Adaptive fuzzy leader clustering of complex data sets in pattern recognition. *IEEE Transactions on Neural Networks 3*(5), 794–800.

H. Nomura, I. Hayashi, and N. Wakami (1992). A learning method of fuzzy inference rules by descent method. In *Proc. 1992 IEEE International Conference on Fuzzy Systems*, San Diego, USA, pp. 203–210.

W. Pedrycz (1991). Neurocomputations in relational systems. *IEEE Transactions on Pattern Analysis and Machine Intelligence 13*(3), 289–297.

W. Pedrycz (1992). Fuzzy neural networks with reference neurons as pattern classifiers. *IEEE Transactions on Neural Networks 3*(5), 770–775.

A. Rocha, I. Guilherme, M. Theoto, A. Miyadahira, and M. Koizumi (1992). A neural net for extracting knowledge from natural language data bases. *IEEE Transactions on Neural Networks 3*(5), 819–828.

P. Simpson (1992). Fuzzy min-max neural networks-part 1: Classification. *IEEE Transactions on Neural Networks 3*(5), 776–786.

P. Simpson (1993). Fuzzy min-max neural networks-part 2: Clustering. *IEEE Transactions on Fuzzy Systems 1*(1), 32–45.

I. Suh and T. Kim (1994). Fuzzy membership function based neural networks with applications to the visual servoing of robot manipulators. *IEEE Transactions on Fuzzy Systems 2*(3), 203–220.

S. Sulzberger, N. Tschichold-Gurman, and S. Vestli (1993). FUN: Optimization of fuzzy rule based systems using neural networks. In *Proc. 1993 IEEE International Conference on Neural Networks*. San Francisco, USA, pp. 312–316.

H. Takagi and I. Hayashi (1991). NN-driven fuzzy reasoning. *International Journal of Approximate Reasoning 5*(3), 191–212.

H. Takagi, N. Suzuki, T. Koda, and Y. Kojima (1992). Neural networks designed on approximate reasoning architecture and their applications. *IEEE Transactions on Neural Networks 3*(5), 752–760.

T. Takagi and M. Sugeno (1985). Fuzzy identification of systems and its applications to modeling and control. *IEEE Transactions on Systems, Man, and Cybernetics 15*(1), 116–132.

H. Ushida, T. Yamaguchi, K. Goto, and T. Takagi (1994). Fuzzy-neuro control using associative memories, and its applications. *Control Engineering Practice 2*(1), 129–145.

L. Wang and J. Mendel (1992). Fuzzy basis functions, universal approximation, and orthogonal least-squares learning. *IEEE Transactions on Neural Networks 3*(5), 807–814.

R. Yager (1994). Modeling and formulating fuzzy knowledge bases using neural networks. *Neural Networks 7*(8), 1273–1283.

T. Yamakawa, E. Uchino, T. Miki, and H. Kusanagi (1992). A neo fuzzy neuron and its applications to system identification and prediction of the system behavior. In *Proc. Second International Conference on Fuzzy Logic and Neural Networks, IIZUKA-92*. Iizuka, Japan, pp. 477–483.

J. Zhang, A. Morris, and G. Montague (1994). Fault diagnosis of a CSTR using fuzzy neural networks. In *Proc. AIRTC'94. IFAC Artificial Intelligence in Real-Time Control*. Valencia, Spain, pp. 191–196.

PART II
LEARNING IN MULTI-MODULE SYSTEMS

6

A HYBRID LEARNING MODEL OF ABDUCTIVE REASONING

Todd R. Johnson
Jiajie Zhang*
Hongbin Wang*

*Department of Pathology
and Center for Cognitive Science
The Ohio State University*

** Department of Psychology and
Center for Cognitive Science
The Ohio State University*

1 INTRODUCTION

Abduction is the process of generating a best explanation for a set of observations. Symbolic models of abductive reasoning tend to be far too search-intensive (e.g., Peng & Reggia, 1990), whereas connectionist models (e.g., Thagard, 1989) have difficulty explaining higher level abductive reasoning, such as the generation and revision of explanatory hypotheses. This chapter proposes a hybrid learning model for abduction that tightly integrates a symbolic Soar model (Newell, 1990) for generating and revising hypotheses with Echo, a connectionist model for evaluating explanations (Thagard, 1989). In this model, Soar's symbolic knowledge compilation mechanism, chunking, acquires rules for forming and revising hypotheses and for taking actions based on the evaluations of these hypotheses. Thus, chunking models the problem solver's shift from slow, deliberate reasoning to quick, automatic reasoning. To complement this, Echo learns to provide better hypothesis evaluations by acquiring explanatory strengths based on the frequencies of events from past experience. Since Echo does not have a learning mechanism, it was extended by adding the Rescorla-Wagner learning rule (Rescorla and Wagner, 1972). This hybrid model is motivated and supported by experimental results from the literature.

2 ABDUCTION

Abductive reasoning is the process of generating a best explanation for a set of observations (e.g., Peng & Reggia, 1990; Josephson & Josephson, 1994). An explanation is a relation between one or more hypotheses and the datum or data they account for. Consider the radar task, a tactical decision making task in which a person uses radar information to determine whether an approaching craft is friend or foe. In the radar task, the observations are the current set of information available about a craft, such as the type of craft (air, surface or subsurface), its speed and course, whether it has responded to a warning and so on. The explanations relate hypotheses about the nature and intent of the craft to the observations. For example, if an aircraft is heading toward your ship and is not on a commercial air route, you might consider two explanations: 1) the craft is hostile (a single hypothesis); or 2) the craft is a commercial plane that is off course (two hypotheses, commercial and off course). Your decision about what to do next depends, in part, on your confidence in these explanations. If your ship is in immediate danger and you feel that the hostile aircraft explanation is more likely, you might decide to take defensive action. On the other hand, if your confidence in the commercial aircraft explanation is much higher than the hostile aircraft explanation, then, despite the threat of immediate danger, you might decide to collect additional data or issue a warning.

3 MOTIVATION FOR A HYBRID MODEL

The hybrid model described in this chapter is motivated by the following observations and empirical results concerning the relationship between symbolic and connectionist processes and human abductive reasoning.

To successfully solve abductive problems people must learn to quickly generate plausible hypotheses for one or more observations, and then integrate these hypotheses into a coherent explanation for the entire set of observations. Symbolic search-based approaches have traditionally performed well at modeling hypothesis generation and modification. Likewise, symbolic knowledge compilation can learn explicit rules based on a single problem solving episode, but it cannot easily learn explanatory strengths from previous experience. In contrast, connectionist learning techniques can easily acquire explanatory strengths, but cannot quickly acquire explicit rules.

For example, based on a single problem-solving episode of identifying an aircraft as hostile, Soar's chunking mechanism can learn an explicit rule that says that under certain general conditions, it should consider a craft to be hostile, but even after many episodes there is no direct way for chunking to learn the probability (or some measure of certainty) that a craft is hostile, given the conditions in the rule. Papageorgiou and Carley (1993) noted this problem with their Soar model of a simplified radar detection task. In contrast, connectionist learning techniques can easily acquire and use such probabilistic knowledge because they are sensitive to the past frequency of events (e.g., Gluck & Bower, 1988), but generally speaking connectionist techniques cannot easily learn explicit, complex rules. These differences suggest that a hybrid Soar/connectionist architecture in which Soar learns complex rules while the connectionist component acquires explanatory strengths might lead to significantly improved models of human learning for multicausal abductive tasks.

Additional support for a hybrid model can be found in the literature on hypothesis evaluation. The processes that people use to determine confidence in an explanation appear to involve a variety of interacting factors. These factors include: explanatory breadth (the amount of the data explained), parsimony (some measure of simplicity), strength of explanatory relations, base rates, the reliability of each datum, knowledge of and confidence in alternative hypotheses, and how thoroughly the explanation space has been searched for alternatives. Researchers in a number of fields have studied the use of these factors and their role in the overall evaluation process, but so far no clear picture has emerged. For example, Shustack and Sternberg (1981) found that the strength of alternatives affects a person's belief in a hypothesis; however, Downing, Sternberg and Ross (1985), using a more complex task, found that the strength of alternatives has little effect on a person's belief.

Symbolic models of hypothesis evaluation have two major problems. First, they have difficulty combining the factors needed to evaluate hypotheses. For example, many symbolic models (e.g., for a review see Josephson & Josephson, 1994) have been based on an evaluation function that considers the number of hypotheses in an explanation and the number of observations that are not explained by those hypotheses. This works for some situations, but for many others it is important to consider other factors, such as those listed above. Downing, Sternberg and Ross' (1985) research illustrates the difficulty of using simple linear combinations of factors to model hypothesis evaluation.

The second problem with symbolic approaches is that they tend to lead to a combinatorial explosion. If a person generates n hypotheses to account for various subsets of the observations, there are up to 2^n ways to combine these hypotheses into explanations. The evaluation function must be applied to each of these explanations. If a person were to employ such a method, his or her working memory would quickly become overloaded by the number of relevant combinations.

Echo's connectionist model of hypothesis evaluation addresses the problems with symbolic models. Echo is based on the theory of explanatory coherence (TEC), which proposes that people prefer explanations that best cohere with their beliefs (Thagard, 1989). TEC defines coherence (and incoherence) in terms of principles that relate hypotheses and observations. For example, a hypothesis coheres with the observations that it explains and also with analogous explanations, but incoheres with hypotheses that provide alternative explanations. Echo implements these principles by representing propositions (hypotheses and observations) as units in a connectionist net, and explanatory relations of coherence and incoherence by excitatory and inhibitory links, respectively. Link weights represent the strengths of explanatory relations, and additional data support units represent the reliability of data. Unit activations represent how well a unit coheres with other propositions in the net, a kind of confidence in a proposition. By synchronously updating activation values, Echo applies the principles of explanatory coherence in parallel. When the net settles, the unit activations represent the coherence (evaluation) for each proposition. This eliminates the problems with symbolic models as follows. First, Echo uses parallel constraint satisfaction to combine a wide range of factors in parallel. These factors include: parsimony, explanatory strength, explanatory breadth, reliability of data, strength of alternatives, analogies, contradictory evidence and explanations that are themselves explained. To our knowledge, no other theory of hypothesis evaluation combines as many factors. Second, the set of hypotheses that form the best explanation emerges from Echo's connectionist net; potential combinations of hypotheses do not need to be deliberately enumerated.

Research in a number of domains supports Echo as a model of human hypothesis evaluation. Thagard used Echo to model conceptual change in scientific discovery (Thagard, 1992a) jury decisions in murder cases (Thagard, 1989) and adversarial problem solving (Thagard, 1992b). Ranney and Thagard (1988) used Echo to model how beginning students solve physics problems and Miller and Read (1991) used Echo to study how people perceive social relationships. Read and Marcus-Newhall (1993) evaluated Echo's predictions using a series of simple social situations in which people were asked to judge their belief in several explanatory hypotheses. Their research shows that Echo can predict both the hypothesis preferred by the subjects as well as the subjects' belief levels for each hypothesis.

Research on implicit acquisition and use of event frequencies supports the hybrid Soar/Echo architecture. When conditional probabilities and base rates of occurrence are presented explicitly in terms of numeric values, they are very difficult to learn and utilize (see Kahneman, Slovic & Tversky, 1982). However, when they are presented in terms of real events and occurrences, they can often be learned implicitly and used correctly (e.g., Christensen-Szalanski & Bushyhead, 1981; Medin & Edelson, 1988). A number of studies indicate that the learning of frequency of occurrence is usually implicit (unconscious) and automatic. The Soar/Echo hybrid architecture is consistent with these results, because Echo appears to Soar as an opaque mechanism that automatically and constantly provides confidence values for hypotheses. Soar sees only the results of Echo's evaluations. It knows nothing about the acquisition or evaluation processes within Echo and does not ever deliberately call upon Echo. Thus, to Soar Echo is an implicit mechanism that supplies appropriate information based on the current situation and previous experience.

The hybrid model is also consistent with Kintsch's construction integration (CI) theory of discourse comprehension (Kintsch, 1988). Kintsch reviewed a variety of comprehension data that strongly suggests that people generate a wide range of possible meanings for a word using context-independent rules and then use a spreading activation process to integrate these meanings into a single discourse interpretation. The Soar/Echo hybrid model seeks to extend this approach from discourse comprehension to abduction in general. The approach differs from CI in at least two ways. First, since the connectionist evaluation process is embedded in Soar, the architecture is more readily applicable to a wide range of complex problem solving tasks. Second, the Soar/Echo model shows how symbolic hypothesis generation rules are acquired and how frequency acquisition, in combination with rule learning, alters the comprehension process.

4   A HYBRID LEARNING MODEL OF ABDUCTION

This section presents an overview of the hybrid learning model, followed by detailed information on Soar and Echo.

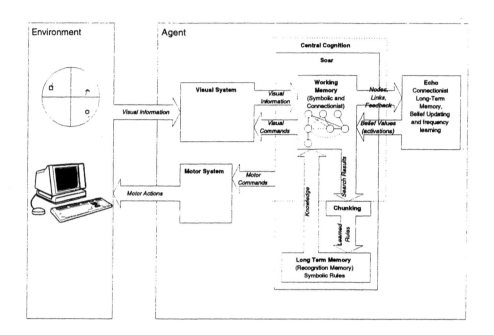

Figure 1   The major architectural components of the hybrid Soar/Echo learning architecture.

4.1   Overview

The major architectural components of the hybrid Soar/Echo architecture are shown in Figure 1. It consists of four major components: (1) Soar for modeling deliberative problem solving (forming and revising hypotheses), interaction with the environment (through the perceptual and motor system), and symbolic rule learning; (2) Echo for evaluating hypotheses, updating beliefs and acquiring event frequencies; (3) a visual system that mediates between the external environment and central cognition; and (4) a motor system that translates motor intentions from central cognition into motor commands.

Consider how these components interact during a radar detection task scenario. Information presented on the radar and other parts of the display flows from the environment, through the visual system and into Soar's working memory. This information is limited by the visual system's focus of attention. Objects near the center of attention show up with the most details, whereas objects far from the center only register as visual events. The symbolic problem-solving knowledge encoded in Soar uses this information to begin to build, in working memory, a situation model of the environment. This model contains the observations as well as hypotheses about the nature of the situation. The model is organized into a network in which nodes represent observations and hypotheses, and links represent explanatory relations. This network is shared between Soar and Echo. As Soar constructs the network, Echo augments the network with additional links and nodes that are needed to support the connectionist belief updating process. Echo also provides link weights and activation values based on a long-term memory of event frequencies. Once the network is specified, Echo updates the node activations, which become values in Soar's working memory that Soar interprets as belief values. Soar then uses these belief values to decide what to do next. It might decide to accept a hypothesis, reject a hypothesis, discount one or more observations, collect additional data, or take some other action appropriate to the task. These actions can lead to changes in working memory and in the environment. As the environment changes, the changes flow back into Soar's working memory, where Soar uses them to update its situation model. Changes to the situation model are detected by Echo and result in updated activation values.

Figure 2 illustrates how Soar and Echo are integrated. Soar solves problems by applying a sequence of operators that lead from an initial problem state to a goal state. Soar generates the operator sequence by repeatedly executing decision cycles (DC). In a single DC, Soar fires all matching production rules (the elaboration phase) until no more rules match. These rules can propose operators, prefer or reject operators, and modify working memory elements representing the current state. Next, Soar uses the decision procedure to select the best operator. Echo is run just before Soar's elaboration phase. Within a single Soar DC, Echo synchronously updates the activations for each unit until either the net settles into a stable state or more than a specified number of synchronous cycles (not Soar DCs) have been run. Echo then inserts these activations into Soar's working memory. To Soar, the activations are indistinguishable from information produced by production rules. Echo is like a continuously running background process that is given time slices at the beginning of each decision cycle. At the second DC, Echo continues to run, but it does so by taking into account any changes (deletions and/or additions) that Soar has made.

Learning takes place in both Soar and Echo. As Soar reasons about what to do (both in terms of cognitive and external actions), it learns recognition knowledge that allows it to reason faster in similar future situations. This is done through Soar's learning mechanism, chunking, which compiles the results of search into new production rules for long-term memory. Thus, chunking mod-

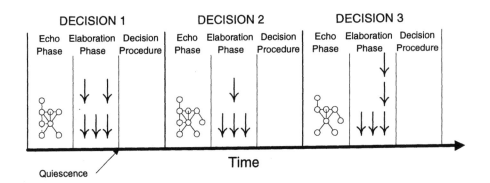

Figure 2 Echo is interleaved with Soar's decision cycle. By placing Echo just before the elaboration phase, the belief values produced by Echo appear to Soar as implicit information, automatically flowing into working memory from an impenetrable source. The diagram illustrates how the network can change from decision cycle to decision cycle.

els the shift from slow, deliberative reasoning to quick, automatic reasoning. Event frequencies are acquired through Echo, using a connectionist learning technique as described later. This technique depends, in part, on feedback from Soar concerning the correctness of the current hypotheses.

4.2   Soar

In the hybrid model, deliberative problem solving and symbolic rule acquisition are modeled using the Soar architecture. In Soar, problem solving is viewed as search in a hierarchy of problem spaces. A problem space consists of a set of states, a set of operators that transform one state into another, an initial state and a goal state. Problems are solved by searching for a sequence of operators that transforms the initial state into the goal state.

Soar has a working memory and a long-term memory. Working memory contains the current hierarchy of problem spaces including their current states and operators. Elements in working memory are represented as objects with relations and attributes. Knowledge for proposing, selecting and directly implementing problem spaces and operators is represented in long-term memory as production rules. If multiple rules simultaneously satisfy their conditions, all of them are fired in parallel.

Whenever a problem space lacks knowledge needed to proceed, an impasse occurs and a subgoal is set up to acquire the knowledge. For example, if a problem space in the radar detection tasks needs to get additional information about an aircraft, but does not have knowledge about how to do this, then Soar will automatically set up a subgoal so that it can select a different problem space in which to search for knowledge about how to collect additional information. This space might involve reasoning in a space of possible experiments, or might indicate how to access external sources of information in order to find a procedure for getting the appropriate information. Once the desired information has been produced, it is passed back to the original problem space, thereby resolving the impasse so that problem solving can continue.

Whenever an impasse is resolved, a production rule, called a chunk, is built. The conditions (i.e., the "if" part) of the chunk test for the situation that led to the impasse. The action (i.e., the "then" part) of the chunk produces knowledge that allows the problem space to avoid the impasse. For example, after problem spaces are searched to decide how to collect additional information, a chunk is built that can immediately produce that result in similar future situations. Thus, if the agent were again given the same problem, the top problem space would immediately know what to do, so an impasse would not occur. Soar's learning mechanism attempts to generalize chunks as much as possible by replacing conditions that test for specific elements of the situation with variables. Because of this, knowledge learned via chunking can transfer to situations that are not completely identical to the original situation.

4.3   Echo

Echo is a connectionist implementation of Thagard's Theory of Explanatory Coherence (TEC) (Thagard, 1989). Thagard has proposed that people prefer the explanation that best coheres with their beliefs. TEC specifies seven principles that define coherence (and incoherence): 1) *symmetry*: If P and Q cohere, then Q and P cohere; 2) *explanation*: If $P_1...P_m$ together explain Q, then $P_1...P_m$ cohere with each other and with Q; however, the degree of coherence is inversely proportional to the number of propositions $P_1...P_m$; 3) *analogy*; 4) *data priority*: observations have a degree of acceptability on their own; 5) *contradiction*: If P contradicts Q, then P and Q incohere; 6) *competition*: If P and Q are part of competing explanations and are not explanatorily related, then P and Q incohere; and 7) *acceptability*: The acceptability of a proposition depends on its coherence with other propositions.

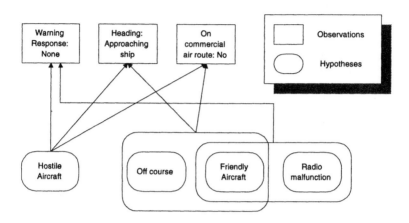

Figure 3 A partial situation model as it appears in Soar's working memory. Arrows lead from hypotheses to the observations they explain. In this situation, a craft that is approaching the subject's ship has failed to respond to a warning message and is not on a commercial air route. Two main hypotheses are being considered: (1) the craft is hostile; and (2) the craft is friendly, but has a malfunctioning radio and is flying off course.

These principles are implemented in a connectionist model, called Echo, that combines the principles in parallel to determine the coherence of hypotheses. Unlike symbolic theories of multicausal hypothesis evaluation, Echo does not provide an evaluation of complete multicausal hypotheses, and it does not require these to be enumerated and represented. Instead, Echo evaluates each individual hypothesis that has been generated to account for some of the observations. The hypotheses with the highest activations represent the most coherent hypotheses for the observations. If these hypotheses are part of the same explanation, then they represent the current best explanation; however, if they are part of competing explanations, they represent the best alternative explanations.

Echo makes use of a connectionist network in which units represent observations and hypotheses and symmetric links among units represent explanatory or contradictory relations. In the network, explanatory links are excitatory and contradictory links are inhibitory. For example, the situation in Figure 3 is represented by the network shown in Figure 4. Hypotheses and observations are represented by units in the network. The only major change is the addition of inhibitory links among competing hypotheses and excitatory links among cohypotheses. Units representing observations are connected to special data activation units (not shown in the diagram), since observations are assumed to

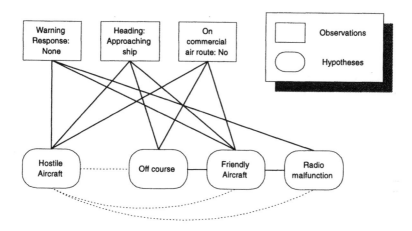

Figure 4 Echo network for the situation shown in Figure 3. Units represent observations and hypotheses. Solid lines represent excitatory links. Dashed lines represent inhibitory links.

have a certain degree of activation independent of any hypotheses. The amount of activation and the weight between the special unit and the observation provide a way to represent the importance of the observation. Activation values on the nodes range from -1 to 1. These values represent how well the hypothesis coheres with the observations and hypotheses in the net. Unit activations are synchronously updated according to the formula:

$$a_j(t+1) = a_j(t)(1-\theta) + \begin{cases} net_j(\text{max}-a_j(t)) & \text{if } net_j > 0 \\ net_j(a_j(t)-\text{min}) & \text{otherwise} \end{cases}$$

Where a_j, is the activation of unit j, θ is a decay parameter that decrements the activation of each unit on each cycle, min is the minimum activation, max is the maximum activation and $net_j = \sum_i w_{ij}a_i(t)$.

This process is repeated for a number of cycles until either no units have changed more than a specified amount or a specified number of cycles have been run. The process of spreading activation results in a combined application of the principles of explanatory coherence to the evaluation of individual hypotheses.

The primary problem with Echo as a process model, as many researchers have noted (see open peer commentary in Thagard, 1989), is that it assumes that humans have the ability to consider all of the interdependencies between an explanation and the available data. O'Rorke (1989) has also pointed out that Echo models abduction as an automatic unconscious process, whereas most complex abductive tasks appear to require conscious deliberative reasoning. These problems can be avoided by integrating Echo with Soar. Most of the criticism of Echo is based on Thagard's models in which he first builds a network containing all relevant observations and hypotheses and then runs the network once. In contrast, the hybrid model combines deliberate abductive reasoning (generating and revising hypotheses and explanatory links) with Echo's automatic hypothesis evaluation. As we noted earlier, a number of experiments support this model.

Echo itself does not have a learning algorithm. In the hybrid model, Echo is augmented with the Rescorla-Wagner (Rescorla & Wagner, 1972) learning rule. This rule is used to change the weights between observations and hypotheses based on feedback about the correct hypothesis for a given set of observations. The Rescorla-Wagner rule was selected for two reasons. First, an appropriate model of human frequency acquisition must acquire frequencies without a large number of training trials. Second, the hybrid model hypothesizes that communication between the deliberate and implicit components is limited to information that appears in working memory. The Rescorla-Wagner rule meets both of these requirements.

The Rescorla-Wagner learning rule works as follows. Let w_{ij} denote the strength of association between observation o_i and hypothesis h_j. (Instead of using a for all units, here we use o and h for observation and hypothesis units separately.) If h_j is a correct hypothesis for observation o_i (based on feedback from Soar), then the weight change is $\Delta w_{ij} = \eta o_i(\max_j - \sum_{i \in O} w_{ij})$, where η is the learning rate, o_i reflects the reliability of the observation, $\max_j$ is the maximum possible level of associative strength that can be associated with h_j, and $\sum_{i \in O} w_{ij}$ is the total associative strength for the hypothesis h_j that connects all observations present on that trial. If the hypothesis h_j is an incorrect hypothesis for observation o_i (again, the feedback is from the Soar component), then the associative strength between o_i and h_j decreases. The weight change is $\Delta w_{ij} = -\eta o_i \sum_{i \in O} w_{ij}$. After a series of trials, w_{ij} will reflect the conditional probability of the hypothesis h_j given the observation o_i.

Two small modifications were required to use the Rescorla-Wagner rule in Echo. First, Δw_{ij} is computed using the present activation of h_j instead of the sum of the inputs to h_j. This is done because the activation of hypothesis units in

Echo are determined only after many cycles, and thus are not equivalent to the present sum of the inputs. Second, each link weight is updated according to the formula:

$$
w_{ij}(t+1) = \begin{cases} \text{max} & \text{if } w_{ij}(t) + \Delta w_{ij} > \text{max} \\ 0 & \text{if } w_{ij}(t) + \Delta w_{ij} < 0 \\ w_{ij}(t) + \Delta w_{ij} & \text{otherwise} \end{cases}
$$

After learning, the conditional probability of each hypothesis h_j given the observation o_i is given by w_{ij}/max.

5 EVALUATIONS: EXPERIMENT AND SIMULATION

This section tests the model on an important component of abductive skill—the acquisition and use of frequency of occurrence information. Due to the nature of this part of the task, the emphasis here is on the connectionist component, Echo, and the Rescorla-Wagner learning rule. We first present the experiment on frequency learning and order effect. Then we present the simulation on frequency learning.

5.1 Experiment: Frequency Learning and Order Effects

The experimental task was implemented on the Combat Information Center (CIC) simulator developed by Towne (1995) for the US Navy. Figure 5 shows a simplified radar display of the CIC simulator. It shows an unknown airplane (the square with a line that indicates direction and velocity) heading toward the Naval ship, which is at the center of the radar display. The captain of the ship can check whether the target is on or off a commercial air route by clicking the route button to display all available routes. He can also send a radio verbal warning to request the target to identify itself. The target may or may not respond to the warning. In this experiment, when it responds to the warning, it always identifies itself as a commercial airplane. The target can be either friendly or hostile. The task is to use the information about the air route and the information about the identity (ID) obtained from the radio warning to

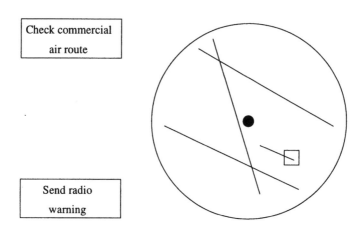

Figure 5   A simplified radar display on the CIC simulator. See text for details.

identify whether the target is friendly or hostile. The constraint of the task is that the two evidence items (Route and ID) can only be obtained sequentially, one at a time. The order can be either Route followed by ID or ID followed by Route.

The experiment tests two hypotheses. The first hypothesis is about frequency learning. In a given geopolitical environment, there are certain conditional probabilities about whether the target is friendly or hostile given the two evidence items. When subjects are trained on the task many times with a fixed base rate and conditional probabilities, they can implicitly and accurately acquire the frequency information. The second hypothesis is about the order effect (e.g., Hogarth & Einhorn, 1992). Previous studies show that when frequency information is accurately and implicitly learned in actual events, certain biases such as the base rate fallacy can be eliminated. We test the hypothesis that even if frequency information is acquired implicitly and accurately, the order effect, a special type of bias, still exists. That is, when the two evidence items are presented one by one in different temporal orders, the final evaluations of hypotheses about the friendliness of the target are different.

Method

Subjects. The subjects were 40 undergraduate students in introductory psychology courses at The Ohio state University who participated for course credit.

Design and Procedure. There were two evidence items: Route and ID. Route indicates whether the target is on or off a commercial air route. ID indicates whether there is any response from the unknown target to a radio warning issued from the ship. The two evidence items were presented in two different orders: Route-ID order in which route information was collected first, followed by ID information; ID-Route order in which ID information was collected first, followed by Route information. After having collected both evidence items, subjects made a forced-choice response indicating whether the unknown target was friendly or hostile. After each response, subjects were given feedback indicating whether the response was correct or incorrect. Each subject performed 50 trials. The conditional probabilities of hostility and friendliness for a given set of evidence items are shown in Table 1 under "T." For half of the 40 subjects, the two evidence items were always presented in the Route-ID order for all 50 trials; for the other half, in the ID-Route order for all 50 trials. The 50 trials for each subject constituted the learning phase for the acquisition of frequency information.

After 50 trials, each subject was given a written questionnaire requesting belief evaluations about the hostility and friendliness of the unknown target after the presentation of a baseline fact and each of the two evidence items. In the questionnaire, Route was always negative (the plane was not on a commercial route) and ID was always positive (the plane indicated that it was a commercial plane). For half of the 20 subjects receiving each of the two training orders (Route-ID and ID-Route), the evaluation order of the evidence items was Route-ID; and for the other half, the evaluation order was ID-Route. For example, an evaluation order of Route-ID is shown in Figure 6. The written questionnaire constituted the evaluation phase for belief evaluations. Thus, this experiment was a 2 x 2 between-subject design, with the two learning orders as one factor and the two evaluation orders as another factor.

Results

Frequency Learning. The responses of the 50 trials by each subject were aggregated across the 40 subjects for the Route-ID and ID-Route learning orders. The aggregated results were transformed into conditional probabilities, which are shown in Table 1. It is obvious from Table 1 that the conditional probabilities acquired by the subjects for both the Route-ID and ID-Route learning orders are nearly identical to the theoretical values. This implies that subjects had correctly acquired the frequency information of events for different conditions.

1. You see a plane which is getting closer to your ship. On a
   scale from 0 to 100 (with 0 being total disbelief and 100
   total belief) please rate your belief in the following
   hypotheses:

   (a) How likely do you think the plane is hostile?

   (b) How likely do you think the plane is friendly?

2. After consulting commercial air routes, you discover that the
   plane is not on a commercial air route. Given this new
   information, please answer the following questions. Again,
   express your answer on a scale of 0 to 100, with 0 being
   total disbelief and 100 being total belief.

   (a) How likely do you think the plane is friendly?

   (b) How likely do you think the plane is hostile?

3. When you asked the plane to identify itself, the plane
   identifies itself as a commercial airplane. Given this new
   information, please answer the following questions. Again,
   express your answer on a scale of 0 to 100, with 0 being
   total disbelief and 100 being total belief.

   (a) How likely do you think the plane is friendly?

   (b) How likely do you think the plane is hostile?

Figure 6   The questionnaire for the Route-ID evaluation order.

Table 1   Conditional probabilities of a friendly aircraft after 50 trials.
F: Friendly, E: Experimental, S: Simulation, T: Theoretical.

Route	ID	p(F | Route)			p(F | ID)			p(F | Route, ID)		
		E	S	T	E	S	T	E	S	T
+	+	.79	.79	.80	.74	.79	.80	.89	.94	.94
+	−	.79	.79	.80	.29	.20	.20	.59	.52	.50
−	+	.24	.20	.20	.74	.79	.80	.44	.53	.50
−	−	.24	.20	.20	.29	.20	.20	.14	.07	.06

Belief Evaluation. The results of belief evaluations after the learning phase are
shown in Figure 7. For both learning orders, there was a clear order effect: when

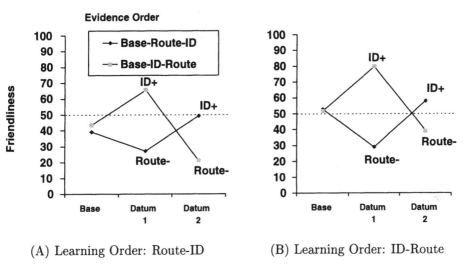

(A) Learning Order: Route-ID   (B) Learning Order: ID-Route

Figure 7 The evaluations of friendliness for the two different evaluation orders under the two different learning orders.

the two evidence items (positive ID, negative Route) were presented in different temporal orders, the final friendliness evaluations of the unknown target were different. This order effect for evaluations was a recency effect, as predicted by Hogarth and Einhorn's (1992) model: the final evaluation of friendliness was determined by the last evidence item. For the Route-ID evaluation order, the last evidence ID was positive, producing a more friendly evaluation. In contrast, for the ID-Route evaluation order, the last evidence Route was negative, producing a more hostile evaluation.

5.2 Simulation

The simulation used the network shown in Figure 8. To compare the simulation with the subjects, 60 simulated subjects, each played 50 trials. At the end of each trial, link weights were updated according to the formula given earlier.

Method

Subjects. Sixty simulated subjects were trained on the network. *Design and Procedure.* The order effect of the presentation of the evidence items was not considered in this simulation because the Rescorla-Wagner rule cannot deal

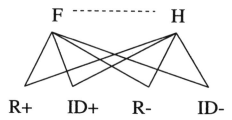

Figure 8　Network used in the frequency learning simulation. F: Friendly, H: Hostile, R+: On commercial route, R-: Not on commercial route; ID+: Aircraft identifies itself as commercial flight, ID-: Aircraft does not respond to identification request.

with temporal orders. The 50 trials used in the experiment were the 50 trials for the simulated subjects. The presentations of the 50 trials were randomized for each simulated subject. The conditional probabilities of outcomes given conditions of the two evidence items were identical to those in the experiment. The initial weights between observations and hypotheses were set at .02. The maximum weight, max, was .04. Each learning trial consisted of the following three steps. First, an input pattern (observation activations) was presented to the network. Second, Echo's activation rule was used to update the activations of all the units in the network in parallel until the network settles down to a stable state. Third, the activations of the two output units (F and H in Figure 8) were compared with the correct values and the differences were used to change the weights according to the modified Rescorla-Wagner rule.

Result

The final weights of the 60 simulated subjects were averaged. These weights were used to estimate the conditional probabilities of friendliness and hostility for different combinations of the two evidence items. As described earlier, the conditional probability of each hypothesis h_j given the observation o_i is given by $w_{ij}/$max. Table 1 shows the conditional probabilities acquired by the network. They are nearly identical to the theoretical values, as well as to the empirical values.

5.3 Discussion

The experimental results supported our two hypotheses: (a) frequency information was learned implicitly and accurately and (b) there was an order effect as predicted by Hogarth and Einhorn's model. The unique contribution of the experiment is that it shows that the order effect could not be eliminated even if the frequency information was learned implicitly and accurately. This is in contrast with previous studies, which show that when frequency information is learned implicitly and accurately, certain biases such as the base rate fallacy can be eliminated.

The simulation results on frequency learning with the Rescorla-Wagner rule were nearly identical to both the theoretical and the empirical values. It indicates that Rescorla-Wagner rule can account for both theoretical and empirical data on frequency learning. In addition to the Rescorla-Wagner rule, a simple recurrent net (Elman, 1990) and a reinforcement learning net (Sutton, 1988) were used to simulate the order effect. The simulation results show that both types of networks could produce order effects for the order used for training but they could not be generalized to a new order not present in the training. Other types of networks are being examined for the order effect. The objective is to find a single architecture that can not only learn frequency information but also produce the full range of order effects.

6 SUMMARY

This chapter described a hybrid learning model of abductive reasoning, along with a variety of experimental evidence to support the model. The model uses the symbolic Soar architecture for deliberate problem solving, hypothesis generation, and hypothesis modification. It uses Echo, a connectionist hypothesis evaluation mechanism, to integrate individual hypotheses into a coherent hypothesis that best explains the observations. Symbolic learning is done using Soar's knowledge compilation mechanism, which can quickly acquire abstract rules. Connectionist learning is done using a modified Rescorla-Wagner learning rule, which enables Echo to acquire conditional probabilities through experience.

The hybrid Soar/Echo model is based, in part, on the hypothesis that frequency acquisition and hypothesis evaluation are done using an implicit, automatic process. This assumption was tested in an experiment in which subjects solved a series of abductive tasks with an underlying frequency distribution and then were asked to estimate conditional probabilities based on a series of evidence items. The experiment showed that subjects accurately acquired the expected probabilities, but also exhibited a recency order effect when asked to estimate belief in a hypothesis given serially presented evidence. The simulation of the same experiment demonstrated that Echo, combined with the Rescorla-Wagner learning rule, could acquire the expected frequencies, but is not appropriate for modeling the order effect. This suggests that frequency acquisition and serial belief combination are independent processes. To improve the model, different learning rules and alternative networks are being explored for possible inclusion in the hybrid model.

Acknowledgements

This research was supported in part by Grant No. N00014-95-1-0241 from the Office of Naval Research, Cognitive Science Program and by a Summer Fellowship to Hongbin Wang from the Center for Cognitive Science at The Ohio State University.

REFERENCES

[1] J. J. J. Christensen-Szalanski and J. B. Bushyhead, (1981). "Physicians' use of probabilistic information in a real clinical setting," *Journal of Experimental Psychology: Human Perception and Performance*, vol. 7, no. 4, pp. 928–935.

[2] C. J. Downing, R. J. Sternberg, and B. H. Ross, (1985). "Multicausal inference: Evaluation of evidence in causally complex situations," *Journal of Experimental Psychology: General*, vol. 114, no. 2, pp. 239–263.

[3] J. Elman, (1990). "Finding structures in time," *Cognitive Science*, vol. 14, p. 179.

[4] M. A. Gluck and G. H. Bower, (1988). "From conditioning to category learning: An adaptive network model," *Journal of Experimental Psychology: General*, vol. 117, no. 3, pp. 227–247.

[5] R. M. Hogarth and H. J. Einhorn, (1992). "Order effects in belief updating: The belief adjustment model," *Cognitive Psychology*, vol. 24, pp. 1–55.

[6] J. R. Josephson and S. G. Josephson, eds., (1994). *Abductive Inference: Computation, Philosophy, Technology.* New York, NY: Cambridge University Press.

[7] D. Kahneman, P. Slovic, and A. Tversky, (1982). *Judgment under uncertainty: Heuristics and biases.* New York, NY: Cambridge University Press.

[8] W. Kintsch, (1988). "The role of knowledge in discourse comprehension: A construction integration model," *Psychological Review,* vol. 95, no. 2, pp. 163–182.

[9] D. L. Medin and S. M. Edelson, (1988). "Problem structure and the use of base-rate information from experience," *Journal of Experimental Psychology: General,* vol. 117, no. 1, pp. 68–85.

[10] L. Miller and S. Read, (1991). "Problem structure and the use of base-rate information from experience," in *Cognition in close relationships,* pp. 69–99, Hillsdale, NJ: Lawrence Erlbaum Associates.

[11] A. Newell, (1990). *Unified Theories of Cognition.* Cambridge, MA: Harvard University Press.

[12] P. O'Rorke, (1989). "Coherence and abduction," *Behavioral and Brain Sciences,* vol. 12, p. 484.

[13] C. P. Papageorgiou and K. Carley, (1993). "A cognitive model of decision making: Chunking and the radar detection task," Tech. Rep. 93.45, Carnegie Mellon University, Pittsburgh, PA.

[14] Y. Peng and J. A. Reggia, (1990). *Abductive Inference Models for Diagnostic Problem-Solving.* New York: Springer-Verlag.

[15] M. Ranney and P. Thagard, (1988). "Explanatory coherence and belief revision in naive physics," in *Proceedings of the Tenth Annual Conference of the Cognitive Science Society,* (Hillsdale, NJ), pp. 426–432, Lawrence Erlbaum Associates.

[16] S. J. Read and A. Marcus-Newhall, (1993). "Explanatory coherence in social explanations: A parallel distributed processing account," *Journal of Personality and Social Psychology,* vol. 65, no. 3, pp. 429–447.

[17] R. A. Rescorla and A. R. Wagner, (1972). "A theory of Pavlovian conditioning: Variations in the effectiveness of reinforcement and non-reinforcement," in *Classical Conditioning II: Current Research and Theory* (A. H. Black and W. F. Prokasy, eds.), pp. 64–69, New York, NY: Appleton-Century-Crofts.

[18] M. W. Shustack and R. J. Sternberg, (1981). "Evaluation of evidence in causal inference," *Journal of Experimental Psychology: General*, vol. 110, no. 1, pp. 101–120.

[19] R. S. Sutton, (1988). "Learning to predict by the methods of temporal differences," *Machine Learning*, vol. 3, pp. 9–44.

[20] P. Thagard, (1989). "Explanatory coherence," *Behavioral and Brain Sciences*, vol. 12, pp. 435–502.

[21] P. Thagard, (1992a). *Conceptual Revolutions*. Princeton, NJ: Princeton University Press.

[22] P. Thagard, (1992b). "Adversarial problem solving: Modeling an opponent using explanatory coherence," *Cognitive Science*, vol. 16, no. 1, pp. 123–149.

[23] D. Towne, (1995). *CIC: Tactical Decision Making (Version 2.0)*. Behavioral Technology Laboratory, University of Southern California.

A HYBRID AGENT ARCHITECTURE FOR REACTIVE SEQUENTIAL DECISION MAKING

Ron Sun
Todd Peterson

Department of Computer Science
The University of Alabama

1 INTRODUCTION

How does an autonomous agent that interacts with an environment learn to survive in the environment and make the most out of it? More specifically, how can it develop a set of coping skills that are highly specific (geared toward very particular situations) and thus highly efficient but, at the same time, acquire sufficiently general knowledge that can be readily applied to a variety of different situations? Although humans seem to possess such abilities and seem to be able to achieve an appropriate balance between the two sides, existing AI systems fall far short.

There has been a great deal of work demonstrating the difference between procedural knowledge and declarative knowledge (or conceptual and subconceptual knowledge; e.g., Anderson 1982, 1990, Keil 1989, Damasio et al. 1990, Sun 1994). It is believed that a balance of the two is essential to the development of complex cognitive agents. For example, one way to learn a sequential decision task, such as navigating a maze (see Figure 1 for an example), is through trial and error: repeated practice gradually gives rise to a set of procedural skills that deal specifically with the practiced situations and their minor variations. However, such skills may not be transferable to truly novel situations, since they are so embedded in specific contexts and tangled together. In order to deal with novel situations, the agent needs to discover some general rules. Generic knowledge helps to guide the exploration of novel situations, and reduces the time (i.e., the number of trials) necessary to develop specific skills in new situations. Generic knowledge can also help in communicating the process and the skill of navigation to other agents. If properly used, generic knowledge

Figure 1   Navigating a maze.

that is extracted on-line during learning can help to facilitate the very learning process itself.

There has been various work that deals only with one type of knowledge or the other, which include: work on reinforcement learning and work on autonomous systems (such as Mahadevan and Connell 1992, Barto et al. 1990); rule learning and encoding, including connectionist versions of them (such as Sun 1992b, Towell and Shavlik 1993). There are also existing AI models combining both types of knowledge, but they often simply juxtapose the two and they often do not perform integrated learning (cf. Gat 1992, Schneider and Oliver 1991, Hendler 1987). Anderson (1982, 1990) and Gelfand et al. (1989) address mostly top-down learning. We will instead explore the possibility of a two-level integrated connectionist architecture in this chapter. The basic desiderata for this work include: the agent should be autonomous and reactive, it should adapt to its environment, the learning process should be on-line (in real-time), and should also be integrated (that is, different types of representations should be developed simultaneously along side each other).

In the rest of this chapter, we introduce a novel architecture by first identifying the two-level structuring used in the architecture, and then discussing the realization of one level with a connectionist reinforcement learning network and the realization of the other level with a connectionist rule network. We present some (partial) experimental results that demonstrate the learning capability of the model, which is sometimes over and above those of the constituent parts.

2 THE ARCHITECTURE

2.1 A Two-Level Architecture

There have been various two-level architectures proposed, such as Hendler (1987), Gelfand et al. (1989), Schneider and Oliver (1991), and Sun (1992a, 1994). Among them, CONSYDERR (Sun 1992a) is the most integrated one. It consists of a concept level and a feature level. The representation is localist in the concept level, with one node for each concept, and distributed in the feature level, with a non-exclusive set of nodes for one concept. Rules as implemented in the concept level capture generic and conceptual knowledge that are available to an agent, and diffused representation of rules in the feature level captures associative and embodied knowledge (skills) to a certain extent. There are two-way connections between corresponding representations in the two different levels. Based on the interaction of the two levels, the architecture is capable of producing, in a massively parallel manner, a number of important commonsense reasoning patterns: evidential rule application, similarity matching, mixed rule application and similarity matching, inheritance (including both top-down and bottom-up inheritance), and so on.

Based on CONSYDERR, we will present a more complete and integrated architecture to tackle the problem of exploring both procedural and declarative knowledge in one framework. The architecture is named CLARION, or *Connectionist Learning with Adaptive Rule Induction ON-line*. It consists of two levels: the top level is a rule level and the bottom level is a reactive level. See Figure 2. The reactive level contains reactive routines (Agre and Chapman 1990), or procedural knowledge, acquired through connectionist reinforcement learning; and the rule level contains rules, or declarative knowledge, acquired through rule extraction (and a variety of other different methods).

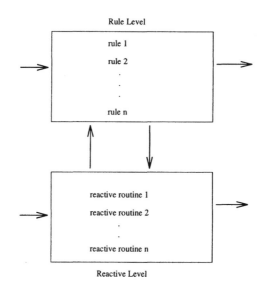

Figure 2   The CLARION architecture.

2.2   Reinforcement Learning

Let us consider the reactive level first. First of all, there is the question of what is the appropriate learning procedure to be used in this level to develop specific reactive routines (Brooks 1991, Maes and Brooks 1990, Agre and Chapman 1990). In a sequential decision-making situation such as navigation, there is seldomly any uniquely correct action. In general, for each situation, there are various possible responses that are roughly equally good, and thus, supervised learning procedures do not seem applicable since they require the a priori determination of a uniquely correct output for each input, or otherwise the learning will not converge (cf. Yamauchi and Beer 1994). However, for each situation, there are indeed good actions and bad actions; we might measure the goodness of an action through a feedback signal (a reinforcement signal) ranging from, say, -1 to 1, with 1 being extremely good and -1 being extremely bad and many other possibilities in between. Thus, we can adopt the reinforcement learning paradigm: we want to make a certain amount of adjustment to some parameters to increase the chance of selecting the actions that receive positive reinforcement and to reduce the chance of selecting the actions that receive negative reinforcement (Barto et al. 1990).

What is more difficult to handle is the sequential nature of the world and the sequential behaviors that are necessary for an agent to survive in the world (Waltz 1991), especially in tasks such as navigation and the like. In order to deal with the sequential nature of the world and to generate sequential behaviors, the agent needs a way of remembering the past and foreseeing the future; or in other words, the agent needs to take into consideration temporal information, beyond mere instantaneous feedback (including the temporal credit assignment problem). [1]

A good solution is to use the temporal difference learning method, as described by, e.g., Watkins (1989), and Sutton (1990). In this method, there is an evaluation function and an action policy. The evaluation function generates a value, $e(x)$, for a current state (input) x, which measures the goodness of x. An action a is chosen according to a certain action policy, based on the evaluation function $e(x)$. An action performed leads to a new state y and a reinforcement signal r. We then modify (the parameters of) the evaluation function so that $e(x)$ is closer to $r + \gamma e(y)$, where $0 < \gamma < 1$ is a discount factor. In other words, we update the function $e(x)$ so that

$$r + \gamma e(y) - e(x)$$

is smaller. At the same time, the action policy is also updated, to strengthen or weaken the tendency to perform the chosen action a, according to the error in evaluating the state: $r + \gamma e(y) - e(x)$. That is, if the situation is getting better because of the action, increase the tendency to perform that action; otherwise, reduce the tendency. In other words, the learning process is dependent upon the temporal difference in evaluating each state.

A variation of this method is *Q-learning* (Watkins 1989), in which the policy and the evaluation function are merged into one function $Q(x, a)$, where x is the current state and a is an action. An action a is chosen based on the values of $Q(x, a)$, given x and considering all the possible a's. The updating of $Q(x, a)$ is done based on minimizing

$$r + \gamma e(y) - Q(x, a)$$

---

[1]The solution offered by symbolic AI is explicit symbolic planning. The problem with this approach is two-fold: one is the high computational complexity inherent in this approach, and the other is the unnaturalness in describing many simple sequential behaviors (Agre and Chapman 1990, Brooks 1991). We need a more viable way.

where $e(y) = \max_a Q(y, a)$, that is, the temporal difference in evaluating the current state and the action chosen. In terms of both simplicity and performance, Q-learning is the best among similar options (Lin 1992). [2]

Reactive routines developed through the above reinforcement learning can exhibit sequential behaviors without explicit (symbolic) planning, since through successive updates of the evaluation (or Q) function, the agent can learn to take into account future steps in longer and longer sequences. The agent may eventually converge to a stable evaluation function (Watkins 1989) or even find an optimal sequence (that maximizes the reinforcement received). Thus the agent accomplishes sequential plans, on the basis of action decision making using moment-to-moment environmental input.

To implement Q-learning, we chose to use a four-layered network (see Figure 4), in which the first three layers form a backpropagation network for computing Q-values and the fourth layer (with only one node) performs stochastic decision making. [3] The output of the third layer (i.e., the output layer of the backpropagation network) indicates the Q-value of each action (represented by each individual node), and the node in the fourth layer determines probabilistically the actual action to be performed based on a Boltzmann distribution (Watkins 1989):

$$p(a|x) = \frac{e^{1/\alpha Q(x,a)}}{\sum_i e^{1/\alpha Q(x,a_i)}}$$

Here α controls the degree of randomness of the decision-making process and can become very small when learning stabilizes, so action selection can become (almost) deterministic (when needed). The training of the backpropagation network is based on minimizing the following:

$$err_i = \begin{cases} r + \gamma e(y) - Q(x, a) & \text{if } a_i = a \\ 0 & \text{otherwise} \end{cases}$$

where i is the index for an output node representing the action a_i. The backpropagation procedure is then applied as usual to adjust weights. This learning process performs, to a certain extent, structural credit assignment (with backpropagation) as well as temporal credit assignment (with Q-learning).

---

[2]There are a number of possible solutions from connectionist models, such as recurrent backpropagation networks; but they require supervised learning and therefore are unsuitable to the tasks we set out to tackle.

[3]To ensure adequate explorations, the action policy needs not to be deterministic. A stochastic decision process can be used, so that different actions can have their chances of being tried in accordance with their respective probabilities, to ensure various possibilities are all looked into.

In sum, the combination of Q-learning and backpropagation facilitates the development of reactive routines, or procedural knowledge, in the bottom level. Such development is based solely on the agent independently exploring a particular world without any external teacher or instruction. Using Q-learning in the model allows sequential behavior to emerge.

2.3 Constructing Rules

The other major aspect of the CLARION agent architecture is rule acquisition and refinement, which constitutes the other side of the equation: we need both the intuitive, reactive, and reflexive aspect of cognition and the deliberative, analytic, and reflective aspect. The latter is better handled by explicit symbolic representation and processes (Smolensky 1988, Sun 1994).

Let us consider in detail how such symbolic representation can come into existence. We need a simple and efficient way of acquiring rules and other structures, suitable for our domain. Because of the nature of navigation and other similar tasks, symbolic representations needed are relatively simple (compared with, e.g., the task of understanding natural language). We will thus mainly focus on simple propositional rules.

In terms of learning propositional rules, there is a substantial amount of work in the AI learning literature. However, in this architecture, there is an especially important factor that needs to be taken into account and made use of: that is, there is a connectionist network in the bottom level that is trained with the reinforcement learning procedure and is capable of performing specific reactive routines. Because of the embodied performance capability of this network, we can extract information from it, and thereby make general rules. In this way, there is no more need for a separate learning mechanism for the top level (although there can be), beside the one for extracting information from the bottom level. Learning in the reactive level serves a dual purpose, and thus the architecture is parsimonious.

The basic idea is as follows: if some action decided by the reactive level is successful,[4] then there might be general knowledge that can be extracted; the agent extracts a rule that corresponds to the action selected by the reactive level and adds the rule extracted to the rule network; in so doing, the agent will remove more specialized rules in the rule network and keep only the most

---

[4]Here, being successful could mean a number of different things. The algorithmic details will be specified later.

general one; then, in subsequent interactions with the world, the agent tries to verify the extracted rule, by considering the result of applying the rule: if the result is not successful, then the rule should be made more specific and exclusive of the current case; if the result is successful, the agent may try to generalize the rule, to make it more universal. In this algorithm, specialization and generalization is done with the previously extracted rules only, so that no search is needed. The Q-values at the bottom level and the reinforcement received by the agent provide suitable measures for rule extraction and generalization. See the section *Experiments* for more details.

Of particular relevance to such rule extraction are Fu (1991) and Towell and Shavlik (1993). However, these rule extraction algorithms can only be applied in the end of the training of the network. Once extracted, the rules are fixed; there is no dynamic modification on the fly (unless, of course, the rules are re-extracted from retrained networks). On the other hand, in CLARION, we can extract and modify rules dynamically, while the connectionist network is being trained. In other words, the connectionist reinforcement learning algorithm and the rule induction algorithm can work together, simultaneously. In this way, we can utilize the synergy of the two algorithms. Dynamicaly extracting and modifying rules also helps the agent to adapt to changing environments, by allowing the addition of new rules and the removal of existing rules at any time.

Now let us look into detailed implementation of such declarative knowledge in the connectionist network of the top level. A question is how we wire up a rule involving conjunctive conditions in a connectionist fashion. There are a number of previous attempts that we may draw upon (Sun 1992b, Towell and Shavlik 1993). When given a set of rules, a link can be established between a concept in the condition of a rule to the conclusion of the rule. If the concept in the condition is in positive form, the link carries a positive weight w; otherwise, it carries a negative weight $-w$. In addition, if there is more than one rule that leads to the same conclusion, an intermediate node is created for each such rule: all the concepts in the condition of one rule are linked to the same intermediate node, and then all the intermediate nodes are linked to the node representing the conclusion. See Figure 3. Sigmoidal functions are used for node activation. The threshold of a node is set to be $n * w - \theta$, where n is the number of incoming links (the number of conditions leading to the conclusion represented by this node), and θ is a parameter, selected along with w to make sure that the node has activation approximately equal to 0.9 or above, when all of its conditions are satisfied, and has activation approximately equal to 0.1 or below, when some of its conditions are not met.

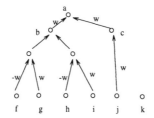

Figure 3 A network for representing rules. (1) $b \ \ c \longrightarrow a$, (2) $\neg f \ \ g \longrightarrow b$, (3) $\neg h \ \ i \longrightarrow b$, (4) $j \longrightarrow c$

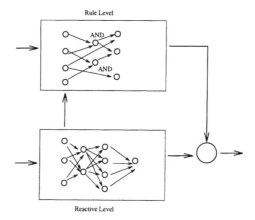

Figure 4 The refined CLARION architecture.

The rule level formed in the above way is complementary to the reactive level, since it extracts general rules that can be applied to novel situations. However, the reactive level has more flexibility: it can adapt itself gradually and allows stochastic exploration. Therefore, the two levels supplement each other and form a synergistic whole. See Figure 4.

3 SOME EXPERIMENTS

Let us examine some simple experiments with CLARION. For the following experiments, we use a simple maze shown in Figure 5 as the primary setting. The reward for an agent reaching the goal is 1, and the punishment for hitting a wall is -0.1. In the maze, wherever it is at, the agent has sensory inputs regarding its immediate left, front, and right side, indicating whether there is a wall, an opening, or the goal; the agent can move forward, turn to the left, or turn to the right.

With the CLARION model as in Figure 4, we first choose (optimize) the structures and parameters of backpropagation and Q-learning and keep them fixed: in the backpropagation network, there are three input units (one for each side of the agent) and three output units (one for each possible action), there are 8 hidden units, the weight update rate is 0.1, the momentum parameter is 0.7, network weights are randomly initialized between -1 and 1; the Q-value discount rate is 0.9, the randomness parameter for stochastic decision making is set at 0.3. We then run many experiments with variations of other CLARION parameters: (1) different rule extraction thresholds, (2) using rule extraction only vs. using rule extraction plus generalization, and (3) different types of top-down training, that is, different ways of using rules extracted to train the bottom level to improve its performance during learning.

Below are a few of the experiments on sequential navigation in mazes. We want to demonstrate that, at least under the given circumstances, (1) it is possible to extract reasonably good rules with the simple algorithm in CLARION, (2) rules extracted do help the transfer of skills to new environments, and (3) extracting rules may also speed up the learning process itself.

3.1   Rule Extraction

In extracting rules, we want to find a set of generic rules each of which must be correct with respect to the training environment.

Here is one typical example, using the maze in Figure 5. In this experiment, both rule extraction and generalization are included, and top-down training is minimal (i.e., successful applied rules are used to update the corresponding Q-values only once). Rule extraction is determined by both (1) the reward received at a step and (2) the difference in Q-values between two consecutive steps. The threshold for the amount of immediate reward required in order to extract a rule decreases gradually over a trial (starting at 0.3, until reaching 0); but the threshold for the difference in Q-values of two consecutive states (i.e., $r + \gamma e(y) - Q(x, a)$, which indicates if an action leads to an improved situation) increases gradually (starting at -0.2, until reaching 0). The idea is that since at the beginning of the learning, Q-values are randomly initialized and not yet tuned (and thus not reliable), we should rely more on direct feedback of reinforcement

Figure 5   The initial maze. The starting position is marked by 'S' in which the agent faces upward to the upper wall. The goal is marked by 'G'.

(i.e., external reward), and later we shall rely more and more on differences in Q-values and less and less on direct reward. Throughout the learning, rules at the top level are selected to be applied 80% of the time; successfully applied rules are generalized. Unsuccessfully applied rules are eliminated, and corresponding adjustments are carried out.

Let us examine the situation for each *episode*, i.e., for an exploration which starts at a certain position and terminates when reaching the prescribed goal. In each rule extracted, we use three numbers to represent conditions: the three numbers indicate the left, front, and right side of the agent; 1 means a wall, 0 means an opening, -1 means the goal, and ? means "don't care". As shown in Figure 6, after going through the first episode, one rule was extracted: "0 -1 1 go forward" (i.e., "if you see the goal in front, go forward"). The second episode did not produce other rules, because of the high setting for the reward threshold for rule extraction. The same goes for episode 3, although this threshold got lowered but the Q difference threshold got incremented. At episode 4, a new rule was generated "1 0 0 go forward" (Figure 6). After a successful application of the rule, three generalizations of the rule were produced. After a successful application of a generalized rule, two generalizations of that rule were produced in turn. Then, one correct rule was erroneously deleted, because Q-values were not perfectly tuned yet. At the end of episode 4, there were 4 rules. In episode 5, two rules were extracted. One faulty rule "1 ? ? go forward" was deleted; thus a suppressed earlier rule "1 0 ? go forward" that was the special case of the deleted rule re-emerged. In the end, there were 7 rules in total. At this point, the performance of the model on the maze was already nearly perfect; however, learning can still continue to fine-tune the rule set (not included here).

With both rule extraction/generalization and Q-learning, the performance of the model as a whole improves gradually. Figure 7 shows that the number of steps (actions) taken per episode goes down over the course of the five episodes.

```
At the end of episode 1:
0 -1 1 go forward

At the end of episode 2:
0 -1 1 go forward

At the end of episode 3:
0 -1 1 go forward


episode 4 :

extraction
1 0 0 go forward

generalization
1 ? 0 go forward
? 0 0 go forward
1 0 ? go forward

generalization
1 ? ? go forward
? 0 ? go forward

deletion
? 0 ? go forward

At the end of episode 4:
1 ? ? go forward
? 0 0 go forward
1 ? 0 go forward
0 -1 1 go forward


episode 5 :

extraction
0 1 1 turn left
0 1 0 turn left

deletion
1 ? ? go forward

At the end of episode 5:
1 0 ? go forward
0 1 0 turn left
0 1 1 turn left
? 0 0 go forward
1 ? 0 go forward
0 -1 1 go forward
```

Figure 6   Rule extraction and generalization. In each rule, the three numbers indicate the left, front, and right side of the agent; 1 means a wall, 0 means an opening, −1 means the goal, and ? means "don't care".

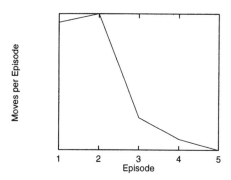

Figure 7 The performance curve.

3.2 Transfer Performance

We will now show that combining rules and Q-learning does help to improve the transfer performance of CLARION. We first train a model on the maze shown in Figure 5; we then apply it to the two larger mazes as shown in Figure 8 and 9. We compare the transfer performance of (1) Q-learning alone, Q-learning and rule extraction (without generalization), and (3) Q-learning and rule extraction/generalization.

The parameters for rule extraction and/or generalization are the same as above. Rules (extracted and/or generalized) are applied 80% of the time in making action decisions. The top-down training now occurs 10 times: that is, each successfully applied rule is used to update the corresponding Q-value for 10 times. After being trained on the initial maze for a total of 10 episodes, the model is applied to a new maze. In testing it in a new maze, we turn the randomness parameter in Q-learning to a very low value 0.01, to ensure that the reactive level will perform its best. Figure 10 shows the comparison of transfer performance, where the transfer performance is measured by the average number of the steps (actions) taken in one episode in a new maze. (An episode terminates if the agent reaches the goal or fails to reach the goal within 3000 steps.) This data is obtained by averaging the results over 20 trials, each consisting of the initial training in the smallest maze and 10 test episodes in a new maze. As demonstrated in the figure, rules help to drastically improve the transfer performance, in either one of the two new mazes, with either extraction alone or with both extraction and generalization. In both of the two new mazes, Q-learning with rule extraction works the best. Q-learning with both rule extraction and generalization is slightly worse off than with extraction only, but still signifi-

Figure 8   The second maze.

Figure 9   The third maze.

cantly better than Q-learning alone. A t test was performed that showed that
the differences were statistically significant ($p < 0.05$). It is a strong indication
of the advantage of the CLARION model, as hypothesized earlier.

Note also that the performance of the model on the initial maze, after the
training of 10 episodes, is near optimal. As a matter of fact, it usually reaches
the near optimal level of performance way before the end of a trial (of 10

	Maze 2	Maze 3
1	418.80	2993.20
2	116.50	1831.50
3	166.10	2191.90

Figure 10 Comparisons of transfer. (1) Q-learning alone, (2) Q-learning and rule extraction, and (3) Q-learning and rule extraction/generalization. Column 2 shows the results with maze 2. Column 3 shows the results with maze 3.

episodes). Therefore, the above comparison is indeed on the transfer capability of different versions of the model, not on the training efficiency of these versions.

3.3   Learning Speedup

We will show here that combining rules and Q-learning also helps to speed up learning in the initial maze (Figure 5). We will compare the learning performance of (1) Q-learning alone, (2) Q-learning and rule extraction (without generalization), and (3) Q-learning and rule extraction/generalization.

The parameters for rule extraction and generalization are the same as above. Rules are applied 80% of the time in action decision making. The top-down training occurs 10 times, in order to fully utilize rules extracted to help to train the Q-learning module. Figure 11 shows the comparison of learning speeds, where the learning speeds are measured by the total number of all the steps (actions) taken in one trial that is composed of (uniformly) 10 episodes. The data are obtained by averaging over 20 trials. As can be seen from Figure 11, a combination of Q-learning and rule extraction works the best, and is significantly better than Q-learning alone. Q-learning with both rule extraction and generalization is slightly better than Q-learning alone (which, we believe, indicates that the generalization process can be further improved).

However, it should be noted that we get mixed results when we reduce top-down training to a minimum (as in the first experiment). Although Q-learning with rule extraction still performs the best, it is not as good as shown before. Moreover, in this case, Q-leaning with both rule extraction and generalization performs the worst among the three. See Figure 12.

	Maze 1
1	2718.00
2	2262.25
3	2565.55

Figure 11 Comparisons of learning speeds. (1) Q-learning alone, (2) Q-learning and rule extraction, and (3) Q-learning and rule extraction/generalization.

	Maze 1
1	3587.15
2	2882.65
3	3973.90

Figure 12 Comparisons of learning speeds. (1) Q-learning alone, (2) Q-learning and rule extraction, and (3) Q-learning and rule extraction/generalization.

4 DISCUSSIONS

4.1 Non-Markovian Processes

Although it seems simple, the maze setting used in the experiments, as seen by the agent, is non-Markovian: because the agent can only sense the existence of a wall or an opening on each of the three sides, it cannot distinguish different locations in the maze. For example, when going down a long corridor, from the agent's viewpoint, it is always in the same "state" after moving forward, since its sensory inputs remain the same (i.e., $1, 0, 1$). Only when it reaches the end of the corridor, it suddenly sees a change in state. But it has no explanation for the change, since from the state $1, 0, 1$, with the action "go forward", it may wind up being in the state $1, 0, 1$ or being in the state $0, 1, 1$ (the end of the corridor). Such a situation is clearly non-Markovian.

Although we can enhance the sensor of the agent, or include a location identification (such as "square number 12") in the input, to make it Markovian, we chose not to. The reason is that we want to test the agent model in a realistic and difficult setting. Although it has been proven that Q-learning works in

Markovian worlds (Watkins 1989), it is not yet clear, theoretically, how well Q-learning can perform in non-Markovian worlds. Some have identified serious problems that may result in a non-Markovian world (such as "perceptual aliasing"; Whitehead and Lin 1995) and proposed solutions for them, for example, by using a recurrent backpropagation network that uses hidden layers as memory. We show here that CLARION, using simple Q-learning in a feedforward backpropagation network, can manage to work despite the non-Markovianness in the maze environment.

4.2 Cognitive Justification

Let us discuss the cognitive justification for each level separately first. For the reactive level, although there is no direct psychological evidence for Q-learning per se, voluminous psychological data exist that lend support to reinforcement learning. For example, Sutton and Barto (1981) describe in detail how a variant of reinforcement learning algorithms can be used to account for classical conditioning data. In terms of higher-level human learning, Anderson (1982) demonstrates the use of *strengthening*, which is similar to tuning of Q-values, in accounting for arithmetic learning. The idea of such learning can also be traced to the Law of Effect of Thorndike (1911). So, the use of reinforcement learning in modeling procedural skill in navigation tasks is not arbitrary but well motivated from the cognitive modeling perspective.

In terms of the rule level, existing psychological data support the rule induction process in CLARION. Various operations used in the above algorithm correspond clearly to what were termed *generalization* and *discrimination* in Anderson (1982); since the data presented by Anderson for such operations are translatable to the present framework, the corresponding operations in CLARION can be justified on the basis of these psychological data.

Due to the shared characteristics between CLARION and CONSYDERR (Sun 1994, 1995), the two-level structuring in this architecture can also be justified cognitively. First, there are cognitive arguments related to the aforementioned distinction of declarative and procedural knowledge: Smolensky (1988) proposed the distinction of conceptual (publicly accessible) and subconceptual processing; Dreyfus and Dreyfus (1987) proposed the distinction of analytical and intuitive thinking; in addition, although controversial, the distinction of conscious and subconscious processes is well known (cf. James 1890). All of them strongly believed in the need for incorporating both in cognitive models, because each side of the dichotomy serves a unique cognitive function and is thus indispensable. Second, as described in Damasio et al. (1990) and LaDoux (1992), there is also ample biological evidence that indicates the existence of multiple pathways (in visual, language, and other modal processing), some of which lead to conscious awareness, while others do not; one type is *cortical* while the other is *subcortical*. For example, LaDoux (1992) described one pathway as from stimulus to thalamus to cortex, which produces conscious, conceptual thoughts, and another pathway as from stimulus to thalamus then to amygdala, which can lead directly to brain stem and effect actions without any conceptual processing. A two-level model approximates the separation of the two kinds of pathways, incorporating the aforementioned distinctions.

4.3   Hybrid Models

Let us now turn to the form of the model. Hybrid models (connectionist and symbolic, reactive and deliberate, rules and non-rules, representation and non-representation, etc.) have been quite popular recently. These models include Hendler (1987), Gelfand et al. (1989), Anderson (1990), Schneider and Oliver (1991), Miikkulainen and Dyer (1991), and Sun (1992a, 1994, 1995), among many others. See Sun and Bookman (1994) for an overview. However, some have objected to such an approach, claiming that such research will most likely be frustrated by its lack of "a consistent conceptual framework". In our view, hybridness does not necessarily mean inconsistency; quite to the contrary, it can be consistent or even principled. From the experiments reported here, we see that there is a performance advantage in combining rules and reactive routines/reinforcement learning; from the cognitive perspective (see the previous subsection), the two-level architecture is principled as well as consistent, since it is based on the theories of the dichotomy of the conceptual and the subconceptual. This work serves as one demonstration of the promise of the hybrid approach in developing agent models.

4.4   Comparisons

Let us compare CLARION with other models. Although CLARION shares much similarity with ACT as described in Anderson (1982, 1983, 1990), it succeeds in explaining two issues that Anderson (1982, 1983) does not address. First, while Anderson takes a top-down approach towards learning (from declarative to procedural knowledge), CLARION is mostly bottom-up (mostly, from procedural to declarative one); therefore, it does not rely on existing, externally given, verbally imparted knowledge as much as ACT does. CLARION is able to learn while acting in the real environment, without an external teacher providing correct input/output mapping or instructions of any form. Second, a more significant difference is in the representation: in ACT, both declarative and procedural knowledge are represented in an explicit, symbolic form (i.e., semantic networks plus production rules), and thus it fails to explain, from a representational viewpoint, the differences in conscious accessibility between the two types of knowledge. (Declarative knowledge is consciously accessible while procedural knowledge is mostly inaccessible; Shiffrin and Schneider 1977 and LaDoux 1992.) CLARION, on the other hand, is successful in accounting for the difference based on a judicious use of the two different forms of representation — the rule level is clearly explicit/symbolic, while the other level with a backpropagation network is implicit and contains embedded knowledge.

In terms of complexity, CLARION is similar to Mitchell et al. (1991), Carbonell et al. (1991), and a number of other cognitive architectures found in the AI literature, in that many different modules and learning methods are incorporated and elaborate mechanisms are developed. Different from other architectures is the fact that in this architecture, representations (including both symbolic representation as in the top level and implicit representation as in the bottom level) are mainly discovered through exploration by the agent, instead of being given. Besides avoiding the practical problem of hand-coding knowledge, such representations are (1) grounded in the external world, (2) more specifically geared towards the particular environment that the agent is in, and (3) can be more adaptive to changing environments.

In the area of hybrid models, while some connectionists try to implement all types of knowledge in one particular kind of connectionist network or another (e.g., Shastri and Ajjanagadde 1990, Miikkulainen and Dyer 1991, Sun 1992a), CLARION, among some others (as cited before), attempts to develop a principled dichotomy in their architectures. While some existing models that incorporate the dichotomy tend to simply juxtapose the two sides of the dichotomy (connectionist and symbolic, reacting and planning), CLARION attempts to explore their synergy, in learning as well as in performance (transfer). While some models explore top-down learning (advice taking; such as Gelfand et al 1989, Maclin and Shavlik 1994), CLARION explores bottom-up learning to show how conceptual/symbolic knowledge emerges through interacting with the world. In addition, CLARION is capable of *on-line* learning (learning during the task performance), and *integrated* learning, developing connectionist and symbolic representation along side of each other.

Let us also compare CLARION with other rule extraction algorithms. Fu (1991) proposed a search-based algorithm to extract conjunctive rules: to find rules, we first search for all the combinations of positive conditions that can lead to a conclusion; then, in the second phase, with a previously found combination of positive conditions, we search for negative conditions that should be added to guarantee the conclusion. Towell and Shavlik (1993) used rules of an alternative form, the *N-of-M* form:

> *If N of the M conditions, a_1, a_2, ..., a_M, is true, then the conclusion b is true.*

It is believed that some rules can be better expressed in such a form, which resembles more the weighted-sum computation in connectionist networks, in order to avoid the combinatorial explosion and to discern structures. A four-step procedure is used to extract such rules, by first grouping similarly weighted links and eliminating insignificant groups, and then forming rules with remaining groups. These rule extraction algorithms can only be applied after the complete training of a connectionist network. Once extracted, the rules are fixed. On the other hand, CLARION can extract and modify rules dynamically, while the connectionist network is being trained, in order to utilize their synergy and to adapt to changing environments. But the rules extracted in CLARION are simpler in form and may not be exhaustive. Gordon and Grefenstette (1992) try to explain reactive behavior with existing knowledge (rules) and then generalize these explanations into generic rules. Thus, they also require complete training first, and they need extensive domain knowledge in their agents to begin with.

4.5   The Need for Two Levels

From the previous discussions, the necessity of having the two-level architecture can be summed up as follows:

- Without the reactive level, the agent will not be able to represent reactive routines accurately (with numeric calculation and probabilistic firing), which may not be captured by simpler mechanisms (such as productions used in Anderson 1982).

- Without learning in the reactive level, the agent will not be able to learn from experience, and therefore will not be able to either dynamically acquire the reactive routines in the bottom level (cf. Brooks 1991), nor the more generic rules in the top level (as in the current model).

- Without the top level, the agent will not be able to (1) represent generic knowledge and (2) explicitly access and communicate that knowledge to other agents (i.e., the explanation capability, which is absent in Sutton 1990, Brooks 1991). Being able to represent generic knowledge is important when novel situations are encountered (Gordon and Grefenstette 1992). The explicit access and explanation capability is also important in order to facilitate cooperation among agents.

- Without rule learning (extraction and generalization), the agent will not be able to acquire *dynamically* generic knowledge for the top level, and therefore has to resort to a pre-wired and/or externally given knowledge in the top level.

4.6 Further Work

In addition to the previously discussed modules in CLARION, there can also be other modules. Among them, *episode replay* (or "world models"; Lin 1992, Sutton 1990) is the training and modification of the reactive routines with previously encountered episodes. The reason for replaying is to fully use available information from previous exploration, to speed up learning and to reduce learning cost. The process can be hypothesized to roughly correspond to an "incubation" period in human learning. *Meta-rules* are the rules that determine actions based on the reflection on an agent's own cognitive states: its own knowledge of something or the lack of it (cf. Perlis 1985). For example, when an agent determines that it has no knowledge about a particular situation x, it then decides to apply a default action d. Or, when an agent determines that it has contradictory decision rules regarding a situation, it then applies a higher-level conflict resolution mechanism. Or, more important, if an agent determines that it is stuck or looping, then certain meta-level actions may be taken to get out of a dead-end or a loop, by e.g. increasing randomness (α) in stochastic decision making. Another kind of rule learning in CLARION is *advice taking* or *learning by being told* (Michalski 1983). When an external instruction in the form of a rule is given, the advice taker then wires it into the rule network in the proper place and connects it to existing representations, in the same way as specified earlier (provided that the form of advice is simple and the range is limited; in general, advice taking is a complex problem). We can go one step further in this two-level architecture, by performing *rule assimilation*, which is the process by which rules (advice) given externally, besides being wired up in the top level, are assimilated into reactive routines and become more effective (Anderson 1982, Dreyfus and Dreyfus 1987, Maclin and Shavlik 1994). We train the bottom level according to rules given in the top level, using either re-

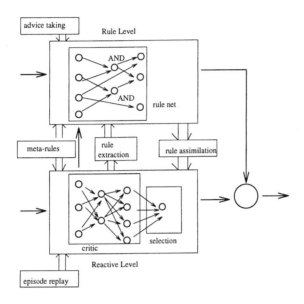

Figure 13   The CLARION architecture with additional modules.

inforcement learning or supervised learning. Altogether, CLARION can contain all the modules as shown in Figure 13.

CLARION, as is, does not yet capture the full range of cognitive processes involved in the maze navigation task. There are at least the following components involved in this task: perception, internal decision making, and motor output, while CLARION accounts for only one of them. Although CLARION is not complete in functionalities, it is, nevertheless, meant to be a generic cognitive model. In other words, it should be able to account for many different phenomena in many different domains, including modeling motor skills, modeling perception, as well as modeling decision making. (We believe that the same two representations and their interaction are essential to many different aspects of cognition; see the earlier arguments.)

Another extension that is worth exploring is generating reinforcement signals internally. In general cases, the world in which the agent lives does not provide a simple, scalar reinforcement signal, but simply changes into a new state after a certain action is performed. An appropriate level of reinforcement has to be determined internally within the agent. We posit that such a signal is internally determined from the goals, needs, and desires of the agent, and the reinforcement is derived from measuring the degree of satisfaction of these goals, needs, and desires. Such determination is context dependent. For example, when an animal is hungry, if an action leads to the discovery of food, a high level of reinforcement is expected; when an animal has just finished eating, finding more food may only create boredom and thus the action may receive neutral or even negative reinforcement (Waltz 1991). Therefore, (implicit or explicit) representation of the goals, needs, and desires of an agent is necessary, and a match of a new state to such representation needs to be computed in order to generate (context-dependent) reinforcement signals.

In order to fully test the model, experiments have been carried out in more complex domains, where inputs are continuous, state spaces are huge, environments are nonstationary, and no simple rule exists. These experiments are reported elsewhere.

5 SUMMARY

This chapter describes a hybrid connectionist agent architecture that utilizes both rules and reactive routines. We show that the combination of the two types of knowledge yields synergistic results, in terms of both expediting learning and facilitating transfer of knowledge. The integration thus has a performance advantage besides being cognitively plausible.

ACKNOWLEDGMENTS: This work is supported in part by Office of Naval Research grant number N00014-95-1-0440. We wish to thank Dave Waltz, Helen Gigley, Susan Chipman, and Diana Gordon for comments, and Ed Merrill for useful discussions.

REFERENCES

[1] P. Agre and D. Chapman, (1990). What are plans for? In: P. Maes, ed. *Designing Autonomous Agents*. Elsevier, New York.

[2] J. Anderson, (1982). Acquisition of cognitive skill. *Psychological Review*. Vol.89, pp.369-406.

[3] J. Anderson, (1983). *The Architecture of Cognition*, Harvard University Press, Cambridge, MA

[4] J. Anderson, (1990). *Rules of the Mind.* Lawrence Erlbaum Associates. Hillsdale, NJ.

[5] A. Barto, R. Sutton, and C. Watkins, (1990). Learning and sequential decision-making. In: M. Gabriel and J. Moors (eds.), *Learning and Computational Neuroscience.* MIT Press. Cambridge, MA.

[6] R. Brooks, (1991). Intelligence without representation. *Artificial Intelligence.* 47, pp.139-160.

[7] J. Carbonell, C. Knoblock, and S. Minton, (1991). Prodigy: an integrated architecture for planning and learning. In: *Architectures for Intelligence.* Lawrence Erlbaum Associates, Hillsdale, NJ.

[8] A. Damasio et al, (1990). Neural regionalization of knowledge access. In: *Cold Spring Harbor Symp. on Quantitative Biology*, Vol.LV. CSHL Press.

[9] H. Dreyfus and S. Dreyfus, (1987). *Mind Over Machine.* The Free Press, New York, NY.

[10] L. M. Fu, (1991). Rule learning by searching on adapted nets, *Proc. of AAAI'91*, pp. 590-595.

[11] E. Gat, (1992). Integrating planning and reacting in a heterogeneous architecture. *Proc. AAAI*, pp. 809-815.

[12] J. Gelfand, D. Handelman and S. Lane, (1989). Integrating knowledge-based systems and neural networks for robotic skill acquisition, *Proc. IJCAI*, pp. 193-198.

[13] D. Gordon and J. Grefenstette, (1992). Explanations of empirically derived reactive plans. *Proc.of Machine Learning Conference.* pp. 198-203.

[14] J. Hendler, (1987). Marker passing and microfeature, *Proc. 10th IJCAI*, pp. 151-154, Morgan Kaufman, San Mateo, CA.

[15] W. James, (1890). *The Principles of Psychology.* Dover, New York.

[16] F. Keil, (1989). *Concepts, Kinds, and Cognitive Development.* MIT Press. Cambridge, MA.

[17] J. LeDoux, (1992). Brain mechanisms of emotion and emotional learning. In: *Current Opinion in Neurobiology.* Vol.2, No.2, pp. 191-197.

[18] L. Lin, (1992). Self-improving reactive agents based on reinforcement learning, planning, and teaching. *Machine Learning.* Vol.8, pp. 293-321.

[19] R. Maclin and J. Shavlik, (1994). Incorporating advice into agents that learn from reinforcements. *Proc. of AAAI-94*. Morgan Kaufmann, San Meteo, CA.

[20] P. Maes and R. Brooks, (1990). Learning to coordinate behaviors, *Proc. of National Conference on Artificial Intelligence*. pp. 796-802. Morgan Kaufmann, San Mateo, CA.

[21] S. Mahadevan and J. Connell (1992), Automatic programming of behavior-based robot with reinforcement learning. *Artificial Intelligence*. Vol.55, pp. 311-365.

[22] R. Michalski, (1983). A theory and methodology of inductive learning. *Artificial Intelligence*. Vol.20, pp. 111-161.

[23] R. Miikkulainen and M. Dyer, (1991). Natural language processing with modular PDP networks and distributed lexicons. *Cognitive Science*. 15(3). pp. 343-399.

[24] T. Mitchell, J.Allen, P. Chalasani, J. Cheng, O. Etzioni, M. Ringuette, and J. Schlimmer, (1991). Theo: a framework for self-improving systems. In: *Architectures for Intelligence*. Lawrence Erlbaum Associates, Hillsdale, NJ.

[25] D. Perlis, (1985). Language with self reference I. *Artificial Intelligence*.

[26] W. Schneider and W. Oliver (1991), An instructable connectionist/control architecture. In: K. VanLehn (ed.), *Architectures for Intelligence*, Lawrence Erlbaum Associates, Hillsdale, NJ.

[27] L. Shastri and V. Ajjanagadde, (1990). From simple association to systematic reasoning, Technical Report MS-CIS-90-05, University of Pennsylvania, Philadelphia, PA.

[28] R. Shiffrin and W. Schneider, (1977). Controlled and automatic human information processing II. *Psychological Review*. 84. pp. 127-190.

[29] P. Smolensky, (1988). On the proper treatment of connectionism. *Behavioral and Brain Sciences*, 11(1). pp. 1–74.

[30] R. Sun, (1992a). A connectionist model for commonsense reasoning incorporating rules and similarities, *Knowledge Acquisition*, Vol.4, pp. 293-321.

[31] R. Sun, (1992b). On Variable Binding in Connectionist Networks, *Connection Science*, Vol.4, No.2, pp.93-124.

[32] R. Sun, (1994). *Integrating Rules and Connectionism for Robust Commonsense Reasoning*. John Wiley and Sons, New York, NY.

[33] R. Sun, (1995). Robust reasoning: integrating rule-based and similarity-based reasoning. *Artificial Intelligence*. 75. pp. 241-295.

[34] R. Sun and L. Bookman, (eds.) (1994). *Computational Architectures Integrating Neural and Symbolic Processes*. Kluwer Academic Publishers. Boston, MA.

[35] R. Sutton, (1990). Integrated architectures for learning, planning, and reacting based on approximating dynamic programming. *Proc. of Seventh International Conference on Machine Learning*.

[36] R. Sutton and A. Barto, (1981). Towards a modern theory of adaptive networks: expectation and prediction. *Psychological Review*, Vol.88, No.2, pp. 135-170.

[37] E. Thorndike, (1911). *Animal Intelligence*. Hafner, Darien, Connecticutt.

[38] G. Towell and J. Shavlik, (1993). Extracting refined rules from knowledge-based neural networks, *Machine Learning*.

[39] D. Waltz, (1991). How to build a robot. *Proc. of Conf. on Simulation of Adaptive Behaviors*.

[40] C. Watkins, (1989). *Learning with Delayed Rewards*. Ph.D Thesis, Cambridge University, Cambridge, UK.

[41] S. Whitehead and L. Lin, (1995). Reinforcement learning of non-Markov decision processes. *Artificial Intelligence*. 73 (1-2). pp. 271-306.

[42] B. Yamauchi and R. Beer, (1994). Integrating reactive, sequential and learning behavior using dynamic neural networks. *Proc. of Conf. on Simulation of Adaptive Behaviors*.

8

A PREPROCESSING MODEL FOR INTEGRATING CASE-BASED REASONING AND PROTOTYPE-BASED NEURAL NETWORK

Maria Malek*,
Bernard Amy**

*TIMC-LEIBNIZ, INPG** LEIBNIZ, INPG*

1 INTRODUCTION

Generally, a Case-Based Reasoning (CBR) system is divided into two major modules: a *case base* and a *problem solver*. Cases in the case base describe the previous solved problems. This base forms the memory or the library of the CBR system. The problem solver in its turn is composed of two components: a *case retriever* and a *case adapter*. Given a new input problem, the case retriever identifies the most appropriate cases (in some similarity sense) in the case base and feeds them to the case adapter. The case adapter then examines the retrieved cases and tries to solve the new problem by adapting these cases (Aamodt and Plaza 1994), (Barletta 1991), (Riesbeck and Schank 1989).

It is obvious that the more the retrieval phase is efficient the more the overall performance of the CBR system is increased. Hence, a particular attention must be paid to the design and the implementation of this phase. In the literature, two widely used approaches are distinguished: flat memory systems and hierarchical organization of cases (Kolodner 1993).

In a flat memory system, cases are stored sequentially in a simple file. They are retrieved by applying a matching function sequentially to each case in the list. The advantage of this approach is that the whole case library is searched, so accuracy is a function of the matching function quality. In addition, adding new cases is cheap (incrementality). However, retrieval process becomes very expensive in time when the case base becomes rather big.

Hierarchical organization of cases provides a means of clustering cases so that cases that share many features are grouped together. Building such a hierarchy takes a lot of time, but it can be used very efficiently during the retrieval phase. Now, adding cases is a complex operation ; besides, it is hard to keep the structure optimal as cases are added. The study of some inductive approaches like ID3/C4 (Quinlan 1992) have shown that the costs of altering large case bases are very high and lead sometimes to a re-compilation of the complete case base after each alteration (Bamberger and Goos, 1993), (Manago et al. 1993). This shows that using hierarchical approaches makes retrieval more efficient, but it considerably complicates the learning phase because of the complex architecture of the structure used (Utgoff, 1989).

This paper describes a hybrid system which integrates CBR with an incremental neural network. The proposed system makes the retrieval process efficient and at the same time maintains a continuous learning process. The proposed case hierarchy contains two memory levels. At the lower one, cases are gathered into groups by similarity. The upper level contains prototypes, each of which represents one group of cases of the lower levels. This upper level memory is used as an indexing system during the retrieval phase.

In section 2, incremental prototype-based neural networks are described, in section 3 the hybrid model using a prototype-based neural network to index the case base is described. In section 4, a comparative study of this model with some inductive approaches (C4.5 and ID5R) is proposed.

2   PROTOTYPE-BASED INCREMENTAL NEURAL NETWORKS

Learning a given class of objects by accumulating representative exemplars of the class and slightly modifying existing ones is the approach used by prototype-based incremental networks. Each hidden network unit represents a *prototype*. These prototype units are grouped into their corresponding classes, each class identified by a category label. The first implemented model using this method commercially known as the Nestor Learning System (NLS) is also described in (Reilly et al. 1982). An incremental prototype-based neural network which is based on a "Grow and Learn" (Gal) algorithm is described also in (Alpaydin 1991).

In this section, the incremental prototype-based neural network model (ARN2) proposed in (Azcarraga and Giacometti 1991) is described. Figure 1 shows the architecture of the basic model. The network is composed of three layers:

- The input layer that contains one unit for each attribute.

- The output layer that contains one unit for each class.

- The hidden layer that contains one unit for each prototype and whose value is represented by the reference vector w_i^t.

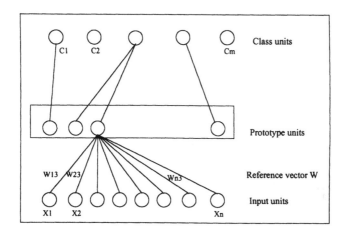

Figure 1 General architecture of a prototype-based network

This model operates either in *supervised learning mode* or in *operating mode*. The input vector at cycle t is denoted by X^t and is associated with a class unit C_x^t when the network is in supervised learning mode. Comparison between the current input and the different prototypes is achieved by means of a similarity measure m_i^t which computes, using some pre-defined measure $M(X^t, w_i^t)$, the similarity between the input vector and the individual reference vectors.

An influence region of a reference vector w_i^t having n components is defined as the locus of points in the space that register a measure of similarity equal or greater than a given threshold Θ (Figure 2). In *learning mode*, the network learns to associate a training example to its correct class. Let U^t be the set of prototype units having the current input X^t within their influence regions:

- If U^t is empty, then a new prototype is created (we call this *assimilation*).

■   Otherwise a winner-take-all competition strategy selects the winning pro-
    totype U_s which registers the highest measure of similarity:

    1. If the wining prototype belongs to the same category then the network
       fine-tunes itself to make the winning prototype even more similar to
       the training input (we call this *accommodation*); this is achieved by
       applying the Grossberg learning law to this prototype (Hecht-Nielsen
       1990).

    2. Otherwise, the influence region of the activated unit is decreased in
       order to exclude the wrong classified example (we call this *differenti-
       ation*). This example is then reintroduced to the network.

Experience shows that the learning procedure may cause the creation of a considerable number of prototype units near the boundaries of classes in the input
space. This situation can be avoided by introducing an uncertain region between two classes in which *differentiation* is not allowed (Giacometti 1992).
This region presents vectors that cause nearly the same activation to two prototypes, each one representing a class. As a result, the network is unable to
learn new cases that falls into this region (*boundary cases*) (Figure 2).

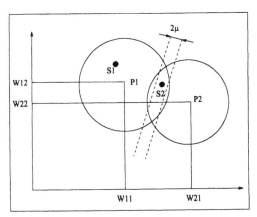

Figure 2   Suppose that we have a two-dimensional space, P1 and P2 are two
prototypes which are associated to different classes. The two spheres represent
the influence regions of these prototypes. S1 is a situation vector which activates
P1. S2 is a situation vector which activates P1 and P2 and which falls into an
uncertain region. The network is unable to give a decision for S2.

3 PROTOTYPE-BASED INDEXING SYSTEM

In this section the Prototype-Based Indexing System (*PBIS*) is described. The general architecture is first presented, then each module is presented in detail, and, last, the integration mode and levels are studied.

3.1 General Architecture of the System

The system has two essential components which are the symbolic component and the connectionist one (Figure 3). The symbolic component contains the case memory and other methods used during the CBR process, such as the k-nearest neighbor algorithm, which is used during the retrieval phase. The connectionist component contains the prototype-based incremental neural network described in the previous section.

The control part of the system is composed of two modules: the interaction administrator and the knowledge transfer module. The interaction administrator supervises the two components during both learning and retrieval modes. The knowledge transfer module controls data exchange between the two components.

Memory Organization

The idea is to construct a simple indexing system that contains two levels of memory (Malek and Rialle 1994):

1. Memory that contains *prototypical cases.*

2. Memory that contains *instances* or real cases.

The *prototype* memory is used during retrieval phase as an indexing system in order to decrease retrieval time.

The first memory level is composed of the hidden layer of the incremental prototype-based network described in previous section. The second memory level is a simple flat memory in which cases are organized into zones of similar cases. These two levels are linked together: to each prototype unit, is associated

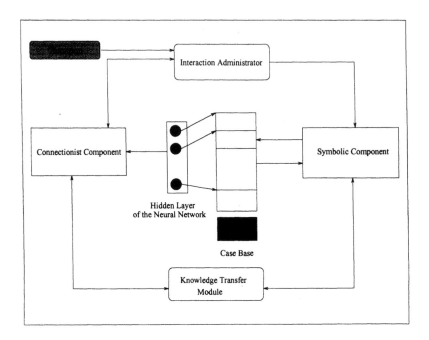

Figure 3   General architecture of the system

a memory zone which contains all instances belonging to this prototype. In addition, a memory zone is reserved for *boundary* cases which falls into an uncertain region as well as for cases that are not classified elsewhere. These cases form a group of *atypical* cases (or unusual cases). Figure 4 illustrates the memory organisation.

3.2   The Interaction Administrator

The interaction administrator controls the learning process during the supervised learning mode, and the retrieval process during the operating mode. These two processes are now described in details in the next.

Learning Process

Initially, the network contains no prototypes and the case base contains one zone: the *atypical zone*. Let's suppose that one wants to construct the prototype memory given a training set S. Instances of S are initially placed into the

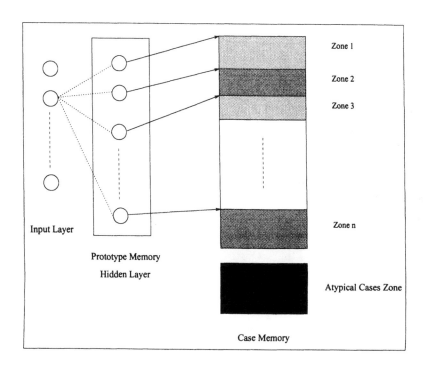

Figure 4 The case memory is composed of two levels: prototype memory and instance memory which are linked together.

atypical zone. *No boundary* instances are learned by the network, *boundary* instances are kept into the atypical zone. In fact, the network can forget many previously learned instances after each epoch; these *lost* instances are then retrieved from their memory zone and are replaced into the atypical zone. The Learning Procedure is re-executed again until stabilization of the atypical zone or a maximum number of times. (see the next two algorithms):

Learning Procedure

> Repeat (n_{max} times) or (until stabilisation of the atypical zone)
>> For each instance **i** belonging to the atypical zone do
>>> (**Example Learning i**) /* see next algorithm*/
>> For each instance i in the case memory
>>> If i does not belong to the associated prototype then
>>>> /* This is a lost instance */
>>>> Remove this instance from this zone

Add it to the atypical zone

Once an instance i is presented to the neural network, the following supervised learning procedure is applied:

Example Learning i
If no prototype units is activated then
Create a new prototype unit /* *assimilation* */
Associate to this prototype a new memory zone
Add this instance to this memory zone
Else If **i** falls into an uncertain region then
/* This is a boundary instance */
Keep **i** into the atypical memory zone
Else If **i** belongs to the activated prototype then
fine-tune this prototype /* *accommodation* */
add **i** to the associated memory zone
Else /* i does not belong to the activated prototype */
Decrease the influence region of the activated unit to exclude **i**
/* *differentiation* */
(**Example Learning i**)
/* Re-learn the example to the network */

Retrieval Process

Once the system is trained, it can operate in retrieval mode. Let's suppose that a new problem is presented to the system. The interaction administrator "reasons" like this :

1. First it searches an instance in the atypical memory which is similar *enough* to the current problem (this is achieved by using a threshold), if such a case exists then it is retrieved.

2. If such a case does not exist so the new problem is presented to the network and the following procedure is executed:

If only one class unit is activated then
Retrieve the most activated prototype.
Else If many class units are activated

Determine the memory zones associated to the activated
prototypes
Retrieve the k-most similar cases from these memory zones
/* Apply then the k-nearest neighbour algorithm to determine
the winning class */
Else /* no prototype is activated */
Retrieve the k-most similar case from the *atypical* memory zone
/* Apply then the k-nearest neighbor algorithm to determine
the winning class */

It is worth mentioning here that at any moment, the system can switch from
the *retrieval mode* to the *learning one* in order to learn new cases and then
returns back to the *retrieval mode*.

3.3   The Knowledge Transfer Module

The knowledge transfer module controls data exchange between the two components. The knowledge transfer can be done from the symbolic component
to the connectionist one or vice-versa. During the learning process, prototypes
are modified by accommodation, differentiation or assimilation. Consequently,
many boundary instances could become no boundary and vice-versa. In addition, some prototypes can be reduced to approximately a single point in the
input space.

Instances which are in the atypical zone and which are no longer boundary are
transferred to the connectionist component during the learning process. On the
other hand, prototype units whose influence radius is less than a given threshold
are considered as single instances and thus are removed from the network and
added to the atypical zone.

Thus, the role of the knowledge transfer module is to maintain prototypical
cases in the connectionist module and boundary and particular instances in
the atypical memory zone.

3.4   Integration Mode and Levels

In (Hilario 1995) and (Orsier 1995), a taxonomy of hybrid systems is proposed: this taxonomy is based on the mode and level of integration. The integration mode refers to the way in which the neural and symbolic components are configured. Four integration schemes are identified: chainprocessing, subprocessing metaprocessing and coprocessing. The integration level refers to the way interaction between the two module is performed.

In PBIS, the connectionist component is used as an indexing system, so the network is considered as a preprocessor because the system input is preprocessed by the network in order to determine the active memory zones that should be used by the CBR retriever.

On the other hand, two integration levels are distinguished in PBIS:

1. A high-level integration, where control and data are transferred via the interaction administrator and the knowledge transfer module.

2. A low-level integration, where each prototype unit is linked to a memory zone. This makes the two components sharing the same data structure.

4   COMPARISON WITH TWO INDUCTIVE INDEXING APPROACHES: C4.5 AND ID5R

Inductive approaches to indexing in a CBR systems are suitable where case outcomes are well-defined and when there are enough examples. They aim to construct inductively a model by generalising from specific examples. These methods have two advantages (Berletta 1991):

1. They can automatically analyze the cases to determine the best features for distinguishing them

2. The cases are organized for retrieval into a hierarchical structure that increases the retrieval time by only the log of the number of cases

C4.5 (Quinlan 1992) is an inductive method that generates a decision tree classifier from an initial set of cases. It is a descendent of the ID3 algorithm (Quinlan 1968). Each leaf in the tree indicates one prototype of a class. A decision node specifies some test to be carried on a single attribute value.

A decision tree can be used to classify a case by starting at the root of the tree and moving through it until a leaf is encountered. The class of the case is predicted to be that recorded at the leaf.

To construct a decision tree, Quinlan has pointed out that selecting an attribute with a lowest E-score is equivalent to selecting an attribute with a highest information gain. The E function is an information theoretical metric based on entropy, the attribute with the lowest E-score is assumed to give a good partition of instances into subproblems for classification and so is placed at the root of the tree. C4.5 is not incremental: this means that one needs to build a new decision tree to learn an additional case.

ID5R is an incremental method to build a decision tree (Utgoff 1989). The idea is to maintain sufficient information to compute the E-score for an attribute at a node, making it possible to change the test attribute at a node to one with the lowest E-score. The algorithm allows at each moment to restructure the whole tree and to expand it if possible.

In order to compare PBIS to C4.5 and ID5R methods, the MONK's problems that were used to compare different learning algorithm performances are chosen (Thrun et al. 1991).

The MONK's problems rely on an artificial robot domain, in which robots are described by six different attributes:

1. x_1: head_shape $\in$ {round, square, octagon}

2. x_2: body_shape $\in$ {round, square, octagon}

3. x_3: is_smiling $\in$ {yes, no}

4. x_4: holding $\in$ {sword, balloon, flag}

5. x_5: jacket_color $\in$ {red, yellow, green, blue}

6. x_6: has_tie $\in$ {yes, no}

The learning task is a binary classification task. Each problem is given by a logical description of a class. Robots belong either to this class or not. Instead of providing a complete class description to the learning problem, only a subset of all 432 possible robots with its classification is given. The learning task is then to generalise over these examples.

The MONK's Problems are:

1. Problem M1: (head_shape = body_shape) or (jacket_color = red)
   From 432 possible examples, 124 were randomly selected for the training set. There is no noise.

2. Problem M2: exactly two of the six attributes have their *first* value. From 432 possible examples, 169 were randomly selected. There is no noise.

3. Problem M3: (jacket_color is green and holding a sword) or (jacket_color is not blue and body_shape is not octagon)
   From 432 examples, 122 were selected randomly. Among them there is 5% of noise.

4.1   Experimental Results

Table 1 presents results of comparison of C4.5, ID5R and PBIS for the M1 problem. Table 2 presents results for the M2 problem and Table 3 presents results for the M3 problem. The complexity of the generated structures (number of Leaves and Prototypes) and the classification and generalization accuracies of the three approaches are compared in the next.

Table 1   M1 Problem, NbN is the number of nodes in the tree, NbP is the number of leaves in the tree or the number of prototype units in the network, TrS is the classification accuracy on the training set, TeS is the generalisation accuracy on the test set

Method	NbN	NbP	TrS	TeS
C4.5	15	28	90.3%	76.6%
ID5R	34	52	100%	79%
PBIS	-	22	100%	86.11%

ID5R registers classification and generalization accuracies which are higher than those registered by C4.5, but the decision tree generated by ID5R (34 nodes,

Table 2 M2 Problem

Method	NbN	NbP	TrS	TeS
C4.5	27	46	85.5%	65.3%
ID5R	64	99	100%	69.23%
PBIS	-	67	100%	75.93%

Table 3 M3 Problem

Method	NbN	NbP	TrS	TeS
C4.5	8	17	96.7%	92.6%
ID5R	14	28	100%	95.28%
PBIS	-	28	100%	89.58%

52 Leaves, for M1 problem) is more complex than the one generated by C4.5 (15 nodes, 28 Leaves, for M1 Problem). This means that using ID5R as an indexing system increases the accuracy of the retrieval phase but also increases the retrieval time because of the complex structure of the generated tree.

PBIS generates a neural network with an acceptable number of prototypes which is smaller than the ID5R one (22 for M1, 67 for M2 and 28 for M3 problems). The fact of using a *parallel* network with such a number of prototypes decreases considerably the retrieval time.

PBIS registers a 100% classification accuracy because it is able to learn most kinds of cases (*no boundary, boundary, lost*) (see previous section). The generalisation accuracies registered by PBIS are better than the ones registered by ID5R, for M1 and M2 problem.

ID5R and PBIS are both incremental. Adding a new case in ID5R is a complex operation because it leads to a whole restructuration of the generated tree (Utgoff 1989), whereas in PBIS, this is achieved by simply adding the new case to the suitable memory zone and by modifying only one unit in the neural network (assimilation, accommodation or differentiation of a prototype).

5 SUMMARY

This paper describes a hybrid system which integrates CBR with an incremental neural network in order to improve the continuous learning process in a CBR system.

To deal with the continuous learning problem, an incremental neural network is used for dynamic memory organisation.

In literature, two wide approaches for memory organization are distinguished: flat memory systems and hierarchical organisation of cases. In a flat memory system, cases are stored sequentially in a simple file. The advantage of this approach is that adding new cases is cheap (incrementality). However, retrieval process becomes very expensive when the case base becomes rather big. Hierarchical organization of cases provides a means of clustering cases so that cases that share many features are grouped together. Building such a hierarchy is time consuming, but it can be used very efficiently during the retrieval process. Now, adding cases is a complex operation and it is hard to keep the structure optimal as cases are added. This shows that using hierarchical approaches makes retrieval more efficient but it considerably complicates the learning phase.

The proposed system makes retrieval efficient, and at the same time, maintains a continous learning process. The proposed case hierarchy contains two levels of memory. At the lower one, cases are gathered into groups by similarity. The upper level contains prototypes, each of which representing one group of cases of the lower level. This upper level memory is used as an indexing system during the retrieval phase.

Experiences show that PBIS registers good classification and generalization accuracies in comparison with some inductive approaches for indexing like C4.5 and ID5R. PBIS is now under evaluation on a real medical domain.

Acknowledgements

This research is partially supported by the MIX ESPRIT. Project-9119

REFERENCES

[1] A. Aamodt and E. Plaza. Case-Based Reasoning: Foundational Issues, Methodological Variations, and System Approaches. *AICOM*, 7(1), March 1994.

[2] E. Alpaydin. Gal : Networks That Grow When They Learn and Shrink When They Forget. Technical Report, International Computer Science Institute, May 1991.

[3] A. Azcarraza and A. Giacometti. A Prototype-Based Incremental Network Model for Classification Task. In *Neuro-Nimes*, 1991.

[4] S.K. Bamberger and K. Goos. Integration of Case-Based Reasoning and Inductive Learning Methods. In *First European Workshop on CBR*, Number 1, November 1993.

[5] R. Barletta. An Introduction to Case-Based Reasoning. *AI Expert*, August 1991.

[6] A. Giacometti. *Modèles Hybrides de l'Expertise*. PhD thesis, Telecom-Paris, 1992.

[7] R. Hecht-Nielsen. *Neurocomputing*. Addison-Wesley Publishing Company, 1990.

[8] M. Hilario. An Overview of Strategies for Neurosymbolic Integration. In *Connectionist-Symbolic Integration: From Unified to Hybrid Approaches, IJCAI Workshop*, 1995.

[9] J. Kolodner. *Case-Based Reasoning*. Morgan Kaufmann Publishers, Inc, 1993.

[10] M. Malek and V. Rialle. A Case-Based Reasoning System Applied to Neuropathy Diagnosis. In *Second European Workshop, EWCBR-94*, Lecture Notes in Computer Science. Springer-Verlag, November 1994.

[11] M. Manago, K. Althoff, E. Auriol, R. Traphoner, S. Wess, and N. Conruyt and F. Maurer. Induction and Reasoning from Cases. In *First European Workshop on CBR*, Number 1, November 1993.

[12] L.R. Medsker and D.L. Bailey. *Models and Guidelines for Integrating Expert Systems and Neural Networks*, chapter 8, pages 153–171. CRC Press, Inc., 1992.

[13] B. Orsier. Etude et Application de Systèmes Hybrides NeuroSymboliques. PhD thesis, Université Joseph Fourrier, Grenoble, 1995.

[14] J.R. Quinlan. Induction of Decision Trees. *Machine Learning*, (1): #81–106, 1986.

[15] J.R. Quinlan. *C4.5*. Morgan Kaufmann Publishers, 1992.

[16] D.L. Reilly, L.N. Cooper, and C. Elbaum. A Neural Model for Category Learning. *Biological Cybermetics*, 1982.

[17] C.K. Riesbeck and R.C. Schank. *Inside Case-Based Reasoning*. Lawrence Erlbaum Associates, 1989.

[18] S.B. Thrun, J. Bala, E. Bloedorn, I. Bratko, B. Cestnik, J. Cheng, K. De Jong, S. Dzroski, S.E. Fahlman, D. Fisher, R. Hamann, K. Kaufman, S. Keller, I. Kononenko, J. Kreuziger, R.S. Michalski, T. Mitchell, P. Pachowicz, Y. Reich, H. Vafaie, W. Van de Welde, W. Wenzel, J. Wnek, and J. Zhang. The Monk's Problems: A Performance Comparison of Different Learning Algorihms. Technical Report CMU-CS-91-197, Carnegie Mellon University, December 1991.

[19] P.E. Utgoff. Incremental Induction of Decision Trees. *Machine Learning*, (4): #161–186, 1989.

9

A STEP TOWARD FULLY INTEGRATED HYBRID SYSTEMS

Bruno Orsier*
Abderrahim Labbi**

Laboratory for Artificial Brain Systems
The Institute for Physical and Chemical Research
*** Department of Computer Science*
University of Geneva

1 INTRODUCTION

This work is primarily intended to find new ideas that could guide the design of more powerful neurosymbolic hybrid systems. In this chapter, *hybrid system* means "functional hybrid system" as defined by Hilario (see chapter 2 of this book). Although a great number of such systems have already been proposed, their architectures remain relatively conventional. That is, such systems are made of components which function in a rather isolated way and interact rather loosely.

For instance, in the theorem prover SETHEO (Goller 1994, Kurfess 1989), a neural network implements an heuristic evaluation function that controls the selection of inference steps at decision points. More precisely, each applicable inference step is rated by an evaluation function that estimates the probability that it will lead to a proof in the current proof context (Goller 1994). Although SETHEO is a very successful hybrid system that has lead to original ideas (see chapter 18 in this book), its architecture is conventional in the sense that using the neural network is like calling any procedure. Actually, the implementation of the heuristic function by means of a neural network does not influence the functioning of the whole hybrid system. That is, the neural network component could easily be replaced by any other procedure able to weight each applicable inference step.

On the contrary, an hybrid system like SYNHESYS (Giacometti et al. 1992, Orsier et al. 1994) is made of two components that can interact in a stronger way. The first component is a rule-based expert system, while the second component is a prototype-based neural network. Each component takes the same vector V as input, and produces the class to which V belongs. Both components can also interact according to a variety of schemes, the simplest being the following: by means of backward chaining, the expert system checks or explains the output of the neural network. It happens that the backward chaining can be made faster via a direct link between the two components: to each rule R_i is associated a neural unit U_i, which is then connected to each prototype unit. The weights of these new connections are learned with a variant of Hebb's rule. The units U_i compute a value which is interpreted by the backward chaining as a measure of the pertinence of R_i with respect to the current input V. This means that the backward chaining favors the rules whose associated units are strongly activated. When this mechanism is enabled, the backward chaining examines around 60% fewer rules. In such a system, it is not so easy to replace the neural component by any other component: the symbolic and neural components are indeed more strongly coupled.

This mechanism in SYNHESYS can be seen as an attempt to build what Medsker (1992, 1994) calls a fully integrated hybrid system linking symbolic and subsymbolic computing. According to Medsker (1994, p. 44), "fully integrated expert system/neural network models share data structures and knowledge representations; the benefits of full integration include robustness, improved performance, and increased problem solving capabilities." However, Medsker (1994, p. 46) explains that there are several issues: "full integration has limitations caused by the increased complexity of the inter-module interactions. First, there is the complexity of specifying, designing, and building fully integrated models. Second, there is a distinct lack of tools on the market that facilitate full integration. Finally, there are important questions in verifying, validating and maintaining fully integrated systems."

The work presented in this chapter addresses Medsker's first issue by proposing an architecture, NESSY3L, involving a gradual transition between several levels. The key idea consists of inserting intermediate levels between a neural level and a symbolic level; in order to smooth the transition, such intermediate levels should have both symbolic and neural features, and will be called *neurosymbolic* levels. Compiling rules into a neural network is a basic way to develop such a neurosymbolic level.

Although intuitively appealing, such fully integrated hybrid systems are very complex and costly to build; therefore, they will not be profitable for every application. A preliminary step of this work has been to find a suitable application domain. Mobile robotics presents several advantages as an application domain for fully integrated hybrid systems:

- To some extent, neural networks can be realized in hardware, and thus can offer a welcome computing power; for instance, Masa et al. (1993) describe a VLSI neural network able to classify a vector of $I\!R^{70}$ in 50 nanoseconds (or 20,000,000 vectors in one second); because its surface is 6.5×4 mm^2, their network could easily be embedded into a real robot.

- Conventional hybrid systems have already been successfully experimented with in this field (see for instance the famous ALVINN (Pomerleau et al. 1991, Pomerleau 1993)); therefore, they can offer a basis for fully-integrated hybrid systems; less conventional hybrid systems are also being experimented with (see chapter 7 of this book).

- Hardware/software architectures dedicated to robot piloting are already very complex (Reignier, 1994); consequently, they will offer enough matter and ideas for designing fully integrated hybrid systems with various levels.

Mobile robotics being a wide field, this chapter is focused on reactive obstacle avoidance. Section 2 is dedicated to a new neural network model; such networks, called *versatile*, are actually dynamic systems that are always converging toward attractors. Changes in their environment lead these networks to progressively converge toward another attractor point, say A. In case another change happens during this convergence, the network gives up A and begins a new convergence toward another attractor point, say B. One of the aims of this work is to try to exploit this property. Because these networks can encode rules, they are used as the intermediate level of NESSY3L. Section 3 details the whole NESSY3L architecture, which is composed of four multilayer perceptrons, one versatile network, and a symbolic level. NESSY3L takes ultrasonic measures as input, and produces the linear and angular velocities that are needed to pilot a robot. Results obtained with NESSY3L are presented and discussed in section 4.

2 VERSATILE NETWORKS

2.1 A New Neural Network Model

This section describes how real-time decision making can be carried out by using a particular competitive neural network. The network proposed has the ability to process dynamic information emerging from an unexpectedly changing environment. Its dynamics are described by a system of differential equations with external input, and such dynamics are shown to be convergent (by means of the Cohen & Grossberg principle) when external inputs are clamped, and globally asymptotically stable when the external input changes (Labbi 1993). Therefore, the network can perform a mapping from the environment space to a decision space.

2.2   What Does the Versatility Stand For?

When designing a decision system (a pattern classifier, recognizer, or associator), we usually suppose that the information being processed by the system to compute a decision (output) remains unchanged (static) during the whole processing period, called the System's Autonomy Period (SAP). These systems are usually unable to process dynamic information emerging from a changing environment since the internal states of such systems can not be forced to take into account sudden environmental changes. Herein, two kinds of information processing systems are distinguished:

- Time Unconstrained Systems (TUS), where the duration of the SAP is not crucial in the decision context, and the environment data is supposed to remain unchanged during the whole processing period. This class includes off-line running systems.

- Time Constrained Systems (TCS), where it is necessary to take into account all the information changes that may occur while computing a decision based on initial information. In this case, the system should be able to *recant* and dynamically change its internal state, when tending toward a first decision, without resetting its variables to a conventional value, e.g. zero. The ability of such systems to adapt continuously their behavior in changing environments has a biological support, and is crucial for real-time processing (Hirscj 1989). Those systems are called *versatile*.

2.3   Network Architecture and Dynamics

The network presented here deals with the second class of decision systems (TCS). To model dynamic information processing in such systems, a competitive network is proposed in this section; it is derived from a continuous nonlinear model introduced by Grossberg (1982) for studying real-time adaptive behavior of individuals subject to changes in a complex environment.

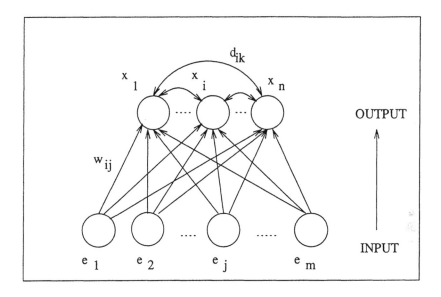

Figure 1 The versatile network architecture.

The network architecture consists of two layers (see Figure 1), the input layer includes the external input variables $e_k, k = 1, ..., m$, which encode the external information received by the system, and the decision (output) layer includes neurons $x_i, i = 1, ..., n$. Concerning the connection topology, there are excitatory (bottom-up) connections between the input and decision layers (weights $w_{ik} \geq 0$), and inhibitory (lateral) connections (weights $d_{ij} \geq 0$) between neurons of the decision layer to allow competition.

$$\frac{dx_i}{dt} = -c_i.x_i + (1 - x_i).(\sum_{k=1}^{k=m} w_{ik}.f_k(e_k))$$
$$- (1 + x_i).(\sum_{j=1}^{n} d_{ij}.g_j(x_j)) \qquad i = 1, ..., n \qquad (9.1)$$

The network dynamics is governed by the differential system (9.1) which includes an excitation term $(\sum_{k=1}^{m} w_{ik}.f_k(e_k))$ induced by external inputs e_k, and a feedback term $(\sum_{j=1}^{n} d_{ij}.g_j(x_j))$, which represents the lateral inhibition part of the input of x_i transmitted by the other decision neurons. $d_{ij} = d_{ji}$ and $d_{ii} = 0$ is assumed. The excitation (resp. inhibition) term includes a state dependent positive signal function f_k (resp. g_j) of sigmoidal type. According to (9.1), the activities of the decision neurons x_i remain into the interval

$[-1, 1]$. In (Labbi 1993), the network dynamics are shown to be convergent for any clamped input E on one hand; on the other hand, the dynamics are also shown to be globally asymptotically stable, which is equivalent to say that the network defines a mapping from the environment space to the decision space. The condition for the dynamics to be globally asymptotically stable is:

$$\min_{i \in \{1,\dots,n\}} c_i > ||D||_1 \tag{9.2}$$

2.4   Versatile Networks and Hybrid Systems

Such versatile networks will be used to develop the neurosymbolic level of NESSY3L. Because they are localist networks, they can encode a set of rules (Labbi 1993), and thus they provide the dual nature (neural/symbolic) that is needed for such neurosymbolic levels.

The general form of the rules that can be encoded is (Labbi 1993):

$$R_i \equiv \text{If } (e_1 \in [a_1, b_1] \text{ and } e_2 \in [a_2, b_2] \dots \text{ and } e_m = \text{TRUE})$$
$$\text{Then } Decision = D_i$$

Each decision D_i is associated to a unit x_i in the decision layer of the network architecture, and an excitatory connection w_{ij} (bottom-up) between an input unit e_j and a unit x_i is simply set as $\frac{1}{p_i}$ where p_i is the total number of input variables occurring in the *premise* of the rule R_i. Concerning the inhibitory connections d_{ik} (lateral) between the units x_i, their weights can be set equal to some value d in order to allow a same strength of inhibition between each two competing units.

This representation of symbolic knowledge into a neural network has two main attractive properties (see for instance (Sun 1991) for a more detailed discussion):

- Parallel processing of the data by running all the rules in parallel according to a competition process.

- Distributed encoding of rules into the network's connections. This property makes a rule activated even when not all of the input units are completely

specified. This capability is usually hard to achieve in a symbolic processing system since it is based on predicate logic where one has to specify
completely all the facts to be considered.

2.5 An Example

This section presents the versatile network that constitutes the neurosymbolic
level of the hybrid system NESSY3L detailed in section 3. This level is primarily intended to pilot the mobile robot in a reactive way. A few basic basic
rules like the following can be sufficient as a starting point:

right obstacle $\longrightarrow$ slow left rotation
front obstacle $\longrightarrow$ stop translation $\wedge$ slow right rotation

Such rules are quite easy to translate into a versatile network that makes the
following four decisions compete: stop translation, slow left rotation, slow right
rotation, stop rotation. The network obtained is shown by Figure 7.

The different weights (d_{ij}, c_i, w_{ik}) of the system (9.1) are iteratively adjusted,
starting from the values given in section 2.4, and varying them until the network gives reasonable output values and provided that the condition 9.2 is
respected. Figure 2 shows the matrix of weights (w_{ij}), while Figure 3 presents
the activations of the output units of the versatile network in order to illustrate
these continuous convergence changes that characterize these networks.

3   NESSY3L

3.1   Obstacle Avoidance

In this section, the problem of reactive obstacle avoidance in mobile robotics is
addressed with NESSY3L, a hybrid architecture motivated by the considerations of section 1. This problem of obstacle avoidance can basically be defined
in the following way: a robot should avoid obstacles while wandering through
an unknown or partially known environment.

The robot considered here is a mobile device surrounded by a ring of 24 ultrasonic sensors (Figure 4) which measure distances between the robot and
obstacles. A pilot, be it a human being or a computer program, has several

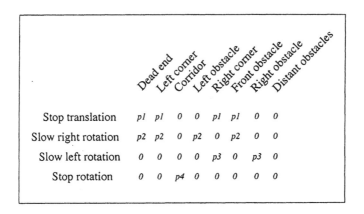

	Dead end	Left corner	Corridor	Left obstacle	Right corner	Front obstacle	Right obstacle	Distant obstacles
Stop translation	p1	p1	0	0	p1	p1	0	0
Slow right rotation	p2	p2	0	p2	0	p2	0	0
Slow left rotation	0	0	0	0	p3	0	p3	0
Stop rotation	0	0	p4	0	0	0	0	0

Figure 2 Matrix of weights. $(p_i) = (1/4;\ 1/4;\ 1/2;\ 1)$. Actually, it has not been necessary to adjust the initial values.

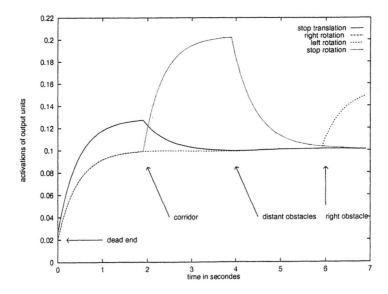

Figure 3 Activations of the output units of the versatile network.

commands at its disposal:
  move(distance, linear velocity, linear acceleration)
  turn(orientation, angular velocity, angular acceleration)
  stop()
For the moment, NESSY3L has only been tested on a simulated version of this robot. The robot simulator MOLUSC (Reignier 1994) offers the environment of Figure 5 where the various components of NESSY3L have been trained and tested. NESSY3L uses four multilayer perceptrons that have been designed and trained with the Stuttgart Neural Network Simulator (Zell et al. 1995), and one versatile network simulated with another program. The robot simulator communicates with all these neural networks via Unix pipes.

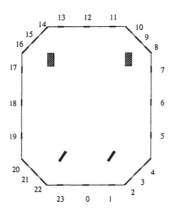

Figure 4 Positions of the 24 ultrasonic sensors surrounding the robot.

The whole architecture NESSY3L is presented by Figure 7, and its three levels are commented in the next sections. As shown by Figure 7, NESSY3L takes a subset of the ultrasonic measures as input, and produces, at each Δt (= 2s currently), the desired linear and angular velocities (other parameters of *move* and *turn* take default values).

3.2 Neural Level

This level gathers neural networks that merely rely on a distributed processing of information; no precise meaning can be assigned to their hidden units.

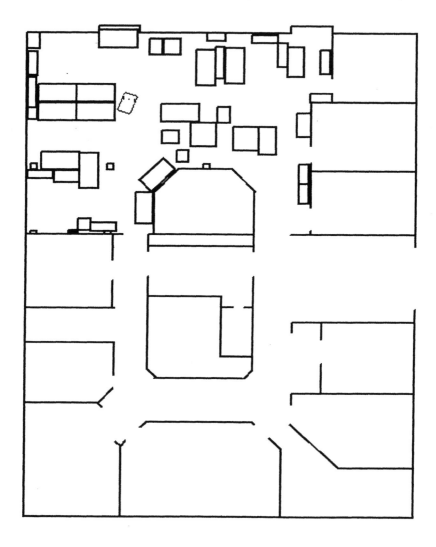

Figure 5 Training and testing environment for NESSY3L. This environment is offered with the robot simulator MOLUSC (Reignier 1994). The simulated robot can be distinguished in the upper left part of the figure.

At this level, ultrasonic measures are pre-processed through three multilayer perceptrons (Bishop 1995, Cichocki et al. 1993) which have previously been taught how to answer 1 when an obstacle is close to the robot and 0 otherwise. Since they identify obstacles respectively situated at the left, right and front of the robot, they are named MLP_L, MLP_R, MLP_F. Obtaining training sets for these networks is simple but not painless; the operator of the simulator pilots the robot in parts of the environment of Figure 5, and regularly tells whether he identifies some close obstacles. Sensor values and operator's decisions are recorded in order to form training and test sets. The networks are then trained using the backpropagation rule (Amari 1993) until at least 90% of the examples are correctly classified. Unknown examples are then used in order to measure the generalization capability of the networks. For example, here are the results of the front obstacle detector (which also takes the linear velocity into account, since the recognition of an obstacle may depend on the speed of the robot):

	Number of examples in test set	Percentage of good answers
test1	198	94.4%
test2	363	83.5%
test3	515	87.5%

These results are rather good, since all data are noisy (thus it is not possible to correctly classify 100% of the examples). $\{MLP_X; \; X = L, R, F\}$ are therefore able to detect their respective obstacles, to a certain extent. By combining their outputs, it is possible to identify the eight situations of Figure 6.

After obstacle detection, another multilayer perceptron (MLP_S) selects one of these height possible situations (distant obstacles, right obstacle, right corner, etc.). In the current NESSY3L prototype, MLP_S has only been taught how to perform the corresponding Boolean mapping. But its usefulness could be greatly improved if it were trained in the following way: the MOLUSC operator pilots the robot, and tells which of the height possible situations he identifies; the ouputs of MLP_X and his decision are recorded and constitute the training set of MLP_S. Consequently MLP_S could be trained so that it would compensate for the weaknessess of the three MLP_X.

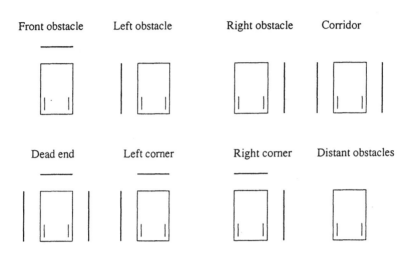

Front obstacle   Left obstacle   Right obstacle   Corridor

Dead end   Left corner   Right corner   Distant obstacles

Figure 6   Height situations that can be identified by combining the outputs of the three networks $\{MLP_X;\ X = L, R, F\}$.

3.3   Neurosymbolic Level

This level gather all components of the hybrid system that have both connectionist and symbolic features, for instance localist neural networks.

In NESSY3L, the activations of the 8 units corresponding to the height possible situations are fed into the versatile network (Figure 7), which is the only component of the neurosymbolic level.

NESSY3L's versatile network is presented in section 2.5. This network is primarily intended to react smoothly to the changes in the environment, which can be nonsmooth. Figure 3 shows how such changes (for instance, changing from corridor to distant obstacles) lead the network to progressively converge toward another attractor point, A. In case another change happens during this convergence, the network will give up A and begin a new convergence toward another attractor point, B. One of the aims of this work is to try to exploit this property, which can be very useful in robotics.

However, because the various weights of this network are choosen in an empirical way for the moment (see a discussion of this issue in section 4), it is not possible to impose precise positions to the attractor points of this network.

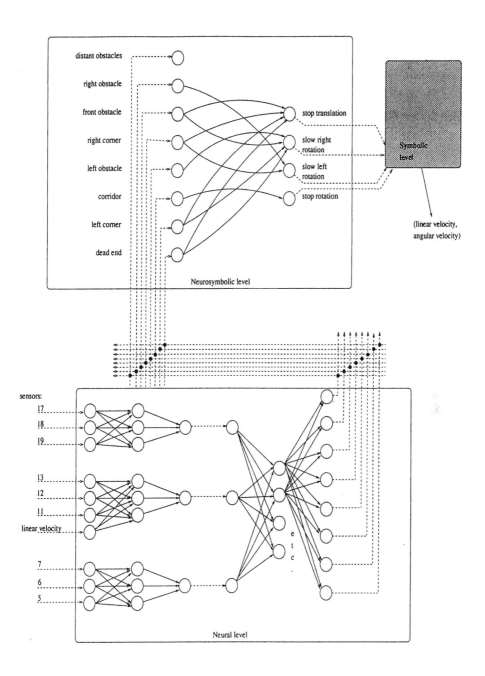

Figure 7 The various components of the system NESSY3L and their interactions.

Consequently, the activations of the output units cannot be used as the parameters of the *move* and *turn* commands. In order to solve this issue, some modeling is necessary, and it is best conducted at the symbolic level.

3.4 Symbolic Level

Simple functions are called at the symbolic level in order to produce the linear and angular velocities. For example,

$$\text{linear velocity} = 100 \times (1 - \text{Activation}(stop\ translation))^2$$

This symbolic level is rather degenerated in its current state; it should be enhanced because in some cases, calling such simple functions is not sufficient. For instance, if Activation(*slow right rotation*) = Activation(*slow left rotation*), a logical reasoning is needed in order to choose between a rotation to the left and a rotation to the right. This case also shows why it is not easy to use a neural network to define a mapping between the output activations of the versatile network and the parameters of the commands.

Another way to develop the symbolic level is to tackle other important issues in robotics, like goal planning, that would be easier to address at the symbolic level than at neural or neurosymbolic level.

4 RESULTS AND DISCUSSION

A first version of NESSY3L has been developed and integrated into the robot simulator MOLUSC. As the main result, the robot is capable to slowly wander through a room (see Figure 8). Some difficulties are encountered when the robot is faced to particular situations (see Figure 8). The problems of Figure 8 are due to a robot that "hesitates" (it makes a small left turn and then a small right turn, and so on) and does not turn quickly enough. The precise cause of these "hesitations" is not well understood at this time; each of the three levels can be responsible, as also can be their combination. In order to clarify this point, new tools have to be developed. For instance, a graphical interface showing the activations of the output units of each network could be very helpful.

The main criticism against NESSY3L seems to be its complexity with respect to the difficulty of the task and to the results currently obtained. The criticism

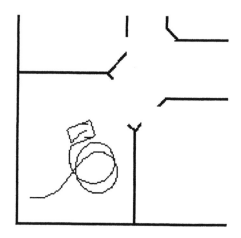

Figure 8 Trajectory of the robot during a six minutes experiment.

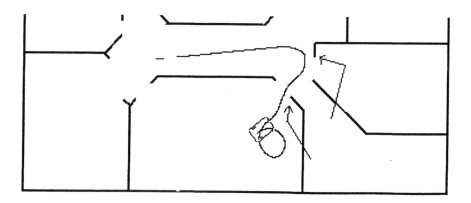

Figure 9 Another robot trajectory, showing some problems. The robot is capable to turn, but is not quick enough, and hits the walls (see arrows).

is justified. However, the aim of this work is not to solve the problem of obstacle avoidance in a perfect and minimal way. The main aim consists in providing an application suited to a fully integrated hybrid system. Such an application must be complex enough, so that the integration of various components and levels into a single architecture may be justified. Therefore, the complexity of NESSY3L should be examined with regard to the future tasks that could be achieved by the system. For instance, it seems possible to integrate a symbolic planner determining subgoals to be followed, and to add to the versatile network a set of rules trying to achieve these subgoals. Another aim of NESSY3L is to conduct a preliminary study on the usefulness of versatile networks. At the end of this study, the main obstacle to their use is the lack of a learning rule for the various weights. Without such a rule, it remains difficult to assign a precise position to attractors in the decision space; therefore it is not currently possible to let the intermediate level pilot the robot without the symbolic level. The recent research results of J. Howse (1995) may lead to a solution.

Actually NESSY3L is a starting point for a study on fully integrated hybrid systems. Although they are quite attractive, very few seem to be currently available (Medsker 1992, 1994).

As a hybrid system, NESSY3L already offers several advantages:

- Multilayer perceptrons (and versatile networks, in the future) offer their learning capabilities, and therefore relieve the designer of tedious modeling problems;

- Any symbolic system is allowed, since the other levels impose not constraints on the symbolic level; thus, NESSY3L is not limited to rule-based symbolic systems.

NESSY3L offers several future prospects:

- Taking time into account: better obstacles detectors could maybe be realized with recurrent networks like the Simple Recurrent Network (Elmann 1990), and new situations could be detected with such networks (see Bartell and Cottrell (1991) for a study of the movement of billiard ball). Temporal reasoning can also be achieved at the symbolic level.

- Use of other networks: in order to quickly build a prototype, very simple backpropagation networks have been used in NESSY3L, but other networks may be more suited, like prototype-based networks (Azcarraga and Giacometti 1991) which could help to identify obstacles.

- Other coupling between levels: the symbolic level could adjust the parameters of the neurosymbolic level (d_{ij}, c_i, w_{ik}) in real-time; it could also activate new input units of the versatile network, in order to influence the versatile decisions. Such coupling seem to be the key of "full integration."

5 SUMMARY

This chapter describes NESSY3L, a three-level hybrid system, composed of:

- A neural level, gathering neural networks that merely rely on a distributed processing of information, like multi-layer perceptrons.

- A neurosymbolic level, gathering components of the hybrid system that have both connectionist and symbolic features, for instance localist neural networks. A particular model of recurrent localist neural network, the so-called versatile neural network model, is also presented in this chapter.

- A symbolic level, gathering all other components of the system.

This architecture is currently dedicated to the problem of reactive obstacle avoidance in mobile robotics. With regard to this problem, the main features of each level can be summarized as follows:

neural level	numeric classification
symbolic level	symbolic decision making logical reasoning with complex rules or other knowledge
neurosymbolic level	parallel application of many simple rules

Although this is not achieved in the current prototype, such an architecture is intended to facilitate inter-level fine-grained communications in order to obtain a kind of fully integrated hybrid system.

ACKNOWLEDGMENTS

The authors would like to thank Mr. P. Reignier and Mr. J. Crowley (Laboratory LIFIA-IMAG, Grenoble, France) for their permission to use the robot simulator MOLUSC and for their useful help. The first author acknowledges partial support from the Swiss *Fonds National de la Recherche Scientifique* and from the Japanese *Science and Technology Agency*.

REFERENCES

[1] Shun ichi Amari. Backprogation and stochastic gradient descent. *Neuro-computing*, 5:185–307, 1993.

[2] A. P. Azcarraga and A. Giacometti (1991). A prototype-based incremental neural network for classification tasks. In *Proc. of the 4th International Conference on Neural Networks and their Applications*, Nîmes, France. EC2.

[3] B. T. Bartell and G. W. Cottrell (1991). A model of symbol grounding in a temporal environment. In *Proc. of the IEEE International Joint Conference on Neural Networks*, volume I, pages 805–810.

[4] C. M. Bishop (1995). *Neural Networks for Pattern Recognition*. Oxford University Press.

[5] A. Cichocki and R. Unbehauen. *Neural Networks for Optimization and Signal Processing*. Wiley, 1993.

[6] J. L. Elman (1990). Finding structure in time. *Cognitive Science*, (14): 179–211.

[7] A. Giacometti, I. Iordanova, B. Amy, A. Vila, et al, (1992). A hybrid approach to computer aided diagnosis in electromyography. In *Proc. of the 14th An. Int. Conf. IEEE Engineer. in Med. and Biol. Soc.*, volume 14.

[8] C. Goller, (1994). A connectionist control component for the theorem prover SETHEO. In Hilario [10], pages 88–93.

[9] S. Grossberg (1982). *Studies of Mind and Brain: Neural Principles of Learning, Perception, Development, and Motor Control*. Reidel Press.

[10] M. Hilario, editor (1994). *ECAI94 Workshop "Combining Symbolic and Connectionist Processing,"* Amsterdam, August.

[11] M. W. Hirsch (1989). Convergent activation dynamics in continuous time networks. *Neural Networks*, 2: 331–349.

[12] J. W. Howse (1995). *Gradient and Hamiltonian Dynamics: Some Applications to Neural Network Analysis and System Identification.* PhD thesis, University of New Mexico.

[13] F. Kurfess and M. Reich, (1989). Logic and reasoning with neural nets. In R. Pfeifer et al., editors, *Connectionism in Perspective*, pages 365–376. Elsevier Science Publishers B. V. North-Holland.

[14] A. Labbi (1993). Neural networks for decision making in dynamic environments. In *Proc. of the 3rd International Conference on Artificial Neural Networks*, Amsterdam, Springer-Verlag, pages ??

[15] P. Masa, K. Hoen, and H. Wallinga (1993). 20 million patterns per second vlsi neural network pattern classifier. In *Proc. of the 3rd International Conference on Artificial Neural Networks*, Amsterdam, Springer-Verlag, pages 1058–1061.

[16] L. R. Medsker and D. L. Bailey (1992). Models and guidelines for integrating expert systems and neural networks. In Kandel and Langholz, editors (1992). *Hybrid Architectures for Intelligent Systems.* CRC Press, chapter 8, pages 154–171.

[17] L. R. Medsker, (1994). *Hybrid Neural Networks and Expert Systems.* Kluwer Academic Publishers, the Netherlands.

[18] B. Orsier, B. Amy, V. Rialle, and A. Giacometti, (1994). A study of the hybrid system SYNHESYS. In Hilario [10], pages 1–9.

[19] D. A. Pomerleau (1993). *Neural Network Perception for Mobile Robot Guidance.* Kluwer Academic Publishers, the Netherlands.

[20] D. A. Pomerleau, J. Gowdy, and C. E. Thorpe (1991). Combining artificial neural networks and symbolic processing for autonomous robot guidance. *Engng Applic. Artif. Intell.*, 4(4): 279–285.

[21] P. Reignier (1994). Fuzzy logic techniques for mobile robot obstacle. *International Journal on Robotics and Autonomous Systems*, 12: 143–153. ISSN 0921 8890.

[22] R. Sun (1991). *Integrating Rules and Connectionism for Robust Reasoning.* PhD thesis, Brandeis University, Waltham, Massachusetts.

[23] A. Zell et al (1995). *SNNS, Stuttgart Neural Network Simulator, User Manual, Version 4.1.* Institute for Parallel and Distributed High Performance Systems, University of Stuttgart, Germany. http://vasarely.informatik.uni-stuttgart.de/snns/snns.html.

10

A DISTRIBUTED PLATFORM FOR SYMBOLIC–CONNECTIONIST INTEROPERATION

José C. González
Juan R. Velasco
Carlos A. Iglesias*

Universidad Politécnica de Madrid
* Universidad de Valladolid
SPAIN

1 INTRODUCTION

Symbolic and connectionist approaches are obviously complementary for problem solving, leading to a growing interest in hybrid systems: those involving the cooperation of both approaches in a single integrated system. However, some general problems may be observed in current literature on the subject. These problems, usual in new research arenas, may render the achievement of advances in the field difficult:

- First, most of the research effort until now has addressed specific applications, generating specific hybrid solutions. Such results rarely evolve toward general models of hybridization.

- Second, applications are usually developed in a purely *ad hoc* manner. Portability, re-usability, scalability and, finally, applicability to real world problems are seriously hampered.

- In this situation, comparing the plausibility, generality and performance of different approaches, models or implementations (in general, any kind of experimental research) becomes an impossible task.

The underlying cause behind this is the lack of theories (conceptual models of reference), methodologies and tools for research and development purposes. Fortunately, some recent works represent considerable contributions in these areas (e.g., Medsker 1995 or, in this volume, chapters 2, 3, and 5).

To address these aforementioned problems, a framework devised for the interoperation of heterogeneous systems is proposed as a well-suited approach. The main characteristics of this approach are identified in section 2. These objectives have nurtured the design of a platform (section 3) and the adaptation of a methodology (section 4) for the development of heterogeneous systems in general, and of symbolic-connectionist hybrids in particular. Some examples are then explored (section 5) and the current research conducted around the platform is overviewed (section 6). A brief summary concludes this chapter.

2   A SOFTWARE INTEROPERATION APPROACH

Symbolic connectionist hybridization represents only one particular case of heterogeneous systems interoperation. A framework suitable for developing the hybrid systems under investigation should at least feature the following capabilities:

- Modularity: Hybrid systems/models should be developed from basic building blocks comprising symbolic, connectionist or fusion modules (those involving the tight coupling of both paradigms), as well as other hardware/software systems (e.g., data acquisition systems, statistical modules, mechanical actuators, etc.)

- Encapsulation: These components should be encapsulated in order to offer homogeneous interfaces.

- Cooperation: Mechanisms suitable for intelligent cooperation should be supported to allow complex interactions among the components of the framework.

- Distribution: Components should be capable of working in distant environments. This requirement can be due to external constraints (such as the execution of individual components in specialized hardware/software platforms), or to the very nature of the problem.

- Ease of use: Any solution to the problem of software interoperation involves some cost, imposing discipline on researchers/developers to force the use of languages, software development methodologies, or tools. However, the overload imposed on researchers to integrate particular pre-existing components in this framework and to organize the interaction of these components should be reduced to a minimum. In any case, such overload should be fully justified in terms of the inherent benefits of this approach.

- Openness: Facilities have to be foreseen for the interoperation of these components with other distributed frameworks currently under development by companies and research institutions.

These considerations lead the authors to propose a multiagent architecture as the most adequate technology for building a common platform for the MIX project (*MIX: Modular Integration of Connectionnist and Symbolic Processing in Knowledge-Based Systems*, European Information Technology Programme, project ESPRIT–9119). An overview of the project objectives and methodology can be found in (Hilario et al. 1994), and a complete description of the MIX platform in (González et al. 1995).

Multiagent architectures belong to the broader field of Distributed Artificial Intelligence. To summarize, we call agents autonomous entities capable of carrying out specific tasks by themselves or through cooperation with other agents. Multiagent systems offer a decentralized model of control, use the mechanisms of message-passing for communication purposes, and are usually implemented from an object-oriented perspective.

3 THE MIX PLATFORM

3.1 Architecture

The MIX architecture consists of two basic entities: the agents and the network through which they interact. The basic functionalities and interfaces of the network constitute the network model. Although different agent models can be integrated, one has been adopted as standard for the current implementation. Moreover, some features are introduced that make this platform especially suitable for symbolic/connectionist hybridization. The starting point for the implementation of the platform has been the formal agent model proposed and implemented by Domínguez (1992).

From an external perspective, an agent is structured as a set of elements:

- Services: functionality offered to other agents.

- Goals: self-imposed tasks (functions that an agent carries out in self-interest, not to meet a demand from another agent).

- Resources: information on external resources (services, libraries, ontologies, groups, etc.)

- Internal objects: data structures shared by all the processes that are launched by the agent to carry out service requests or to achieve goals.

- Control: specification of how service requests are handled by the agent.

At the network level, a yellow-page service is offered by a specialized agent, the *Yellow_Pages* (YP) agent. At birth, agents register with a particular YP agent, giving their net address, and information on the services they offer and the services they might need. Agents can also subscribe to "groups." Groups refer to dynamic sets of agents, and can be used as aliases in service petitions. Thus, these petitions can be addressed to an individual agent, to the agents subscribed to a group, or to all the agents offering the service. The YP agent responds to a registration request providing all the information that an agent needs to know (e.g., the addresses of the agents offering services that it will request). Such information is updated continually by the YP agent.

A YP agent acts as a sort of active repository, not as a router. It registers and diffuses information regarding the structure of a set of agents who cooperate in a particular application. Therefore, different YP agents can be simultaneously active, even in the same machine (provided they use distinct ports for communication). By using the information received from the YP agent, the remaining "application" agents can establish direct communication links, thus making the risk of network collapse (due to saturation of the communication channels in the YP agent) negligible.

Several communication primitives are implemented, including different synchronization mechanisms (synchronous, asynchronous and deferred communications) and higher level protocols, as Contract Net (Smith 1980).

The relationship between the MIX architecture and other models designed for agent interoperation is explored in depth in (González et al. 1995), in particular with AOP: Agent Oriented Programming (Shoham 1993), and with the work around KQML: Knowledge Query and Manipulation Language (Finin and Fritzson 1994). On the other hand, the MIX network model is related to those of EMMA: Enterprise Modeling and Management Architecture (Sycara and Roboam 1992), and the I^3 Reference Architecture (Genesereth and Ketchpel 1994).

3.2 The Knowledge Level

One important problem regarding the exchange of messages in a set of agents is how to facilitate the mutual understanding of the content of these messages. The adopted solution permits the inclusion of a parameter in message headers expressing the language used to codify its content. Moreover, the content can make reference to concepts in an ontology shared by the sender and the recipient agents alike. The current implementation includes tools for the automatic translation of messages written in a reduced version of CKRL (Common Knowledge Representation Language) both to and from C++ code. CKRL was designed by the MLT consortium (project ESPRIT–2154) as an interchange language for symbolic machine learning algorithms (Causse et al. 1993).

On the other hand, it is always possible to compose the content of messages in a free format. But, in this case, sender and recipient need to agree previously on the structure of the body of the messages that they interchange.

3.3 Agents Specification: MIX-ADL

With the MIX project in mind, a specialized language (Agent Description Language, MIX-ADL) has been designed to simplify the specification of the agents cooperating in solving a problem in a hybrid framework.

A MIX-ADL file consists, briefly, of two sections:

- A preamble containing headers, needed predominantly to specify the locations where relevant resources can be found:
  - Net address of the machine where the YP agent for all the agents in the file will be found.
  - Default language that will be used to codify messages sent by all the agents included in the file.
  - Default ontologies for concepts in the application domain.
  - C++ source or object libraries used for low-level service implementation.
- The body of the MIX-ADL specification describes the structure of a set of agents. Agent classes and instances can be declared, leading to a hierarchical organization with inheritance of structure, in the style of the object-oriented paradigm.

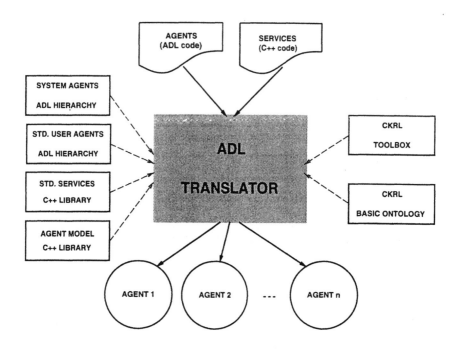

Figure 1   The MIX platform.

3.4   The MIX ToolBox

Finally, some tools have been implemented to translate the MIX-ADL description files to standard C++ programs and for subsequently compiling them. A scheme of the platform is shown in figure 1. It is made up of four elements:

■   ADL translator: this translates the MIX-ADL description of a particular set of agents into a set of independent executable programs (one program per agent). These agents can cooperate in the same application, possibly together with other agents compiled in the same or other machines in a distributed and heterogeneous environment. In this task, the translator uses the following three complementary sources.

- MIX C++ libraries: these offer the basic low-level functionality of the platform, including all the typical mechanisms of multiagent libraries as well as general purpose objects and functions.

- CKRL toolbox: this serves for translating CKRL descriptions to C++ classes and objects and C++ objects to CKRL descriptions.

- Standard ADL agent definitions and CKRL ontologies.

Users of the platform have to write the ADL specification of their applications and, eventually, a library containing some objects and functions that implement services, goals, etc. The result obtained from the platform using these elements is a set of executable programs: the agents.

3.5 Types of Coupling

One of the most appealing features of the MIX architecture from the point of view of symbolic–connectionist integration is the possibility of dealing with two levels of integration. By default, our agents are loosely coupled. It means that inter-agent communication is carried out via message passing. However, a more tight coupling mechanism is often needed (mainly for the sake of efficiency). This happens when there is a continuous flow of interaction among agents. Such is the case of the SETHEO system (Goller 1994; Suttner and Ertel 1990).

SETHEO is a theorem prover that uses a neural module to guide the search for a solution across the problem space search tree. When the prover arrives at a situation where several paths could be tried, the neural module suggests the most promising branch to follow.

The MIX-ADL language permits the specification of a group of agents that will be treated as a strongly coupled society. Only part of the services offered by the society as a whole are exported (and thus made visible from the outside). The remaining internal services are offered only to the agents in the society. The petition of these internal services is executed by the platform as a function call instead of using message passing. However, the specific method used for service handling is kept hidden from the user.

4   A METHODOLOGY FOR MULTI-AGENT HYBRID SYSTEMS DEVELOPMENT

As stated in section 1, lack of methodology is a serious drawback in current hybrid systems development. In the MIX project, the CommonKADS methodology (Breuker and Van de Velde 1994; Wielinga et al. 1992) (another product of an European project, ESPRIT–5248) has been adopted and adapted to specific needs in the field of hybrid systems.

CommonKADS is a model-based approach to the development of knowledge-based systems. In this approach, knowledge acquisition is no longer viewed as the simple transfer of knowledge from a human expert to a computer system, but rather as a modeling process. The result of this process is a set of complementary models: Organization, Task, Agent, Communication, Expertise and Design models. The Expertise model plays a pivotal role in the methodology. It represents the problem solving knowledge used by an agent to perform a task.

Obviously, CommonKADS was not originally conceived as a conceptual framework for the development of distributed systems. This is the reason behind the problems found in adopting the methodology for hybrid systems development. The main drawbacks detected concern Agent and Communication models. Firstly, CommonKADS takes into consideration only two kinds of agents: knowledge-based systems and users. But the most difficult problems arise in relation to the Communication model: (1) It only considers human–computer interaction. (2) It does not deal with multi-partner transactions in a natural way. (3) It does not permit a flexible and dynamic assignment of tasks to agents. These are the most important aspects of the original methodology for which modifications have been required. A fully developed example of application of this methodology to the analysis, design and implementation of a hybrid fuzzy-connectionist system can be found in (Iglesias et al. 1996).

5   EXAMPLES

5.1   A Connectionist Agent

In this section, one of the many possible ways of encapsulating a neural net in a MIX agent is shown. This agent is not proposed as a general model, but as an illustrative example. A neural net can be viewed as a reactive agent offering a set of functions, such as loading/saving the structure of the net from a file, training (or testing) the net from (against) a set of input/output patterns, initializing the weights of links to particular values, initializing learning parameters, activating the net (obtaining the output for a given input), or even storing input/output patterns for learning purposes. From this plausible point of view, each one of these functions has to be modeled as a service.

The MIX-ADL description of a neural class according to this perspective is included in the Appendix. In this piece of ADL code, only the specification of the service *Activate* (for defining the activating function of the agents belonging to this class) has been included. This service is in charge of processing an input pattern and replying to the calling agent with the corresponding output. In line with the above specification, the body of the requesting and replying messages should have a fixed format according to concepts defined in a CKRL ontology. The activation function is a simple C++ function (in the file *neural_agent.C*) that can make calls to external programs or object libraries compiled from other languages.

Services may have associated cost functions. In this case, we can use the cost function to transmit an estimation of the error committed by the neural net to the calling agent. When the neural agent receives a request to carry out the *activate* service according to the Contract Net protocol, it first evaluates the cost function, and sends back the estimate of the error to the petitioner. Then, this agent analyzes the received bids, selects the agent or agents best suited to achieving the contract according to a particular criterion, and asks them finally to provide the service.

5.2 A Simple Hybrid System

In this section, an example will be shown to illustrate how to model a hybrid system using the MIX toolbox. Let's suppose a simple industrial process that predicts the value of one distinguished variable from the values of a set of observed variables (e.g., acquired through sensors). Two different learning agents (a neural net and an algorithm for the induction of decision trees) have been considered for predicting the desired value for the variable.

As seen in figure 2, there are six agents offering different services. A learning group is defined, because different learning systems are used for the same prediction purpose. The following agents are involved:

- *Interface* agent: allows the user to order a number of actions, such as starting and ending the process.

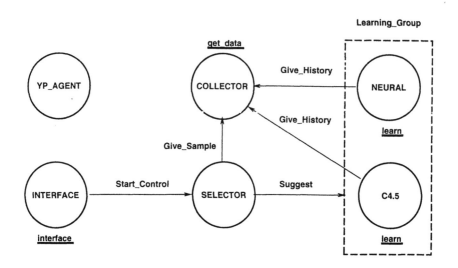

Figure 2 Agents structure of a simple hybrid.

- *Collector* agent: supplies samples from the industrial process modeled, and stores them in a history file to allow the learning systems to work.

- *Selector* is the agent who obtains new samples from Collector and asks the learning agents (as a group) for a suggestion.

- *Neural* and *C4.5* (neural and symbolic agents) provide suggestions. From time to time they ask Collector for the latest history, in order to update their knowledge.

The ADL code used to specify this application is shown in the Appendix. Once this program has been translated, the agents are compiled into separate executable programs, which could even be running on different computers. This is a typical loosely coupled, stand alone system whose interest is the reduction of error in the prediction of the output variable.

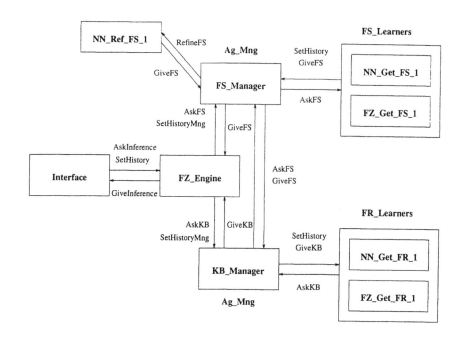

Figure 3 Fuzzy-neural cooperative learning model.

5.3 An Advanced Case Study: Fuzzy-Neural Hybridization

In this section, a particular model of fuzzy-neural hybrid is described. This model has been derived from a rigorous CommonKADS analysis and design process, implemented in MIX-ADL, and evaluated for an application in the MIX project: the presetting of a steel temper mill (Pican et al. 1996). From a previous work using a multi-layer perceptron, general hybrid models have been developed and applied by the MIX consortium to this problem to achieve an improved performance. In the case presented here, the learning capabilities of both connectionist and fuzzy systems are used together. The implemented prototype follows a fuzzy-neural cooperative learning model (figure 3).

- Fuzzy sets are extracted inductively from the past experience by neural nets and by fuzzy clustering algorithms, both methods being integrated in an intelligent stand-alone hybrid model.

- The complete problem space is partitioned into a set of regions, each one with its own associated fuzzy knowledge base. The identification of regions is carried out by neural nets (Kohonen's self-organizing maps) and fuzzy clustering algorithms

- Fuzzy rules are acquired inductively (in each region of the problem space) by neural nets and by fuzzy techniques, integrated in an intelligent stand-alone hybrid model.

- In a future version, fuzzy sets will be tuned (refined) on line, for a continuous adaptation to the real processes under modeling.

An *intelligent stand-alone model* is a compound of an agent *manager* and a set of learning agents which are joined to form a public group. The *manager* selects the best acquired knowledge base. It can also decide the different regions in which the learning agents should work. Depending on the results obtained by the different learning agents, the *manager* can learn which agents work better under certain circumstances. Thus, the *manager* performs meta-processing. The fuzzy-neural cooperative model consists of three instances of this basic intelligent stand-alone model, and a protocol is defined for communication between the *managers* of the different parameters to be optimized. The main difference with the simple stand-alone model is that first one selects a certain learning agent for working in one region, but the global knowledge base is built from different learning agents. These learning agents can be pure symbolic, pure neural or hybrid (fusion) agents. Each region can be optimized by different agent sets.

6   CURRENT WORK

Release 1.2 of the MIX platform is already available via anonymous ftp from ftp://ftp.gsi.dit.upm.es/pub/mix/. This platform is currently being used by the MIX consortium to test different hybrid models for three different applications. The first one is the optimization of a motor/gear-box combination for a turbo-charged engine. The second one consists of the control of a roll-mill in a steel making company (Pican et al. 1996). The last application pertains to the medical domain: a monitoring system for an intensive care unit.

In addition to this, the platform is being used in three other areas: communication network management (Cáncer et al. 1996), distributed control of fossil-fired power plants (Velasco et al. 1996) and natural language processing.

Further improvements are being included or considered for inclusion in future releases of the platform:

- A KQML-compatible set of performatives could be offered. KQML (Finin et al. 1994) is both a language and a protocol designed for interchanging knowledge. It has been developed as part of the ARPA Knowledge Sharing Effort. A KQML API would be used in order to allow the interoperation of MIX and KQML agents.

- A knowledge agent is being implemented with the CLIPS rule-based shell (Giarratano and Riley 1993) capable of interpreting knowledge-oriented performatives.

- A subset of the KIF (Knowledge Interchange Format) language (Genesereth et al. 1992), also developed in the framework of the Knowledge Sharing Effort, is being considered for inclusion as another native language of the platform.

- Regarding the network model, a federation architecture for YP agents is being designed. The reason for this improvement is to assure system functioning in case of failure of the (only) YP agent responsible for a particular application. In such a situation, alternate YP agents would take charge of managing the application agents affected by the problems.

From the point of view of hybridization, the main issues to be addressed in the near future are:

- The development of a sufficiently large and versatile set of agents apt for symbolic–connectionist integration.

- The design of a set of hybrid models capable of representing a significant proportion of the work carried out in this field and suitable for tackling challenging classes of problems.

- The rigorous evaluation of hybrid models in comparison to pure symbolic and connectionist approaches.

The approach presented here should assist in making the relative benefits and strengths of these models evident, thus guiding future research in this field.

7 SUMMARY

A Distributed Artificial Intelligence approach is proposed as a convenient way for designing an open platform for the integration of connectionist and symbolic systems. In this chapter, our particular perspective on the problems faced in the field of connectionist–symbolic hybridization is introduced. Also a multiagent architecture is put forward as a convenient way of addressing these problems and, following on, the software platform developed for the MIX ESPRIT project is presented. Then, an enhanced version of CommonKADS is proposed as a useful methodology for building hybrid systems.

To conclude: comprehensive methodologies and effective tools have an important role to play in the challenges faced by the field of hybrid systems. This work represents an attempt in this direction, offering a solid basis for further research.

ACKNOWLEDGEMENTS

This research is funded in part by the Commission of the European Communities under the ESPRIT Basic Research Project *MIX: Modular Integration of Connectionist and Symbolic Processing in Knowledge-Based Systems*, ESPRIT–9119. The MIX consortium is made up of the following institutions: Institute National de Recherche en Informatique et en Automatique (INRIA–Lorraine/CRIN–CNRS, France), Centre Universitaire d'Informatique (Université de Genève, Switzerland), Institute d'Informatique et de Mathématiques Appliquées de Grenoble (France), Kratzer Automatisierung (Germany), Fakultät für Informatik (Technische Universität München, Germany) and Dept. Ingeniería de Sistemas Telemáticos (Universidad Politécnica de Madrid, Spain).

This work would have never been carried out without the experience accumulated and the tools developed by Mercedes Garijo and Tomás Domínguez in their Multiagent System Model, that constitutes the basis for the MIX agent model. We are also indebted to Jaime Alvarez and Andrés Escobero (from our group) and Marc Vuilleumier (from Université de Genève, Switzerland) for their contribution to the implementation of the platform.

APPENDIX

ADL DESCRIPTION OF A SIMPLE HYBRID

```
#DOMAIN "ijcai-example"
#YP_SERVER "tcp://madrazo.gsi.dit.upm.es:6050"
#COMM_LANGUAGE ckrl
#ONTOLOGY "example.ckrl"

CLASS Neural_Class -> Basic_Class
    RESOURCES
        REQ_LIBRARIES:  "neural_agent.C"
        REQ_ONTOLOGIES: "neural.ckrl, learning.ckrl"
        REQ_SERVICES:   give_history
        SUBSCRIBE_TO:   Learning_Group
    INTERNAL_OBJECTS
        a_net, l_net -> neural::neural-net
        param ->        neural::learning-parameters
        error ->        learning::error-estimate
    GOALS
        learn: CONCURRENT Learning_Function
    SERVICES
        activate: Activation_Function
                  REQ_MES_STRUCT learning::input-data
                  ANS_MES_STRUCT learning::output-data
              COST Error_Estimation_Function
                  REQ_MES_STRUCT learning::input-data
                  ANS_MES_STRUCT learning::error-estim
        ...
END Neural_Class

AGENT YP_Agent -> YP_Class
END YP_Agent

AGENT Interface -> Basic_Class
    RESOURCES
        REQ_LIBRARIES: "inter_funct.C"
        REQ_SERVICES: start_control;
                      finish_in_order
    GOALS
        interface: CONCURRENT Inter_Function
END Interface

AGENT Selector -> Basic_Class
    RESOURCES
        REQ_LIBRARIES: "selec_funct.C"
```

```
        REQ_SERVICES:
            give_sample;
            activate
                CONTRACT_POLICY Eval_Function
                    REQ_MSG_STRUCT example::Cost
    SERVICES
        start_control: CONCURRENT Start_Function
END Selector


AGENT Collector -> Basic_Class
    RESOURCES
        REQ_LIBRARIES: "collec_funct.C"
    INTERNAL_OBJECTS
        history -> History
    GOALS
        get_data: CONCURRENT Get_Data_Function
    SERVICES
        give_sample: Give_Sample_Function
                ANS_MSG_STRUCT example::Vector
        give_history: Give_History_Function
                REQ_MSG_STRUCT example::Depth
                ANS_MSG_STRUCT example::Vector
END Collector


// ****************************************
//            Learning Agents
// ****************************************

AGENT Neural -> Neural_Class
END Neural

AGENT C45 -> Basic_Class
    RESOURCES
        REQ_LIBRARIES: "symbolic_agent.C"
        REQ_SERVICES: give_history
        REQ_ONTOLOGIES: "c45.ckrl","learning.ckrl"
        SUBSCRIBE_TO: Learning_Group
    INTERNAL_OBJECTS
        a_tree, l_tree -> c45::decision-tree
        param -> c45::learning-parameters
        error -> learning::error-estim
    GOALS
        learn: CONCURRENT C45_Function
    SERVICES
        activate: CONCURRENT Decision_Function
                REQ_MSG_STRUCT learning::input-data
                ANS_MSG_STRUCT learning::output-data
            COST C45_cost_function
                REQ_MSG_STRUCT learning::input-data
                ANS_MSG_STRUCT learning::error-estim
END C45
```

REFERENCES

Breuker, J. and W. Van de Velde (Eds.) (1994). *COMMONKADS Library for Expertise Modelling*. Amsterdam, The Netherlands: IOS Press.

Cáncer, A., J. J. Sánchez, and M. Garijo (1996, April). A multi-agent system for cooperative network-faults management. In *Proceedings of the First International Conference on the Practical Applications of Intelligent Agents and Multi-Agent Technology, PAAM-96*, London, UK, pp. 279–294.

Causse, K. et al. (1993, May). Final discussion of the Common Knowledge Representation Language (CKRL). Deliverable D2.3, MLT Consortium, ESPRIT project 2154, Laboratoire de Recherche en Informatique, Université de Paris Sud, Orsay, France.

Domínguez, T. (1992). *Definición de un Modelo Concurrente Orientado a Objetos para Sistemas Multiagente*. Ph. D. thesis, Dep. Ingeniería de Sistemas Telemáticos, E.T.S.I. Telecomunicación, Universidad Politécnica de Madrid.

Finin, T. and R. Fritzson (1994, July). KQML: A language and protocol for knowledge and information exchange. In *Proceedings of the Thirteenth International Workshop on Distributed Artificial Intelligence*, Lake Quinalt, WA, pp. 126–136.

Finin, T., J. Weber, G. Wiederhold, M. R. Genesereth, R. Fritzson, D. McKay, J. McGuire, R. Pelavin, S. Shapiro, and C. Beck (1994, February). Specification of the KQML agent–communication language plus example agent policies and architectures. Draft document, The DARPA Knowledge Sharing Initiative. External Interfaces Working Group, Baltimore, MD.

Genesereth, M. R., R. E. Fikes, et al. (1992). Knowledge Interchange Format, Version 3.0. Reference manual. Technical Report Logic-92-1, Computer Science Department, Stanford University, Stanford, CA.

Genesereth, M. R. and S. P. Ketchpel (1994, July). Software agents. *Communications of the ACM, Special Issue on Intelligent Agents 37*(7), 48–53.

Giarratano and Riley (1993). *Clips Manuals, Version 6.0*. Houston, TX: Software Technology Branch, Lyndon B. Johnson Space Center, NASA.

Goller, C. (1994). A connectionist control component for the theorem prover SETHEO. In *Proceedings of the ECAI-94 Workshop on Combining Symbolic and Connectionist Processing*, Amsterdam, The Netherlands, pp. 88–93.

González, J. C., J. R. Velasco, C. A. Iglesias, J. Alvarez, and A. Escobero (1995, November). A multiagent architecture for symbolic-connectionist integration. Technical Report MIX/WP1/UPM/3.2, Dep. Ingeniería de Sistemas Telemáticos, E.T.S.I. Telecomunicación, Universidad Politécnica de Madrid.

Hilario, M., C. Pellegrini, and F. Alexandre (1994, May). Modular integration of connectionist and symbolic processing in knowledge-based systems. In *Proceedings of the International Symposium on Integrating Knowledge and Neural Heuristics*, Pensacola, Florida, pp. 123–132.

Hilario, M. (1997). An overview of strategies for neurosymbolic integration. (Chapter 2 of this volume).

Iglesias, C. A., J. C. González, J. R. Velasco, and K. Eder (1996, January). Prototype of a fuzzy-neural hybrid model. Implementation report. Technical Report MIX/WP2/UPM/2.0, Dep. Ingeniería de Sistemas Telemáticos, E.T.S.I. Telecomunicación, Universidad Politécnica de Madrid.

Khosla, R. and T. Dillon (1997). Task structure and computational level: Architectural issues in symbolic-connectionist integration. (Chapter 3 of this volume).

Magdalena, L. (1997). A first approach to a taxonomy of fuzzy-neural systems. (Chapter 5 of this volume).

Medsker, L. R. (1995). *Hybrid Intelligent Systems*. Boston, MA: Kluwer Academic Publishers.

Pican, N., F. Alexandre, and P. Bresson (1996, February). Artificial neural networks for the presetting of a steel temper mill. *IEEE Expert 11*(1), 22–27.

Shoham, Y. (1993, March). Agent-oriented programming. *Artificial Intelligence 60*(1), 51–92.

Smith, R. G. (1980). The contract net protocol: High-level communication and control in a distributed problem solver. *IEEE Transactions on Computers C-29*, 1104–1113.

Suttner, C. and W. Ertel (1990, January). Using connectionist networks for guiding the search of a theorem prover. Technical Report 342/8/90 A, Institut für Informatik, Technische Universität München, München, Germany.

Sycara, K. and M. Roboam (1992). EMMA: An architecture for enterprise modeling and integration. In N. M. Avouris and L. Gasser (Eds.), *Distributed Artificial Intelligence: Theory and Praxis*, pp. 197–213. Boston, MA: Kluwer Academic Publishers.

Velasco, J. R., J. C. González, C. A. Iglesias, and L. Magdalena (1996, June). Multiagent based control systems: A hybrid approach to distributed process control. *Control Engineering Practice 4*(6), 839–845. (Extended version of a paper previously published in the *Preprints of the 13th IFAC Workshop on Distributed Computer Control Systems, DCCS-95*, A. E. K. Sahraoui and J. A. de la Puente, editors, Toulouse, France, 1995).

Wielinga, B. J., A. T. Schreiber, and J. A. Breuker (1992). KADS: A modeling approach to knowledge engineering. *Knowledge Acquisition 4*(1), 5–53. (Special Issue, The KADS Approach to Knowledge Engineering).

PART III

REPRESENTING SYMBOLIC
KNOWLEDGE

11

MICRO-LEVEL HYBRIDIZATION IN THE COGNITIVE ARCHITECTURE DUAL

Boicho Kokinov

Institute of Mathematics
Bulgarian Academy of Sciences
and
Cognitive Science Department
New Bulgarian University

1   INTRODUCTION

After a long and exhausting war between the representatives of the symbolic and connectionist approaches (this war stimulated, however, the clarification of the limitations and advantages of both approaches) a growing group of peace-makers emerged who tried to integrate the advantages of both approaches and to fill in the gap between them (Hendler, 1989a, Hinton, 1990, Barnden & Pollack, 1991, Thornton, 1991, Sun & Bookman, 1992, Sun & Bookman, 1994, Dinsmore, 1992, Holyoak & Barnden, 1994. However, a mini-war started between the peace-makers themselves on the issue of how to sign the peace treaty: with the surrender of one of the approaches or with their parity. Some researchers supported the connectionist-to-the-top view that symbol structures and symbol processing should emerge from the work of a neural network (called a unified approach in chapters 2 and 4 of this volume and connectionist symbol processing in Elman, 1990, Pollack, 1990, Smolensky, 1990, Touretzky, 1990, Smolensky, Legendre, Miyata, 1992, Smolensky, 1995, while others supported the synergistic hybrid approach bringing together connectionist and symbolic machines in a single system or model Hendler, 1989b, Hendler, 1991, Lange & Dyer, 1989, Sun, 1991. Strangely enough, no one suggested building connectionist systems on the top of a symbolic system.

The former approach is called *vertical integration* in this chapter because it is based on the clear philosophical view that symbols and symbol processing are a macro-level description of what is considered as a connectionist system at the micro level (like the relationships between Newtonian Mechanics and

197

Quantum Mechanics, or between Thermodynamics and Statistical Physics). This approach has the shortcoming of losing some of the advantages of the connectionist approach (e.g., its dynamic properties) when using it for symbol processing.

The latter approach (the hybrid one) is called *horizontal integration* in this chapter as it considers the symbolic and connectionist approaches as being at the same level of description and combines elements of different approaches or systems built up within different paradigms (e.g., a connectionist system performing learning and perception and a symbolic system performing reasoning) in order to use the advantages of both approaches. The hybrid approach has, however, no clear and unified philosophy and is often criticized as being eclectic. It needs a general philosophy and a first step in this direction is presented in the next section.

Theoretically there might exist a third approach to integration which is called a *unifying approach* in this chapter (which is, however, different from the unified approach in chapters 2 and 4 referred to here as vertical integration). An approach is called unifying one if it is more general than both the connectionist and symbolic approaches and they can be considered as particular cases of it. One such candidate will be discussed in this chapter.

On the other hand the vertical and horizontal integration approaches might be viewed as complementary and a meta-level integration of these approaches is also possible. Thus Sun (1995) suggests a hybrid approach implemented as a "pure" connectionist system using both local and distributed representations. The meta-level integration possibilities will be discussed further on the example of the architecture described in this chapter.

2   THE MICRO-LEVEL HYBRIDIZATION APPROACH

The author of this chapter considers the symbolic and the connectionist approaches as equally important and equally contributing to the understanding of human cognition. Moreover, he shares the view that no single formal approach can completely describe human cognitive processes, as they are complex enough, and this is the main reason for building hybrid models of human cognition.

The symbolic approach is a discrete one while the connectionist approach is a continuous one and that is why they can be considered as complementary formal descriptions each capturing different aspects of human cognition. (Similarly the light has been described both as a particle and a wave).

Many aspects of human cognition are better described by the symbolic approach while many others are described by the connectionist one (ref. chapters 2 and 4). Here only two very important characteristics of human cognition will be stressed. These are often underestimated but are considered as basic features in the DUAL approach.

- The ability to categorize and to describe portions of the continuous world around us as separate entities and relations between them. The symbolic approach is best suitable for modeling this aspect — it describes human knowledge of the world as a system of discrete symbolic structures and human cognitive processes as processes of building and manipulation of such structures;

- The dynamic properties of all cognitive processes which are characterized by continuous and smooth changes of the mental state following both the internal dynamics of the cognitive system itself and the external dynamics of the continuously changing environment — these properties are best handled by the connectionist approach.

These two features are, however, characteristics of *every* cognitive process and therefore instead of having two or more subsystems each designed according to one of the approaches these characteristics are needed at the micro level so that every macro-level cognitive process can benefit from them. In this way a new idea emerged – to have a DUAListic cognitive architecture consisting of a huge number of small elements (called micro-agents) each of them being hybrid, i.e., consisting of a symbolic and a connectionist part. In other words, *instead of hybridization at the macro level a hybridization at the micro level is being proposed*. One important characteristic of all the possible architectures of that kind is that they will produce *emergent computation* reflecting the collective behavior of all micro-agents.

In short, the micro-level hybridization approach is a particular type of horizontal integration. It follows the general philosophy that *it is a matter of principle to use two different and complementary formalisms (a discrete and a continuous one) for describing and explaining human cognition*. It uses integrated symbolic and connectionist mechanisms in modeling *every* cognitive process and therefore it is crucial to ground the hybridization on the micro level.

Now coming back to the possibility of building a unifying approach it seems that the micro-level hybridization approach can also be considered as a first approximation of such a unifying approach. Varying the proportions of symbolic and connectionist processing capabilities of the micro-agents, a whole spectrum of hybrid models will arise. In the particular case of micro-agents having only connectionist parts, a purely connectionist system will emerge, while in the particular case of micro-agents having only symbolic parts, a purely symbolic system will emerge. Neural nets are examples of the first class, while cellular automata and classifier systems are examples of the second type. It is also clear that there is a continuum of possibilities differing in the balance of the symbolic and the connectionist abilities the micro-agents have. Actually, the micro-agents in different models may differ drastically in their symbolic capabilities, starting with simple micro-agents performing only marker passing, going through micro-agents being able to perform some specialized (and possibly complex) procedures and ending with micro-agents being universal Turing machines.

3 THE DUAL COGNITIVE ARCHITECTURE

The DUAL cognitive architecture (Kokinov, 1994b, 1994c) is one particular example of the micro-level hybridization approach that has been developed and implemented as a generalization of and a common basis for various models of particular cognitive processes: memory (Kokinov, 1989), similarity judgments (Kokinov, 1992), word-sense disambiguation (Kokinov, 1993), and analogical reasoning (Kokinov, 1994a).

DUAL micro-agents consist of a connectionist part (*c-component*), which computes the continuous dynamic changes of the activation levels of the micro-agents and of a symbolic part (*s-component*), which is able to perform local marker-passing and some specialized symbolic procedures. From the symbolic perspective the micro-agents represent various concepts, objects, events, situations, facts, rules, plans, actions, etc. They might represent static facts as well as built-in procedural knowledge. A frame-like representation scheme is used. The connectionist aspect of DUAL is used for representing context (Kokinov, 1994a), (Kokinov, 1994b), (Kokinov, 1995). Context is represented in a distributed way by the relevance factors of all micro-agents to the current situation. Current goals and currently perceived elements are considered relevant as well as memory elements which have been considered relevant in the very recent past. All memory elements connected with these elements are also associatively relevant. The degree of connectivity of the particular element with all other currently relevant elements is used as a measure of relevance, called associative relevance. It is represented by the activation level of the corresponding micro-agent. Thus the activation level of the micro-agent within the connectionist aspect represents the relevance of the knowledge represented by the micro-agent within the symbolic aspect.

The micro-agents representing entities being perceived at the moment as well as micro-agents representing current goals of the cognitive system are called *source nodes* and have a constant level of activation for the period of time they are on the input or goal list. There is a relatively slow decay process so that all currently active nodes can be considered as sources of activation for a period of time. In this way, the micro-agents with a high level of activation correspond to descriptions tightly connected both with the perceived and memory-activated elements, i.e., they represent elements of the context with a graded degree of membership.

A cognitive system built on the DUAL cognitive architecture consists of a large number of simple and highly interconnected micro-agents, each of them performing a specific task and/or representing some specific declarative knowledge. The micro-agents are connected with each other — some of the links are permanent, while others are dynamically created and removed by the micro-agents themselves. Each micro-agent exchanges information only with its neighbors. The behavior of the whole system emerges from the collective behavior of the micro-agents that work in parallel. At each particular moment only some of the micro-agents are active and only they can contribute to the computation. Moreover, every micro-agent acts at its own rate that depends on its activation level. In this way even faced with the same problem at the macro level, the cognitive system will behave differently in different contexts as the activity distribution will be different due to the differences in the perception-induced context (the objects perceived from the environment) and in the memory-induced context (the concepts being active in the preceding memory state). That is, at different occasions different groups of micro-agents with different activity distribution will act together to perform the computation and consequently different behavior will emerge.

The differences in the behavior due to differences in the perception-induced context (reflecting differences in the environment) are called context effects, while the differences in the behavior due to differences in the memory-induced context (reflecting differences in the preliminary setting of the cognitive system) are called priming effects. Both the perception-induced and memory-induced contexts are represented in the same way — by the distribution of activation over the network of micro-agents. That is why the same mechanisms are used for explaining the context and priming effects.

Both the availability of the knowledge structures represented by the micro-agents and the rate of performing of the actions which the micro-agents are capable of are affected by the micro-agent's level of activation. Low activation level will even block both their availability for other micro-agents and their actions. Let us consider a simple example: the context-sensitive behavior of the marker-passing process. All micro-agents are capable of local marker-passing (i.e., they can pass the received markers to their immediate neighbors over specific links). However, their actual performance depends on their activation level, i.e., the rate at which the markers are passed to the micro-agent's neighbors is proportional to its activation level. In particular, the micro-agents will not pass the markers farther when their activation level is below a certain threshold. As a result in different contexts the markers started from the same nodes and wandering through the same network will pass along different ways, i.e., different results will be produced.

4   THE AMBR MODEL OF ANALOGICAL REASONING

AMBR is a computer model of human analogical reasoning built up on the basis of DUAL (Kokinov, 1994a).

The simulation system models human commonsense reasoning, solving problems in the area of cooking and boiling water, eggs, etc., both in the kitchen and in the forest. The knowledge base of the simulation program contains about 300 nodes and 4,000 links. Here are some example situations related to heating water and known to the system from beforehand: A) successfully heating water in a pot on the plate of a cooking stove, B) failing to heat water on the fire in a wooden vessel, and C) successfully heating water by means of an immersion heater in a glass.

A simplified version of a target problem used in a psychological experiment has been used as a target problem in the simulation: *how can you heat water in a wooden vessel when you are in a forest, having only a knife, a match box and an ax.* The problem is represented in the following way: the reasoner should look for a situation in which the water is in a wooden vessel and which will cause another situation in which the water will be hot and will still be in the wooden vessel.

The system runs continuously and so its memory is always in some particular memory state when a manually encoded representation of the target problem is presented to it and the corresponding memory structures are being activated, simulating the process of problem perception. In this way both the preliminary distribution of activation in working memory and the activation arising from the perception process are responsible for the resulting memory state which, on its turn, determines the results of the retrieval, mapping and transfer processes. The retrieval, mapping and transfer processes are emergent processes, they emerge from the collective behavior of the many active micro-agents in the DUAL architecture. Thus, for example, the mapping process involves an emergent subprocess of semantic similarity judgment which is performed by the distributed marker-passing processes described in the previous section. All these processes depend on the distribution of activation which changes continuously and in this way become context-sensitive.

The simulation experiment consists of several runs of the program in slightly different conditions varying the additional input nodes (corresponding to additionally perceived casual objects from the environment) and the distribution of activation at the initial moment (corresponding to different preliminary settings). It has been demonstrated that the behavior of the system varies with the variations of the context in accordance with the psychological data. For example, typically the system finds situation A as a base for analogy and fails in solving the problem (the same happens to most subjects in psychological experiments); with some priming (preactivation of the concept of immersion heater) the system finds the situation C as a base for analogy and finds a solution of the problem (putting a hot knife in the water); and in simulating the perception of a stone during the problem solving process (putting the concept of a stone on the input list), the system finds a different solution (using a hot stone instead of a hot knife).

The simulation system has demonstrated both AMBR's capability of analogical problem solving and its ability to produce priming effects in accordance with the data produced in psychological experiments. The simulation experiments have made also a prediction about some specific context effects (the perception of a stone will increase the probability for generation of a solution involving stone although the concept of a stone is not explicitly mentioned in the problem's description).

5   COGNITIVE RATIONALE AND PSYCHOLOGICAL EXPERIMENTS

The basic motivation for developing DUAL and AMBR is to propose architectures and models that will reflect both human ability to perform specific tasks (in AMBR's case — analogical problem solving) and the dynamics of that performance.

Psychological experiments (Kokinov, 1990) have demonstrated strong priming effects on problem solving. Moreover, they have demonstrated a particular dynamics of these priming effects: the degree of those effects decreases in the course of time according to an exponential law, i.e., the memory-induced context changes in a continuous manner.

Recent experiments (Kokinov, 1996) have confirmed AMBR's prediction about the context effects. Moreover, it has been demonstrated that elements from both the central and the peripheral parts of the perceived environment can cause context effect and change human behavior; however, the degree of these context effects decrease from the center toward the periphery in a continuous way.

The system's behavior is in accordance with all these findings. It is the combination of discrete symbolic abilities (like mapping of two structures and transfer of their parts) and their continuous dynamics which is reflected in DUAL and AMBR by the symbolic and connectionist aspects, respectively.

6   SUMMARY

The basic claim of this chapter is that modeling human cognition requires at least two complementary formal descriptions: a discrete and a continuous one, reflecting two different basic properties — the ability to categorize and the dynamics of the cognitive processes. Moreover, both formalisms are needed in describing each particular cognitive process. For this reason a micro-level hybridization approach has been proposed. The basic idea is that cognitive processes emerge from the collective behavior of a great number of micro-agents, each of them being hybrid (having a symbolic and a connectionist component). The DUAL cognitive architecture is one particular example developed within the micro-level hybridization approach. Several cognitive models have been built up on the basis of this architecture. They were able to reproduce some patterns of human behavior, including its dynamics and context-sensitivity.

The micro-level hybridization approach is considered also as a way of unifying symbolic and connectionist processing. This approach can also be combined with connectionist symbolic processing approaches to produce a "pure" connectionist system that will, however, keep dualistic representations and processing mechanisms.

Historically, John Anderson (Anderson, 1983) can be considered as the precursor of such type of micro-hybridization approach. However, his ACT* architecture has a central mechanism — the interpreter — and cannot be described as producing emergent computation. Moreover, the connectionist type of spreading activation is restricted only to the declarative memory.

An approach much more similar to DUAL has been proposed in (Hofstadter & Mitchell, 1994, Mitchell, 1994, Hofstadter, 1995, French, 1995). The micro-agents in Copycat and Tabletop are called "codelets" and perform simple symbolic tasks; their performance is determined by their "urgency" which is a numeric value although it is not computed by a connectionist type mechanism. The declarative and procedural knowledge is, however, separated and different mechanisms are used for their activation.

Smolensky, who follows the vertical integration approach, has recently argued for integrating the symbolic and connectionist principles of processing (Smolensky, et al., 1992, Smolensky, 1995), considering them as dualistic and equally important. This is, however, a direction of integration orthogonal to the one presented in the current chapter.

Moreover, in the future development of DUAL the micro-level hybridization approach can be combined with the vertical integration approach: this is the meta-level integration possibility mentioned in the introduction. The idea is to implement both the connectionist and the symbolic parts of the micro-agents by neural networks, but to keep the properties of both parts different — the ability for structure representation (e.g. Smolensky's tensor product representation) and the ability for continuous dynamic change of context. Activation (which might be the same physical variable) is used for two different purposes in both cases — for representation and for relevance, respectively. To keep this difference between the representation and the dynamic parts of the micro-agents seems important according to the general philosophy of horizontal integration approach proposed in this chapter.

Acknowledgements

This research has been partially supported by grant OHN406: "Context and Priming Effects on High-Level Cognitive Processes" from the Bulgarian National Science Foundation.

REFERENCES

[1] Anderson, J. (1983). *The Architecture of Cognition*, Cambridge, MA: Harvard Univ. Press.

[2] Barnden, J. & Pollack, J. (1991). *High-Level Connectionist Models, Advances in Connectionist and Neural Computation Theory*, vol. 1, Norwood, NJ: Ablex Publ. Corp.

[3] Dinsmore (1992). *The Symbolic and Connectionist Paradigms: Closing the Gap.* Hillsdale, NJ: Lawrence Erlbaum Associates, Inc.

[4] Elman, J. (1990). Finding Structure in Time. *Cognitive Science*, vol. 14, pp. 179-211.

[5] French, R. (1995). *The Subtlety of Sameness: A Theory and Computer Model of Analogy-Making.* Cambridge, MA: MIT Press.

[6] Hendler, J. (1989a). Hybrid Systems (Symbolic/Connectionist). Special Issue of *Connection Science*, vol. 1(3).

[7] Hendler, J. (1989b). Marker Passing over Microfeatures: Towards a Hybrid Symbolic/Connectionist Model. *Cognitive Science*, vol. 13, pp. 79-106.

[8] Hendler, J. (1991). Developing Hybrid Symbolic/Connectionist Models. In: Barnden J. & Pollack J. (eds.) *High-Level Connectionist Models, Advances in Connectionist and Neural Computation Theory*, vol. 1, Norwood, NJ: Ablex Publ. Corp., 165-179

[9] Hinton, G. (ed.) (1990). Connectionist Symbol Processing. Special Issue of *Artificial Intelligence*, vol. 46 (1-2).

[10] Hofstadter, D. (1995). *Fluid Concepts and Creative Analogies*. New York: Basic Books.

[11] Hofstadter, D. & Mitchell, M. (1994). The Copycat Project: A Model of Mental Fluidity and Analogy-Making. In: Holyoak, K. & Barnden, J. (eds.) *Analogical Connections, Advances in Connectionist and Neural Computation Theory*, vol. 2, Norwood, NJ: Ablex Publ. Corp., pp.31-112

[12] Holyoak, K. & Barnden, J. (eds.) (1994). *Analogical Connections, Advances in Connectionist and Neural Computation Theory*, vol. 2, Norwood, NJ: Ablex Publ. Corp.

[13] Kokinov, B. (1989). About Modeling Some Aspects of Human Memory. In: Klix, Streitz, Waern, Wandke (eds.) *MACINTER II*, Amsterdam: North-Holland, pp. 349-359

[14] Kokinov, B. (1990). Associative Memory-Based Reasoning: Some Experimental Results. In: *Proceedings of the 12th Annual Conference of the Cognitive Science Society*, Hillsdale, NJ: Lawrence Erlbaum Associates, Inc., pp. 741-749

[15] Kokinov, B. (1992). Similarity in Analogical Reasoning. In: B. du Boulay & V. Sgurev (eds.) *Artificial Intelligence V*. Amsterdam: Elsevier, pp. 3-12

[16] Kokinov, B. (1993). Context-Sensitive Word-Sense Disambiguation. *International Journal on Information Theories and Applications*. vol. 1(10), pp. 47-50

[17] Kokinov, B. (1994a). A Hybrid Model of Reasoning by Analogy. In: K. Holyoak & J. Barnden (eds.) *Analogical Connections, Advances in Connectionist and Neural Computation Theory*, vol.2, Norwood, NJ: Ablex Publ. Corp., pp. 247-318

[18] Kokinov, B. (1994c). The Context-Sensitive Cognitive Architecture DUAL. In: *Proceedings of the 16th Annual Conference of the Cognitive Science Society*. Hillsdale, NJ: Lawrence Erlbaum Associates, Inc., pp. 502-507

[19] Kokinov, B. (1994b). The DUAL Cognitive Architecture: A Hybrid Multi-Agent Approach. In: A. Cohn (ed.) *Proceedings of ECAI'94*. New York: John Wiley & Sons, Ltd., pp. 203-207

[20] Kokinov, B. (1995). A Dynamic Approach to Context Modeling. In: P. Brezillon & S. Abu-Hakima (eds.) *Proceedings of the IJCAI-95 Workshop on Modeling Context in Knowledge Representation and Reasoning*. LAFORIA 95/11, pp. 199-209

[21] Kokinov, B., Yoveva, M. (1996). Context Effects on Problem Solving. In: *Proceedings of the 18th Annual Conference of the Cognitive Science Society*. Hillsdale, NJ: Lawrence Erlbaum Associates, Inc., pp. 586-590

[22] Lange, T. & Dyer, M. (1989). High-Level Inferencing in a Connectionist Network. *Connection Science*, vol. 1, pp. 181-217.

[23] Mitchell, M. (1994). *Analogy as Perception*. MIT Press, Cambridge, MA.

[24] Pollack, J. (1990) Recursive Distributed Representations. *Artificial Intelligence*, vol. 46 (1-2), pp. 77-105

[25] Smolensky, P. (1990). Tensor Product Variable Binding and the Representation of Symbolic Structures in Connectionist Systems. *Artificial Intelligence*, vol. 46 (1-2), pp.159-216

[26] Smolensky, P., Legendre, G. & Miyata, Y. (1992). Principles for an Integrated Connectionist/Symbolic Theory of Higher Cognition. TR-CU-CS-600-92

[27] Smolensky, P. (1995). Constituent Structure and Explanation in an Integrated Connectionist/Symbolic Cognitive Architecture. In: Macdonald, C. & Macdonald, G. (eds.) *The Philosophy of Psychology: Debates on Psychological Explanation*. Oxford, UK: Basil Blackwell.

[28] Sun, R. (1991). Connectionist Models of Rule-Based Reasoning. In: *Proceedings of the 13th Annual Conference of the Cognitive Science Society*. Hillsdale, NJ: Lawrence Erlbaum Associates, Inc., pp. 437-442

[29] Sun, R. (1995). Robust Reasoning: Integrating Rule-Based and Similarity-Based Reasoning. *Artificial Intelligence*, vol. 75(2), 241-295.

[30] Sun, R. & Bookman, L. (1992). *Integrating Neural and Symbolic Processes: The Cognitive Dimension*. AAAI Press.

[31] Sun, R. & Bookman, L. (1994). *Computational Architectures Integrating Neural and Symbolic Processes: A Perspective of the State of the Art*. Dordrecht, The Netherlands: Kluwer Academic Publishers.

[32] Touretzky, D. (1990). BoltzCONS: Dynamic Symbol Structures in a Connectionist Network. *Artificial Intelligence*, vol. 46 (1-2), pp. 5-46

[33] Thornton, C. (1991) Special Issue on Hybrid Models. *AISB Newsletter*, No 78.

AN INTEGRATED SYMBOLIC/CONNECTIONIST PARSING ARCHITECTURE

Suzanne Stevenson

Department of Computer Science,
and Center for Cognitive Science,
Rutgers University

1 INTRODUCTION

Language is the prototypical rule-governed domain of human intelligence, with linguistic representations involving tree-structured forms with rich featural specifications and elaborate relations among non-neighboring nodes. Traditional artificial intelligence approaches to natural language processing (NLP) have therefore emphasized the complex symbolic manipulations involved in understanding human language. In addition to the necessity of creating complex representations, these systems also face the challenge of determining an effective approach for resolving linguistic ambiguities in order to focus on a single interpretation of the input. Ambiguity is pervasive at all levels of linguistic representation, and yet people usually have no difficulty in determining the intended interpretation of a sentence. Much recent work in psycholinguistics has suggested that numeric information, such as lexical frequencies and co-occurrence probabilities, play a central role in linguistic ambiguity resolution (e.g., MacDonald, Pearlmutter, and Seidenberg 1994; Spivey-Knowlton, Trueswell, and Tanenhaus 1993; Juliano and Tanenhaus 1994). At the same time, computational linguists have begun to develop automatic methods for resolving ambiguity that are based on statistical models of word co-occurrences derived from large text corpora (e.g., Hindle and Rooth 1993; Schutze 1993; Weischedel et al. 1993). However, pure statistical models are not able to capture sophisticated grammatical knowledge, nor do they appear sufficient to model human behavior.[1] Effective modeling of both linguistic knowledge and performance requires a computational framework that successfully integrates

---

[1] For example, Hindle and Rooth found that a statistical model of PP attachment, based on lexical associations derived from a large corpus, achieved only 80% accuracy even when tested on (previously unseen) sentences from the same corpus (Hindle 1993). The areas in

higher level symbolic processing abilities with the numeric information that crucially focuses the understanding process onto a coherent interpretation.

Connectionism is an obvious candidate for a computational framework that can synthesize a large number of probabilistic influences on linguistic performance. However, the emphasis within connectionist NLP has been on demonstrating that connectionist networks have specific capabilities needed to support linguistic processing—for example, showing that connectionist networks can encode recursive structures (Reilly 1992; Sopena 1992), perform transformational mappings (Chalmers 1992), or make generalizations over linguistically relevant subfeatures (McClelland and Kawamoto 1986). Connectionist researchers have yet to bring together all these pieces within a model that can achieve the level of sophisticated structural knowledge that is evidenced within current linguistic theories. Much progress must be made before purely connectionist models will be capable of supporting the symbolic functionality needed for modeling highly structured representations.

In order to focus on higher level language processing issues while maintaining the advantages of the connectionist paradigm, a number of researchers have instead taken a hybrid approach to the design of an NLP system. Typically, the sub-processes of the system are divided between traditional symbolic mechanisms and purely connectionist modules, according to whether those sub-processes emphasize symbolic or numeric processing (e.g., Hendler 1987; Kimura, Suzuoka, and Amano 1992; Kwasny and Faisal 1992; Waltz and Pollack 1985; Wermter and Lehnert 1989). A common practice in this "divide-and-conquer" approach is to augment a traditional symbolic parser with a special purpose connectionist module to perform a particular generalization task or evidence-combining function. A conceptual drawback of hybrid approaches of this kind is that the symbolic and connectionist processing components are not integrated within a unifying computational framework. Furthermore, an approach that segregates symbolic and connectionist processing fails to recognize that parallel distributed processing is not only advantageous for capturing and integrating numeric evidence, it is also particularly appropriate for encoding the symbolic constraint-based formalisms of recent linguistic theories. Thus, hybrid models that use connectionist networks only as individual decision-making sub-processes are not exploiting the full power of distributed processing for parsing natural language.

---

which the model did not perform adequately involved grammatical distinctions which their simple association metric could not capture.

By contrast, the architecture described here, known as the competitive attachment model, takes a fully integrated hybrid approach to natural language parsing (Stevenson 1994). In the model, both symbolic and numeric processing are achieved within a computational framework of parallel distributed processing. Instead of augmenting an existing symbolic parser with connectionist sub-modules, the approach here incorporates very simple symbolic processing capabilities into each node of a connectionist network. Both symbolic and connectionist computations are carried out by the same simple and uniform processing nodes of the parsing model. Symbolic and connectionist algorithms do not form discrete, modular sub-processes, but instead tightly interact within individual network nodes to determine the correct syntactic parse of an input. Although the symbolic processing abilities are quite restricted, their integration within the network enables the model to focus on higher level linguistic processing issues by providing the capabilities necessary to encode a recent constraint-based linguistic theory. The resulting parallel distributed processing of both symbolic and numeric information has been shown to concisely explain a number of human behaviors in syntactic ambiguity resolution (Stevenson 1993a, 1993b, 1994).

The remainder of this chapter presents the design of the competitive attachment model and the consequences of that design. Section 2 describes the precise nature of the hybrid solution that was developed. Section 3 summarizes the results of experiments using the implemented model, which demonstrate its viability as a natural language parsing mechanism. Section 4 raises some issues for further research in the development of hybrid models. Section 5 concludes with some of the contributions of the competitive attachment model.

2 THE COMPETITIVE ATTACHMENT MODEL

2.1 Network Structure

The competitive attachment (CA) parsing model uses a localist representation in which network nodes directly represent syntactic parse tree structures. The model has two types of nodes corresponding to the two types of information that must be represented. Phrasal nodes represent the syntactic phrases of a parse tree. Each phrase consists of three nodes, with feature values encoding relevant grammatical information; see Figure 1. Attachment nodes represent

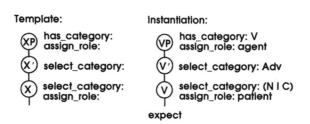

Figure 1 A syntactic phrase template and a sample instantiation of its nodes with lexically-specified symbolic features.

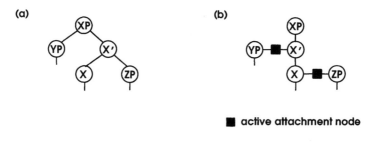

■ active attachment node

Figure 2 (a) The basic configuration of a syntactic phrase. (b) Representation of these attachments as sister relations in the parsing network.

the tree structure relations between two different syntactic phrases; that is, they explicitly represent what is normally drawn as a link in a parse tree diagram between nodes from two different phrases. In the model, each attachment node connects two potential *sisters* in the parse tree; see Figure 2. The set of fully activated attachment nodes in the network represents the model's current hypothesis regarding the syntactic structure of the linguistic input it has seen.

The parsing network is activated incrementally in response to the list of words of an input sentence. The current word triggers the activation of a phrasal template, whose symbolic features are initialized according to the lexical entry for the word, as shown in Figure 1. At the same time, the parser activates a set of attachment nodes that represent the potential attachment of the current phrase at each of the attachment sites along the right edge of the partial parse tree represented within the network; see Figure 3. After the current phrase has been connected to the developing parse tree structure, the network begins an output/update processing loop that interleaves marker passing and spreading activation (described below). When the numeric activation has stabilized, the

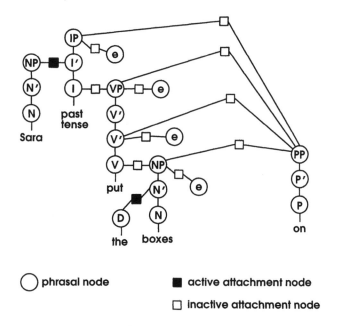

Figure 3 The CA network parsing the sentence *Sara put the boxes on the table*, at the point of processing the word *on*. Newly established attachment nodes connect the current phrase (the prepositional phrase triggered by *on*) to the right edge of the existing parse tree. Recall that attachment nodes connect potential sisters in the parse tree. Attachments to empty (e) nodes represent unfilled attachment sites.

set of activated attachment nodes represents the preferred parse tree structure for the input processed thus far; compare Figure 4(a) with the partial parse tree that it represents in Figure 4(b). At this point, the next input token is read and the competitive attachment process repeated.

2.2 Symbolic Processing

Simple symbolic features are used to implement a subset of a linguistic theory known as Government-Binding theory, or GB (Chomsky 1981; Rizzi 1990). In GB theory, there are no phrase structure rules to define possible syntactic structures; instead, grammaticality is determined by the simultaneous application of simple constraints within local sub-structures of a parse tree. For example,

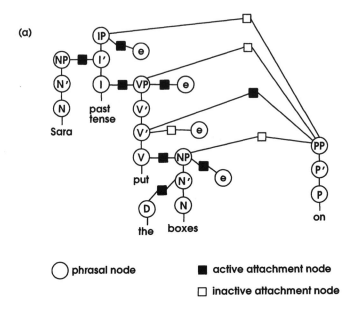

(a)

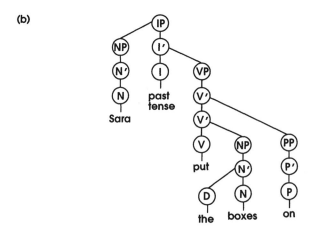

(b)

Figure 4 (a) The CA network parsing the sentence *Sara put the boxes on the table*, after determining the best attachment for the current phrase (triggered by the word *on*). (b) The partial parse tree represented by the network in (a).

a rule-based approach to grammar may have a number of context free rewrite rules for all different types of verb phrases, such as:

VP ⇒ V NP

VP ⇒ V PP

VP ⇒ V NP PP

VP ⇒ V S

VP ⇒ V NP S

By contrast, in GB all verb phrases are assumed to have the same general structural configuration: VP ⇒ V $\{XP\}^{*}$. The number and value of the objects within the VP (the XP phrases) are constrained to match the lexical information stored with individual verbs.[2] In a similar manner, all such complex rule-based information can be replaced by simple and general constraints that apply across a number of different structures.

Two aspects of this type of constraint-based linguistic theory make it particularly appropriate as the underlying linguistic formalism for a hybrid connectionist parser. First, a parallel distributed processing framework can accurately model the simultaneous application of multiple constraints defined by the theory. Second, the simplicity of the grammatical constraints avoids the need for complex symbolic processing mechanisms. In the CA model, each network processing node is augmented with the following restricted symbolic capabilities: storing simple features (atomic features or a list of atomic features) within a finite number of labeled slots, comparing the values of two features, and propagating features to neighboring nodes.

The two types of nodes in the network play very different roles in the symbolic processing. First, the phrasal nodes create the symbolic features and initiate their propagation through the parsing network. In GB, determining satisfaction of certain constraints requires comparing the features of two nodes that are not necessarily directly connected in the parse tree. However, the nodes must be in a precisely specified structural configuration. The parsing network must both verify the structural relation between the two nodes and evaluate their featural

---

[2] The verb phrase in this example is simplified, since in the version of the theory assumed here, all syntactic phrases are assumed to have three levels of structure (XP, X′, X), rather than two.

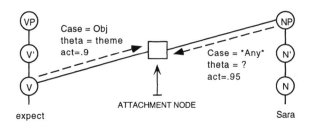

Figure 5 The representation of the attachment of an NP as direct object of (sister to) a verb.

compatibility. In order to support this functionality, a new approach to marker passing was developed that constrains the communication of features according to symbolic information from GB (Stevenson 1993a, 1994). The method uses only local information at each potential source and destination node in deciding whether or not to propagate a feature. The distributed algorithm ensures that all marker passing paths conform to a valid syntactic configuration for the feature being communicated.

The final landing site for a symbolic feature is an attachment node. The symbolic features of an attachment node encode all of the information relevant to the syntactic relation represented by the node. For example, the attachment node in Figure 5 receives features from its phrasal nodes indicating that the verb (V node) assigns to its object a *thematic* role (the role of the object within the predicate of the verb) and a *Case* (e.g., nominative or objective), and that the noun phrase (NP) requires a thematic role and is compatible with any Case. The features that originate at the phrasal nodes are thus evaluated at the attachment nodes to determine to what degree the grammatical constraints on an attachment structure are satisfied. Each attachment node unifies the features it receives and applies a simple constraint-checking algorithm to verify that the symbolic constraints imposed by GB are met. In the example in Figure 5, the algorithm will test the thematic role and Case compatibility of the features received by the attachment node. The constraint-checking algorithm is uniform across all attachment nodes in the network. The distributed constraint-checking algorithm, in conjunction with the restricted marker passing method, constitute a distributed implementation of the constraints of the linguistic theory.

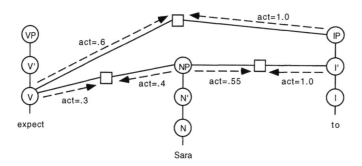

Figure 6 An example of an ambiguous attachment structure, and the apportionment of output activation from the phrasal nodes to the competing attachment nodes.

2.3 Numeric Processing

Because of linguistic ambiguity, there may be more grammatical attachment nodes than can be activated within a single parse tree. Just as phrasal nodes are the originators of the symbolic features that determine the grammaticality of an attachment node, phrasal nodes are also the source of numeric activation that must be focused onto a consistent subset of the grammatical attachment nodes. For example, Figure 6 shows an ambiguous attachment structure in which the verb may take either the NP (a noun phrase) or the IP (a sentential phrase) as its direct object, and the NP may attach as either the object of the verb or the subject of the IP. If all three of the possible attachment nodes is activated, however, an inconsistent parse tree would result.[3] The V node and the NP node each must choose a single attachment node to activate, and the choices must be consistent with each other.

To focus activation onto valid parse tree structures, the phrasal nodes use a competitive spreading activation method (Reggia 1987), which distributes proportionately more numeric output to the attachment nodes that they prefer.[4] The attachment nodes compete for the activation that is output from the phrasal nodes, and apply an evidence-combining function to the input they receive. This numeric evidence is a large component of the activation level of

---

[3] Activation of all the nodes would entail that the verb has two objects, and the noun phrase is both the object of the verb and the subject of the IP.

[4] The competitive distribution of activation obviates the need for inhibitory links in the network, allowing a more direct correspondence between the network and the parse tree that it represents.

an attachment node, reflecting the combined preference from its two phrasal nodes for including the attachment in the parse tree structure.

The competitive relations among the attachment nodes propagate through the network to ensure that the local attachment decisions enforced by the phrasal nodes form a globally consistent set of attachment relations. For example, in Figure 6, because each phrasal node must activate exactly one attachment node, the network will settle on an attachment configuration in which the attachments between the V and IP nodes, and between the NP and I' nodes, are fully activated. It is important to note that this set of attachment decisions is made through a gradual process of focusing activation onto the appropriate attachment nodes. Furthermore, the results may change in response to changes in the numeric influences on the network nodes. For example, frequency information stored with lexical entries affects the amount of activation distributed by phrasal nodes to different attachment possibilities. This allows the model to account for the influence of lexical frequencies on the resolution of ambiguities within psycholinguistic experiments.

2.4 Interaction Between Symbolic and Numeric Processing

The model takes the novel approach of integrating symbolic and numeric processing *within* individual nodes in the network. This raises the issue of defining the interaction between the two types of processing within a node. Currently, each component can affect the other in a single way. First, the symbolic processing computations affect the activation level of an attachment node through a numeric parameter called the state value. The state value of an attachment node is a numeric representation of the degree to which the attachment node meets the grammatical constraints on its symbolic features. The state value is combined with the input from the phrasal nodes to yield the activation level of the attachment node.[5] Second, the numeric functions in turn affect the marker passing algorithm of the symbolic processing component. Only nodes with activation levels above a given threshold are able to propagate symbolic information to their neighbors. The numeric thresholding of marker passing helps to focus symbolic and numeric information within the preferred parse tree structure. The tightly coupled, but restricted, integration of symbolic and

---

[5] Unredeemable constraint violations cause the state value of a node, and subsequently its activation value, to be zero.

numeric processing thus is crucial to achieving correct parsing behavior within the network.

2.5 Uniformity of Symbolic and Numeric Processing

The parsing architecture developed here illustrates that a complex symbolic processor is not a necessary component of a hybrid model. In the CA model, symbolic features are restricted to atomic values (or a list of atomic values), and symbolic processing is limited to propagation (marker passing) and equality testing. Furthermore, the algorithms for symbolic and numeric computation in the network are quite similar to each other at an information processing level. Both symbolic features and numeric activation are distributed by the phrasal nodes to the attachment nodes, which in turn combine the symbolic and numeric evidence that they receive to determine their strength of preference for inclusion in the parse tree. Thus, phrasal nodes and attachment nodes play complementary evidence-distributing and evidence-combining roles, respectively, in the network. Furthermore, these roles apply consistently to both dimensions of symbolic and numeric evidence. The symbolic and numeric components of each type of node therefore apply analogous computations to the two types of information. In other words, although the approach developed here is *hybrid* in the sense of integrating symbolic and numeric information types, it is *uniform* in the sense of consistency across symbolic and numeric processing algorithms.

3 RESULTS

In a hybrid connectionist model, three aspects of the system must be tested: the symbolic processing methods, the numeric activation functions, and the interaction of the two. Although symbolic and numeric computations are interleaved in the CA parser, it is possible to test them independently. The symbolic processing capabilities were tested by turning off the numeric activation functions and tracing the paths of all the different types of features through a test suite of network configurations. The marker passing method successfully constrains features to be passed only between phrasal nodes in syntactically valid configurations defined by the linguistic theory. Figure 7 illustrates an example of the type of syntactically-constrained communication paths that are supported by the CA marker passing method. In the sentence *Who does Mary say that Joan*

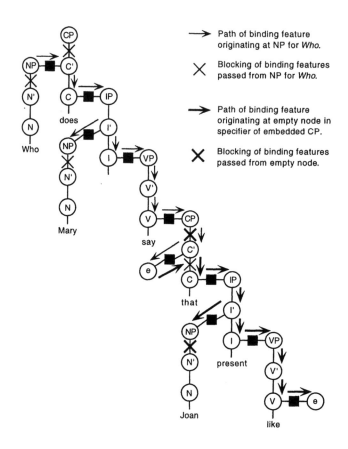

Path of binding feature
originating at NP for *Who*.

Blocking of binding features
passed from NP for *Who*.

Path of binding feature
originating at empty node in
specifier of embedded CP.

Blocking of binding features
passed from empty node.

Figure 7   The restricted paths of two features through the network: from
Who to the empty node in the middle of the tree (thin lines), and from *that*
empty node to the one at the bottom right of the tree (thick lines).

likes?, the word *Who* must be understood as the logical object of the verb
likes. The appropriate interpretation of *Who* is accomplished by an explicit
binding relation between the two positions in the parse tree. Using only local
feature comparisons at each potential source and destination node along the
path, the CA network ensures that the word *Who* and the object position of
likes are in a grammatical configuration. The same marker passing method is
applied consistently by all nodes in the parser to verify all constrained syntactic
relations maintained within the network.

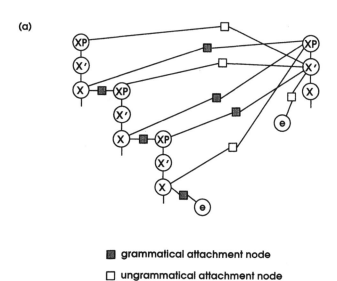

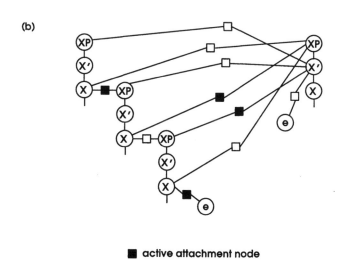

Figure 8 A sample network configuration for the numeric simulations. All attachment nodes shown simultaneously compete for activation.

The numeric activation functions required a more complex testing procedure. The goal was to verify that the numeric processing functions can in fact focus activation within the network onto a consistent parse tree structure. The activation functions were tested independently of the symbolic features in an attempt to abstract away from particular linguistic configurations that arise from some arbitrarily chosen lexicon, and to instead test the network on all possible structural configurations. The numeric experiments tested the ability of the network to attach an input phrase to the right edge of a developing parse tree. The depth of the right edge of the existing tree was varied from zero to five; within each structure, all combinations of grammatical and ungrammatical attachment nodes was systematically tested. Figure 8(a) gives an example of the type of network configuration that was tested, in which the existing parse tree (on the left) has a depth of three phrases, and three of the new attachments are grammatical. Figure 8(b) shows the attachment nodes that are activated in this configuration.

The total number of numeric experiments resulting from the established testing parameters was 1,365. In all but 16 cases—less than 2% of the experiments— the parsing network stabilized in a valid parse tree representation. Note that it is not true that any subset of grammatical attachment nodes represents a valid syntactic tree, and therefore this result does not trivially follow from the way attachment nodes are established. Furthermore, the parser did not just settle on some arbitrary set of grammatical attachments, but behaved consistently and predictably across the set of experiments. For example, across all configurations tested, the network activated the most recent attachments possible (due to decay of activation), and always activated sets of attachments that required less restructuring of the existing tree structure.

Finally, numerous experiments have been performed by running the model on actual linguistic input, testing the symbolic processing and numeric decision-making together. As mentioned above, these experiments demonstrate that the parser exhibits psycholinguistically interesting behavior in resolving ambiguities. The model conforms with human preferences in resolving a number of types of syntactic ambiguity, and mimics human ability or inability to recover from early choices that turn out to be incompatible with later input in the sentence. Furthermore, many of the test sentences entailed trees with depths of more than five phrases, and these examples showed no degradation in attachment decision performance. Together, the successes of the large number of symbolic, numeric, and integrated experiments provide confidence in the CA approach as a viable hybrid connectionist parsing architecture.

4 ISSUES IN THE DESIGN OF HYBRID MODELS

An issue that arises in developing any hybrid connectionist model is how to coordinate the symbolic and numeric processing. As mentioned in the introduction, many hybrid approaches have used connectionist networks as subcomponents of a symbolic processing model. The control strategy in such an approach is straightforward: a traditional symbolic model initializes a connectionist network, triggers its operation, and evaluates the results. Since the connectionist network has no knowledge of the symbolic processor, there is no coordination of symbolic processing within the operation of the network. In a more integrated approach, as in the CA model, the coordination of symbolic and numeric processing plays a crucial role. If network processing nodes have both symbolic and numeric capabilities, they cannot be entirely independent, or there were would be no beneficial interaction. On the other hand, if the symbolic and numeric information at a node continually affect each other, the control of activation within the network becomes greatly complicated. In the current version of the CA model, the symbolic and numeric propagation of information is interleaved in blocks of time, rather than at each tick of the network clock. This avoids each type of information being overly sensitive to small changes in the other. However, symbolic and numeric processing should ideally proceed in truly concurrent fashion, and future research will investigate the control of finer grained interaction between the two types of computation.

Another issue faced by any connectionist model, hybrid or pure, is scalability. In a hybrid model with tight coupling of symbolic and numeric computations, scalability along both dimensions has to be dealt with simultaneously. Increasing the syntactic coverage of the CA model, for example, clearly means adding to the symbolic capabilities, but may also entail an increase in the complexity of the numeric competitions that must be resolved. For example, augmenting the symbolic knowledge may require more than just the addition of features; it may also involve employing a finer grained parallelism to achieve more efficient distribution of the features. Since all nodes have both symbolic and numeric capabilities, finer grained parallelism for the symbolic features will mean possible changes to the numeric processing functions, to accommodate the increased connectivity of the network. Thus, the conceptual elegance of a fully integrated symbolic and numeric model relies on developing computational methods for handling the complexity of interaction inherent in the close coupling of symbolic and numeric processing.

5 SUMMARY

A hybrid approach to NLP that fully integrates symbolic processing within a connectionist framework has two important motivations: (1) the ability to directly encode the simultaneous local constraints of current linguistic theories, and (2) the use of spreading activation to capture the diverse performance effects that play a large role in resolving ambiguity. The competitive attachment model demonstrates that a restricted set of symbolic extensions to a connectionist framework can yield useful computational mechanisms for modeling human linguistic behavior. Furthermore, the model serves as a testbed for research into the control of fine-grained interaction between symbolic and numeric computation, which is necessary to exploit both advances in connectionism and the advantages of symbolic processing methods.

REFERENCES

[1] Chalmers, D. (1992). "Transformations on Distributed Representations." In N. Sharkey (Ed.), *Connectionist Natural Language Processing: Readings from Connection Science*. Dordrecht, The Netherlands: Kluwer.

[2] Chomsky, N. (1981). *Lectures on Government and Binding: The Pisa Lectures*. Dordrecht, The Netherlands: Foris Publications.

[3] Hendler, J. (1987). "Marker-passing and Microfeatures." *Proceedings of the Tenth International Joint Conferences on Artificial Intelligence*, 151–154.

[4] Hindle, D. and M. Rooth (1993). "Structural Ambiguity and Lexical Relations." *Computational Linguistics* **19:1**, 103–120.

[5] Juliano, C. and M. Tanenhaus (1994). "A Constraint-Based Lexicalist Account of the Subject/Object Attachment Preference." *Journal of Psycholinguistic Research* **23:6**, 459–471.

[6] Kimura, K., T. Suzuoka, and S. Amano (1992). "Association-Based Natural Language Processing with Neural Networks." *Proceedings of the 30th Annual Meeting of the Association for Computational Linguistics*, 224–231.

[7] Kwasny, S. and K. Faisal (1992). "Connectionism and Determinism in a Syntactic Parser." In N. Sharkey (Ed.), *Connectionist Natural Language Processing: Readings from Connection Science*. Dordrecht, The Netherlands: Kluwer.

[8] MacDonald, M., N. Pearlmutter, and M. Seidenberg (1994). "Lexical Nature of Syntactic Ambiguity Resolution." *Psychological Review* **101:4**, 676–703.

[9] McClelland, J. and A. Kawamoto (1986). "Mechanisms of Sentence Processing: Assigning Roles to Constituents." In J. McClelland, D. Rumelhart, and the PDP Research Group (Eds.), *Parallel Distributed Processing: Explorations in the Microstructure of Cognition, Volume 2*. Cambridge, MA: MIT Press.

[10] Reggia, J. (1987). "Properties of a Competition-Based Activation Mechanism in Neuromimetic Network Models." *Proceedings of the First International Conference on Neural Networks*, San Diego, II-131–II-138.

[11] Reilly, R. (1992). "A Connectionist Technique for On-Line Parsing." *Network* **3:1**.

[12] Rizzi, L. (1990). *Relativized Minimality*. Cambridge, MA: MIT Press.

[13] Sopena, J. (1992). "ERSP: A Distributed Connectionist Parser That Uses Embedded Sequences to Represent Structure." Manuscript, University of Barcelona, Spain.

[14] Schütze, H. (1993). "Part-of-Speech Induction from Scratch." *Proceedings of the 31st Annual Meeting of the Association for Computational Linguistics*, 251–258.

[15] Spivey-Knowlton, M., J. Trueswell, and M. Tanenhaus (1993). "Context Effects in Syntactic Ambiguity Resolution: Discourse and Semantic Influences in Parsing Reduced Relative Clauses." *Canadian Journal of Experimental Psychology* **47:2**, 276–309.

[16] Stevenson, S. (1993). "Establishing Long-Distance Dependencies in a Hybrid Network Model of Human Parsing." *Proceedings of the 15th Annual Conference of the Cognitive Science Soc.*, 982–987.

[17] Stevenson, S. (1993). "A Competition-Based Explanation of Syntactic Attachment Preferences and Garden Path Phenomena." *Proceedings of the 31st Annual Meeting of the Association for Computational Linguistics*, 266–273.

[18] Stevenson, S. (1994). "Ambiguity Resolution in a Hybrid Network Model of Human Parsing." Doctoral dissertation, University of Maryland. Available as a Rutgers Center for Cognitive Science Technical Report, RuCCS TR-18.

[19] Waltz, D., and J. Pollack (1985). "Massively parallel parsing: A strongly interactive model of natural language interpretation." *Cognitive Science* **9**, 51–74.

[20] Weischedel, R., M. Meteer, R. Schwartz, L. Ramshaw, and J. Palmucci (1993). "Coping with Ambiguity and Unknown Words through Probabilistic Models." *Computational Linguistics* **19:2**, 359–382.

[21] Wermter, S. and W. Lehnert (1989). "A Hybrid Symbolic/Connectionist Model for Noun Phrase Understanding." *Connection Science* **1:3**, 255–272.

13

A HYBRID SYSTEM FRAMEWORK FOR DISAMBIGUATING WORD SENSES

Xinyu Wu

Michael McTear

Piyush Ojha

Haihong Dai*

School of Information & Software Engineering
University of Ulster at Jordanstown, UK

*Department of Computer Science
Queen's University of Belfast, UK

1   INTRODUCTION

The task of word sense disambiguation (WSD) is to choose, for a word with multiple senses in a particular context, which of its senses is the "correct"one for the context. In order to carry out the WSD tasks, a system must have sufficient background knowledge about various information sources. Although knowledge acquisition has been recognized as a very difficult problem in AI, it is undeniable that knowledge will be able to provide valuable help in language understanding. Up to now much research effort has been put on solving the WSD problem using a number of different approaches (e.g. Cottrell 1989, Hirst 1987, Stevenson 1990, Waltz 1985, Wu 1994a), and although some encouraging results can be found in the literature, progress is still considered limited.

In this chapter, a hybrid system SYMCON is presented to solve the problem of WSD by considering both syntactic and semantic information. The system combines distributed and localist connectionist techniques with symbolic methods. It consists of three sub-systems: a *distributed simple recurrent network* (SRN), a *localist connectionist network*, and a *knowledge-based symbolic subsystem*. The development of such a hybrid system is based on the observation that, on the one hand, pure connectionist systems and pure symbolic systems both have impressive results in Natural Language Processing (NLP) and exhibit complementary strengths. On the other hand, however, they both still have some serious limitations. Therefore, a hybrid system that combines connectionist and symbolic techniques promises to be more powerful than systems operating within only one paradigm (Dyer 1991, Hendler 1989, Lange 1989b, Wermter 1989).

In relation to the SYMCON system, three key issues will be addressed in this chapter: first, the integration of symbolic and connectionist processing; second, the representations of concepts in the connectionist network; and third, the incorporation of syntactic and semantic information in the system. The rest of the chapter is organized into eight sections. In section 2, previous work on WSD using connectionist systems and networks with high-level inferencing capabilities is briefly reviewed. In sections 3 to 6, the SYMCON framework is overviewed and the three system components are discussed respectively. Some initial experimental results are presented in section 7, and a distributed representational scheme is discussed in section 8. Last, a summary is provided in section 9.

2   PREVIOUS APPROACHES AND RELATED WORK

In order to accomplish WSD tasks, systems are generally required to have sufficient background knowledge and the ability of using that knowledge to conduct reasoning. In the past, connectionist systems were regarded as incapable of performing such high-level inferencing due to the fact that they had difficulties in coping with the so-called variable binding problem (Fodor 1989).

Since mid-eighties, attempts have been made to incorporate high-level reasoning abilities into connectionist systems. Some examples are the work described in (Dolan 1989) and (Touretzky 1988). They use the energy minimization metaphor to settle into individual variable bindings or rule firing. These systems are capable of representing and using explicit rules, although they operate serially at the knowledge level and may be inefficient for complex problems.

As a result of previous investigations on the issue of high-level inferencing in connectionist systems, the variable binding problem appears to be the major concern and has been the focus of much research work, in which various approaches have been explored to solve the problem. Examples of some important contributions were the work by Lange and Dyer, and Sun (Lange 1989a, Lange

1989b, Sun 1992, Sun 1993). In Lange and Dyer's work, a structured localist connectionist network was developed with additional facilities to deal with multiple role bindings. In Sun's work, a discrete neuron formalism was proposed and applied to solving the variable binding problem.

With regard to accomplishing WSD tasks, the work by Lange and Dyer is the most relevant to our work reported in this chapter. In fact, the development of the SYMCON framework was inspired by their approach to constructing a localist network with inferencing capabilities.

As described in (Lange 1989b), a structured connectionist network, called ROBIN, has been developed for natural language understanding. This system is able to conduct high-level inferencing by using an additional layer of signature nodes to handle the variable binding problem. The signature nodes in ROBIN are simple activation patterns that uniquely identify a concept bound to relevant roles. They are integrated within a connectionist network, and allow multiple role bindings to be propagated through the network in parallel for rule application and dynamic inference path instantiation. As claimed in (Lange 1989b), however, there are some potential problems with this model. This is mainly because the localist representation is used in the network. As a result, the number of signature nodes will increase very rapidly for large network models, which may cause problems. ROBIN also lacks lexical information of concepts, the knowledge of which is important for WSD.

The SYMCON system is constructed based on similar ideas as in the development of ROBIN. However, there are a number of important differences. First, a distributed representational scheme (i.e., microfeatures) is used to represent concepts and handle variable bindings in SYMCON. This can avoid the problem of excessive number of signature nodes for large networks. Second, lexical information is encoded by using semantic microfeatures. The WSD process makes full use of such semantic knowledge. Third, a simple recurrent network is incorporated to pre-process concepts based on the available lexical information. Fourth, although the localist network in SYMCON has a similar structure as in ROBIN, the knowledge base is conceptually separated from the network to form a symbolic sub-system. This enables SYMCON to take advantages of knowledge-based techniques with respect to issues such as knowledge acquisition and system scaling-up. In sections 3 to 6, the overall organization of SYMCON and its sub-systems are discussed.

3   THE SYMCON SYSTEM - A BRIEF OVERVIEW

As the name implies, the system consists of connectionist and symbolic components. It is, therefore, able to take advantages of both methods.

A high-level reasoning capability is needed because domain knowledge is necessary to understand a piece of text so as to disambiguate any ambiguous words. Although it has been argued in (Gale 1992) that there exists a knowledge acquisition bottleneck, it is undeniable that knowledge will be able to provide valuable help in language understanding. A key issue is that an effective way must be found to incorporate the knowledge in NLP systems. Thus, an attempt has been made in constructing the SYMCON system by integrating a knowledge-based system with connectionist systems.

The basic structure of the SYMCON system is depicted in figure 1. First, a simple recurrent network is used to learn the semantic relationships among concepts and generate categorical constraints in a sentence. Second, a knowledge-based symbolic sub-system is used to conduct high-level inferencing by associating domain knowledge with specific cases presented in the text to be processed. The system also maintains multiple role-bindings and propagates them through a localist network. The third sub-system is the localist connectionist network, which completes the task of selecting the best interpretation among multiple alternatives and potential ambiguous inference paths by spreading activation. The output of the system will therefore be the correct inference on the ambiguous text presented to the system.

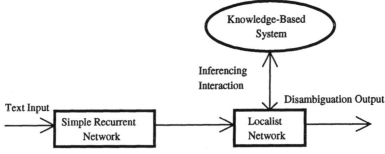

Figure 1. The basic structure of the SYMCON system.

As described above, the SYMCON system integrates three different types of sub-systems. The three sub-systems must co-operate and be able to work as a whole. It is therefore desirable to find a unified way to represent words and their senses (i.e., concepts) in SYMCON. Otherwise, it would be awkward if three different representations had to be used.

Microfeatures have been chosen as a means of representing word concepts. In SYMCON, a word concept is represented by two different groups of microfeatures, namely *categorical microfeatures* and *semantic microfeatures* (Wu 1995b).

Categorical microfeatures are features that describe the nature of the category to which the words belong. They contain syntactic information as well as some semantic information. They are also used to maintain links with knowledge cases in the symbolic sub-system. The creation of the categorical microfeatures is carried out by abstracting the most general terms in the hierarchy that describe the concept and its syntactic category. Sample concepts encoded by such categorical microfeatures are used to train the recurrent network to complete the prediction task. Semantic microfeatures are features which are extracted from word definitions in a machine readable dictionary (MRD) (Guo 1989, Wilks 1990). They represent the precise meanings of words and contain mainly semantic information. The method of establishing the semantic microfeatures has been reported elsewhere (Wu 1995b), but will be described briefly later in this chapter (Section 8).

4 THE SIMPLE RECURRENT NETWORK

A SRN was first applied to NLP by Elman (Elman 1990, Elman 1991). The main task of the SRN in SYMCON is to learn semantic relationships among concepts, and therefore, to predict the categorical constraints of the next concept in a sentence, given the current concept. That is, when given the current concept, the trained network is capable of deciding within which categories the next concept should come from (Wu 1994b).

The network was trained by using a corpus of sentences generated from a ten-rule context-free grammar. In training, the standard back-propagation learning algorithm (Rumelhart 1986) was used. The processing in the SRN is based on categorical features. The trained network is capable of predicting within which category/categories the next word should come from, given the current word described by a set of microfeatures.

As a sub-system of SYMCON, SRN is mainly used for pre-processing in the system. It is efficient for disambiguating words which have strong categorical constraints in a particular context. The following is an example to disambiguate the word STAR in the sentence (which is borrowed from Charniak 1983):

> *The astronomer marries a star.*

As a noun, STAR has three possible senses: (1) celestial body; (2) asterisk; (3) celebrated person.

All the words in the sentence (except articles) are represented by categorical microfeatures and input to the SRN when the disambiguating process begins. Since the SRN was trained by using a sample vocabulary including the word MARRY, it is able to predict that the next word after *marries* should have a strong link with the HUMAN category by assigning a relatively large value to the feature of HUMAN such as

$$v_{HUMAN} = 0.95$$

as well as

$$v_{ANIMAL} = 0 \text{ and } v_{PHYSICAL\_OBJECT} = 0.$$

When STAR is input to the SRN, only the third sense (i.e., celebrated person) passes through the network. This is because only this sense has the desired values in corresponding categorical microfeatures. In this case, therefore, the WSD task is accomplished by the SRN alone.

Apart from predicting the categories of each concept in a sentence, however, if the senses of an ambiguous word have similar categorical constraints, the SRN is unable to produce any helpful semantic information to choose the correct sense. For instance, a slightly more complex sentence (as shown below) is input to the SRN:

> *Peter put the bug into a dustbin, because the police were coming.*

The ambiguous words is BUG, which has two meanings here: (1) small insect; (2) secret listening device. After the processing in the SRN, the network is unable to distinguish the two meanings of BUG, as they can both be the expected concept after word PUT. Therefore, the two senses of BUG are all passed to the localist network which will be co-operating with the knowledge-based symbolic sub-system to conduct further inferencing. This example, which is borrowed from (Lange 1989b) with slight changes, will be used throughout the rest of this chapter to explain the way in which SYMCON works.

5 THE KNOWLEDGE-BASED SUB-SYSTEM

Any system which deals with the WSD task must have the capability of performing high-level inferencing to make explanations and predictions from what is known about the world (Fu 1989, Towell 1991, Towell 1994). Traditional knowledge-based systems are capable of applying general knowledge rules stored in the knowledge base to perform inferencing (e.g. Dyer 1983).

The SYMCON system combines a knowledge-based symbolic sub-system with localist and distributed connectionist networks. With this special structure, SYMCON is able to perform inference and select the best interpretation from among multiple alternative inference paths, and therefore to accomplish the disambiguation task.

At the present, the SYMCON's knowledge base is hand-built, and made up of conceptual frames (which correspond to conceptual frame nodes in the localist network) and rules needed for reasoning in a given domain. Each frame (i.e., a case) is connected to one or more roles which have relations with the sense nodes in the localist network. A frame can be related to one or more other frames, which indicates the general knowledge rules. Similarly the corresponding roles may be related to other relevant roles. In order to explain how the knowledge base is structured in the symbolic sub-system, the BUG example mentioned above is used.

The word *bug* is ambiguous, which can be interpreted as either a *small insect* or a *secret listening device*. When presented with the first phrase, *Peter put the bug into the dustbin*, most people would conclude that Peter transferred an *insect* into a *dustbin* for the purpose of *clearing away*. However, when the second phrase *because the police were coming* appears, the interpretation of the word *bug* would change to *secret listening device*, and word *dustbin* should be comprehended as an *opaque object* which helps to complete the hiding plan, thus obtains the correct interpretation of the sentence. General knowledge rules necessary for conducting such inferences are incorporated in the knowledge base.

The functionality of this knowledge-based sub-system is similar to that of the inference layer of the conceptual nodes in ROBIN (Lange 1989b). However, it is conceptually a separate component in SYMCON. The knowledge base is organized according to the categorical and semantic microfeatures of the word concepts in a particular domain. It is integrated with the localist network by using the signature-like nodes with distributed representations (i.e., microfeatures).

Figure 2 provides a general view based on a portion of the knowledge base. It can be seen that the knowledge base is structured with conceptual frames and their relevant rules. Each rule is encoded by a set of microfeatures, and corresponds to the role node in the localist network, which connects to its relevant sense nodes that are represented by the same set of microfeatures.

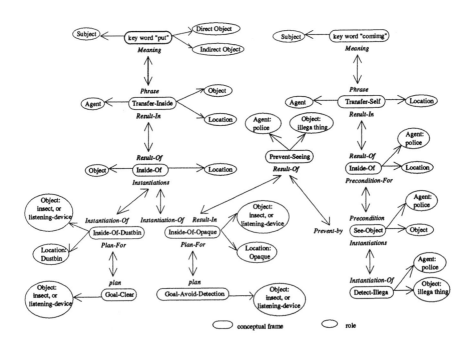

Figure 2. A part of the knowledge base in SYMCON.

6 THE LOCALIST CONNECTIONIST NETWORK

The purpose of incorporating a localist network in the hybrid system is to spread activations among various alternative inference paths and allow the automatic selection of the most highly activated path as the best interpretation, and thus, to obtain the correct sense of an ambiguous word. Another important reason for using a localist network is that it is parallel at the knowledge level, which means that multiple inference paths can be pursued simultaneously in the network. Furthermore, with activations spreading in the network, related concepts under consideration provide evidence and feedback to one another. They do not need the complicated and expensive backtracking rules to force a change in re-interpretation like traditional symbolic approaches do.

6.1 The Basic Network Architecture

The basic architecture of the localist connectionist network in SYMCON is similar to that of ROBIN (Figure 3, using the same example as above with only part of the nodes and connections are shown). The network consists of two layers and three types of nodes. The bottom layer contains conceptual frame nodes and role nodes which correspond to the conceptual frames and roles in the knowledge-based sub-system respectively. The top layer contains only one type of nodes: sense nodes which are connected to the relevant role nodes in the bottom layer. Each sense node and role node is represented by a distributed pattern, which, in this case, are twenty semantic microfeatures with an additional ten categorical features used in SRN. The strategy of determining the semantic microfeatures and assigning their values will be discussed later.

The inferencing rules specified in the knowledge-based sub-system are mirrored by the connection weights among conceptual frame nodes in the localist network. For example, the weighted connection from conceptual frame node *Transfer-Inside* to *Inside-Of* encodes the *Result-Of* relationship, and the activation will be propagated along that structure.

6.2   Propagation of Activation for Disambiguation

Before propagating the activation in the localist network, a sentence is pre-processed in the SRN for the categories anticipation as discussed earlier. The results will influence the initial activation values assigned to the frame nodes. If a desired category of a concept predicted by the SRN is similar to a role node, then the frame node to which the role node is connected will be given a higher initial activation value. The links among the conceptual frame nodes, role nodes and sense nodes are established according to the rules in the knowledge base. With these original links and initializations, the activation of all types of nodes starts to spread in the localist network to perform the WSD functions (Wu 1995a).

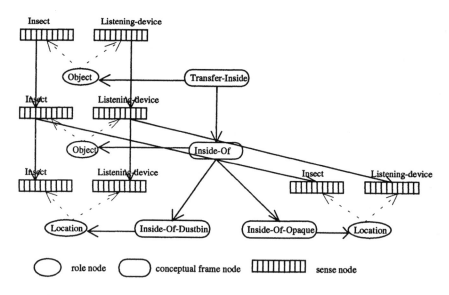

Figure 3. Basic architecture of the localist connectionist network.

7   INITIAL EXPERIMENTAL RESULTS

The BUG example is used here again to report some experimental results of a prototype based on the SYMCON framework. The sentence is first input to the SRN for pre-processing. Because the two meanings of the word BUG can both be the expected concept according to their categorical features, the recurrent network is unable to disambiguate. Thus, the two senses are passed to the localist network and the related conceptual frames are also activated in the knowledge-based system to conduct further inferencing.

The establishment of the weights among the conceptual frame nodes in the localist network are influenced by knowledge structures and rules stored in the knowledge base, and the activation values of the frame nodes are calculated accordingly. The activation values of the sense nodes in the localist network are also computed in a similar way (Lange 1989b, Wu 1995a).

Figure 4 shows the changing course of the activations of the sense nodes *Insect* and *Listening-device* obtained from the localist network. The activation level of the sense nodes is shown vertically, and the iteration number is given horizontally. The word BUG is first interpreted as a *Insect* because of strong evidence from the inferred context *Dustbin-Clearing*. With the propagation of activations throughout the network, the activations accumulate for sense node *Listening-device* because the inference path involving the *Police* and *Detect-Illegal* is activated. After a number of processing cycles, the activation process stabilizes when *Listening-device* gains greater activations than *Insect*. Thus, it is chosen as the correct meaning of the ambiguous word BUG in the sentence.

It can be seen from figure 4 that in the first five processing cycles, both sense nodes of *Insect* and *Listening-device* receive activations from lexical input BUG. In the following ten cycles, activations on *Insect* and *Listening-device* all decay until the sense node of *Insect* receives activations from the newly-activated frame node *Inside-Of-Dustbin*. Thus, the activations on the sense node *Insect* begin to increase while the activations on *Listening-device* continue to decay, and this state lasts for about five cycles. Activations of the sense node *Listening-device* start to climb because of the feedback from the inference path involving *Police* and *Detect-Illegal*. At the same time, activations on *Insect* decay because of lack of support from the new evidence. After another thirty to thirty-five processing cycles, *Listening-device* is more highly activated than *Insect*, and this remains till the network completely stabilizes.

One important observation of our initial experiments is that the distributed representation of concepts is effective for WSD. Because lexical information, encoded in microfeatures, is available for inferencing, the system is able to disambiguate ambiguous words efficiently.

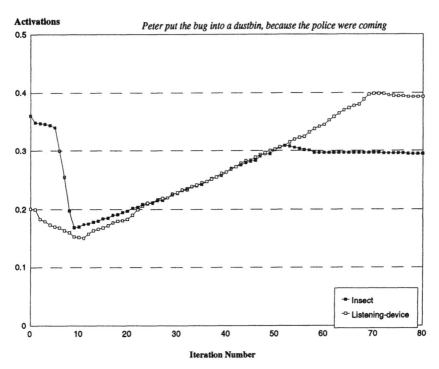

Figure 4. The activations of the two sense nodes in the network.

8   REPRESENTATIONAL SCHEME IN SYMCON

In order to disambiguate different word senses, the senses themselves must first be represented in a machine-tractable manner. Many different representational ideas have been reported in the literature, e.g., (Alshawi 1985, Kawamoto 1988, Sharkey 1991, Wilks 1990). The effectiveness of each of the approaches depends on the underlying system methodology used for WSD.

In SYMCON, two types of information about words, namely categorical and semantic information, are used for WSD. The categorical information is encoded by a set of categorical microfeatures that describe the nature of a category to which the words belong. This type of microfeatures is established by classifying words in a certain domain into a number of categories. This step abstracts specific concepts using more general terms. Then these general terms are grouped into 10 features describing the basic meaning and categorical constraints of a concept. Table 1 shows the categorical microfeatures used along with some examples used to train the SRN. As discussed in section 4, the predication task of the SRN is accomplished based on categorical microfeatures.

Categorical Microfeatures	Examples
AGENT	John, astronomer, police, diver, shark
ACTION	eat, put, marry
TRANSFER	eat, put, throw, move
PATIENT	shark, star, diver, ball
INSTRUMENT	fork, washing-machine, ball
LOCATION	church, washing-machine
HUMAN	John, astronomer, diver
ANIMAL	shark, cat
PHYSICAL-OBJECT	ball, fork, star
EDIBLE	cake, shark, food

Table 1. Categorical microfeatures of the concepts and examples.

The semantic information which describes the precise meanings of concepts can be modeled in a number of different ways. For example, it may be represented by semantic microfeatures created in an *ad hoc* manner (Sutcliffe 1992), as we did in developing the prototype system to encode sense nodes and conceptual frame nodes. However, this approach faces a difficult task in choosing appropriate microfeatures to represent word sense accurately, especially when dealing with a very large vocabulary. It has been realized that the creation of an effective machine-tractable dictionary (MTD) is a very important task for the SYMCON system (Wu 1995b), in which precise word meanings are to be represented by semantic features extracted from word sense definitions in a machine readable dictionary (MRD).

It has been found in related research (Guo 1989) that all words in a dictionary can be defined by a finite set of semantic primitives. All other work on the same topic also indicates that it is possible to create such a natural set of primitives. An algorithm has been proposed and implemented for extracting semantic microfeatures from an MRD (Wu 1995b).

The algorithm begins at the first word in a pre-determined vocabulary. Related definitions are retrieved from the MRD. The definitions of the defining words are also retrieved, and so on. This process is an iterative one and the number of iterations is initially set to a threshold value. Links are established between the word and all its senses. As a result, a directed graph is created, in which the starting node is the node to be defined, and other nodes are words defining the senses of a previous word.

It is possible that a loop may be formed if the definition of a sense node contains a word that has already been established in the graph. In this case, if the word is the starting word, the process stops and the word comprising the sense node becomes one of the microfeatures for the word to be defined. If the word is not the starting word, the iterative process also stops and the word being pointed at by the sense node will be chosen as a microfeature of the word to be defined. If there is not any loop when the specified number of iterations have been completed, the graph will have a tree-like structure. All the key words contained in the leaf nodes will be included in the set of microfeatures for the word to be defined. The complete set of microfeatures for the vocabulary will then be the union of all the microfeature sets for individual words.

The feature-extracting process is repeated for all words in the vocabulary until every word has obtained a microfeature set. Individual sets are then combined to form a complete microfeature set for the vocabulary. After completing the above process, all microfeatures are combined to represent concepts in the SYMCON's lexicon, based on which WSD tasks are accomplished.

9   SUMMARY

In this chapter, SYMCON, which is a hybrid system framework for WSD, is described. It consists of three sub-systems: (1) a simple recurrent network; (2) a knowledge-based system; (3) a localist connectionist network. It has been shown that with this special hybrid structure, SYMCON is capable of tackling the WSD problem and is also potentially powerful than systems relying on only one processing paradigm.

REFERENCES

[1] Alshawi, H., Boguraev, B. and Briscoe, T. (1985). "Towards a Dictionary Support Environment for Real Time Parsing," *Proc. of the 2nd European ACL Conf.*, pp. 171-178

[2] Charniak, E. (1983). "Passing Markers: A Theory of Contextual Influence in Language Comprehension," *Cognitive Science*, Vol.7, pp. 171-190

[3] Cottrell, G. W. (1989). *A Connectionist Approach to Word Sense Disambiguation*, London:Pitman

[4] Dolan, C. P. and Smolensky, P. (1989). "Tensor Product Production System: A Modular Architecture and Representation," *Connection Science*, Abingdon, England:Carfax Publishing, Vol. 1, pp. 53-68

[5] Dyer, M. G. (1983). *In-Depth Understand: A Computer Model of Integrated Processing for Narrative Comprehension*, MIT Press

[6] Dyer, M. G. (1991). "Symbolic Neuroengineering for Language Processing: A Multi-Level Research Approach," *Advances in Connectionist and Neural Computation Theory*, edited by J. Barnden and J. Pollack, Norwood

[7] Elman, J. L. (1990). "Finding Structure in Time," *Cognitive Science*, Norwood, NJ:Ablex Publishing, Vol. 14, pp. 179-211

[8] Elman, J. L. (1991). "Distributed Representations, Simple Recurrent Networks, and Grammatical Structure," *Machine Learning*, Vol. 7, pp. 195-225

[9] Fodor, J. A. and Pylyshyn, Z. W. (1989). "Connectionism and Cognitive Architecture: A Critical Analysis," *Cognition*, Vol. 28, pp. 3-71

[10] Fu, L. (1989). "Integration of Neural Heuristics into Knowledge-Based Inference," *Connection Science*, Vol. 1, No. 3, pp. 325-340

[11] Gale, W. A., Chirch, K. W. and Yarowsky, D. (1992). "A Method for Disambiguating Word Sense in a Large Corpus," *Computers and the Humanities*, Vol. 26, No. 5-6, pp. 415-439

[12] Guo, C. M. (1989). "Deriving a Natural Set of Semantic Primitives From Longman Dictionary of Contemporary English," *Proc. of the 2nd Irish Conf. on AI and Cognitive Science*, Dublin, pp. 218-227

[13] Hendler, J. A. (1989). "Marker Passing Over Microfeatures: Towards a Hybrid Symbolic/Connectionist Model," *Cognitive Science*, Norwood, NJ:Ablex Publishing, Vol. 13, pp. 79-106

[14] Hirst, G. (1987). *Semantic Interpretation and the Resolution of Ambiguity*, Cambridge University Press, Cambridge, England

[15] Kawamoto, A. H. (1988). "Distributed Representations of Ambiguous Words and Their Resolution in a Connectionist Network," *Lexical Ambiguity Resolution*, edited by S. Small, Morgan Kaufmann, Los Altos CA, pp. 195-228

[16] Lange, T. E. and Dyer, M. G. (1989a). "Frame Selection in a Connectionist Model of High-Level Inferencing," *Proc. of the 11th Annual Conf. of the Cognitive Science Society*, pp.706-713

[17] Lange, T. E. and Dyer, M. G. (1989b). "Higher-Level Inferencing in a Connectionist Network," *Connection Science*, Vol. 1, No. 2, pp. 181-217

[18] Rumelhart, D. E., Hinton, G. E. and Williams, R. J. (1986). "Learning Internal Representations by Error Propagation," *Parallel Distributed Processing, Explorations in the Microfeature of Cognition*, Volume 1: *Foundations*, edited by D. E. Rumelhart and J. L. McClelland, MIT Press, pp. 318-362

[19] Sharkey, N. E. (1991). "Connectionist Representation Techniques," *Artificial Intelligence Review*, Vol. 5, pp. 143-167

[20] Stevenson, S. (1990). "A Parallel Constraint Satisfaction and Spreading Activation Model for Revolving Syntactic Ambiguity," *Proc of the 12th Annual Conf. of Cognitive Science Society*, USA, pp. 396-403

[21] Sun, R. (1992). "On Variable Binding in Connectionist Networks," *Connection Science*, Vol. 4, No. 2, pp. 93-124

[22] Sun, R. (1993). "Beyond Associative Memories: Logics and Variables in Connectionist Models," *Information Sciences*, 70, pp. 49-73

[23] Sutcliffe, R. F. E. (1992). "Constructing Distributed Semantic Lexical Representations Using a Machine Readable Dictionary," *AI and Cognition Science'92*, Edited by K. Ryan and R. F. E. Sutcliffe, Springer-Verlag, pp. 210-223

[24] Touretzky, D. S. and Hinton, G. E. (1988). "A Distributed Representation Production System," *Cognitive Science*, Vol. 12, pp. 423-466

[25] Towell, G. (1991). *Symbolic Knowledge and Neural Networks: Insertion, Refinement, and Extraction*, PhD Thesis, Computer Science Department, University of Wisconsin at Madison, USA

[26] Towell, G. and Shavlik, J. (1994). "Knowledge-Based Artificial Neural Networks," *Artificial Intelligence*, Vol. 70, pp. 119-166

[27] Waltz, D. and Pollack, J. B. (1985). "Massively Parallel Parsing: A Strongly Interactive Model of Natural Language Interpretation," *Cognitive Science*, Vol. 9, pp. 51-74

[28] Wermter, S. and Lehnert, W. G. (1989). "A Hybrid Symbolic/ Connectionist Model for Noun Phrase Understanding," *Connection Science*, Vol. 1, No. 3, pp. 225-272

[29] Wilks, Y., Fass, D. and Guo, C.M. et al. (1990). "Providing Machine Tractable Dictionary Tools," *Machine Translation*, No. 5, pp. 99-154

[30] Wu, X., McTear, M. and Ojha, P. C. (1994a). "Pronoun Disambiguation Using a Hybrid System," *Proc. of the 14th International Conf. on AI, KBS, Expert System and Natural Language Processing*, Vol. 3, Paris, pp. 67-76

[31] Wu, X., McTear, M. and Ojha, P. C. (1994b). "Learning Semantic Relationships and Syntactic Roles in a Simple Recurrent Network," *Proc. of International Conf. on New Methods in Language Processing*, Manchester England, pp. 23-29

[32] Wu, X., McTear, M. and Ojha, P. C. (1995a). "Word Sense Disambiguation by a Hybrid Approach," *Proc. of the 5th Scandinavian Conf. on Artificial Intelligence (SCAI '95)*, Trondheim, Norway, pp. 281-292

[33] Wu, X., McTear, M., Ojha, P. C. and Dai, H. (1995b). "A Representation Scheme for a Hybrid Natural Language Processing System," *Proc. of the 1995 IEEE International Conf. on Systems, Man, and Cybernetics*, Vancouver, Canada, Vol. 4, pp. 3162-3167

14

A LOCALIST NETWORK ARCHITECTURE FOR LOGICAL INFERENCE

Nam Seog Park
Dave Robertson

Department of Artificial Intelligence
University of Edinburgh

1 INTRODUCTION

The primary interest of this chapter is in understanding how systems which are described in a symbolic specification style may be implemented using a connectionist architecture. As a focus of attention, techniques have been developed for *compiling* Horn clauses into a connectionist network. This offers significant practical benefits but also forces limitations on the scope of the compiled system. Executable symbolic specifications are (in the right hands) effective for describing systems and are comparatively easy for designers to understand. However, they normally require extra *machinery*, in the form of an interpreter or theorem proving system in order to be executed. For many applications (particularly when the system is to be implemented in hardware) such extra mechanisms are both inefficient and structurally complex. Connectionist systems, on the other hand, use structurally simple components, may provide very fast inference and have no need of a separate interpreter, but are difficult to use directly for specification because of the mass of connections between elements. By providing automatic translation from symbolic to connectionist representations, one should be able to cancel out the deficiencies of each style whilst retaining the advantages of both. Unfortunately, this type of compilation is not straightforward; since an *interpreter* has to be merged into the connectionist networks, the compilation process has to take into account not only the Horn clauses themselves but also the strategy, which is intended to be used for drawing inferences from them. It also appears that some fundamental aspects of symbolic inference are difficult to translate directly into a connectionist framework. In particular, it has proved to be difficult to provide a full translation of term unification (in the style of common Horn clause languages like Prolog) and this has, in turn, placed awkward limitations on the forms of inferences which could be supported. The purpose of this chapter is to propose a localist network architecture which removes some of these fundamental limitations, resulting in a connectionist system which extends expressive power in achieving symbolic inference.

2   A TARGET SYMBOLIC MODEL

2.1   Symbolic Knowledge

Since a localist connectionist architecture is to be designed as a connectionist model which translates symbolic knowledge (described in the form of rules and facts) into a network, defining a symbolic expression to describe them is necessary. The symbolic expression that has been chosen to describe the target symbolic knowledge is a subset of first-order Horn clause expressions, which is defined as follows:

Definition: A subset of *first-order Horn clause expressions* is a set of universally quantified expressions in first-order predicate calculus of the form:

$$p_1(\cdots) \wedge p_2(\cdots) \wedge \cdots \wedge p_n(\cdots) \rightarrow q(\cdots),$$

where $p()_i$'s and $q()$ are all positive atomic expressions. The conjunction of $p()_i$ is the antecedent and the $q()$ the consequent. An expression with no antecedent is called a *fact* and an expression which has both antecedent and consequent is called a *rule*.

2.2   Symbolic Inference Procedures

To achieve symbolic style of inference, a localist network architecture also has to merge the strategies which are used for drawing inferences into connectionist mechanisms. Two basic symbolic inference procedures must be embedded into the network structure: *matching* and *substitution* procedures. Connectionist mechanisms which correspond to these two procedures will be designed in such a way that they perform counterparts to the symbolic tasks in a connectionist manner.

Let us consider the following rule:

$$p(X,Y) \rightarrow q(X,Y).$$

When the predicate, $p(a,U)$, is presented to the antecedent of the given rule, a forward chaining symbolic inference system will normally use a matching procedure to see if the antecedent of the rule matches with the presented predicate. This yields a set of substitutions between variables and constant in the matching terms.

$$Match[p(a,U), \; p(X,Y) \rightarrow q(X,Y)] = \{a/X, \; U/Y\}.$$

As the result of match procedure, two types of bindings are obtained: the *constant binding* between a and X and the *variable binding* between U and Y. These bindings are usually differentiated using different symbol names in a symbolic inference system (a constant symbol for a constant binding and a variable symbol for a variable binding).

Once a set of bindings is obtained from the match procedure, these bindings are then used for the symbolic substitution procedure. The substitution procedure takes the matched formula and consistently substitutes all occurrences of variables in the formula using the binding set. This procedure may be represented as follows:

$$Substitute[\{a/X,U/Y\}, \; p(X,Y) \rightarrow q(X,Y)] = [\, p(a,U) \rightarrow q(a,U)].$$

From the result of this substitution, a symbolic inference system can apply the *modus ponens* inference rule to infer the new logical assertion, $q(a,U)$.

In a symbolic system, these symbolic procedures are clearly separated and are usually implemented as independent modules. In a connectionist system, however, knowledge representation and inference procedures cannot be easily separated because inference procedures have to be represented either in the form of weights on the network or in the embedded structure of networks. In addition, there exists a wide range of algorithms to implement symbolic inference procedures in a symbolic inference system. We are, however, much more constrained in a connectionist system because of the uniformity of network components and the simplicity of their computing abilities. Nevertheless, any connectionist system which wishes to resemble a symbolic style of inference must have connectionist mechanisms which represent symbolic knowledge and perform some form of matching with substitution.

3   A NETWORK ARCHITECTURE

The localist network architecture proposed in this chapter is a connectionist model which encodes symbolic rules and facts in first-order Horn clause expressions into a set of corresponding structured networks called *structured predicate networks* (SPNs) and performs symbolic inferences over these networks.

When a set of rules and facts are given, this input is compiled into SPNs by the knowledge compiler using algorithm devised. The general structure of a SPN is demonstrated in Figure 1.

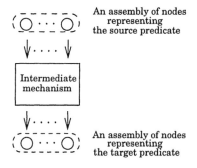

Figure 1   The structure of SPNs.

As can be seen, each SPN consists of three parts: an assembly of nodes for a source predicate, an assembly of node for a target predicate, and an intermediate mechanism between them. The corresponding source and target predicates are the antecedent and consequent predicates of a rule when the SPN is built to support forward chaining and vice versa to support backward chaining. In the case of a fact SPN, the source predicate is a base form of the fact given and the target predicate is a special assembly of nodes introduced to represent result bindings generated as a result of inference. This intermediate mechanism performs similar tasks to the two previously mentioned symbolic inference procedures during inference.

In many cases, a set of rules and facts share the same base predicate (by having the same predicate name and arity) and this allows their SPNs to be connected to each other through this common predicate when they are encoded. When performing inference, this series of connected SPNs is used to draw a chain of inference, which is carried out in a standard way over the network by activating a group of nodes and propagating the activation through these SPNs.

4   COMPONENTS OF SPNS

4.1   Basic Neuron-Like Elements

Before we define neuron elements that will be used to build SPNs, it may be helpful to explain two time scales which will be used throughout this chapter: a *phase* is a minimum time interval in which a neural element performs the basic computations (sampling its inputs and thresholding); an *oscillation cycle* is a window of time in which neuron elements show their oscillatory temporal behaviors. Each oscillation cycle consists of several phases and the number of phases in one oscillation cycle limits the number of distinct entities (constants and variables) which participate for bindings during inference.

To build SPNs, three basic neuron elements are required. Unlike ordinary nodes found in conventional neural network models, these elements have special temporal behaviors hypothesised. An ordinary node samples and sums all its inputs in a given cycle of the time and thresholding the sum to decide its output. Whereas the neuron-like elements sample their inputs over several phases of an oscillation cycle and determine their output patterns, depending on the input patterns sampled during this time period. The detailed behavior of each type of element is differentiated based on a type of input pattern they sample and a type of output pattern they produce in each oscillation cycle. On becoming active, these elements continually produce the output (oscillating) for the duration of inference.

Definition: The **neuron-like elements**[1] that will be used to build SPNs are defined as follows:

- a **π-btu element** becomes active on receiving one or more spikes in different phases of any oscillation cycle. On becoming active, a π-btu element produces an oscillatory spike that is in phase with the driving inputs;

- a **τ-or element** becomes active on receiving one or more spikes within a period of oscillation. On becoming active, a τ-or element produces an oscillatory pulse train whose pulse width is comparable to the period of an oscillation cycle;

- a **multiphase τ-or element** becomes active on receiving more than one input in different phases within a period of oscillation. On becoming active, a multiple τ-or element produces an oscillatory pulse train whose pulse width is comparable to the period of an oscillation cycle.

A threshold, n, associated with each neuron-like element indicates that the element will fire only if it receives n or more spike inputs in the same phase.

Figure 2 shows graphical notation of each neuron-like element and its temporal characteristics.

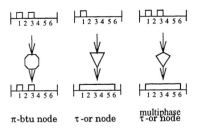

Figure 2   Temporal behaviors of the neuron-like elements.

4.2   Entity Nodes

Symbolic inference systems use symbols to represent components of knowledge. Each symbol is represented using a unique symbolic name and this unique

---

[1]The τ-or and multiphase τ-or elements are the same as defined in Shastri & Ajanagadde [1] and a π-btu element is newly defined.

name is used to distinguish not only each symbol from the others but also each symbolic binding from the others. A variable symbol can unify with a constant, a variable, or even with a function in some inference systems but cannot unify with two different constants at the same time. During unification, the system must always be able to identify which variable has been unified.

For proper representation of symbolic entities, the proposed network architecture introduces an entity node.

Definition: An **entity node** is a pair of π-btu elements. The left element is used to represent a variable role of the entity and the right element a constant role. A symbolic entity name may be used as a label of an entity node. Symbolically an entity node is represented using the notation, $entity\_name[\phi,\phi]$, where the left position of the bracket represents the state of the left π-btu element and the right position that of the right π-btu element. The symbol "ϕ" denotes the state in which the element is inactive. The subscripts, $left$ or $right$, are used as a suffix of a symbolic entity name to differentiate the left element from the right one. The notations, $entity\_name_{left}[\phi]$ or $entity\_name_{right}[\phi]$ are used to indicate each state of the left or right π-btu element.

When an entity node is used to represent a constant, only its right element becomes active during a chain of inference. Whereas when the entity node is used to represent a variable, only its left node becomes active. However, when it is used to represent an argument of the predicate, either or both its elements may become active during a chain of inference.

4.3   Predicate Assemblies

A predicate is a basic structured unit of symbolic rules and facts. To represent predicates, an assembly of nodes, called a *predicate assembly*, is used. Like a symbolic predicate, a predicate assembly also has associated arity since each predicate assembly is composed of n entity nodes that correspond to the n arguments.

When a predicate is encoded using a predicate assembly, it is always represented in the form of base predicate which is defined as follows:

Definition: A **base predicate** of an n-ary predicate, $p(A_1, A_2, \ldots, A_n)$, is a predicate which has the same predicate name p followed by the n argument names, $arg_1, arg_2, \ldots, arg_n$. All predicates which share the same predicate name and arity have the same base predicate.

A more detailed definition of a predicate assembly is as follows:

Definition: An n-ary **predicate assembly** is composed of n entity nodes, $arg_1, arg_2, \ldots, arg_n$. Each of these entity nodes is called an *argument node*. We use the notation, *pred_name:*{ $arg_1[\phi,\phi]$, $arg_2[\phi,\phi]$, $\ldots$, $arg_n[\phi,\phi]$} to represent an n-ary predicate assembly symbolically. When any individual argument node needs to be named, a prefix *"pred_name:"* is used before a symbolic name of the argument node.

Figure 3 depicts the structure of a predicate assembly graphically.

Figure 3   The structure of a predicate assembly.

5   REPRESENTING DYNAMIC BINDINGS

Representing dynamic bindings in a connectionist system has been recognized as one of the main technical obstacles to achieving a symbolic style of inference (see a survey in Park et al [2]). The network architecture proposed here adopts the basic idea of the *temporal synchrony approach* which is credited to Ajjanagadde & Shastri [3]. However their approach can only represent constant bindings and fails to represent variable bindings (limiting the inferential power of their system). The binding mechanism used in this chapter is based on the extended temporal synchrony mechanism described in Park et al [2].

To help the understanding of this mechanism, let us consider the constant a, the variable U, and the two arguments arg_i and arg_j. Before setting up the bindings, they first need to be represented using entity node as follows:

$$a[\phi, \phi], \ U[\phi, \phi], \ arg_i[\phi, \phi], \ arg_j[\phi, \phi].$$

A constant binding and a variable binding between these entity nodes can be represented in the following ways:

- the constant binding between a and arg_i, $\{a/arg_i\}$, is represented by activating the right element of $a[\phi,\phi]$ and $arg_i[\phi,\phi]$ ($a_{right}[\phi]$ and $arg_{i_{right}}[\phi]$) in the same phase, say the first phase, which results in $a[\phi,1]$ and $arg_i[\phi,1]$, where the number 1 stands for the first phase;

- the variable binding between U and arg_j is represented by activating their left elements ($U_{left}[\phi]$ and $arg_{j_{left}}[\phi]$) in a different phase, the second phase for example, which results in $U[2,\phi]$ and $arg_j[2,\phi]$, where the number 2 indicates the second phase.

Basically the in-phase activation between two or more entity nodes represents temporal bindings between them. By changing synchronous activity among entity nodes, different temporal bindings can be obtained easily. A constant binding and a variable binding are distinguished by which element of an entity node become active.

6   BUILDING SPNS FOR RULES

A symbolic rule is encoded by building the antecedent and consequent predicate assemblies and the intermediate connectionist mechanism between them. Since predicates of the rule are easily encoded using two base predicate assemblies, the main concern is how to decide the structure of the intermediate mechanism. The complexity of its structure depends on the following factors:

- *type of an argument*: if a constant argument or repeated variable argument appears in the antecedent predicate, a consistency checking sub-mechanism is inserted into the intermediate mechanism. This sub-mechanism forces the condition that any constant filler which will get bound to a constant argument should be the same as the constant argument and any constant fillers which get bound to repeated arguments should be the same constant;

- *argument matching between the antecedent and consequent*: if the same argument appears both in the antecedent and consequent, a binding propagation sub-mechanism is required between those argument nodes to propagate dynamic bindings from the antecedent to the consequent predicate assembly. Those arguments which only appear in the antecedent do not need this sub-mechanism; however those arguments which only appear in the consequent require a special sub-mechanism called the binding generation sub-mechanism;

- *binding interaction between different groups of unifying arguments*: if there are more than one different groups of unifying arguments in the antecedent of the rule, the appropriate bindings in one unifying argument group may need to be propagated to the other unifying argument groups when both of them are assigned the same variable filler.

When encoding each symbolic rule, the knowledge compiler must examine all the above factors and has to decide the structure of the intermediate mechanism required. The complexity of the intermediate mechanism of a rule therefore depends on the complexity of the conditions that the syntax of the symbolic rule imposes.

To exemplify this encoding procedure, let us consider the following example rule:

$$p(X, X, Y) \rightarrow q(X, Y).$$

Encoding the rule starts with constructing the base predicate assemblies of the predicates appearing in the rule, $p(X, Y, Z)$ and $q(X, Y)$. Then the intermediate mechanism between them is built, which involves the following procedure to determine the required sub-mechanisms.

First of all, a number of groups of unifying arguments is examined. The antecedent of the give rule has two groups of unifying arguments (the X's and the Y's). The required sub-mechanism in this case is a consistency checking sub-mechanism for the repeated X's in the antecedent so that any fillers which get bound to these repeated arguments should be the same constant or unifiable ones.

Second, the matching between arguments in the antecedent and those of in the consequent must be checked. The variable arguments X and Y appear both in the antecedent and consequent of the rule. Therefore binding propagation sub-mechanisms are needed between the first two arguments of p and the first argument of q and between the third argument of p and the second argument of q.

Finally, binding interaction between different groups of unifying arguments will be accommodated. When the same variable filler is assigned to both groups of unifying arguments, X's and Y, the binding obtained from the argument group X's must be propagated to the argument group Y. Therefore, we need binding interaction sub-mechanisms between them to support this.

After this analysis, the knowledge compiler automatically figures out the necessary sub-mechanisms for the intermediate mechanism and builds the corresponding network to the given rule (refer to Park et al [4] for a more detailed algorithm).

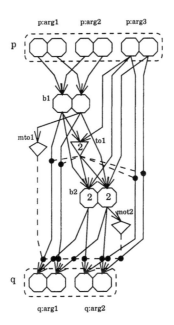

Figure 4   The network which encodes the rule $p(X, X, Y) \to q(X, Y)$.

Figure 4 shows the corresponding SPN which encodes the given rule. Two base predicate assemblies are shown at the top and bottom of the network and between them is the intermediate mechanism. The $b1_{right}$ and $mto1$ connections provide the consistency checking sub-mechanism for the repeated arguments, *p:arg1* and *p:arg2* (corresponding X's in the given rule). The links from *b1* to *q:arg1* and those from *p:arg3* to *q:arg2* are the binding propagation sub-mechanisms for the arguments corresponding to X and Y in the given rule. The nodes *b1*, *to1*, *b2* are used as the binding interaction sub-mechanism between two different groups of unifying arguments *X*'s and *Y*. And the node *mot2* is used to check the consistency of the bindings generated after binding interaction. The links drawn in a solid line are excitory and those in a dashed line are inhibitory. The eight black dots which are connected with a dashed line near to the bottom of the network are used to reduce the complexity of the network in the drawing. On becoming active, any inhibitory sources connected to one of these black dots send the same inhibitory signal to the the rest of dots.

7 BUILDING SPNS FOR FACTS

Symbolically, an n-ary fact is represented by the fact name followed by *n* constant arguments. And this has the same structure as that of ordinary predicate except that it has pre-established bindings. When a fact is encoded, one operation that can be performed against the encoded fact is posing a query predicate to the network to see if the proposed query matches with the encoded fact. Since fillers of the posed query can be a mixture of constants and variables, two types of consistency need to be forced during this match procedure. If the fact, *p(a,a,b)*, is encoded, for example, posing the query *p(a,X,X)* requires the intermediate mechanism to check both constant and variable consistency between fillers and arguments of the encoded fact.

This sort of query processing is relatively easy in symbolic inference systems because matching between two predicates is done by a symbolic pattern matching. The bindings produced are easily shared by other variables using pointers. However, it is difficult to achieve in a connectionist manner because of the following reasons:

■   it requires built-in mechanisms for consistency checking (for both constant fillers and variable fillers);

■   unlike symbolic system, the result bindings should be explicitly represented over certain nodes and this should be achieved by automatic propagation of bindings during inference.

The proposed network architecture tackles these problems by using an additional predicate assembly, called a *fact assembly*, and the intermediate mechanism. To encode each fact, the fact encoding mechanism requires two predicate assemblies, a base predicate assembly and a fact assembly. The fact assembly has the same structure as an ordinary predicate assembly and is used to represent the result of inference involving the fact. The base predicate assembly provides the basic structure of facts to be encoded. All facts which share the same predicate name and the same arity are associated with the same base predicate assembly. This allows parallelism in inference over encoded facts. The consistency checking mechanisms will be built into the intermediate mechanism, which will connect between the base predicate assembly and the fact assembly.

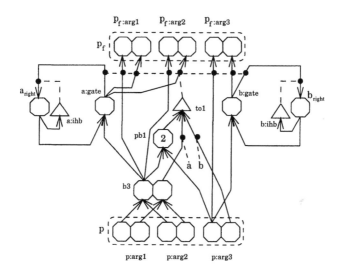

Figure 5   Encoding of the fact, $p(a, a, b)$.

Figure 5 shows the detailed structure of the intermediate mechanism required to encode the fact, $p(a,a,b)$. We can see the fact assembly p_f and its base predicate assembly p. Between them is the intermediate mechanism which involves the consistency checking sub-mechanisms and the binding propagation sub-mechanism. The node $b3$ is used to collect initial bindings from the repeated constant arguments (a's in the given fact). The fact inhibitory links between $b3_{right}$ and $to1$, between $p{:}arg3_{right}$ and $to1$, are used for constant consistency checking. The nodes, $b3_{left}$, $p{:}arg3_{left}$, $pb1$, and $to1$ and related links between them are used for variable consistency checking. The links between $b3$ and $p_f{:}arg1$, $p_f{:}arg2$ and those between $p{:}arg3$ and $p_f{:}arg3$ are used as the binding propagation sub-mechanism. When a posed query violates any forced consistency conditions, $to1$ will be activated and this prevents the fact assembly, p_f, from becoming active. Otherwise, the initial bindings will propagate from the base predicate assembly to the fact assembly. Consequently, each argument node of the fact assembly will be activated by the binding propagation sub-mechanism and will represent the result of unification occurred during inference. The nodes *a:gate* and *b:gate* are used to activate the appropriate argument nodes of the fact assembly and their corresponding constant node at the same time. The nodes *a:ihb* and *b:ihb* are used to make each constant node become active only once during a chain of inference. Once constant nodes *a* and *b* become active, their activation makes associated *ihb* nodes active and, as a result, all inputs coming to these constant nodes will be inhibited.

8   PERFORMING INFERENCE

Once a set of symbolic rules and facts are encoded into a network, the inference system can perform either forward chaining or backward chaining over the network (to support both, separate intermediate mechanisms have to be built).

Forward chaining is started by presenting a predicate to the system. The presented predicate has the form $pred\_name(t_1, t_2, \ldots, t_m)$, where t_i's are either constants or existentially quantified variables. Presenting a predicate to the system involves specifying the bindings between the presented predicate and its corresponding base predicate assembly in the network. Setting up the initial bindings is done as follows:

■   assign each entity node (called a filler node) to each filler which appears in the input predicate

■   activate each filler node and the corresponding argument of the base predicate in a unique phase in such a way that: if the filler is a constant, activate both the right π-btu element of the filler and the argument nodes; if the filler is a variable, activate both the left π-btu element of the filler and the argument nodes.

Once these initial bindings are set up using temporal synchrony, these bindings are then propagated to the consequent predicate assembly and, as a result, its arguments will represent the result of inference. In Figure 4, for instance, presenting the input fact, *p(a, U, U)*, to the network will set up initial bindings, { *a/p:arg1, U/p:arg2, U/p:arg3* } by activating the filler nodes and their corresponding argument nodes in the following phases:

$$a_{right}[1], \ U_{left}[2],$$
$$p:\{arg1[\phi,1], \ arg2[2,\phi], \ arg3[2,\phi]\},$$

where the numbers specify the particular phases. These activations propagate to the q predicate assembly through the intermediate mechanism and activate its argument nodes

$$q:\{arg1[2,1], \ arg2[2,1]\},$$

which represents the result of inference $q(a,a)$ and the result of unification generated during the inference $\{U/a\}$.

Backward chaining over encoded facts is also started by posing a query predicate to the network. The query predicate has the same form as that used in forward chaining. Posing a query predicate sets up the initial bindings between the posed query and the corresponding base predicate assembly (the consequent predicate assembly in case of a rule) in the same way as shown for forward chaining. The result of inference is then obtained by propagating these initial bindings to the antecedent predicate assembly and the associated fact assemblies if any. An associated fact assembly will only be activated if it matches with the query predicate posed. If the posed query contains variable fillers, the arguments of the activated fact assembly will represent the result of unification obtained from the inference. Therefore, after a query is posed to the network, the final result of backward chaining is obtained by observing the states of each fact assembly and its base predicate asembly in the network.

For example, posing the query, $q(a, U, V)$, to the network shown in Figure 5 will set up initial bindings, $\{a/p:arg1, \ U/p:arg2, \ V/p:arg3\}$, by activating the filler nodes and their corresponding argument nodes in the following phases:

$$a_{right}[1], \ U_{left}[2], \ V_{left}[3],$$
$$p:\{arg1[\phi,1], \ arg2[2,\phi], \ arg3[3,\phi]\}.$$

These initial bindings then propagate into the intermediate mechanism, including the consistency checking sub-mechanism. Since the posed query does not violate the consistency condition, these bindings propagate to the fact asembly through the binding propagation sub-mechanism. As a result, the arguments of the fact assembly and their corresponding constant nodes will be activated as follows:

$$b_{right}[3],$$
$$p_f:\{arg1[\phi,1],\ arg2[2,1],\ arg2[3,3]\}.$$

This represents that the encoded fact, $p_f(a,a,b)$, matches with the posed query and the result of unification obtained from the second and third argument nodes of the fact predicate is $\{U/a, V/b\}$.

9   SOME RELATED WORK

Applying temporal synchrony for a connectionist model to support various inference is found in the early work of Fahlman [5] in the form of an abstract computational mechanism in which temporal synchrony is represented in the notion of *marker passing*. Each node in the network stores a small number of discrete markers. These markers propagate between nodes under the supervision of the network controller to achieve dynamic bindings in a symbolic style of inference. Thus nodes in his system were required to have high computational ability such as storing, matching, and selectively propagating marker bits. Later, Clossman [6] used synchronous activity to represent argument-filler bindings for a connectionist model of categorization and learning without efficient encoding mechanisms for rules and facts. Ajjanagadde & Shastri [3] proposed a connectionist dynamic binding mechanism using temporal synchrony. They also suggested integrated rule and fact-encoding mechanisms which cooperate with their dynamic binding mechanism. Later, Shastri & Ajjanagadde [1] built a connectionist model for reflexive reasoning (called SHRUTI) on the basis of their mechanisms. It provides an efficient connectionist mechanism for dynamic bindings based on temporal synchrony together with encoding mechanisms for rules and facts involving n-ary predicates.

Since the basic connectionist binding mechanism using temporal synchrony is inspired by SHRUTI's dynamic binding mechanism, it is interesting to compare their system with ours. First, Shastri & Ajjanagadde's binding mechanism only represents constant bindings explicitly. It represents variable bindings by inactivity of argument nodes during inference. It does not therefore differentiate one variable binding from others, which is a basic, and fundamentally important feature of symbolic inference. Second, Shastri & Ajjanagadde's rule and fact-encoding mechanisms do not consider all the conditions that symbolic rules and facts may impose. In particular, a sub-mechanism for binding interaction between arguments is not considered in their system at all. However our model can represent groups of unifying arguments even when it is not known to which individual the variable in those arguments is bound. Finally, the proposed fact-encoding mechanism does not need different network configurations for yes-no and and wh-type query processing (as is the case in Shastri & Ajjanagadde's system). These two query procedures are merged into one fact-encoding mechanism. This mechanism does not even require two separate stages of wh-type query processing because the result of unification is automatically represented on each argument node of the fact assembly during query processing.

Other connectionist systems which tried to achieve Horn clause calculus-based expressive power, without using the temporal synchrony approach, can be found in Hölldobler & Kurfeß' CHCL [7] and Sun's CONSYDERR [8]. CHCL can handle unification over arbitrary first-order terms. However, the total number of nodes required in their system is quadratic in the size of its knowledge base. CONSYDERR also provides a compilation mechanism of rules and facts in a subset of Horn clause and is able to handle various knowledge representation issues, but the need for high computational ability of the assemblies adopted and the use of abstraction which hides network details is beyond simple summation with thresholding.

10 SUMMARY

Any connectionist knowledge-based system which aspires to imitate symbolic inference should be able to represent variables and constants and unification between them not only within a group of unifying arguments but also across many groups of unifying arguments. The proposed localist network architecture is a step in this direction. In the proposed inference system, both constant and variable entities are represented using entity nodes. Also, arguments of a predicate are represented using the same entity nodes. This representation together with the connectionist dynamic binding mechanism enables the proposed architecture to deal with both constant and variable bindings without additional mechanisms. The use of a predicate assembly to represent rules and facts allows the inference system to represent easily the result of inference and unification on each argument node. The various intermediate mechanisms adopted in the rule and fact encoding mechanisms provide a way of representing not only a group of unifying arguments but also many groups of such arguments, with consistency checking between them.

In summary, the proposed inference system provides a mechanism which translates a significant subset of Horn-clause into a connectionist representation, which may be executed very efficiently (not only in a forward chaining but also in a backward chaining style). However, in order to have the full expressive power of Horn clause FOPC, we need to add the ability to represent structured terms as arguments of a predicate and unbounded recursion in rules. Currently, no connectionist system has provided a convincing solution to all these problems (given the established problems of decidability for full FOPC) and we know that to do so, in general, we would have to sacrifice one of the most attractive features of this class of system: its ability to guarantee an answer in finite time.

ACKNOWLEDGMENTS

This work was partly supported by the Ministry of Science & Technology, Korea, and the British Council under grant SCOT/KOR/2923/37/A.

REFERENCES

[1] Shastri, L., and Ajjanagadde, V., "From simple associations to systematic reasoning: A connectionist representation of rules, variables, and dynamic bindings using temporal synchrony" *Behavioral and Brain Sciences*, Vol. 16, No. 3, 1993.

[2] Park, N. S., Robertson, D., and Stenning, K., "An extension of the temporal synchrony approach to dynamic variable binding in a connectionist inference system" *Knowledge-Based Systems*, Vol. 8, No. 6, 1995, pp. 345–357.

[3] Ajjanagadde, V., and Shastri, L., "Rules and variables in neural nets" *Neural Computation*, Vol. 3, 1991, pp. 121–134.

[4] Park, N. S., Robertson, D., and Stenning, K. Oscillation of neurons, dynamic bindings, and a symbolic knowledge representation with an embedded inference mechanism, In D. Levine, B. Brown, and T. Shirey (Eds.), *Oscillation in Neural Systems*, Lawrence Erlbaum Associates, Inc., in print.

[5] Fahlman, S. E., *NETL: A System for Representing Real-World Knowledge*, MIT Press, 1979.

[6] Clossman, G., A model of categorization and learning in a connectionist broadcast system, Ph.D. dissertation, Department of Computer Science, Indiana University, 1988.

[7] Hölldobler, S. H., and Kurfeß, F., "CHCL - A connectionist inference system" In B. Fronhöfer, and G. Wrightson (Eds.) *Parallelization in Inference Systems*, Lecture notes in computer science, Springer, 1991, pp 318–342.

[8] Sun, R., "On variable binding in connectionist networks" *Connection Science*, Vol. 4, No. 2, 1992, pp 93–124.

15

A DISTRIBUTED ASSOCIATIVE MEMORY FOR SYMBOLIC REASONING

James Austin

University of York, UK

1   INTRODUCTION

There have been a number of neural models of reasoning Sun (1994) which have mainly been aimed at explaining human cognitive processes. This chapter briefly introduces the Advanced Uncertain Reasoning Architecture (AURA), aimed at the implemention of practical reasoning systems. Thus, it considers the aspect of implementation efficiency on currently available computing platforms.

One of the essential features of most forms of reasoning is the ability to match a piece of input information with a potentially very large amount of stored knowledge. For practical reasoning systems neural networks offer a very efficient matching process. If a conventional multi-layer network is considered, this can be trained to take a piece of input data (expressed as a pattern) and perform a match with the data (or knowledge) stored in the network. The result of the matching process will be an output label, expressed in the firing of the output neurons. As such, the neural network operates as a distributed associative memory (AM). In this mode, the neural network is able to recall an association using one pass through the network. The speed of this operation is much faster than found in conventional listing approaches to matching, where a piece of input data is compared with a list of potentially matching data. Through training, the neural network AM is able to form a very efficient and compact representation of the associations. In addition to their ability to perform fast match, the network is able to recall stored patterns when the inputs are not exactly like the patterns seen during training but are similar (in a pattern sense). These two features (partial match and speed) are exploited in the system described here to produce flexible and fast reasoning.

Although most neural networks can be used in this way, a major problem is the time required to train the network, especially if the input patterns are large. The approach taken here avoids long training times through the use of correlation matrix memories (CMM). The work shows that a simple neural network architecture that uses a distributed representation can be used for rule matching. Unlike other approaches, the method uses distributed representation of inputs and outputs, and a distributed representation for the storage of rules. The advantage of this is a space efficient system that operates at very high speeds when implemented in conventional computing technology.

Although the approach described here could be used to implement other types of reasoning (e.g., for a frame-based approach see Jackson (1994)), we concentrate on rule based reasoning because this is the most common methodology used in industry. The main aim of this chapter is to describe how rule matching is achieved. The process of rule chaining, backtracking etc. is not considered.

2   CAPABILITIES OF THE METHOD

The system is able to match logical rules in the form:

A and B $\rightarrow$ C

That is if A is true and B is true then this implies that C is true.

The system supports binary variables (i.e. true or false), variable names, pre-condition matching and instantiation processes. Both AND and OR logical connectives are supported in the pre-conditions of rules. Furthermore, the system supports binding between A (the variable name) and 4 (the value) (expressed as A:4). The system can cope with rule conflicts, such as occurs when two (or more) rules successfully match a set of pre-conditions, and cause multiple outputs from the network. One of the most novel features of the system is its capability of matching partial input data to pre-conditions of rules at high speed.

3 THE NEURAL NETWORK ARCHITECTURE USED

A multi-layer neural network can support the fast match of one pattern to elicit the recall of another. In the current system the input to the neural network consists of rule pre-conditions and the output of the network rule post-conditions. To train the neural network we cannot use conventional error back propagation methods because this takes a long time to train a set of patterns. Also it does not permit new patterns to be learned without training all other patterns at the same time (on-line learning). This is a problem for practical production systems because they will typically need new rules to be added without a significant training time. Furthermore, storage of all rules for re-training the network may not be possible.

The approach taken here is based on previous work on a neural associate memory (ADAM, Austin and Stonham (1987)) which used a two-layer network architecture with (1) binary weights (2) Hebbian learning (3) L-max hidden layer encoding. The ADAM network consists of two Correlation Matrix Memories (CMM, see Willshaw, Buneman and Longuet-Higgins (1969) for an example) connected to each other. This can be seen as two layers of fully connected neurons with binary (1 or 0) weights. The conventional sum of products activation function is used, but the system uses an L-max non-local output thresholding. The hidden layer pattern is not generated through error descent learning, but is chosen by the system. This can be done because no generalization is needed between the pattern associations stored; only between a given pattern and the input. All the patterns used by the system (including the hidden layer patterns) are made up of a fixed number, L, of bits set to one in an array. The benefit of this is to ensure that the input to hidden pattern association can be reliably recalled using the L-max threshold method. L-max operates during recall by selecting the L highest responding neurons in the hidden layer and sets their outputs to one, all other outputs are set to zero. Each neuron is trained using simple Hebbian learning, i.e. if the particular neuron input is set to one and output of the neuron is set to 1 then the weight connecting the input to the neuron is set to one. This is used for both the first and second layer neurons. A detailed description of ADAM can be found in Beale and Jackson (1990).

The storage capacity of CMMs used in ADAM has been discussed in detail in Austin and Stonham (1987), Casasent and Telfer (1992), Willshaw, Buneman and Longuet-Higgins (1969) Nadal, Toulouse (1990) and Turner and Austin (1996). The general result is that if the number of bits set to one in the patterns used by the system are equal to Log_2 of the total number of bits in the pattern then maximum storage is obtained. The result of this is that although the size of the network can be large, and thus the number of weights stored is large, the number of weights accessed in any one recall is small. This results in a very practical implementation of the system. A more detailed analysis of the properties of CMMs can be found in Turner and Austin (1996).

Because the storage of information is distributed, there is always a small probability of failure to recall the correct association. This is the cost paid for the fast recall times achieved. However, the recall failure will always consist of extra bits being set to one in the output of the network, thus the output will be the correct result plus some additive noise. This type of error can be corrected through further processing.

The benefits of using L-max encoding are described in detail in Austin and Stonham (1987), Casasent and Telfer (1992). The network allows on-line learning of each association by a single pass through the network. The use of binary weights allows very simple implementation in dedicated hardware (Kennedy and Austin (1994)), although very good processing rates can be achieved using software simulations on conventional computers. In addition, the network training time scales well with the number of training patterns, thus the network can be used for real world-sized problems.

All these features make the use of this type of network attractive. The next section describes how the rule pre-conditions are encoded into the network.

4   RULE PRESENTATION AND BASIC SYSTEM ARCHITECTURE

The pre-conditions of a rule consist of a set of tokens joined with AND and OR terms. The present system deals with rules consisting of sum-of-products notation, for example

A.B + B . C + D → ?

Each 'AND' (product) term is dealt with individually, as though the 3 product terms were 3 distinct sub-rules. i.e.,

A.B → ? B.C → ? D → ?

Thus each rule can be decomposed into sub-rules, each of which will consist of a single product term in the pre-condition and a set of logical consequences.

Pre-conditions → post-conditions.

As described in section 2, the system uses a two-layer network architecture. Training the network starts by placing the pre-conditions on the input to the first layer and the post-conditions on the output layer. The system then generates a hidden layer pattern which is used as the input values for the inputs to the second layer neurons and the output values of the input layer neurons. Thus we have

Pre-conditions → separator → post-conditions.

The hidden layer pattern is called the separator because its action is to ensure that all rules are correctly separated from each other. Once this is done the system uses the Hebbian learning method to train the two layers, which only takes one pass through the data to train all the data.

The success of the training process is dependent on the correct selection of the hidden layer pattern. To ensure that all rules are kept apart from each other, all the hidden layer patterns must be orthogonal with each other. These pattern codes can be generated off-line. However, for optimal storage (size of the network in relation to the number of rules trained) the separator patterns need to be chosen with reference to the rules trained in the network. If this is required, more optimal methods can be used (Brown and Austin (1992)). However, all these methods require iterative training, which can take time to store new rules. The simplest is the test-and-train method described in Austin and Turner (1996). This can be shown to generate a near optimal set of orthogonal codes (i.e., it is a good heuristic method).

5   INPUT REPRESENTATION

Each value and variable name in the pre-conditions of the rules presented to the system is converted to a token, which is a binary pattern with a fixed number of bits set to one. The system that maps the input symbols to tokens is a simple look-up table in a pre-processor, termed the lexical token converter.

The system deals with binary variables by binding a special Boolean truth value to the variable, TRUE or FALSE, for example, A:FALSE. The system allocates constant binary patterns to represent TRUE and FALSE. The notation ":" is used to represent a binding. The system deals with other variables in the same way, by binding the value to the variable name. For example, binding the value 4 to the variable AGE is denoted by AGE:4.

The problem of binding one token with another, as in AGE:4, has been difficult in neural network systems. The issues surrounding this will not be described here, but the approach taken appears to overcome a number of the problems. We use a method that is similar to Dolan and Smolensky (1989), but instead of using continuous tensor products, we use binary tensors, an approach discounted by Smolensky for no obvious reason.

In the present system the aim is to bind two (variable and value) tokens together, to avoid loss of information when the conjunction of tokens is implemented (see later). A binding of A:4 is represented as a rank-two tensor of the tokens representing A and 4. The tensors are concatenated together and presented to the first layer of the network. In addition, all constants that occur in the pre-condition of a rule are bound to a NULL token. This is needed because of the fixed input size to the network.

6   TRAINING THE INPUT CONDITIONS

The first layer of the network is trained by placing the tensored input data onto the inputs to the first layer and generating a new separator for the hidden layer. A simple Hebb learning rule is used in the CMM to associate the inputs with the separator.

7   IMPLEMENTATION OF AND

We now turn our attention to the problem of forming the AND conditionals between the input tensors. We need to be sure that in a rule such as

A:4 . B:5 → S

only fires if both the tensors for A:4 and B:5 are present.

The AND logical connective between the tensors is achieved through the action of the network and not through explicit manipulation of the input bindings. Smolensky used higher order tensors to form the AND logical connectives between the bindings and, although effective, these scaled badly with problem size.

In the present approach, a logical AND connective is achieved by thresholding the output of the network at a fixed level. In the example given above, each token consists of N bits set to one (where N = 2 in the examples). This results in each tensor (e.g., A:4) having N^2 bits set, and a total of approximately $3N^2$ set bits input to the net (this number can be smaller due to tokens sharing bit positions in the input). When this input is presented to the network, each neuron in the hidden layer having activation of $3N^2$ should be set to one because all the bits in the input patterns that match the stored pattern will respond. Thus a threshold set to $3N^2$ will ensure that the output from the first layer of neurons is the separator pattern for the matched rule.

This approach works well for rules with a fixed number of bindings, or a fixed arity (where arity is the number of bindings plus the number of unbound items present in the pre-condition of the rule, after the rule has been separated in to a set of rules containing only a single product term). However, if the arity of the rules that are trained into the network varies then the network can generate false matches. To illustrate this problem, consider the following rules trained into a network:

(i) A:TRUE . B:TRUE → S1

(ii) A:TRUE → S2

where Sn is the n'th separator token. The rule (i) has an arity of 2; rule (ii) has an arity of 1.

Then the network is presented with the bound variable

A:TRUE

which asks if there are any rules that have a pre-condition that matches A:TRUE. The first layer will respond with an activation which is then thresholded to recover the separator for the matching rules. It is not clear what threshold should be chosen to allow rule (ii) to match but not rule (i). If the threshold was set to be equal to the number of bits set to one in the binding A:TRUE, then both rules would fire. This would be exhibited by both separators, S1 and S2, simultaneously appearing in the hidden layer, which is incorrect, and the network is unable to distinguish between the two rules. To overcome this, the network architecture is extended by adding a new set of inputs and associated set of weights to the network for each arity of rule. In effect, each arity has an associated first layer of weights.

In the implementation, a pre-processor determines the arity of the input rule and routes it to the correct arity network. The threshold used at the output is determined according to the rule arity, i.e, for rules of arity A, the threshold, T, is set to N x A, where N is the number of bits set in each binding.

8   ALLOWING COMMUTATIVITY OF INPUT BINDINGS

Although sufficient to perform rule matching, the scheme presented so far cannot cope with commutativity of the input arguments. A network trained on the pre-conditions given above would not recall the correct rule if the order of presentation of arguments was changed.

This is a severe limitation in this and other connectionist implementations. A typical suggestion is that the tokens should be ordered prior to their application to the network. Unfortunately, in the case where variables are missing (due to insufficient information) this produces incorrect orderings.

The solution to this problem described here is to use a superimposed coding. This has been popularly used in database systems for forming compact keys (Knuth (1973), Sacks-Davis and K Ramamohanaro (1983)). The approach is simple and consists of superimposing the bindings together as shown in the example 15.1, for an arbitrary set of 3 bindings. The superimposed binding (SIB) removes all order from the input bindings, thus allowing commutativity of the matching process. This is the input presented to the network. It is important to note firstly that the input to the network is now smaller and more dense. To preserve the storage capacity of the network the binding arrays must be larger. Secondly, because the bindings are superimposed (bitwise OR'ed together) there is a small probability of error due to interference between the bindings. Thirdly, it allows the size of the input query to the network to be independent of the number of variable names (arity) of that the input contains.

$$Input_{SIB} = \bigcup_{all\ n} I_n \qquad (15.1)$$

$$Input_{SIB} = \begin{bmatrix} 0\,0\,1\,1\,0 \\ 0\,0\,1\,1\,0 \\ 0\,0\,0\,0\,0 \\ 0\,0\,0\,0\,0 \\ 0\,0\,0\,0\,0 \end{bmatrix} \cup \begin{bmatrix} 0\,1\,0\,0\,1 \\ 0\,0\,0\,0\,0 \\ 0\,0\,0\,0\,0 \\ 0\,0\,0\,0\,0 \\ 0\,1\,0\,0\,1 \end{bmatrix} \cup \begin{bmatrix} 0\,0\,0\,0\,0 \\ 1\,0\,1\,0\,0 \\ 0\,0\,0\,0\,0 \\ 1\,0\,1\,0\,0 \\ 0\,0\,0\,0\,0 \end{bmatrix} = \begin{bmatrix} 0\,1\,1\,1\,1 \\ 1\,0\,1\,1\,0 \\ 0\,0\,0\,0\,0 \\ 1\,0\,1\,0\,0 \\ 0\,1\,0\,0\,1 \end{bmatrix}$$

The use of the SIB coding method is only possible because the tensor product method of encoding the bindings has been used. By forming tensors, the binding between two tokens does not get lost when SIB coding is used. If the two tokens were not bound together, when superimposed, individual pairs of tokens could not be disambiguated.

The following shows the training stages in the complete system using a small example.

Rule input:

A:TRUE . B:TRUE + C:4 . D:TRUE → X

Decompose into two sub-rules:

A:TRUE . B:TRUE → X
C:4 . D:TRUE → X

Convert lexical items to binary patterns (tokenize) shown by lower case:

a:true . b:true → x
c:4 . d:true → x

Bind variable and value tokens by forming tensors:

a:true . b:true $\rightarrow$ x

c:4 . d:true $\rightarrow$ x

Assign separator tokens:

a:true . b:true $\rightarrow$ S1$\rightarrow$ x

c:4 . d:true $\rightarrow$ S2 $\rightarrow$ x

where Sn is a binary pattern.

Superimpose to form SIBs:

(a:true $\cup$ b:true) $\rightarrow$ S1 $\rightarrow$ x

(c:4 $\cup$ d:true) $\rightarrow$ S2 $\rightarrow$ x

where $\cup$ is bitwise OR.

Train into arity 2 network:

$$(a{:}true \cup b{:}true) * S1 + W_{in_2}^t = W_{in_2}^{t+1}$$
$$(c{:}4 \cup d{:}true) * S2 + W_{in_2}^t = W_{in_2}^{t+1}$$

Where "+" is a bit wise OR over the whole correlation matrix, and $W_{in_2}^t$ is the current CMM for the arity 2 network. Then train the second stage CMM in the arity two network to associate the separator with the output data.

$$S1 * x + W_{out_2}^t = W_{out_2}^{t+1}$$
$$S2 * x + W_{out_2}^t = W_{out_2}^{t+1}$$

Where $W_{out_2}^t$ is the second stage CMM, and "*" represents the outer product of two vectors.

To summarise, when the input data is presented for training, the rules are decomposed to produce one product in each pre-condition and the arity of the rule noted. The variable/value bindings are then formed and the superimposed binding is created. This is then sent to the correct arity network inputs for training. A unique separator code is generated and used as the hidden layer pattern of the arity network. The memory that holds the consequent of the rule is then trained to take the separator and output the post-conditions. During testing, the stages used to prepare the input to the network are identical. The appropriate threshold is applied for the recovery of the separator.

9   SEPARATOR RECOVERY IN THE CASE OF RULE CONFLICTS

If an input matches a number of rules, G, stored in the neural network, then the network will output a number of separators, G, all superimposed in a single binary pattern. The binary pattern representing the recovered separators must be individually identified prior to their presentation to the next layer of the network. To achieve this, a list of valid separators is held and used to identify the individual separator patterns. The efficient implementation of this list is vital for the rapid operation of the system. Because no partial match is required in this stage of the memory, the separator list and match engine can be implemented in standard content addressable memory.

10   OUTPUT PROCESSING

The final output from the system is generated through the second layer of the neural network. Rule consequences supported by the system include both single and multiple bound variables. An example of a multiple output is

pre-condition → A:4 . B:3 . C:TRUE

This indicates that the pre-condition implies A:4 and B:3 and C:TRUE.

The output of the second layer of the net is in the form of concatenated pairs of tokens. Neither the tensor product, nor SIB representation is needed for the output as commutativity in the output tokens is not required.

To support a set of R bindings in the post-condition of a rule, it is necessary to allow R binding fields, or groups of outputs from the second layer of the network. This sets a strict limit on the number of bindings that can be represented for any given implementation. However, it is possible to support more than R output bindings by using a chaining method. In this method, the n'th binding output from the network is either a separator token that can be re-applied directly to the network for another set of consequences, or a null output (indicating no more bindings need to be recalled).

The threshold for the second layer output from the network is set to the number of bits present in the separator token. Once the outputs have been obtained, they converted back to labels used by the external interface. Alternatively, they can be fed back to the input to support rule chaining (not considered here).

11   PARTIAL MATCH CAPABILITY

The basic system described here allows a set of pre-conditions expressed as a set of bindings to be applied to the network so that all the rules and associated post-conditions can be recalled. One of the main aims of the work has been to allow a partial match capability. In this work, partial match means the ability to recall rules when only given a subset of the correct bindings. To illustrate the operation, consider a system with the following rules stored

(i) A:1 . B:3 . C:4 → S1 → X

(ii) A:1 . B:5 . D:2 → S2 → Y

(iii) A:1 . B:6 → S3 → Z

A partial match capability would allow rule (i) to fire when the network was only given the pre-conditions (A:1 . B:3). This can be achieved in the network by (1) applying the pre-conditions to the arity 3 network input and (2) thresholding the output (the arity 3 network output) at a level equal to the number of bits in the input SIB. This is like asking "are there any 3 arity rules that match 2 or more terms". In this case there is a match and the separator (S1) for rule (i) would be output from the network.

This capability can be used to find any sub-set of terms that match the rules stored. The is a very fast and efficient operation, which only requires one pass through the network.

The partial match capability can also cope with more complex problems. Consider the input

> A:1 . B:3 . F:4 . B:6

The operation is now "find all the rules that match any 2 terms in the set of 4 supplied terms". Typically, this is a combinatorial problem, which requires mCn separate match operations where M is greater than n and m is the number of suppled terms and n is the number of terms which must match. If this input were used to search the list of rules given above, both rule (i) and (ii) should match.

12 SUMMARY

This chapter has described the basic rule-matching engine. The system has applications in many areas of machine based reasoning in addition to being of interest to cognitive scientists. It has been shown how a simple two layer neural network can be used to perform complex and fast rule matching. In particular it allows the fast matching of rules without worrying about the order of presentation of the terms within pre-conditions.

13 REFERENCES

[1] J. Austin and T. J. Stonham, (1987), An Associative Memory for Use in Image Recognition and Occlusion Analysis, *Image and Vision Computing*, Vol. 5, No. 4, p. 251-261.

[2] J. Austin and A. Turner (1996), *A simple method for selecting near orthogonal class patterns*, In preparation, University of York.

[3] R. Beale and T. Jackson (1990), *Neural Computing: An introduction*, Adam Hilger.

[4] M. Brown and J. Austin (1992), Optimum Selection of Class Vectors for ADAM, *Proceedings of International Conference on Artificial Neural Networks*, Brighton, UK.

[5] D. P. Casasent and B. A. Telfer (1992), High Capacity Pattern Recognition Associative Processors, *Neural Networks*, Vol. 5. No. 4. p. 687-698.

[6] C. P. Dolan and P. Smolensky (1989), Tensor product production system: A modular architecture and representation, *Connection Science*, No. 1, vol 1. p. 53-68.

[7] T. J. Jackson (1994), *Associative Neural Networks for Frame Based Reasoning*, PhD Thesis, University of York, UK.

[8] J. Kennedy and J. Austin (1994), A Hardware Implementation of a Binary Neural Network, p. 178-185, *Fourth International Conf. on Microelectronics for Neural Networks and Fuzzy Systems*, IEEE Computer Press.

[9] D. E. Knuth (1973), *The Art of Computer Programming*, Vol. 3, Addison Wesley.

[10] J. P. Nadal and G. Toulouse (1990), Information Storage in Sparsely Coded Memory Nets, *Networks*, Vol. 1. p. 61-74.

[11] R. Sacks-Davis and K. Ramamohanaro (1983), A Two Level Superimposed Coding Scheme for Partial Match Retrieval, *Information Systems*, p. 273-280.

[12] R. Sun (1994), *Integrating Rules and Conectionism for Robust Commonsense Reasoning*, John Wiley and Sons, New York.

[13] M. Turner and J. Austin (1996), Analysis of the storage capacity of Correlation Matrix Memories. Submitted to *Neural Networks*.

[14] D. J. Willshaw, O. P. Buneman, and H. C. Longuet-Higgins (1969), Non-Holographic Associative Memory, *Nature*, Vol. 222, June 7, p. 960-962.

16

SYMBOLIC NEURAL NETWORKS DERIVED FROM STOCHASTIC GRAMMAR DOMAIN MODELS

Eric Mjolsness

Machine Learning Systems Group,
Jet Propulsion Laboratory, Caltech

1   INTRODUCTION

This paper outlines a statistical approach to unifying certain symbolic and neural net architectures, by deriving them from a stochastic domain model with sufficient structure. The goal is to derive neural networks which retain some of the expressive power of a semantic network and also some of the pattern recognition and learning capabilities of more conventional neural networks. The domain model is a stochastic L-system grammar, whose rules for generating objects and their parts each include a Boltzmann probability distribution. Using such a domain model in high-level vision, it is possible to formulate object recognition and visual learning problems as constrained optimization problems (Mjolsness 1991) of a restricted form which can be locally optimized by suitable neural network architectures. In ths way, one can semi-automatically produce neural nets for object recognition with some of the representational properties of semantic nets.

In technical content, this paper generalizes the method in several ways: it includes a fairly general recursive grammar in which derivations may have a large but bounded depth; it allows the compositional hierarchy of object and part models or types to be a general graph; it subsumes a specialization hierarchy of object models within the compositional hierarchy; it adds learning as another constrained optimization problem; it introduces a general way to reformulate the optimization problems by "changing variables". However, many restrictions on the expressiveness and functionality of the combined architecture remain. The most important issue not addressed in this paper is the neural network dynamics by which the nonlinear global optimization problem is to be solved, for large systems. There has been substantial progress on this subject for related, less difficult combinatorial optimization problems (Kosowsky and Yuille 1994) (Peterson and Soderberg 1989) (Van den Bout and Miller 1990) and their application to pattern recognition and learning in high-level vision (Gold et al. 1995) (Gold et al. 1996) derived from somewhat simpler stochastic grammars (Mjolsness 1991).

Deriving the unified architecture from a statistical model has several advantages, including the integration of suitable "distance" or "similarity" measures for pattern recognition and learning on structured objects, and the specification of a broad class of domain models for which the symbolic neural network architecture is applicable. In Section 2 we will describe the grammar domain model and how it incorporates compositional and specialization hierarchies (as present in semantic nets) within a parameterized grammar schema. In Section 3 we summarize some of the technical manipulations by which probabilistic parsing and grammatical inference problems can be cast as constrained optimization problems with various cost characteristics, including the derivation of a semantic net-like formulation with instantiation links, and solved by neural networks. Section 4 compares the present approach to symbolic/neural net unification with several related architectures, and concludes.

2   THE GRAMMAR

Our basic modeling tool is neither a neural net nor a symbol processor, but rather a type of stochastic grammar which permits quantitative, probabilistic modeling as well as considerable expressive power. The grammar is "parameterized" because each term carries numerical parameters whose values are determined when the right rule fires. Each rule has a conditional probability distribution on these parameters which could be any Boltzmann distribution; such a distribution by itself is an expressive language for many domains. The presence of multiple rules serves to integrate qualitatively different processes into one model.

As is common in high-level languages, we first design for appropriate expressiveness (now including learning and pattern recognition) and then worry about program transformations which can obtain high performance on a useful class of examples. Here the program transformations include different ways of translating inference problems on grammars to constrained optimization problems and thence to neural architectures which seek good local minima at low cost, as well as transformations within each of these stages. Such transformations

(Mjolsness and Garrett 1990) (Mjolsness 1991) (Mjolsness et al 1991a) can be much more quantitative than conventional program transformations, and introduce great flexibility in the neural "wiring diagrams" that correspond to a given grammar model. They may also include outright approximations, such as our use of deterministic annealing in place of global optimization. This transformational approach gives us new methods with which to explore the inevitable trade-offs between expressiveness and efficiency.

In a parameterized L-system grammar (Prusinkiewicz 1990), rules can fire in parallel and terms can carry parameters which are altered by the rules. Our stochastic grammar rules will be of the form:

$$\textbf{term}(params) \quad : \quad l - condition(params) \rightarrow$$
$$\{\textbf{term1}(params1), \textbf{term2}(params2), ... \mid r - condition(choice - params)\};$$
$$//comments$$
$$E = E(\{paramsi\}, choice - params; params) \qquad //comments$$
$$\ni constraints(\{paramsi\}) \; //comments$$

In this rule schema, E is the energy function in a Boltzmann probability distribution on the parameters $\{paramsi\}$ of the new terms **termi**, given the fixed parent **term** and its fixed *params*. The constraint introduction symbol "$\ni$" is read "such that", and the constraints are predicates (usually conjunctions of equalities or inequalities) which restrict the space of allowed parameter values for the new terms. The optional left and right conditions are predicates, depending on the parent and choice parameters respectively, which must be satisfied for the rule to fire; they are introduced by symbols ":" and "|" which can be read as "for which" and "such that". The optional choice parameters are used to parameterize all the alternative sets of terms, {**termi**}, which could result from the same left hand side, to determine their relative probabilities in the relevant Boltzmann distributions, and to record numerically the choice made. The set of new terms could have just one element, in which case we'll omit the braces, and it is unordered except for any implicit order encoded in the parameters. This form of rule is context-free, but we will also use one context-sensitive rule in which the left hand side is a set of terms rather than a single term.

We now introduce a particular grammar for generating images consisting of sparse point-like features that represent hierarchical objects. A "scene" generates a single scene "object", which recursively generates other "objects" each of which can be randomly deleted, through L generations of a part-whole hierarchy. A generation-L object generates a "point", and the context-sensitive final rule randomly relabels all the points. The "object" terms will be of the form **object**(<level>, <type>, <deriv-trace>, <instance-params>), where <level> is an integer level number l, constrained to increase with each rule firing and to not exceed a maximal derivation depth L; <type> is the object type or model number α; <deriv-trace> is a record of the path to this node in the compositional (part-whole) hierarchy, in the form of a unique sequence $(s_1 s_2 \ldots s_l)$ of slot or sibling numbers; and <instance-params> are possibly analog parameters specifying, for example, the spatial coordinates and orientation of the object.

Each object has an ordered set of slots to be filled by its children in the compositional hierarchy. The children are pre-objects which, if they are not randomly deleted, survive to become objects. The child of an object of type α, whose path index is $(s_1 s_2 \ldots s_l)$, must choose some type β; the choice is constrained by the constant 0/1 array of allowed component types $\text{INA}_{\alpha s_l \beta}$, and recorded in the 0/1-valued choice variables $C_{s_1 \ldots s_l}^{l\beta}$. In detail, the grammar is:

$$
\begin{aligned}
&\textbf{scene} \quad \rightarrow \textbf{object}(l = 0, \alpha = \text{"scene"}, (), x^0); \; E = H^0(x_0) \\
&\textbf{object}\left(l - 1, \alpha, (s_1 \ldots s_{l-1}), x_{s_1 \ldots s_{l-1}}^{l-1}\right) : l < L \\
&\quad \rightarrow \{ \textbf{preobject} \left(l, \beta, (s_1 \ldots s_l), x_{s_1 \ldots s_l}^l\right) \mid 1 \le s_l \le s \; \wedge \; C_{s_1 \ldots s_l}^{l\beta} = 1 \} \\
&\quad\quad E(C, x) = \sum_{s_l} \sum_\beta C_{s_1 \ldots s_l}^{l\beta} H^{(\alpha s_l \beta)} \left(x_{s_1 \ldots s_l}^l, \; x_{s_1 \ldots s_{l-1}}^{l-1}, \; u^{(\alpha s_l \beta)}\right) \\
&\quad\quad \ni C_{s_1 \ldots s_l}^{l\beta} \le \text{INA}_{\alpha s_l \beta} \; \wedge \; \sum_\beta C_{s_1 \ldots s_l}^{l\beta} \\
&\textbf{preobject} \left(l, \beta, (s_1 \ldots s_l), x_{s_1 \ldots s_l}^l\right) \\
&\quad \rightarrow \textbf{object} \left(l, \beta, (s_1 \ldots s_l), x_{s_1 \ldots s_l}^l\right) \mid \omega_{(s)} = 1 ; \; E = -\mu^{(s_l \beta)} \\
&\quad \rightarrow \textbf{nothing} \mid \omega_{(s)} = 0; \; E = 0 \\
&\quad\quad // \; \omega \text{ is a choice param for one object} \\
&\quad\quad // \; \text{So } E(\omega) = -\mu^{(s_l \beta)} \omega_{s_1 \ldots s_l} \\
&\textbf{object} \left(L, \beta, (s_1 \ldots s_l), x_{s_1 \ldots s_L}\right) \\
&\quad \rightarrow \textbf{point} \left(x_{s_1 \ldots s_L}^L\right) ; \; E = 0 \\
&\{ \; \textbf{point} \left(x_{s_1 \ldots s_L}^L\right) \; \} \\
&\quad \rightarrow \{ \; \textbf{imagepoint} \left(x_k = \sum_{(s)} P_{(s)k} x_{(s)}^L\right) \; \}; \; E = 0 \\
&\quad\quad \ni \sum_{(s)} P_{(s)k} = 1 \; \wedge \; \sum_k P_{(s)k} = \prod_{l=1}^L \omega_{s_1 \ldots s_l}^l \le 1 \\
&\quad\quad // \; \text{P is a permutation of } k_{\max} \text{ elements}
\end{aligned}
$$

The object-part recursion proceeds according to a fixed part-whole hierarchy between models (or types, or frames) α and β, if they are related by the constant matrix INA, and will result in a kind of semantic network we call "Frameville" (Mjolsness et al. 1989) (Mjolsness 1994). The other variables may be explained as follows: l is the level number, bounded by L; α is the object type or "frame" index; (s) is a derivation path index consisting of a string of slot indices s_l; x is a set of analog parameters for an object, such as the position vector of its centroid; u is a set of constant analog parameters for a model, such as the expected displacement vector from the parent object's centroid to that of a child object; H is the penalty function (e.g. a quadratic) for deviations from the expected relations between parent and child parameters; C are the 0/1-valued choice parameters recording which frame β was chosen as the type of each preobject child of a given object; ω is the 0/1-valued choice parameter recording whether a preobject was deleted, or survived to become an object; and P is the random permutation that renumbers the level-L objects (now points) as "imagepoints" in an uninformative order. An example two-level derivation is shown below, in which transitions according to the level-1 object rule, the level-2 object rule (in two steps), and the final point renumbering rule are shown:

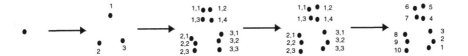

Figure 1   Generating a hierarchical object image

Because the model or "frame" indices α and β are term parameters in the grammar, the two mutually recursive object $\leftrightarrow$ preobject rules are able to subsume many parameterized L-system rules of the form $\alpha(x) \to \{\beta(x)\}$, in which the allowed transitions are given by the INA array. (If several different rules start with the same $\alpha(x)$, we introduce intermediate models $\alpha_r(x)$ to select among them in two steps, $\alpha(x) \to \alpha_r(x) \to \{\beta(x)\}$. This is still encoded in INA, using its ability in this grammar to simulate ISA links.) In this way, the single six-rule grammar above is actually a grammar schema for any number of much larger grammars whose transitions can be tabulated by INA arrays. Considered as a graph on models or "frames", INA is not restricted to being a tree or a directed acyclic graph (DAG). We can compute the joint probability distribution on all the possible parameterized terms which could arise in a derivation of this grammar; it is another Boltzmann distribution (Mjolsness 1991). The problem of finding the most probable derivation giving rise to a given set of level-L final terms is the constrained optimization problem of minimizing the resulting energy function. The objective may be straightforwardly calculated as:

$$E\left(C,\,\omega,\,x\right) = H_0\left(x^0\right)$$

$$+ \sum_{\alpha_1 s_1} C_{s_1}^{1\alpha_1}\left[H^{(\text{scene}s_1\alpha_1)}\left(x_{s_1}^1,\,x^0,\,u^{(\text{scene}s_1\alpha_1)}\right) - \mu^{(s_1\alpha_1)}\omega_{s_1}^1\right.$$

$$+ \omega_{s_1}^1 \sum_{\alpha_2 s_2} C_{s_2}^{2\alpha_2}\left[H^{(\alpha_1 s_2\alpha_2)}\left(x_{s_1 s_2}^2,\,x_{s_1}^1,\,u^{(\alpha_1 s_1\alpha_2)}\right) - \mu^{(s_2\alpha_2)}\omega_{s_2}^2\right.$$

$$+ \ldots + \omega_{s_1\ldots s_{L-1}}^{L-1} \sum_{\alpha_L s_L} C_{s_1\ldots s_L}^{L\alpha_L}$$

$$\times\left[H^{(\alpha_{L-1} s_L\alpha_L)}\left(x_{s_1\ldots s_L}^L,\,x_{s_1\ldots s_{L-1}}^{L-1},\,u^{(\alpha_{L-1} s_L\alpha_L)}\right) - \mu^{(s_L\alpha_L)}\omega_{s_1\ldots s_L}^L\right]\ldots\Big]\Big]$$

i.e.

$$E\left(C,\,\omega,\,x\right) = H_0\left(x^0\right) \tag{16.1}$$

$$+ \sum_{l=1}^{L}\sum_{(s)}\sum_{\alpha\beta} C_{s_1\ldots s_l}^{l\beta} C_{s_1\ldots s_l}^{l-1\alpha}\left(\prod_{k=1}^{l}\omega_{s_1\ldots s_l}^k\right)$$

$$\times\left[H^{(\alpha s_l\beta)}\left(x_{s_1\ldots s_l}^l,\,x_{s_1\ldots s_{l-1}}^{l-1},\,u^{(\alpha s_l\beta)}\right) - \mu^{(s_l\beta)}\omega_{(s)}^l\right]$$

and the constraints are:

$$C,\,\omega,\,P,\,\text{INA} \in \{0,\,1\}$$

$$\omega_{(s_1\ldots s_l)}^l \leq \sum_{\beta} C_{s_1\ldots s_l}^{l\beta} \leq \prod_{k=1}^{l-1}\omega_{s_1\ldots s_l}^k$$

$$x_k = \sum_{(s)} P_{(s)k}x_{(s)} \ \wedge\ \sum_{(s)} P_{(s)k} = 1 \ \wedge\ \sum_k P_{(s)k} = \prod_{k=1}^{L}\omega_{s_1\ldots s_l}^k \leq 1 \tag{16.2}$$

$$C_{s_1\ldots s_l}^{l\beta} \leq \sum_{\alpha}\text{INA}_{\alpha s_l\beta}C_{s_1\ldots s_{l-1}}^{l-1\alpha}$$

Note that the constraint $\omega_{(s)}^l \leq \sum_\beta C_{(s)}^{l\beta} \leq \prod_{k=1}^{l-1}\omega_{(s)}^k$ has been used to simplify the objective in equation (16.1), by removing a product over C's from earlier levels. Note also that the **object** → **{preobject}** grammar rule could be restricted so that it couldn't delete preobjects (and only the preobject deletion rule could do so), e.g. $C^{l-1\alpha}\omega^{l-1} = 1 \Rightarrow \sum_\beta C_{(s\sigma)}^{l\beta} = \max_\beta\text{INA}_{\alpha\sigma\beta}$. But the extra condition would later be eliminated along with the auxiliary variables of equation 10 below.

The mapping from such constrained optimization problems to neural nets is discussed in section 3.2. This particular problem formulation is difficult to work with because it has high polynomial degree ($L + 4$ or more depending on H), making circuit implementations and global optimization difficult, and because there are several sets of variables indexed by the possible derivation paths $(s) = (s_1 \ldots s_l)$, of which there are exponentially many as the maximum depth L increases. If the probability of preobject deletion is not very low, this leads to polynomial or even exponential discrepancies between the number of image points (which is the size of the input data to a recognition problem) and the number of possible intermediate terms which have to be represented to parse, explain or recognize a given scene. So the cost of storing an arbitrary configuration, let alone computing the optimal one, is prohibitive. Reformulating the constrained optimization problem to remove these obstacles is addressed in the next section.

3 PROBLEM REFORMULATIONS

The cost and polynomial degree of the constrained optimization problem (16.1), (16.2) may be improved by repeatedly changing to a better set of variables. In this section we introduce the conditions that must be verified for a change of variables to produce an equivalent Boltzmann probability distribution and optimization problem.

Given a free energy objective, $F_1(x;T)$, depending on some set of variables x and on a fixed global temperature parameter T, and given a constraint predicate on x, $C_1(x)$, we can change variables to another set of variables y, free energy $F_2(y;T)$ and constraint predicate $C_2(y)$ by finding two change-of-variable predicates, $(\Delta_F(Y, X), \Delta_B(X, Y))$ (for the forwards and backwards directions respectively), usually expressed as conjunctions of equality and inequality constraints between supersets X and Y of x and y, such that:

$$C_1 \wedge \Delta_F \Leftrightarrow C_2 \wedge \Delta_B \qquad \text{and}$$

$$C_1 \wedge \Delta_F \wedge C_2 \wedge \Delta_B \Rightarrow \qquad\qquad (16.3)$$

$$F_1(x) - TS_1(X\backslash x) = F_2(y) - TS_2(Y\backslash y) - T\log J(x, y)$$

The first condition says that the constraint space on X and Y is the same, whether it is described by a set of boolean constraints on x and a forward change of variables, or by a set of constraints on y and a backwards change of variables. The second condition says that in this common constraint space, the free energies differ only by entropy terms S_1 and S_2 which account for the logarithm of the volume of the allowed space of auxiliary variables $X\backslash x$ and $Y\backslash y$ (where $\backslash$ is the set difference), and the logarithmic ratio of volume elements of any continuous variables among x and y. The entropy and Jacobian terms arise from the partition function in the statistical mechanics treatment of Boltzmann probability distributions, and may be ignored at zero temperature $(T = 0)$. For simplicity we'll ignore these terms and just verify the equality of objective functions E before and after the change of variables, but it is easy to reinstate the temperature-dependent terms.

3.1   Degree Reduction

If we change to the object "aliveness" variables $A^{l\beta}_{s_1\ldots s_l}$ (Mjolsness et al 1991b) which are 1 or 0 depending on whether an object with path index (s) and type α is in the derivation or not, rather than the "rule choice" variables $C^{l\beta}_{s_1\ldots s_l}$ and $\omega^l_{(s)}$, we can reduce the objective and constraints to low polynomial degree. To this end, we use change of variable equations like $A^{l\beta}_{(s)} = C^{l\beta}_{(s)}\omega^l_{(s)}$, which says that an object is live with type β if and only if it was a preobject with type β and it survived to become an object. For deleted objects, however, we retain the choice variables $\tilde{C}$. In detail, the change of variables is:

$$\Delta_F: \quad \begin{aligned} A^{0,\alpha} &= \delta_{\alpha,\,\text{scene}} \quad \wedge \quad \hat{A}^0 = 1 \quad // \quad (\delta \text{ is the Kronecker delta function}) \\ A^{l\beta}_{(s)} &= C^{l\beta}_{(s)}\omega^l_{(s)} \quad \wedge \quad \hat{A}^l_{(s)} = \omega^l_{(s)} \quad \wedge \quad \tilde{C}^{l\beta}_{(s)} = C^{l\beta}_{(s)}\left(1 - \omega^l_{(s)}\right)(l \geq 1) \end{aligned}$$

$$\Delta_B: \quad C^{l\beta}_{(s)} = A^{l\beta}_{(s)} + \tilde{C}^{l\beta}_{(s)} \quad \wedge \quad \omega^l_{(s)} = \hat{A}^l_{(s)}(l \geq 1) \tag{16.4}$$

The new objective function is:

$$E\left(A,\,x\right) = H_0\left(x^0\right) \;+\; \sum_{l=1}^{L}\sum_{(s)}\sum_{\alpha\beta} A^{l\beta}_{s_1\ldots s_l} A^{l-1\,\alpha}_{s_1\ldots s_{l-1}} \tag{16.5}$$

$$\times \left[H^{(\alpha s_l\beta)}\left(x^l_{s_1\ldots s_l},\, x^{l-1}_{s_1\ldots s_{l-1}},\, u^{(\alpha s_l\beta)} \right) - \mu^{(s_l\beta)} \right]$$

which is a sum of low-degree monomial interaction terms. (In a Hopfield neural network, a quadratic monomial becomes two regular synapses and a cubic monomial becomes three multiplicative synapses.) The H functions may be interpreted as context-dependent "distance" or "similarity" measures between a model β and the set of instantiation parameters $x^l_{s_1 \ldots s_l}$ ultimately constrained by data x_k. The associated constraints for the (A, P, x) variables are:

$$A, \hat{A}, \tilde{C}, P, \text{INA} \in \{0, 1\}$$

$$A^{0, \alpha} = \delta_{\alpha, \text{root}}$$

$$\hat{A}^l_{(s)} = \sum_\beta A^{l\beta}_{(s)}$$

$$\hat{A}^l_{s_1 \ldots s_l} + \sum_\beta \tilde{C}^{l\beta}_{s_1 \ldots s_l} \leq \hat{A}^{l-1}_{s_1 \ldots s_{l-1}}$$

$$A^{l\beta}_{s_1 \ldots s_l} + \tilde{C}^{l\beta}_{s_1 \ldots s_l} \leq \sum_\alpha \text{INA}_{\alpha s_l \beta} A^{l-1\alpha}_{s_1 \ldots s_{l-1}}$$

$$x_k = \sum_{(s)} P_{(s)k} x_{(s)} \quad \wedge \quad \sum_{(s)} P_{(s)k} = 1 \quad \wedge \quad \sum_k P_{(s)k} = \hat{A}^L_{(s)}$$

(16.6)

For these objectives, constraints, and forward and backward changes of variable, the change of variable conditions (3) are proven to hold in Appendix I. The advantage of the new system is that all polynomial degrees are low (3 or 4 rather than L). However, the overly numerous (s)-indexed variables remain.

The objective and constraints of (16.5) and (16.6) may be diagrammed as shown below, in which the small open circles are variables, the ovals represent the models (which store constant database information like u, μ, H, and INA), and the squares are possible terms in a derivation. Each diagram below shows only a representative clique of related variables which interact in one constraint in a conjunction thereof or one summand of the objective function. Links connect variables which share an index. The objective function and the inequality constraint are shown in these two diagrams, with object types on the left and instances (grammatical "object" terms and their associated parameters, x) on the right of each diagram.

Specialization to Point-Matching

We can make contact with previous experiments on nonhierarchical point-matching by specializing the aliveness variable formulation of the constrained optimization problem. If there is only one model accessible after L levels of

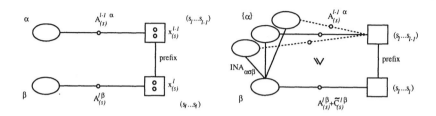

Figure 2   Aliveness variables in objective and constraint.

derivation, say the "point" model, then $A_{(s)}^{L\beta} = \delta_{\beta,\,\text{point}}\hat{A}_{(s)}^{L}$ and we can substitute $x_{(s)} = \sum_{(s)} P_{(s)k} x_k^L$ into the $l = L$ summand of the objective and simplify. By specializing H to include translational an rotational degrees of freedom at every node in the hierarchy, we arrive at the objective

$$
\begin{aligned}
E\left(A,\,x\right) \;=\; & H_0\left(x^0\right) \\[4pt]
+ \; & \sum_{l=1}^{L-1}\sum_{(s)}\sum_{\alpha\beta} A_{s_1\ldots s_l}^{l\beta}\, A_{s_1\ldots s_{l-1}}^{l-1\,\alpha} \\[2pt]
& \times \left[\frac{1}{2\sigma_l^2}\,\|\,x_{s_1\ldots s_l}^{l} - x_{s_1\ldots s_{l-1}}^{l-1} - \Omega_{s_1\ldots s_{l-1}}^{l-1}\cdot y^{\alpha s_l \beta}\,\|^2\right. \\[2pt]
& \left. + \, G\left(\Omega_{s_1\ldots s_{l-1}}^{l-1},\,\sigma_l,\,\sigma_{l-1}\right) - \mu^{(s_l\beta)}\right] \qquad (16.7) \\[4pt]
+ \; & \sum_{k}\sum_{(s)}\sum_{\alpha} A_{s_1\ldots s_{l-1}}^{L-1\,\alpha}\, P_{(s)k} \\[2pt]
& \times \left[\frac{1}{2\sigma_L^2}\,\|\,x_k^{L} - x_{s_1\ldots s_{l-1}}^{L-1} - \Omega_{s_1\ldots s_{l-1}}^{L-1}\cdot y^{\alpha s_l \text{point}}\,\|^2\right. \\[2pt]
& \left. + \, G\left(\Omega_{s_1\ldots s_{l-1}}^{L-1},\,\sigma_L,\,\sigma_{l-1}\right) - \mu^{(s_l \text{point})}\right]
\end{aligned}
$$

and the constraints

$$A, \hat{A}, P, \text{INA} \in \{0, 1\}$$

$$A^{0, \alpha} = \delta_{\alpha, \text{root}}$$

$$\hat{A}^l_{(s)} = \sum_\beta A^{l\beta}_{(s)} \tag{16.8}$$

$$A^{l\beta}_{s_1 \ldots s_l} \le \sum_\alpha \text{INA}_{\alpha s_l \beta} A^{l-1\alpha}_{s_1 \ldots s_{l-1}}$$

along with the constraints

$$\sum_\beta \text{INA}_{\alpha \sigma \beta} \le 1 \tag{16.8 cont.}$$

$$\sum_{(s)} P_{(s)k} = \Theta \left(k + \tfrac{1}{2} \right) \Theta \left(k_{\max} - k + \tfrac{1}{2} \right) \quad \wedge \quad \sum_k P_{(s)k} = \hat{A}^L_{(s)}$$

(Here Θ is the 0/1-valued Heaviside function, used to constrain k to be between 1 and its maximum.) This constrained optimization problem is a hierarchical generalization of a previous nonhierarchical (L=1 or 2) point-matching architecture implemented in (Gold et al. 1995):

$$E(m, A, t, \mu, \nu) = \frac{1}{2\sigma^2} \sum_{ij} m_{ij} \| x_i - t - A y_j \|^2 - \alpha \sum_{ij} m_{ij} - g(A)$$

with constraints $m \in \{0, 1\} \quad \wedge \quad \sum_i m_{ij} \le 1 \quad \wedge \quad \sum_j m_{ij} \le 1.$

Here g is a regularizer on the affine transformation matrix A, and G is a similar regularizer for the affine transformation Ω between levels in the hierarchical object grammar, parameterized by the noise parameters σ. In particular if Ω is regularized to favor rotations, then we obtain a mobile-like hierarchical object model.

3.2 Mapping to Neural Networks

An objective function such as equation (5), and its associated constraints (e.g. that each A is zero or one), can be mapped into an analog neural network by a variety of techniques (Hopfield 1984) (Kosowsky and Yuille 1994) which require that we expand H into a polynomial, and allocate multi-way synapses for each monomial in the resultant polynomial expression for E. The constraints can be treated similarly. Monomials of degree two such as $3xy$ are mapped to a pair of conventional synapses from neuron x to neuron y and back. If the polynomials have a regular structure, the synapse count may be considerably reduced by introducing intermediate variables as in (Mjolsness and Garrett 1990). Convergence can often be greatly accelerated by introducing clocked dynamics as in (Mjolsness and Miranker 1993). The resulting networks will have a localist encoding because of the 0/1-valued A and P variables, which is an inefficient use of space since at least the permutation matrix P is sparse. It is possible that new mappings to localist (Mjolsness and Garrett 1990) or distributed (Plate 1994) (see also chapter 17) representations will eventually allow the same model to run with much less circuitry. Effective use of deterministic annealing methods can also improve the quality of the local minima to which such algorithms converge, for both recognition and learning (Gold et al. 1995) (Gold et al. 1996).

3.3 Eliminate Derivation Indices

The (s) indices still introduce a rapidly, perhaps exponentially growing number of variables, corresponding to all the possible derivations in the grammar. Two further changes of variable can eliminate the excess variables. First, we introduce auxiliary variables P and x at all levels, not just $l=L$, and we eliminate the remaining choice variables $\tilde{C}$. This step introduces trivial dependent "frame instances" in correspondence with the derivation objects. Second, we eliminate the derivation objects and their aliveness variables A in favor of the frame instances and relationships between them and between frames (models) and their instances. These changes are diagrammed in figure 3, using triangles to represent frame instances and showing all relevant variables in two neighboring cliques at levels $(L-2, L-1)$ and $(L-1, L)$. The dotted lines show the introduction of the new link types: the match or instantiation variables "M" between frame models and instances, and the Part-of variables "ina" between instances.

1st Change: Add Instances

The change of variables is:

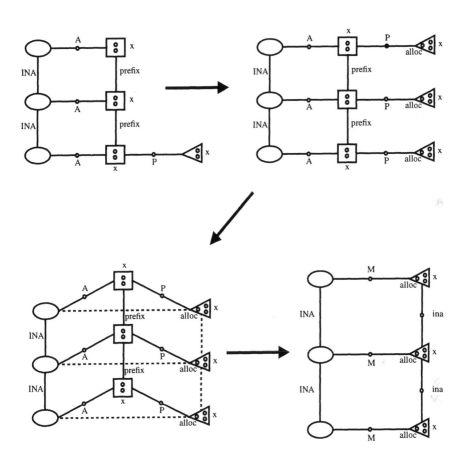

Figure 3 Change of variables to Frameville architecture.

$$A = A \quad \wedge \quad \hat{A} = \hat{A} \quad \wedge \quad P^L = P \quad \wedge \quad x^L = x^L$$

$\Delta_F:$ auxiliary variables : $x_j^l \in \Re \quad \wedge \quad P_{(s)j}^l \in \{l < L\}, \text{alloc}_j^l \in \{0, 1\}$ (16.9)

$$x_j^l = \sum_{(s)} P_{(s)j}^l x_{(s)}^l \quad \wedge \quad \sum_{(s)} P_{(s)j}^l = \text{alloc}_j^l \quad \wedge \quad \sum_j P_{(s)j}^l = \hat{A}_{(s)}^l$$

and inversely

$$A = A \quad \wedge \quad \hat{A} = \hat{A} \quad \wedge \quad P = P^L \quad \wedge \quad x^L = x^L$$

$$\Delta_B: \qquad x^l_{(s)} = \sum_j P^l_{(s)j} x^l_j$$

$$\tilde{C}^{l\beta}_{(s)} \in 0, 1 \quad \wedge \quad \sum_\beta \tilde{C}^{l\beta}_{(s)} \le \hat{A}^{l-1}_{(s)} - \hat{A}^l_{(s)} \qquad (16.10)$$

$$\text{auxiliary variables}: \qquad \tilde{C}^{l\beta}_{(s)} \le \sum_\beta \text{INA}_{\alpha s_l \beta} A^{l-1\alpha}_{(s)} - A^{l\beta}_{(s)}$$

The new objective function is:

$$
\begin{aligned}
E(A, x) \; = \; & H_0\left(x^0\right) \\
& + \sum_{l=1}^{L} \sum_s \sum_{\alpha\beta} \sum_{ij} \text{INA}_{\alpha s_l \beta} A^{l\beta}_{s_1 \ldots s_l} A^{l-1\alpha}_{s_1 \ldots s_l} P^l_{s_1 \ldots s_l, j} P^{l-1}_{s_1 \ldots s_{l-1}, i} \\
& \times \left[H^{(\alpha s_l \beta)}\left(x^l_j, x^{l-1}_i, u^{(\alpha s_l \beta)}\right) - \mu^{(s_l \beta)} \right]
\end{aligned}
\qquad (16.11)
$$

The constraints for the (A, P, alloc, x) variables are:

$$A, \hat{A}, P, \text{alloc}, \text{INA} \in \{0, 1\}$$

$$A^{0,\alpha} = \delta_{\alpha, \text{root}} \quad \wedge \quad x^L_k = x_k \quad \wedge \quad \text{alloc}^L_k = \Theta\left(k + \tfrac{1}{2}\right) \Theta\left(k_{\max} - k + \tfrac{1}{2}\right)$$

$$\hat{A}^l_{(s)} = \sum_\beta A^{l\beta}_{(s)} \quad \wedge \quad \hat{A}^l_{(s)} \le \hat{A}^{l-1}_{(s)} \qquad (16.12)$$

$$A^{l\beta}_{s_1 \ldots s_l} \le \sum_\alpha \text{INA}_{\alpha s_l \beta} A^{l-1\alpha}_{s_1 \ldots s_{l-1}}$$

$$\sum_{(s)} P^l_{(s)j} = \text{alloc}^l_j \quad \wedge \quad \sum_j P^l_{(s)j} = \hat{A}^l_s$$

The validity of this change of variables is proven in Appendix II.

2nd Change: Eliminate Path Indices

Now we eliminate all the exponentially growing derivation path indices *(s)* by eliminating A and P. The change of variables is:

$$x^l = x^l \quad \wedge \quad \text{alloc}_j^l = \text{alloc}_j^l$$

$$\Delta_F: \quad M_{\beta j}^l = \sum_{(s)} A_{(s)}^{l\beta} P_{(s)j}^l$$

$$\text{ina}_{is_l j}^l = \sum_{s_1 \ldots s_{l-1}} P_{s_1 \ldots s_{l-1}, i}^{l-1} P_{s_1 \ldots s_l, j}^l$$

$$\qquad \qquad \qquad \qquad \qquad \qquad (16.13)$$

$$x^l = x^l \quad \wedge \quad \text{alloc}_j^l = \text{alloc}_j^l$$

$$\Delta_B: \quad A_{(s)}^{l\beta} = \sum_j M_{\beta j}^l P_{(s)j}^l \quad \wedge \quad \hat{A}_{(s)}^l = \sum_\beta A_{(s)}^{l\beta}$$

$$P_{()i}^0 = M_{\text{root}\, i}^0$$

$$P_{s_1 \ldots s_l, j}^l = \sum_i \text{ina}_{is_l j}^l P_{s_1 \ldots s_{l-1}, i}^{l-1}$$

This is quadratic in the link variables A, P, M, and ina.

3.4   Frameville with Slots

The resulting objective function and clique diagrams are shown below:

$$E(A, x) = H_0\left(x^0\right)$$

$$+ \sum_{l=1}^{L} \sum_{\alpha\sigma\beta} \sum_{ij} \text{INA}_{\alpha\sigma\beta} \text{ina}_{i\sigma j}^l M_{\alpha i}^{l-1} M_{\beta j}^l$$

$$\times \left[H^{(\alpha\sigma\beta)}\left(x_j^l,\, x_i^{l-1},\, u^{(\alpha\sigma\beta)}\right) - \mu^{(\sigma\beta)} \right] \qquad (16.14)$$

This objective is of polynomial degree five or a little more depending on H. Further reduction down to degree three is possible as in (Mjolsness and Garrett 1990). The constraints for the (M, ina, alloc, x) variables are:

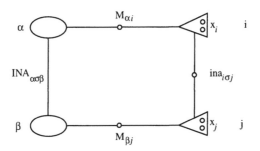

Figure 4   Frameville objective.

M, ina, alloc, INA $\in \{0,\ 1\}$

$$\sum_i M_{\alpha i}^0 = \delta_{\alpha,\,\text{root}} \quad \wedge \quad x_k^L = x_k \quad \wedge \quad \text{alloc}_k^L = \Theta\left(k + \tfrac{1}{2}\right)\Theta\left(k_{\max} - k + \tfrac{1}{2}\right)$$

$$\sum_\beta M_{\beta j}^l = \text{alloc}_j^l$$

$$\sum_{i\sigma} \text{ina}_{i\sigma j}^l = \text{alloc}_j^l$$

$$\sum_j \text{ina}_{i\sigma j}^l = \text{alloc}_i^{l-1}$$

$$\sum_j \text{ina}_{i\sigma j}^l M_{\beta j}^l \leq \sum_\alpha \text{INA}_{\alpha s_l \beta} M_{\alpha i}^{l-1}$$

(16.1

The four constraint cliques relating different kinds of variables are diagrammed as before, in Figure 5. Again, the validity of this change of variables is proven in Appendix II. Note that the $\sum_j \text{ina}_{i\sigma j}^l$ inequalities reflect the possibility of object deletions in the original grammar, which has not been hidden in this particular problem formation.

An earlier version of Frameville (Mjolsness et al. 1989), (Mjolsness 1991), which did not have the slot index σ on INA or *ina* and which specialized INA by restricting it to be a tree, can be derived (for tree INA's) from this version by a further change of variables which we omit. A version including slot indices was related to predicate calculus in (Anandan et al. 1989). Related symbolic optimization architectures include (Malsburg and Bienenstock 1986), (Pinkas 1991), (Stolcke 1989).

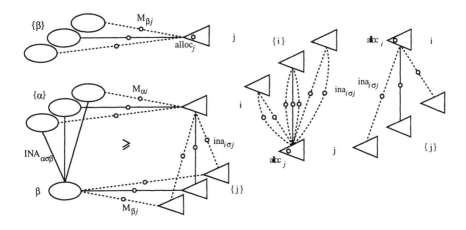

Figure 5   Frameville constraints

Learning in Frameville

Important aspects of the model base such as the constant parameters u and μ which tune the consistency function H, or the INA matrix which specifies the equivalent detailed grammar, may be learned by starting off the recursive object-generation grammar with extra "metagrammar" or "compound grammar" rules which first choose u and/or INA from a prior probability distribution, and then generate a number of scenes (rather than just one as above) which can be used as input to a learning algorithm. The resulting constrained optimization problem for learning the model base parameters u could for example be:

$$E_{\text{learn}}\left(u,\,\mu,\,\{M,\,\text{ina},\,x,\,\text{alloc}\}\,;\text{INA}\right) =$$

$$\sum_{p} E_{\text{recog}}\left(M^{p},\,\text{ina}^{p},\,x^{p},\,\text{alloc}^{p}\,;u,\,\mu,\,\text{INA}\right)$$

$$+\frac{1}{2\sigma_{u}^{2}}\sum_{\alpha\sigma\beta}\left[u^{\alpha\sigma\beta}\right]^{2}+\frac{1}{2\sigma_{u}^{2}}\sum_{\sigma\beta}\left[\mu^{\sigma\beta}\right]^{2}+\tilde{\mu}\sum_{\alpha\sigma\beta}\text{INA}_{\alpha\sigma\beta}$$

$$(16.16)$$

if the prior on u and μ is taken to be Gaussian and that on INA is taken to be independent on each two-valued matrix entry, subject to the INA constraint.

This type of learning problem has been solved efficiently with neural networks for the simpler point-matching problems that arise in nonhierarchical generative grammar models (Gold et al. 1996).

4   CONCLUSION

In this version of the Frameville architecture, by comparison with earlier versions (Mjolsness et al. 1989) (Mjolsness 1994), we can see several advantages and limitations. The depth of a derivation is bounded by the arbitrary integer L. Any number of "distractor" or noise objects can be modelled as parts of a level-one "background" object. The model-side compositional hierarchy $\text{INA}_{\alpha\beta} = \sum_{\sigma} \text{INA}_{\alpha\sigma\beta}$ is a general graph, rather than being limited to a tree or a DAG. The stochastic grammar can be extended to define model-learning as another constrained optimization problem, in which the bias of the learning algorithm is explicitly given by a prior probability distribution on model bases in the compound grammar rather than implicitly given by a neural net wiring diagram. And as before, the number of required variables grows as a low power of the size of the data, and the architecture can be diagrammed with a 3D embedding that suggests control flow strategies.

On the other hand, the Frameville architecture presented here is missing several crucial link types (such as explicit ISA, EQU for equality of frame instances, SIB for siblings in the composition hierarchy, and so on); the data-side dynamic *ina* links are restricted to form a tree (a restriction removed by EQU for translating predicates in (Anandan et al. 1989); see also (Mjolsness et al 1991b); the remaining slot indices σ are inconvenient for large collection objects; all variables remain indexed by their level numbers in the grammar derivation; and we have not exhibited a neural dynamics, or other global constrained optimization algorithm, which can solve the Frameville optimization problems in a scalable way as has been done for less difficult optimization problems.

4.1   Comparison with Other Integration Schemes

Bayesian networks (Pearl 1988) are analogous to derivations of our grammar, in that they have conditionally independent probability distributions forming an underlying stochastic domain model, they can be learned, and they provide a high-level language for integrating multiple process models. They have the important expressive advantage that they are DAGs, rather than trees as our derivations are; so they are "multiple cause models" (Saund 1995). We have formulated context-sensitive deterministic L-system grammars whose derivations are DAGs, for use in biology (Mjolsness et al 1991b), and a similar generalization may be possible here. But in Bayesian networks each node's probability distribution tends to be much less powerful than our Boltzmann distributions, and there is no grammar inducing structure or regularity on the derivation tree. Also there is no analog of the "correspondence" or "variable-binding" problem introduced by relabelling the data according to the random permutation matrix P, which speeds up the computations but limits the expressive power of the Bayesian networks.

A related trend in machine learning is the introduction and formalization of appropriate "structure" in a model class by model-generation procedures. A Minimum Description Length approach to neural net learning (Hinton and Zemel 1994) and Hidden Markov Model-generating neural networks (Baldi and Chauvin 1996) are recent examples. Our grammar schemata may be viewed as procedures for generating models, with appropriate structure, in the following model classes: (1) larger parameterized L-system grammars; (2) simplified semantic networks; (3) Bayesian net-like grammar derivations; (4) constrained optimization problem formulations; and (5) relaxation-based neural networks. A stochastic grammar formalism may be especially expressive in this role.

There are a number of neural network architectures which do variable-binding (Derthick 1990) (Land and Dyer 1988) (Pinkas 1991) (Stolcke 1989), some of which are relaxation-based networks which pose constrained optimization problems. Some of our work on transformations from optimization problems to neural networks could be applied to those systems as well. The stochastic grammar approach avoids the common problem of creating slightly extended implementations of symbolic processing in neural networks, rather than true integration of the advantages of each, by starting with an underlying statistical domain model. From this model emerge domain-specific "distance" or "similarity" measures for pattern recognition and learning on structured objects. If a statistical domain model is simple enough one may derive algorithms close to ordinary neural networks, including learning (Cheng and Titterington 1994). Otherwise, we find mixed logical and numerical processing in a more elaborate architecture. The grammar and therefore the network architecture can be tuned to specific domains (such as high-level vision) by including domain-specific grammar rules (such as the geometric invariances of objects (Mjolsness 1991) which get hard-wired into the resulting neural networks. For highly expressive architectures one generally cannot claim more or less complete expressiveness, only more or less appropriate expressiveness. Further work on the stochastic grammar approach will determine whether such claims should be made about it.

Acknowledgments. Gary Cottrell provided many useful comments in the preparation of this paper. Jennifer Schopf provided considerable assistance with formatting and page layout.

REFERENCES

[1] P. Anandan, S. Letovsky, and E. Mjolsness. Connectionist variable-binding by optimization. *Proceedings of the Cognitive Science Conference*, August 1989.

[2] P. Baldi and Y. Chauvin, Hybrid Modeling, HMM/NN Architectures, and Protein Applications. *Neural Computation*, 8(7):1541-1565, 1996.

[3] B. Cheng and D. M. Titterington. Neural networks: A review from a statistical perspective. *Statistical Sciences*, 9(1):2-54, 1994.

[4] M. Derthick. *Mundane Reasoning by Parallel Constraint Satisfaction*. Morgan-Kaufmann 1990.

[5] S. Gold, A. Rangarajan, and E. Mjolsness. Learning with preknowledge: Clustering with point and graph matching distance measures. *Neural Computation*, 8(4):787-804, 1996.

[6] S. Gold, C. P. Lu, A. Rangarajan, S. Pappu, and E. Mjolsness. New algorithms for 2D and 3D point matching: Pose estimation and correspondence. In: *Neural Information Processing Systems 7*, MIT Press 1995.

[7] G. Hinton and R. Zemel, Autoencoders, Minimum Description Length and Helmholtz Free Energy. *Advances in Neural Information Processing Systems 6*, eds. J. Cowan, G. Tesauro, and J. Alspector, Morgan Kauffman 1994.

[8] J. J. Hopfield. Neurons with graded response have collective computational properties like those of two-state neurons. *Proceedings of the National Academy of Sciences USA*, 81:3088-3092, 1984.

[9] J. J. Kosowsky and A. L. Yuille, The invisible hand algorithm: Solving the assignment problem with statistical physics. *Neural Networks* 7(3):477-490, 1994.

[10] T. Lange, and M. G. Dyer. Dynamic, non-local role-bindings and inferencing in a localist network for natural language understanding. In David S. Touretzky (ed.), *Advances in Neural Information Processing Systems 1*, pp. 545-552. Morgan-Kaufmann, 1988.

[11] C. von der Malsburg and E. Bienenstock. Statistical coding and short-term synaptic plasticity: A scheme for knowledge representation in the brain. In *Disordered Systems and Biological Organization*, 247-252, Springer-Verlag 1986.

[12] E. Mjolsness and C. Garrett. Algebraic transformations of objective functions. *Neural Networks*, 3:651-669, 1990.

[13] E. Mjolsness, C. Garrett, and W. Miranker. Multiscale optimization in neural networks, *IEEE Transactions on Neural Networks* 2(2), March 1991.

[14] E. Mjolsness and W. Miranker. Greedy Lagrangians for Neural Networks: Three Levels of Optimization in Relaxation Dynamics. Technical Report YALEU/DCS/TR-945, Yale Computer Science Department, January 1993.

[15] E. Mjolsness, D. H. Sharp, and J. Reinitz. A connectionist model of development. *Journal of Theoretical Biology*, 152(4):429-454, 1991.

[16] E. Mjolsness. Bayesian inference on visual grammars by neural nets that optimize. Technical Report YALEU/DCS/TR-854, Yale Computer Science Department, May 1991. Available on neuroprose and at URL http://www-cse.ucsd.edu/users/emj .

[17] E. Mjolsness. Connectionist grammars for high-level vision, in *Artificial Intelligence and Neural Networks: Steps Toward Principled Integration*, eds. Vasant Honavar and Leonard Uhr, Academic Press, 1994.

[18] E. Mjolsness, G. Gindi, and P. Anandan. Optimization in model matching and perceptual organization. *Neural Computation* 1(2), 1989.

[19] J. Pearl. *Probabilistic Reasoning in Intelligent Systems: Networks of Plausible Inference.* Morgan-Kaufmann, 1988.

[20] C. Peterson and B. Soderberg. A new method for mapping optimization problems onto neural networks. International Journal of Neural Systems, 1(3), 1989.

[20] G. Pinkas. Energy minimization and the satisfiability of propositional calculus. *Neural Computation* 3(2), 1991.

[21] T. Plate. *Distributed representations and nested compositional structures.* PhD thesis, Department of Computer Science, University of Toronto, 1994.

[22] P. Prusinkiewicz. *The Algorithmic Beauty of Plants.* Springer-Verlag New york, 1990.

[23] E. Saund. A multiple cause mixture model for unsupervised learning. *Neural Computation,* 7(1), 1995.

[24] A. Stolcke. Unification as Constraint Satisfaction in Structured Connectionist Networks. *Neural Computation,* 1(4):559–567, 1989.

[25] D. E. Van den Bout and T. K. Miller, III. Graph partitioning using annealed networks. *IEEE Transactions on Neural Networks,* 1(2):192-203, 1990.

APPENDIX A

We prove the validity, according to the criterion of equation (16.3) with temperature $T = 0$, of the change of variable (16.4) from rule choice variables C to term aliveness variables A..

First we show that the constraints on C (equation (16.2), and the forward change of variables Δ_F (equation (16.4), imply the constraints on A (equation (16.6), i.e. $C_C \wedge \Delta_F \Rightarrow C_A$.

Clearly Δ_F preserves the 0/1-valuedness of all the variables. The condition on $A^{0,\,\alpha}$ is unchanged in C_A from C_C. From $C_C \wedge \Delta_F$ we can calculate $\sum_\beta A^{l\beta}_{(s)} = \omega^l_{(s)}\sum_\beta C^{l\beta}_{(s)} \geq \omega^l_{(s)}\omega^l_{(s)} = \omega^l_{(s)} = \hat{A}^l_{(s)}$; but $\omega^l_{(s)}\sum_\beta C^{l\beta}_{(s)} \leq \omega^l_{(s)}\prod_{k=1}^{l-1}\omega^k_{(s)}$ so $\sum_\beta A^{l\beta}_{(s)} \leq \omega^l_{(s)} = \hat{A}^l_{(s)}$, and we have proven two inequalities implying $\sum_\beta A^{l\beta}_{(s)} = \hat{A}^l_{(s)}$.

The constraints on x and P are direct translations under Δ_F, from C_C to C_A. So we only have to derive the two inequalities on $\tilde{C}$ and A, in C_A. We can calculate $\hat{A}^l_{(s)} + \sum_\beta \tilde{C}^{l\beta}_{(s)} = \sum_\beta A^{l\beta}_{(s)} + \tilde{C}^{l\beta}_{(s)} = \sum_\beta C^{l\beta}_{(s)} \left[\omega^l_{(s)} + 1 - \omega^l_{(s)} \right] = \sum_\beta C^{l\beta}_{(s)}$. But $\sum_\beta C^{l\beta}_{(s)} \leq \prod_{k=1}^{l-1} \omega^k_{(s)}$, which equals $\omega^{l-1}_{(s)}$ for $l \geq 2$ (otherwise $l = 1$ and $\prod = 1 = \hat{A}^0$), which is $\hat{A}^{l-1}_{(s)}$ by Δ_F. This establishes the first inequality. For the second inequality, calculate $A^{l\beta}_{(s)} + \tilde{C}^{l\beta}_{(s)} = C^{l\beta}_{(s)} \left[\omega^l_{(s)} + 1 - \omega^l_{(s)} \right] = C^{l\beta}_{(s)} \omega^{l-1}_{(s)}$, which is$\leq \omega^{l-1}_{(s)} \sum_\alpha \mathrm{INA}_{\alpha s_l \beta} C^{l-1\alpha}_{(s)}$, as required.

So $C_C \wedge \Delta_F \Rightarrow C_A$. Next we must show $C_C \wedge \Delta_F \Rightarrow \Delta_B$. But Δ_B follows trivially from Δ_F alone.

Now we must show that the constraints on A (equation (16.6), and the backward change of variables Δ_B (equation (16.3)), imply the constraints on C (equation (16.2)), i.e. $C_A \wedge \Delta_B \Rightarrow C_C$. Clearly Δ_B preserves the 0/1-valuedness of the ω and P variables. However, the C variables could also take on the value $1+1=2$, except that $C^{l\beta}_{(s)} \leq \sum_\beta C^{l\beta}_{(s)} = \hat{A}^l_{(s)} + \sum_\beta \tilde{C}^{l\beta}_{(s)} \leq \hat{A}^{l-1}_{(s)} \leq 1$.

The constraints on $\sum_\beta C^{l\beta}_{(s)}$ in C_C may be verified as follows. From Δ_B, $\sum_\beta C^{l\beta}_{(s)} = \hat{A}^l_{(s)} + \sum_\beta \tilde{C}^{l\beta}_{(s)} \geq \hat{A}^l_{(s)} = \omega^l_{(s)}$. On the other hand we have already calculated that $\sum_\beta C^{l\beta}_{(s)} = \hat{A}^l_{(s)} + \sum_\beta \tilde{C}^{l\beta}_{(s)} \leq \hat{A}^{l-1}_{(s)}$, which is ≤ 1 for $l = 1$, and $= \omega^{l-1}_{(s)}$ for $l = 2$ (as required for $\sum_\beta C^{l\beta}_{(s)} \leq \prod_{k=1}^{l-1} \omega^k_{(s)}$) and also for all larger values of l. But by induction on l, for $l \geq 2$ we have $\omega^{l-1}_{(s)} = \omega^{l-1}_{(s)} \omega^{l-1}_{(s)} \leq \omega^{l-1}_{(s)} \prod_{k=1}^{l-2} \omega^k_{(s)} = \prod_{k=1}^{l-1} \omega^k_{(s)}$, which establishes $\sum_\beta C^{l\beta}_{(s)} \leq \prod_{k=1}^{l-1} \omega^k_{(s)}$ for all l. As a corollary, we see that $\prod_{k=1}^{l} \omega^k_{(s)} = \omega^{(l-1)l}_{(s)}$, and therefore the constraints on x and P in C_C are a direct translation of those in C_A.

The last constraint in C_C is $C^{l\beta}_{(s)} \leq \sum_\alpha \mathrm{INA}_{\alpha s_l \beta} C^{l-1\alpha}_{(s)}$, which we prove using Δ_B and nonnegativity of $\mathrm{INA}_{\alpha s_l \beta}$ and $\tilde{C}^{l\beta}_{(s)}$: $\sum_\alpha \mathrm{INA}_{\alpha s_l \beta} C^{l-1\alpha}_{(s)} - C^{l\beta}_{(s)} = \sum_\alpha \mathrm{INA}_{\alpha s_l \beta} \left(A^{l-1\alpha}_{(s)} + \tilde{C}^{l-1\alpha}_{(s)} \right) - A^{l\beta}_{(s)} - \tilde{C}^{l\beta}_{(s)} \geq \sum_\alpha \mathrm{INA}_{\alpha s_l \beta} A^{l-1\alpha}_s - A^{l\beta}_{(s)} - \tilde{C}^{l\beta}_{(s)}$, which is ≥ 0 by C_A.

Next we show that $C_A \wedge \Delta_B \Rightarrow \Delta_F$: The conditions on A^0 follow directly from C_A. $\hat{A}^l_{(s)} = \omega^l_{(s)}$ by Δ_B. $C^{l\beta}_{(s)} \omega^l_{(s)} = \left(A^{l\beta}_{(s)} + \tilde{C}^{l\beta}_{(s)} \right) \hat{A}^l_{(s)} = A^{l\beta}_{(s)} \hat{A}^l_{(s)} + \tilde{C}^{l\beta}_{(s)} \hat{A}^l_{(s)}$. Evaluate the summands: $\hat{A}^l_{(s)} = \sum_\beta A^{l\beta}_{(s)}$ implies (for 0/1 variables) that $A^{l\beta}_{(s)} \hat{A}^l_{(s)} = A^{l\beta}_{(s)}$, and $\tilde{C}^{l\beta}_{(s)} \hat{A}^l_{(s)} \leq \hat{A}^l_{(s)} \sum_\beta \tilde{C}^{l\beta}_{(s)} \leq \hat{A}^l_s \left(\hat{A}^{l-1}_{(s)} - \hat{A}^l_{(s)} \right) = \hat{A}^l_{(s)} - $

$\hat{A}^l_{(s)} = 0$, since $\hat{A}^l_{(s)} \leq \hat{A}^l_{(s)} + \sum_\beta \tilde{C}^{l\beta}_{(s)} \leq \hat{A}^{l-1}_{(s)}$. Substituting, we find $A^{l\beta}_{(s)} = C^{l\beta}_{(s)} \omega^l_{(s)}$ as desired. Likewise $C^{l\beta}_{(s)} \left(1 - \omega^l_{(s)}\right) = = \left(A^{l\beta}_{(s)} + \tilde{C}^{l\beta}_{(s)}\right) \left(1 - \hat{A}^l_{(s)}\right) = \tilde{C}^{l\beta}_{(s)} - \tilde{C}^{l\beta}_{(s)} \hat{A}^l_{(s)} + A^{l\beta}_{(s)} \left(1 - \hat{A}^l_{(s)}\right) = \tilde{C}^{l\beta}_{(s)} - 0 + 0$, as desired.

Finally we must translate the objective, assuming $C_C \wedge \Delta_F \wedge C_A \wedge \Delta_B$. Using the calculations in the proof above, we can work out

$$
\begin{aligned}
C^{l\beta}_{s_1\ldots s_l} C^{l-1\alpha}_{s_1\ldots s_l} \left(\prod_{k=1}^{l} \omega^k_{s_1\ldots s_l}\right) &= C^{l\beta}_{s_1\ldots s_l} C^{l-1\alpha}_{s_1\ldots s_l} \omega^l_{(s)} \\
&= \left(A^{l\beta}_{(s)} + \tilde{C}^{l\beta}_{(s)}\right) \left(A^{l-1\alpha}_{(s)} + \tilde{C}^{l-1\alpha}_{(s)}\right) \hat{A}^l_{(s)} \\
&= A^{l\beta}_s A^{l-1\alpha}_s \hat{A}^l_s + \hat{A}^l_s \tilde{C}^{l\beta}_s A^{l-1\alpha}_s + \hat{A}^l_{(s)} \hat{A}^{l-1}_{(s)} \tilde{C}^{l-1\alpha}_{(s)} \left(A^{l\beta}_{(s)} + \tilde{C}^{l\beta}_{(s)}\right) \\
&= A^{l\beta}_s A^{l-1\alpha}_s \hat{A}^l_s + 0 A^{l-1\alpha}_s + \hat{A}^l_{(s)} 0 \left(A^{l\beta}_{(s)} + \tilde{C}^{l\beta}_{(s)}\right) \\
&= A^{l\beta}_s A^{l-1\alpha}_s
\end{aligned}
$$

Substituting this result into equation (16.1), after using $\left(\prod_{k=1}^{l} \omega^k_{s_1\ldots s_l}\right) \omega^l_{(s)} = \prod_{k=1}^{l} \omega^k_{s_1\ldots s_l}$ to simplify the μ term, yields equation (16.5) as desired.

APPENDIX B

We now prove the validity, according to the criterion of equation (16.4) with temperature $T = 0$, of the change of variable (16.9),(16.10) which adds dependent permutation variables P at each level in the hierarchy, and also the change of variable (16.13) which completes the derivation of Frameville.

First we show the validity of the change of variables (16.9), (16.10), from C_A (equation (16.6)) to $C_{A,P}$ (equation (16.12)). For the most part, this change of variables just consists of adding and removing auxiliary variables, i.e. variables in $X\backslash x$ or $Y\backslash y$, in the notation of section 3. These changes would affect the entropy terms (omitted in this paper) in the free energy expressions at nonzero temperature. In C_A, when mapping to $C_{A,\,P}$ via Δ_F, the auxiliary variables are the $\tilde{C}$'s. In $C_{A,\,P}$, when mapping back to C_A via Δ_B, the auxiliary variables are those x_j^l and P_j^l for which $l < L$. Most of the constraints on nonauxiliary variables are explicitly preserved between C_A and $C_{A,\,P}$. There are only a few details to check.

In the forward direction, it is not explicit in C_A that $\hat{A}_{(s)}^l \leq \hat{A}_{(s)}^{l-1}$. It is, however, implicit: $A_{(s)}^{l\beta} \leq A_{(s)}^{l\beta} + \tilde{C}_{(s)}^{l\beta} \leq \sum_\alpha \mathrm{INA}_{\alpha s_l \beta} A_{(s)}^{l-1\alpha} \leq \sum_\alpha \left(A_s^{l-1\alpha} \right) = \hat{A}_{(s)}^{l-1}$; but since $A_s^{l\beta} \in \{0, 1\}$ and $\hat{A}_{(s)}^l = \sum_\beta A_{(s)}^{l\beta} \in \{0, 1\}$, we have $\hat{A}_{(s)}^l = \max_\beta A_s^{l\beta} \leq \max_\beta \hat{A}_{(s)}^{l-1} = \hat{A}_{(s)}^{l-1}$.

We must also check that the required auxiliary variables exist, i.e. that their constraints are consistent. The auxiliary x's are uniquely determined by the regular x's an the auxiliary P's, which are in turn constrained by permutation-like constraints which can be satisfied in many ways. The $\tilde{C}$ variables are constrained by Δ_B to be less than or equal to quantities which are guaranteed by $C_{A,\,P}$ to be nonnegative, so that at least the configuration $\tilde{C} = 0$ is consistent.

Finally we must translate the objective. We first show $A_{(\ s)}^{l\ \ \beta} A_{(\ s)}^{l-1\ \ \alpha} = \mathrm{INA}_{\alpha s_l \beta} A_s^{l\beta} A_{(s)}^{l-1\alpha}$. Since $\sum_\beta A_{(s)}^{l\beta} = \hat{A}_{(s)}^l \in \{0, 1\}$, we know that $A_{(s)}^{l\beta} A_{(s)}^{l\beta'} = \delta_{\beta\beta'} A_{(s)}^{l\beta}$, and likewise $A_{(s)}^{l-1\alpha} A_{(s)}^{l-1\alpha'} = \delta_{\alpha\alpha'} A_{(s)}^{l-1\alpha}$. Therefore

$$
\begin{aligned}
\mathrm{INA}_{\alpha s_l \beta} A_{(s)}^{l\beta} A_{(s)}^{l-1\alpha} \leq A_{(s)}^{l\beta} A_{(s)}^{l-1\alpha} &= A_{(s)}^{l\beta} A_{(s)}^{l\beta} A_{(s)}^{l-1\alpha} \\
&\leq A_{(s)}^{l\beta} \left(\sum_{\alpha'} \mathrm{INA}_{\alpha' s_l \beta} A_{(s)}^{l-1\alpha'} \right) A_{(s)}^{l-1\alpha} \\
&= A_{(s)}^{l\beta} \sum_{\alpha'} \mathrm{INA}_{\alpha' s_l \beta} A_{(s)}^{l-1\alpha'} A_{(s)}^{l-1\alpha} \\
&= A_{(s)}^{l\beta} \sum_{\alpha'} \mathrm{INA}_{\alpha' s_l \beta} \delta_{\alpha\alpha'} A_{(s)}^{l-1\alpha} \\
&= \mathrm{INA}_{\alpha s_l \beta} A_s^{l\beta} A_{(s)}^{l-1\alpha}
\end{aligned}
$$

as desired. Using this fact, and substituting $x_{(s)}^l \sum_j P_{(s)j}^l x_j^l$, we can calculate

$$A_s^{l\beta} A_{(s)}^{l-1\alpha} \left[H^{(\alpha s_l \beta)} \left(x_{(s)}^l, \, x_{(s)}^{l-1}; u^{(\alpha s_l \beta)} \right) - \mu^{(s_l\beta)} \right]$$

$$= \text{INA}_{\alpha s_l \beta} A_s^{l\beta} A_{(s)}^{l-1\alpha}$$

$$\times \left[H^{(\alpha s_l \beta)} \left(\textstyle\sum_j P_{(s)j}^l x_j^l, \, \sum_j P_{(s)i}^{l-1} x_i^{l-1}; u^{(\alpha s_l \beta)} \right) - \mu^{(s_l\beta)} \right]$$

$$= \textstyle\sum_{ij} \text{INA}_{\alpha s_l \beta} A_s^{l\beta} A_{(s)}^{l-1\alpha} P_{(s)j}^l P_{(s)i}^{l-1}$$

$$\times \left[H^{(\alpha s_l \beta)} \left(x_j^l, \, x_i^{l-1}; u^{(\alpha s_l \beta)} \right) - \mu^{(s_l\beta)} \right]$$

in which the last step follows from the winner-take-all constraints $\sum_j P_{(s)j}^l = \hat{A}_{(s)}^l$ and $\sum_i P_{(s)i}^{l-1} = \hat{A}_{(s)}^{l-1}$ for 0/1 variables, in which $\hat{A}_{(s)}^l = 1$ and $\hat{A}_{(s)}^{l-1} = 1$ for any nonzero instance of the above expressions. Substituting this result into the objective of equation (16.5) yields the objective of equation (16.11), as desired. Thus we have proven the validity of the first change of variables.

Now we show the validity of the change of variables (16.13) from $C_{A,\,P}$ (equation (16.12)) to C_M (equation (16.15)). The constraints on x, alloc and INA are unchanged. First we show $C_{A,\,P} \wedge \Delta_F \Rightarrow C_M$. To show that M and ina are 0/1-valued variables, we bound their expressions in Δ_F: $M_{\beta j}^l = \sum_{(s)} A_{(s)}^{l\beta} P_{(s)j}^l \leq \sum_{(s)} P_{(s)j}^l = \text{alloc}_j^l \leq 1$, and $\text{ina}_{is_lj}^l = \sum_{s_1...s_{l-1}} P_{s_1...s_{l-1},\,i}^{l-1} P_{s_1\,...s_l,\,j}^l \leq \sum_{s_1...s_{l-1}} P_{s_1...s_{l-1},\,i}^{l-1} = \text{alloc}_i^{l-1} \leq 1$. The level-0 boundary condition on M is: $\sum_i M_{\alpha j}^l = \sum_{i,\,(s)=()} A_{()}^{0\alpha} P_{()i}^0 = \delta_{\alpha \text{root}} \sum_i P_{()i}^0 = \delta_{\alpha \text{root}} \hat{A}^0 = \delta_{\alpha \text{root}}$, since $\hat{A}^0 = 1$.

For the allocation constraint on M, we calculate that $\sum_\beta M_{\beta j}^l \sum_{(s)} \left(\sum_\beta A_{(s)}^{l\beta} \right) P_{(s)j}^l P_{(s)j}^l \leq \sum_j P_{(s)j}^l = \text{alloc}_j^l$, where we have used $P_{(s)j}^l \leq \sum_j P_{(s)j}^l = \hat{A}_{(s)}^l$. Likewise for the allocation constraints on ina, $\sum_{i\sigma} \text{ina}_{i\sigma j}^l = \sum_{(s)} \left(\sum_i P_{(s)i}^{l-1} \right) P_{(s)j}^l = \sum_{(s)} \hat{A}_{(s)}^{l-1} P_{(s)j}^l = \sum_{(s)} P_{(s)j}^l = \text{alloc}_j^l$, where we have used $\hat{A}_{(s)}^{l-1} P_{(s)j}^l \leq P_{(s)j}^l = P_{(s)j}^l P_{(s)j}^l \leq P_{(s)j}^l \sum_j P_{(s)j}^l = P_{(s)j}^l \hat{A}_{(s)}^l \leq P_{(s)j}^l \hat{A}_{(s)}^{l-1}$. On the other hand, $\sum_j \text{ina}_{i\sigma j}^l = \sum_{(s)} \left(\sum_j P_{(s)j}^l \right) P_{(s)i}^{l-1} = \sum_{(s)} \hat{A}_{(s)}^l P_{(s)i}^{l-1} \leq \sum_{(s)} \hat{A}_{(s)}^{l-1} P_{(s)j}^{l-1} \sum_{(s)} P_{(s)j}^{l-1} = \text{alloc}_i^{l-1}$, where we have used $\hat{A}_{(s)}^{l-1} P_{(s)j}^{l-1} \leq P_{(s)j}^{l-1} = P_{(s)j}^{l-1} P_{(s)j}^{l-1} \leq P_{(s)j}^{l-1} \sum_j P_{(s)j}^{l-1} = P_{(s)j}^{l-1} \hat{A}_{(s)}^{l-1}$.

The rectangle constraint on ina, INA and M is derived in another calculation:

$$\sum_j \text{ina}^l_{i\sigma j} M^l_{\beta j} \;=\; \sum_{(s)} \sum_{(s')} \sum_j A^{l\beta}_{(s')} P^l_{(s')j} P^{l-1}_{(s)i} P^l_{(s\sigma)j}$$

$$=\; \sum_{(s)} \sum_{(s')} A^{l\beta}_{(s')} P^{l-1}_{(s)i} \sum_j P^l_{(s')j} P^l_{(s\sigma)j}$$

$$=\; \sum_{(s)} \sum_{(s')} A^{l\beta}_{(s')} P^{l-1}_{(s)i} \delta_{(s')(s\sigma)} \hat{A}^l_{(s)}$$

$$=\; \sum_{(s)} A^{l\beta}_{(s)} P^{l-1}_{(s)i}$$

$$\leq\; \sum_\alpha \text{INA}_{\alpha\sigma\beta} \sum_{(s)} A^{l-1\alpha}_{(s)} P^{l-1}_{(s)i}$$

$$=\; \sum_\alpha \text{INA}_{\alpha\sigma\beta} M^{l-1}_{\alpha i}$$

So we have shown $C_{A,\,P} \wedge \Delta_F \Rightarrow C_M$. Next we show $C_{A,\,P} \wedge \Delta_F \Rightarrow \Delta_B$. For this we must show $A^{l\beta}_{(s)} = \sum_j M^l_{\beta j} P^l_{(s)j}$ and $P^l_{(s\sigma)j} = \sum_i \text{ina}^l_{i\sigma j} P^{l-1}_{(s)i}$. Substituting from Δ_F, $\sum_j M^l_{\beta j} P^l_{(s)j} = \sum_{(s')} A^{l\beta}_{(s')} \sum_j P^l_{(s')j} P^l_{(s)j} = \sum_{(s')} A^{l\beta}_{(s')} \delta_{(s')(s)} \hat{A}^l_{(s)} = A^{l\beta}_{(s)}$. Likewise, $\sum_i \text{ina}^l_{i\sigma j} P^{l-1}_{(s)i} = \sum_{(s')} P^l_{(s'\sigma)j} \sum_i P^{l-1}_{(s')i} P^{l-1}_{(s)i} = \sum_{(s')} P^l_{(s'\sigma)j} \delta_{(s')(s)} \hat{A}^{l-1}_{(s)} = P^l_{(s\sigma)j}$, as desired. In addition, the relation between A and $\hat{A}$ variables is directly present in $C_{A,\,P}$ and the expression for $P^0_{()i}$ follows from Δ_F: $M^0_{\alpha i} = A^{0\alpha}_{()} P^0_{()i} = \delta_{\alpha\text{root}} P^0_{()i}$. So $C_{A,\,P} \wedge \Delta_F \Rightarrow \Delta_B$.

Now we need to establish the backwards direction, $C_M \wedge \Delta_B \Rightarrow C_{A,\,P} \wedge \Delta_F$, starting with $C_M \wedge \Delta_B \Rightarrow C_{A,\,P}$. That alloc is a 0/1-valued variable is direct. For the A and $\hat{A}$ variables, their expressions are non-negative integers and we can bound them with $A^{l\beta}_{(s\sigma)} \leq \hat{A}^l_{(s\sigma)} = \sum_j \left(\sum_\beta M^l_{\beta j} \right) P^l_{(s\sigma)j} = \sum_j \text{alloc}^l_j P^l_{(s\sigma)j} \leq \sum_j P^l_{(s\sigma)j} = \sum_{ij} \text{ina}^l_{i\sigma j} P^{l-1}_{(s)i} = \sum_i \text{alloc}^{l-1}_i P^{l-1}_{(s)i} = \hat{A}^{l-1}_{(s)}$, which is a 0/1 variable by induction. For the base case, $\hat{A}^0_{()} = \sum_{\alpha i} M^0_{\alpha i} P^0_{()i} = \sum_{\alpha i} M^0_{\alpha i} M^0_{\text{root}i} = \sum_\alpha \delta_{\alpha\text{root}} \sum_i M^0_{\text{root}i} = \sum_\alpha (\delta_{\alpha\text{root}})^2 = 1$, as desired. This proves all the relevant 0/1-valuedness constraints, except those on P.

The summation and 0/1 constraints on P can be established by induction on level number. For l=0, we have $\sum_{()} P^0_{()i} = P^0_{()i} = M^0_{\text{root}i} \leq \sum_\alpha M^0_{\alpha i} = \text{alloc}^0_i$; on the other hand $\sum_\alpha M^0_{\alpha i} = M^0_{\text{root}i} + \sum_{\alpha \neq \text{root}} M^0_{\alpha i} \leq M^0_{\text{root}i} + \sum_{\alpha \neq \text{root}} \left(\sum_i M^0_{\alpha i} \right) = M^0_{\text{root}i}$, so $\sum_{()} P^0_{()i} = \text{alloc}^0_i$. The induction step is: $\sum_{(s\sigma)} P^l_{(s\sigma)j} = \sum_{i\sigma} \text{ina}^l_{i\sigma j} \left(\sum_{(s)} P^{l-1}_{(s)i} \right) = \sum_{i\sigma} \text{ina}^l_{i\sigma j} \text{alloc}^{l-1}_i = \sum_{i\sigma} \text{ina}^l_{i\sigma j} = \text{alloc}^l_j$. From this equality, we can also deduce $\hat{A}^l_{(s)} = \sum_{\beta j} M^l_{\beta j} P^l_{(s)j} = \sum_j \text{alloc}^l_j P^l_{(s)j} = \sum_j P^l_{(s)j}$. Finally $P^l_{(s)j} \leq \sum_j P^l_{(s)j} = \hat{A}^l_{(s)} \leq 1$.

The value of $A^{0\alpha}_{()}$ may be computed as with $\hat{A}^0_{()}$: $A^{0\alpha}_{()} = \sum_i M^0_{\alpha i} P^0_{()i} = \sum_i M^0_{\alpha i} M^0_{\text{root}i} = \delta_{\alpha\text{root}} \sum_i M^0_{\text{root}i} = (\delta_{\alpha\text{root}})^2 = \delta_{\alpha\text{root}}$. That $\hat{A}^l_{(s\sigma)} \leq \hat{A}^{l-1}_{(s)}$ follows from what has already been proven: $\hat{A}^l_{(s\sigma)} = \sum_\beta A^{l\beta}_{(s\sigma)} =$

$$\sum_j \left(\sum_\beta M^l_{\beta j} \right) P^l_{(s\sigma)j} = \sum_j \text{alloc}^l_j P^l_{(\sigma s)j} = \sum_j P^l_{(s\sigma)j} =$$

$$\sum_i \left(\sum_j \text{ina}^l_{i\sigma j} \right) P^{l-1}_{(s)i} \leq \sum_i \text{alloc}^{l-1}_i P^{l-1}_{(s)i} = \sum_i P^{l-1}_{(s)i} = \hat{A}^{l-1}_{(s)}.$$

The last component of $C_{A,P}$ is the INA inequality. It is computed as follows:
$$\hat{A}^l_{(s\sigma)} = \sum_j M^l_{\beta j} P^l_{(s\sigma)j} = \sum_i \sum_j \text{ina}^l_{i\sigma j} M^l_{\beta j} P^{l-1}_{(s)i} = \sum_{\alpha i} \text{INA}_{\alpha\sigma\beta} M^{l-1}_{\alpha i} P^{l-1}_{(s)i} =$$
$$\sum_\alpha \text{INA}_{\alpha\sigma\beta} \sum_i M^{l-1}_{\alpha i} P^{l-1}_{(s)i} = \sum_\alpha \text{INA}_{\alpha\sigma\beta} A^{l-1\alpha}_{(s)}. \text{ So we have proven } C_M \wedge \Delta_B \Rightarrow$$
$C_{A,P}$.

Next we prove $C_M \wedge \Delta_B \Rightarrow \Delta_F$. The expression for ina can be verified simply: $\sum_{(s)} P^l_{(s\sigma)j} P^{l-1}_{(s)i} = \sum_{i'(s)} \text{ina}^l_{i'\sigma j} P^{l-1}_{(s)i'} P^{l-1}_{(s)i} = \sum_{i'} \text{ina}^l_{i'\sigma j} \text{alloc}^{l-1}_i \delta_{ii'} = \text{ina}^l_{i'\sigma j} \text{alloc}^{l-1}_i = \text{ina}^l_{i'\sigma j}$. The expression for M is: $\sum_{(s\sigma)} A^{l\beta}_{(s\sigma)} P^l_{(s\sigma)j} = \sum_{(s\sigma)j'} M^l_{\beta j} P^l_{(s\sigma)j'} P^l_{(s\sigma)j} = \sum_{(s\sigma)j'} M^l_{\beta j} \delta_{j'j} P^l_{(s)j} = \sum_{(s\sigma)} M^l_{\beta j} P^l_{(s\sigma)j} = M^l_{\beta j} \sum_{(s\sigma)i} \text{ina}^l_{i\sigma j} P^{l-1}_{(s)i} = M^l_{\beta j} \sum_{\sigma i} \text{ina}^l_{i\sigma j} \text{alloc}^{l-1}_i = M^l_{\beta j} \text{ina}^l_{i\sigma j} = M^l_{\beta j} \text{alloc}^l_j = M^l_{\beta j}$. The other components of Δ_F are trivial. So we have proven $C_M \wedge \Delta_B \Rightarrow \Delta_F$.

Now we need only translate the objective function. To this end, we use $P^{l-1}_{(s')i} P^{l-1}_{(s)i} = \delta_{(s')(s)} P^{l-1}_{(s)i}$ and $P^l_{(s'\sigma)j} P^l_{(s\sigma)j} = \delta_{(s')(s)} P^l_{(s\sigma)j}$ to calculate

$$\sum_{\alpha\beta} \sum_{ij} \sum_{(s\sigma)} \text{INA}_{\alpha\sigma\beta} A^{l\beta}_{(s\sigma)} A^{l-1\alpha}_{(s)} P^l_{(s\sigma)j} P^{l-1}_{(s)i} H^{(\alpha\sigma\beta)} (x_i, x_j)$$

$$= \sum_{\alpha\beta} \sum_{ij} \sum_{(s\sigma)} \text{INA}_{\alpha\sigma\beta} A^{l\beta}_{(s\sigma)} A^{l-1\alpha}_{(s)} P^l_{(s\sigma)j} P^{l-1}_{(s)i} H^{(\alpha\sigma\beta)} (x_i, x_j)$$

$$= \sum_{\alpha\sigma\beta} \sum_{ij} \sum_{(ss's'')} \text{INA}_{\alpha\sigma\beta} A^{l\beta}_{(s'\sigma)} A^{l-1\alpha}_{(s'')} P^l_{(s''\sigma)j} P^{l-1}_{(s'')i} P^l_{(s\sigma)j} P^{l-1}_{(s)i} H$$

$$= \sum_{\alpha\sigma\beta} \sum_{ij} \text{INA}_{\alpha\sigma\beta} M^l_{\beta j} M^{l-1}_{\alpha i} H^{(\alpha\sigma\beta)} (x_i, x_j) \sum_{(s)} P^l_{(s\sigma)j} P^{l-1}_{(s)i}$$

$$= \sum_{\alpha\sigma\beta} \sum_{ij} \text{INA}_{\alpha\sigma\beta} \text{ina}^l_{i\sigma j} M^l_{\beta j} M^{l-1}_{\alpha i} H^{(\alpha\sigma\beta)} (x_i, x_j)$$

(where we have used the fact that H depends on σ but not (s)) which shows the desired equivalence of objective functions.

PART IV

ACQUIRING DISTRIBUTED
REPRESENTATION

17

STRUCTURE MATCHING AND TRANSFORMATION WITH DISTRIBUTED REPRESENTATIONS

Tony A. Plate

School of Mathematical and Computing Sciences
Victoria University of Wellington

1 INTRODUCTION

One of the barriers to integrating connectionist and symbolic computation is the difficulty of representing recursive structure in a distributed fashion. Hinton (1990) discusses this problem and proposes a framework in which "reduced descriptions" are used to represent parts and wholes in a part-whole hierarchy. Hinton's framework requires that a number of vectors, each a part and together forming a whole, be compressed (reduced) into a single vector of the same dimension as the original vectors. This reduced vector can in turn be used as a part in the representation of some greater whole. The reduction must be reversible so that one can move in both directions in a part-whole hierarchy, i.e., reduce a set of vectors to a single vector (a whole to a part), and expand a single vector to a set of vectors (a part to a whole). In this way, compositional structure can be represented. For reduced descriptions to be truly useful they should be systematically related to their components, so that information about the components can be gleaned from the reduced description without requiring its expansion. It is this property that distinguishes reduced descriptions from pointer-based methods for representing recursive structure, in which the pointer is the "reduced description" but is arbitrary and is unrelated to the components of the object it points to.

Holographic Reduced Representations (HRRs) (Plate 1995) provide an implementation of Hinton's reduced descriptions. In HRRs, circular convolutions are used to construct associations of vectors. These representations of associations differ from those produced by the more familiar outer-product associative operator (as in Smolensky's (1990) Tensor products) in that they are vectors of the same dimensionality as the vectors participating in the associations. This allows the easy construction of representations of objects with recursive structure. HRRs inherit many of the attractive properties of distributed representations of objects, including the ability to represent similar objects by similar representations. In fact, if the objects in two HRRs have similar representations, then the two HRRs will be similar, and the similarity will further depend on the similarity of the structural arrangement of the objects. The most interesting properties of HRRs are related to structural operations that can be performed without unpacking – matching and transformation are described in this chapter.

The next section of this chapter gives a brief overview of HRRs. For more details, consult Plate (1995) or Plate (1994). The third section gives an example of structure matching with HRRs: obtaining fast estimates of the analogical similarity of structured objects. The fourth section describes how HRRs can be transformed structurally without unpacking. The final section compares HRRs to other connectionist representations for complex structure and discuss some general issues.

2   HOLOGRAPHIC REDUCED REPRESENTATIONS

HRRs are a distributed representation for recursive propositional (or frame-like) structures. Objects, predicate labels, and roles are represented by n-dimensional vectors of real numbers. Instantiated propositions are encoded as the sum of role-filler bindings. A binding is the circular convolution (denoted by ⊛) of a role and a filler. The circular convolution of two n-dimensional vectors $\mathbf{x}$[1] and $\mathbf{y}$ ($\mathbf{z} = \mathbf{x} ⊛ \mathbf{y}$) is n-dimensional and has elements

$$z_i = \sum_{k=0}^{n-1} x_k y_{j-k}$$

where subscripts are modulo-n. Circular convolution can be considered as a multiplication operation for vectors, and has algebraic properties in common with scalar and with matrix multiplication: it is associative, commutative, distributive over addition, an identity vector exists, and most vectors have inverses. Circular convolution can also be computed efficiently via the Fast Fourier Transform in $O(nlogn)$ time (see Press, Flannery, Teukolsky, and Vetterling (1992) for algorithms).

---

[1]Bold-face names, e.g., $\mathbf{x}$ are used for vectors.

For example, a simple propositional representation of "Spot bit Jane" is

$$\mathbf{P_{bite}} = \langle \mathbf{bite} + \mathbf{bite_{agt}} \circledast \mathbf{spot} + \mathbf{bite_{obj}} \circledast \mathbf{jane} \rangle,$$

where **bite** is a predicate label, $\mathbf{bite_{agt}}$ and $\mathbf{bite_{obj}}$ are roles, and **jane** and **spot** are fillers. The angle brackets $\langle \cdot \rangle$ indicate that the vector is normalized to have a Euclidean length of one. Bindings do not get confused when added together: $\mathbf{bite_{agt}} \circledast \mathbf{spot} + \mathbf{bite_{obj}} \circledast \mathbf{jane}$ is quite distinct from $\mathbf{bite_{agt}} \circledast \mathbf{jane} + \mathbf{bite_{obj}} \circledast \mathbf{spot}$. Even though some components are associations (the bindings) and some are objects (the predicate label), they are all n-dimensional vectors and can be superimposed straightforwardly. Thus, $\mathbf{P_{bite}}$, the representation for the entire proposition, is also an n-dimensional vector. This makes it simple to use propositions as fillers for roles in other propositions. For example, in the proposition for "Spot bit Jane, which caused Jane to run away from Spot." ($\mathbf{P_{cause}}$, below), $\mathbf{P_{bite}}$ fills the antecedent role of the top-level cause proposition:

$$
\begin{aligned}
\mathbf{P_{bite}} &= \langle \mathbf{bite} + \mathbf{bite_{agt}} \circledast \mathbf{spot} + \mathbf{bite_{obj}} \circledast \mathbf{jane} \rangle \\
\mathbf{P_{flee}} &= \langle \mathbf{flee} + \mathbf{flee_{agt}} \circledast \mathbf{jane} + \mathbf{flee_{from}} \circledast \mathbf{spot} \rangle \\
\mathbf{P_{objects}} &= \langle \mathbf{jane} + \mathbf{spot} \rangle \\
\mathbf{P_{cause}} &= \langle \mathbf{cause} + \mathbf{P_{objects}} + \mathbf{P_{bite}} + \mathbf{P_{flee}} \\
&\quad + \mathbf{cause_{antc}} \circledast \mathbf{P_{bite}} + \mathbf{cause_{cnsq}} \circledast \mathbf{P_{flee}} \rangle
\end{aligned}
$$

The unbound representations for the objects ($\mathbf{P_{objects}}$) and lower-level HRRs ($\mathbf{P_{bite}} + \mathbf{P_{flee}}$) are included in $\mathbf{P_{cause}}$ in order to make the representation for a proposition have some similarity to those objects and other propositions composed of those objects; these components are not necessary for the representation of the structure.

Bindings can be decoded by convolving with the approximate inverse[2] of the role (or filler) vector. For example, the filler in $\mathbf{bite_{agt}} \circledast \mathbf{spot}$ can be found by convolving it with $\mathbf{bite_{agt}^{*}}$ ($\mathbf{x^{*}}$ denotes the approximate inverse of $\mathbf{x}$). The result is a noisy version of **spot**, which must be cleaned up using some sort of autoassociative memory in which the possible fillers have been stored. This clean-up memory must perform closest-match retrieval and must store all vectors, both objects and structures, which can result from decoding a HRR in the system.

---

[2] The exact inverse of a vector under convolution usually exists, but is numerically unstable except under certain conditions. Thus it is usually preferable to use the approximate inverse.

When multiple bindings are superimposed, as in $\mathbf{P_{bite}}$, the other bindings do not interfere with the decoding other than by making it more noisy. The approximate inverse of a vector under convolution is simple to compute: it is a permutation of elements: $\mathbf{x_i^*} = \mathbf{x_{n-i}}$, where subscripts are modulo-n (this is equivalent to reversal of the elements followed by rotation by one position). Thus, like binding, decoding (without cleanup) can be computed in $O(n \log n)$ time.

As a binding operation, convolution has two very useful properties: it is randomizing and similarity preserving. Convolving a role and a filler effectively randomizes with respect to the role and the filler: the binding will not be similar to either the role or the filler (except in special cases). On the other hand, convolution preserves similarity between bindings with similar components: if **jane** is similar to **fred** then **jane** ⊛ **role** will be similar to **fred** ⊛ **role** to approximately the same degree.

The distributed representations for the base-level components, i.e., objects, roles, and labels, are based on random vectors of independently distributed elements with mean zero and variance $1/n$. Representations of similar entities (e.g., **jane** and **fred**) are composed of a base type (**person**) and unique random identifying vectors ($\mathbf{id_{jane}}$ and $\mathbf{id_{fred}}$):

$$\mathbf{jane} = \langle \mathbf{person} + \mathbf{id_{jane}} \rangle$$
$$\mathbf{fred} = \langle \mathbf{person} + \mathbf{id_{fred}} \rangle.$$

The mixing proportions of the various components can be changed to make objects of the same type more or less similar.

HRRs require high-dimensional vectors to work well – even small toy problems require vectors with 512 or 1,024 elements.[3] However, this is not as much of a drawback as it might seem, for two reasons. One reason is that the scaling is very good, thus larger problems do not require much higher dimensionality – tens or hundreds or thousands of objects can be represented using vectors with 2,048 or 4,192 elements. The other reason is that the HRR construction and decoding operations are very fast: binding and decoding can be computed in $O(n \log n)$ time. Clean-up (i.e., finding the closest matching vector in memory) is the only slow operation, but is highly amenable to parallel implementation.

---

[3] Vectors here have dimensions which are powers of 2 only because this makes FFT implementation of convolution simple and efficient.

3   ESTIMATING ANALOGICAL SIMILARITY VIA DOT PRODUCTS OF HRRS

The superficial features of HRRs can reflect their structural composition: if the entities in structures are similar, then the HRRs are similar to the degree that their structures are similar. This allows the estimation of degree of structural match by the dot product of vectors (HRRs). The sensitivity of this representation to various aspects of structural similarity is illustrated using the examples shown in Table 1. These examples are elaborations on an example in Thagard, Holyoak, Nelson, and Gochfeld (1990). The episodes **E1–E5** have different degrees of similarity to the probe on attributes (first-order features), role alignment, and higher-order structure.

Probe:		Spot bit Jane, causing Jane to flee from Spot.	Average dot product with probe		
Episodes for comparison:			Expt1	Expt2	Expt3
E1	LS	Fido bit John, causing John to flee from Fido.	0.70	0.63	0.81
E2	AN^{cm}	Fred bit Rover, causing Rover to flee from Fred.	0.47	0.47	0.69
E3	AN	Felix bit Mort, causing Mort to flee from Felix.	0.39	0.39	0.61
E4	SF	John fled from Fido, causing Fido to bite John.	0.47	0.44	0.53
E5	FOR	Mort bit Felix, causing Mort to flee from Felix.	0.39	0.39	0.39

Table 1   Results of Experiments 1, 2 and 3.

In these episodes Jane, John, and Fred are people; Spot, Fido and Rover are dogs; Felix is a cat; and Mort is a mouse. All of these are *objects*, represented by *token* vectors. Tokens of the same type are considered to be similar to each other, but not to tokens of other types. Bite, flee, and cause are *relations* (i.e., propositions). The argument structure of the cause relation, and the patterns in which objects fill multiple roles constitutes the *higher-order* structure.

The second column classifies the relationship between each episode and the probe using Gentner et al.'s (1993) types of similarity: LS (Literal Similarity) shares relations, object features, and higher-order structure; AN (Analogy, also called True Analogy) shares relations and higher-order structure, but not object features; SF (Surface Feature Similarity, also called Mere Appearance) shares relations and object features, but not higher-order structure; FOR (First-Order Relations or False Analogy) shares relations only. AN^{cm} denotes a *cross-mapped* analogy – it involves the same types of objects as the probe, but the types of corresponding objects are swapped.

The figures shown in Table 1 are the averages over 100 runs, where each run involves a different choice of the random base vectors, and all vectors have $2,048$ elements. The standard deviations of the dot products range from 0.016 to 0.025.

The results for Experiment 1 were obtained with the HRRs constructed as described in Section 2. The literally similar episode **E1**, which is both structurally isomorphic and attributionally similar to the probe, receives the highest score. The superficially similar episode **E4** involves the same predicates and objects as the literally similar episode **E1**, but the higher order structure of **E4** does not match the probe, and it scores lower. The cross-mapped analogous episode **E2** is structurally isomorphic to the probe. However, the types (dog, person, etc.) of corresponding fillers are swapped, which prevents the structural similarity from influencing the dot product, and thus the cross-mapped analogous episode **E2** scores the same as the superficially similar **E4**, which is not structurally isomorphic to the probe. The analogous episode **E3** is also structurally isomorphic to the probe, but none of the objects are similar. Consequently, its structural similarity also does not influence the dot product, and it scores the same as **E5** which only shares relations (and not structure or objects) with the probe.

The superficially similar episode **E4** is attributionally more similar to the probe than the analogous episode **E3** since both **E4** and the probe involve "dog bites person." However, the role alignment of **E4** and the probe is worse: in both **E3** and the probe the bitee flees, but in **E4** the biter flees. The representation as described so far is not sensitive to role alignment, so the superficially similar **E4** achieves a higher score.

3.1   Filler Contextualization (Experiments 2 and 3)

One way to make role structure a surface feature, and thus allow judgement of role alignment by dot-product comparison, is to *contextualize* the representations of fillers. This can be done by incorporating components in the representation of a filler that indicate what other roles it is involved in. This can be viewed as conceptualizing Jane in the probe as a person who flees (a fleer) and a person who gets bitten (a bitee). The degree to which this is done is governed by a mixing proportion, κ. High values of κ correspond to representing Jane mostly by context. The salience of role alignment in a comparison can be altered by changing just κ_p, the κ value used in the probe. The items for comparison can be encoded with a fixed κ, which is fortunate because it would often be impractical to recode all items the probe is being compared against (which could be all the episodes stored in a large data-base) in order to alter the salience of role alignment.

In ordinary HRRs the filler alone is convolved with the role. In contextualized HRRs a blend of the filler and its context is convolved with the role. The context of object in a particular role is defined as the *other* roles the object fills. For example, the context for Spot in the **flee** relation is represented by **context**$_{\text{biter}}$ and the context in the **bite** relation is represented by **context**$_{\text{fled-from}}$.[4] For the purposes of contextualization, the choice of representations for contexts is arbitrary. In the experiments described here role context is the convolution of the predicate label and the approximate inverse of the role, e.g., **context**$_{\text{biter}}$ = **bite** $\circledast$ **bite**$^*_{\text{agt}}$ and **context**$_{\text{fled-from}}$ = **flee** $\circledast$ **flee**$^*_{\text{from}}$. This representation was chosen because it is always a component of the corresponded decoded filler – **bite** $\circledast$ **bite**$^*_{\text{agt}}$ is always produced when a bite agent is decoded. The contextualized filler is the weighted sum of context and filler (the weights are κ and $\sqrt{1 - \kappa^2}$, so that the expected Euclidean length is one). The contextualized HRR for the probe is constructed as follows:

$$\mathbf{P}'_{\text{bite}} = \; < \mathbf{bite} + \mathbf{bite_{agt}} \circledast (\sqrt{1 - \kappa^2_p}\mathbf{spot} + \kappa_p\mathbf{context_{fled-from}})$$
$$+ \; \mathbf{bite_{obj}} \circledast (\sqrt{1 - \kappa^2_p}\mathbf{jane} + \kappa_p\mathbf{context_{fleer}}) >$$

$$\mathbf{P}'_{\text{flee}} = \; < \mathbf{flee} + \mathbf{flee_{agt}} \circledast (\sqrt{1 - \kappa^2_p}\mathbf{jane} + \kappa_p\mathbf{context_{bitee}})$$
$$+ \; \mathbf{flee_{from}} \circledast (\sqrt{1 - \kappa^2_p}\mathbf{spot} + \kappa_p\mathbf{context_{biter}}) >$$

$$\mathbf{P}'_{\text{objects}} = \; < \mathbf{jane} + \mathbf{spot} >$$
$$\mathbf{P}'_{\text{cause}} = \; < \mathbf{cause} + \mathbf{P}'_{\text{objects}} + \mathbf{P}'_{\text{bite}} + \mathbf{P}'_{\text{flee}}$$
$$+ \; \mathbf{cause_{antc}} \circledast \mathbf{P}'_{\text{bite}} + \mathbf{cause_{cnsq}} \circledast \mathbf{P}'_{\text{flee}} >$$

The figures for Experiments 2 and 3 in the table show results obtained for the probe without and with contextualization (Experiment 2 has $\kappa_p = 0$ and

---

[4]It is possible to use the same context in all sub-propositions. This results in terms like **bite**$_{\text{agt}}$ $\circledast$ **context**$_{\text{biter}}$ which are superfluous because they always occur together with the predicate label **bite** and thus do not impart any additional information.

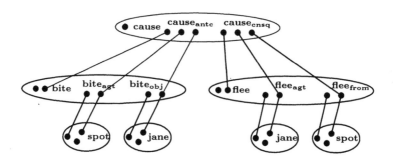

Figure 1 Binding chains for $\mathbf{P_{cause}}$.

Experiment 3 has $\kappa_p = \sqrt{0.5}$). In both Experiments 2 and 3 the items for comparison (**E1–E5**) are encoded with $\kappa = \sqrt{0.5}$, which gives contexts and fillers equal weights in the contextualized fillers.

Note that with no contextualization in the probe and contextualization in the episodes (Experiment 2) the ranking of dot products is the same as when no contextualization is used at all. This is because the contextualized terms in the episodes do not match any terms in the uncontextualized probe and thus are effectively ignored. With contextualization in the probe (Experiment 3), the cross-mapped analogy **E2**, which has matching role alignment but less attribute similarity, becomes more similar to the probe than the superficially similar **E4**, which has more attribute similarity, but non-matching role alignment. Likewise, the structurally similar **E3** also becomes more similar to the probe than both the superficially similar **E4** and the false analogy **E5**.

3.2   Why the HRR Dot Product Reflects Structural Similarity

The HRR for an episode can be expanded to a weighted sum of convolution products. This is illustrated for $\mathbf{P_{cause}}$ in Figure 1. These convolution products contain one or more entities and correspond to the binding chains (hierarchical role/filler paths) in the episode. Consideration of the binding chains shows both why the HRR dot product reflects structural similarity in the presence of similar objects and why it is an unreliable indicator in their absence. Two binding chains (convolution products) are similar if the entities in them are similar. Consequently, the HRRs for two episodes are similar if they have similar binding chains.

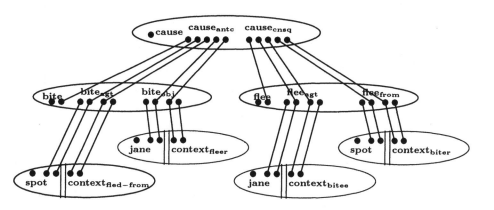

Figure 2   Binding chains for P'_{cause} (the contextualized version of P_{cause}).

The HRR for the uncontextualized probe (Figure 1) is the weighted sum of binding chains (connected dots) and singletons. For example, the rightmost binding chain is $cause_{cnsq} \circledast flee_{from} \circledast spot$. Roles and fillers can be in more than one binding chain.

Literally similar episodes have similar fillers in similar roles and thus will have many similar binding chains, e.g., $cause_{cnsq} \circledast flee_{from} \circledast spot$ from the probe and $cause_{cnsq} \circledast flee_{from} \circledast fido$ from **E1** (these are similar because **spot** and **fido** are similar).

However, by definition analogous episodes do not have similar objects – if episodes share structure and objects they are literally similar. Thus their ordinary (uncontextualized) HRRs will not have many similar binding chains – the structurally corresponding chains are not similar because they involve objects of different types, e.g., $cause_{cnsq} \circledast flee_{from} \circledast spot$ from the probe and $cause_{cnsq} \circledast flee_{from} \circledast felix$ from **E3** (since **spot** and **felix** are not similar).

Superficially similar episodes have some similar fillers in similar roles and thus may still have quite a few similar binding chains. E.g, the superficially similar episode **E4** and the probe both have binding chains for dogs in the agent role of bite ($bite_{agt} \circledast spot$ and $bite_{agt} \circledast fido$), which are similar since the representations for the two dogs are similar.

As shown in Figure 2, contextualization nearly doubles the number of binding chains in the HRR for an episode (and would increase their number more if some entities were involved in more than two relations). The extra binding chains, like $\mathbf{cause_{antc}} \circledast \mathbf{bite_{obj}} \circledast \mathbf{context_{fleer}}$, encode the patterns in which objects fill multiple roles. Analogous episodes will share these binding chains even if the corresponding objects are dissimilar, thus making the HRR dot-product sensitive to this type of structural similarity.

3.3 The Importance of Structural Matching

The ability to perform analogical, or structural, matching is not an esoteric, seldom used ability. Rather, it is essential to any reasoning system based on rules or cases. Rule following requires the ability to perform structural matches between a description of some specific situation and an abstract description of a general situation, and case-based reasoning requires the matching of descriptions at the same level of abstraction. These types of reasoning also require the ability to identify correspondences between descriptions, which can be done with HRRs (Plate 1994). The structural classifications described by Sperdutti, Starita and Goller in Chapter 18 are another example of structural matching between abstract templates and specific instances.

4 TRANSFORMATIONS WITHOUT DECOMPOSITION

One of properties of reduced representations which makes them interesting is the possibility of operating on them without decomposition. This is a type of fast computation with no obvious parallel in conventional symbol manipulation. Various authors have demonstrated that structural transformations without decoding can be performed on Pollack's (1990) RAAMs and on Smolensky's (1990) tensor-product representations. Pollack (1990) trained a feedforward network to transform reduced descriptions for propositions like (LOVED X Y) to ones for (LOVED Y X), where the reduced descriptions were found by a RAAM. Chalmers (1990) trained a feedforward network to transform reduced descriptions for simple passive sentences to ones for active sentences, where again the reduced descriptions were found by a RAAM. Niklasson and van Gelder (1994) trained a feedforward network to do material conditional inference (and its reverse) on reduced descriptions found by a RAAM. This involves transforming reduced descriptions for formulae of the form $(A \rightarrow B)$ to ones of the form $(\neg A \lor B)$ (and vice-versa). Legendre, Miyata, and Smolensky (1991) showed how tensor product representations for active sentences could be transformed to ones for passive sentences (and vice-versa) by a pre-calculated linear transformation. Dolan (1989) showed how multiple variables could be instantiated in parallel, again using a pre-computed linear transformation.

It is straightforward to do transformations like these with HRRs. Consider Niklasson and van Gelder's task, which was to perform the following transformations:

$$
\begin{aligned}
p \rightarrow q &\Rightarrow (\neg p \vee q) \\
(\neg p \vee q) &\Rightarrow (p \rightarrow q) \\
(p \rightarrow (q \vee r)) &\Rightarrow (\neg p \vee (q \vee r)) \\
(\neg p \vee (q \vee r)) &\Rightarrow (p \rightarrow (q \vee r)) \\
(p \rightarrow (q \rightarrow r)) &\Rightarrow (\neg p \vee (q \rightarrow r)) \\
(\neg p \vee (q \rightarrow r)) &\Rightarrow (p \rightarrow (q \rightarrow r))
\end{aligned}
$$

These formulas can be represented by two relations: implication and disjunction. Implication has two roles, antecedent and consequent, and disjunction also has two roles, negative (negated) and positive (these can be duplicated). The following HRRs represent $(\neg p \vee q)$ and $(p \rightarrow (q \vee r))$:

$$
\begin{aligned}
\mathbf{R}_{\neg p \vee q} &= \langle \mathbf{disj} + \mathbf{neg} \circledast \mathbf{p} + \mathbf{pos} \circledast \mathbf{q} \rangle \\
\mathbf{R}_{p \rightarrow (q \vee r)} &= \langle \mathbf{impl} + \mathbf{ante} \circledast \mathbf{p} + \mathbf{cnsq} \circledast \langle \mathbf{disj} + \mathbf{pos} \circledast \mathbf{q} + \mathbf{pos} \circledast \mathbf{r} \rangle \rangle
\end{aligned}
$$

To transform an implication into a disjunction, three changes are necessary: **impl** must be changed to **disj**, **ante** $\circledast$ **x** must be changed to **neg** $\circledast$ **x**, and **cnsq** $\circledast$ **y** must be changed to **pos** $\circledast$ **y**. The first change can be accomplished by convolving the implication with $\mathbf{impl}^* \circledast \mathbf{disj}$, the second by convolving with $\mathbf{ante}^* \circledast \mathbf{neg}$, and the third by convolving with $\mathbf{cnsq}^* \circledast \mathbf{pos}$. In all cases, there are other convolution products such as $\mathbf{impl}^* \circledast \mathbf{disj} \circledast \mathbf{ante} \circledast \mathbf{x}$, but these products can be treated as noise. These three vectors can be superimposed to give a vector which transforms implications to disjunctions:

$$
\mathbf{t_1} = \langle \mathbf{impl}^* \circledast \mathbf{disj} + \mathbf{ante}^* \circledast \mathbf{neg} + \mathbf{cnsq}^* \circledast \mathbf{pos} \rangle.
$$

When $\mathbf{R}_{p \rightarrow q}$ is convolved with $\mathbf{t_1}$, it gives a noisy version of $\mathbf{R}_{\neg p \vee q}$. A similar vector can be constructed to transform disjunctions to implications:

$$
\mathbf{t_2} = \langle \mathbf{disj}^* \circledast \mathbf{impl} + \mathbf{neg}^* \circledast \mathbf{ante} + \mathbf{pos}^* \circledast \mathbf{cnsq} \rangle.
$$

The transformation vectors t_1 and t_2 can be superimposed to give one vector which will transform implications to disjunctions and disjunctions to implications:

$$t = \langle t_1 + t_2 \rangle.$$

This results in more noise products, but these will not make the result unrecognizable if the vector dimension is high enough. The strength of non-noise components in the transformed HRR is $1/\sqrt{k}$ times their strength in the original HRR, where k is the number of components in the transformation vector ($k = 6$ for t).

A simulation of the above task was run, with results checked by decoding their various roles. For example, $t \circledast R_{p \rightarrow (q \rightarrow r)}$ should give $R_{\neg p \vee (q \rightarrow r)}$, which should decode as follows:

$$
\begin{aligned}
t \circledast R_{p \rightarrow (q \vee r)} &\approx \text{disj} \\
t \circledast R_{p \rightarrow (q \vee r)} \circledast neg^* &\approx p \\
t \circledast R_{p \rightarrow (q \vee r)} \circledast pos^* &\approx \text{impl} \\
t \circledast R_{p \rightarrow (q \vee r)} \circledast pos^* \circledast ante^* &\approx q \\
t \circledast R_{p \rightarrow (q \vee r)} \circledast pos^* \circledast cnsq^* &\approx r
\end{aligned}
$$

The various formulae were tried with all possible instantiations of five different variables, which gave 550 different formulae, and 4,800 retrieval tests. For 10 runs with $n = 4,096$, there were an average of 1.2 retrieval errors per run (out of 4,800). Five of the runs had no errors. With lower dimensions, there were more errors. For example, with $n = 2,048$ there were an average of 58.5 retrieval errors per run (over 10 runs).

It turns out that the most difficult thing to do is to leave something untransformed. This is because when one component is left untransformed, all the other components superimposed with it are left untransformed as well. Consider the goal of changing all occurrences of x to y, but leaving other components untransformed. This requires a transformation vector like

$$t = x^* \circledast y + I.$$

The identity vector must be included so that the result will have an untransformed component of the original. However, this cannot target particular bindings in the original – it applies generally. Thus, when it is applied to a HRR like

$$R = x \circledast a + z \circledast b$$

it gives

$$t \circledast R = y \circledast a + x \circledast a + z \circledast b + noise.$$

This problem does not arise when all components are transformed because in that case, the cross terms can be regarded as noise (they will be extremely unlikely to be similar to any other vectors in the system). The only way to solve the problem is to do transformations separately and clean up intermediate results. It would be interesting to see whether a similar difficulty arises with representations developed by RAAMs.

One thing to note when considering transformations on structures is that the result of a transformation will be noisy, and usually can only be cleaned up by decoding and reassembly. This is because the transformed structure will most likely be novel and thus cannot have been stored in clean-up memory. This is different from the situation where chunked structures are decoded, and decoded structures can be cleaned up because they are stored in the clean-up memory.

5 DISCUSSION

5.1 Advantages of Distributed Representations

Holographic Reduced Representations retain nearly all the advantages of distributed representations for objects. Firstly, there is a simple and computationally efficient measure of similarity between two distributed representations: the vector dot product. Similar items can be represented by similar vectors.

Secondly, items are represented in a continuous space. This has two distinct benefits: it allows continuously varying differences in similarity between items, and the representations can be used in systems which learn using gradient descent techniques.

Thirdly, information in the vector is distributed and redundant. This has several benefits: the representations of multiple items can be superimposed – individual items are degraded but still can be recognized; the representations degrade gracefully as noise is added; and redundancy makes it possible to clean up degraded representations using an error-correcting associative memory.

5.2   Scaling properties of HRRs

There are two constraints which determine the scaling properties of HRRs (see Plate (1994) for details):

- The number of components which can be included in one HRR scales linearly with the vector dimension n.

- The number of HRRs (chunks) which can be stored in clean-up memory scales exponentially with n.

The first constraint tends to be the limiting one, so chunks must be kept to a reasonable size. Note that the "number of components" in a HRR depends on the chunking and decoding strategies used. The only components which count towards the size of a chunk are those which must be directly decoded without intermediate cleanup: components inside chunks do not count. Thus, chunking allows structures of unlimited depth to be represented in HRRs.

For toy problems, HRRs seem to require very large vectors compared with other schemes. For example, in the structural-similarity experiments the vectors had 2,048 elements. However, in these experiments the limiting factor on capacity was the number of components in an HRR – with this dimensionality many thousand HRRs can be stored in clean-up memory. A toy problem with a large number of objects in memory in given in Plate (1994). The task involves memorizing times and addition tables for numbers from 1 to 50 and retrieving them based on partial cues. Just over 5,000 objects were stored in memory (2,500 numbers, and just over 2,500 relations). The vector dimension was 512, and no errors were made in over 10,000 trials of retrieving and decoding a relation based on partial information. The vector dimension was low compared with the structural similarity task because chunks only had a maximum of 3 components.

5.3   Chunking

Chunking, i.e., breaking large structures in pieces of manageable size, is readily implementable with HRRs. Chunking makes it possible to use HRRs to store structures of unlimited size, and HRRs provide a method for chunking that has some very attractive properties.

As more items and bindings are stored in a single HRR, the noise on extracted items increases. If too many associations are stored, the quality will be so low that the extracted items will be easily confused with similar items or, in extreme cases, completely unrecognizable. The number of items and bindings in a HRR grows with both the height and width of the structure being represented – $\mathbf{P_{bite}}$ (in Section 2) has 3, while $\mathbf{P_{cause}}$ has 15 (expanded out to the level of **bite**, **bite$_{agt}$**, **spot**, etc.) The number of items and bindings that can be stored for a given degree of quality of decoding grows linearly with the vector dimension (Plate 1994), but using vectors with very high dimension is not a satisfactory way to store large structures. A far superior way is to use chunk information. This involves storing substructures in the clean-up memory, and using them when decoding components of complex structures. For example, to decode the agent of the antecedent of $\mathbf{P_{cause}}$, the antecedent is extracted first. This gives a noisy version of $\mathbf{P_{bite}}$, which can be cleaned up by accessing clean-up memory and retrieving the closest match (which should be $\mathbf{P_{bite}}$). This gives an accurate version of $\mathbf{P_{bite}}$ from which the filler of the agent role can be extracted. Using chunks during decoding like this reduces the effective number of items and bindings in HRRs and thus makes it possible to store structures of nearly unlimited size (although of course the number of chunks in clean-up memory grows with the size of the structure).

Any system that uses chunks must have also have a way of referring, or pointing to the chunks. HRRs provide a very attractive way of constructing chunks because a HRR can provide pointer information, but can also provide information about its contents without dereferencing any pointers. This is what the "reduced" in "Holographic Reduced Representation" refers to – a HRR is a compressed, or reduced, version of the structure it represents. The advantage of having a pointer which encodes some information about what it refers to is that some operations can be performed without following the pointer. This can save much time. For example, nested fillers can be decoded quickly without clean up of intermediate results if very noisy results are acceptable, or the similarity of two structures can be estimated without decoding the structures.

5.4   Comparison to Other Distributed Representations for Propositions

HRRs have much in common with Smolensky's (1990) tensor product representation for propositions: both use a multiplication-like operator to bind together role and filler vectors, both superimpose multiple role-filler bindings to represent propositions, and the algebra of the binding operations is very similar. The major difference between HRRs and tensor products is that the dimensions of HRRs do not expand under recursive composition, because HRRs use reduced descriptions and chunking to represent nested structures. However, keeping the dimensionality of vectors constant has a price: decoding is noiser in HRRs than in tensor products. The high dimensionality of tensor products also allows manipulations like rebinding multiple variables in parallel, which can also be done in HRRs, though the noise is considerable.

HRRs also have much in common with Pollack's (1990) RAAMs. In fact, Smolensky (1990)[5] pointed out that RAAMs can also be viewed as a role-filler binding representation for propositions: the roles are the input-to-hidden weights, the binding operation is matrix-by-vector multiplication.

The major differences between HRRs and RAAMs are as follows:

- RAAMs learn how to encode structures (by learning role matrices using error backpropagation). Consequently, RAAMs may possibly make better use of the representation space – they certainly use lower-dimensional vectors than HRRs. However, the learning is slow.

- RAAMs use a nonlinear operation in encoding. This makes it difficult to analyze scaling properties and to predict how RAAMs will work with novel vectors without trying them out. In contrast, HRRs use a bilinear operation for encoding. Scaling properties of HRRs are easily analyzed, as is performance on novel vectors.

- RAAMs do not use an explicit clean-up memory, although the sigmoid on the output can be regarded as a type of cleanup. Consequently, RAAMs do not provide chunking. They are also very sensitive to noise and require increasing precision to represent deeper structures. In contrast, HRRs allow chunking, and are quite robust to noise and quantization error due to limited precision.

- RAAMs use fixed roles and can only represent predicates of fixed arity. HRRs allow predicates of any arity and a great variety of roles. Furthermore, in HRRs similarity of roles can be expressed through similarity of role vectors.

Another way of representing bindings in connectionist networks is through temporal synchrony in unit activations, as in Hummel and Biederman (1992). However, as Hummel and Holyoak acknowledge, dynamic binding is impractical for

---

[5]Personal communication

storing bindings in long-term memory. Thus, an additional binding principle, and means for translating between representations in long- and short-term memory is still needed. Shastri and Ajjanagadde (1993) describe a method for doing this with localist representations, but it seems unlikely that this method could be used with distributed representations, because it requires intricate connectivity among various types of nodes. Another point about dynamic binding is that it does not provide any systematic method for constructing informative chunk labels.

5.5   The Essence of HRRs

HRRs are intended more as an illustration of how convolution and superposition can be used to represent complex structure than as a strict specification of how complex structure should be represented. The essence of HRRs is as follows:

- It is a distributed representation.

- Proposition-like objects are represented as the superposition of role-filler bindings (and possibly some additional information).

- The representation of a compositional object has the same dimension as the representation of each of its components.

- Roles and fillers are bound together with associative memory operation, like circular convolution, which does not increase dimensionality and is randomizing and similarity preserving.

In any particular domain or application, choices must be made about what will and will not be included in the representation, and about how the representation will be structured. The HRRs described in this chapter consisted of the superposition of fillers and further bindings derived from the context of fillers. In other domains, fewer or different HRR components might be appropriate.

6   SUMMARY

Memory models using circular convolution provide a way of representing compositional structure in distributed representations. They implement Hinton's (1990) suggestion that reduced descriptions should have microfeatures that are systematically derived from those of their constituents. HRRs preserve natural similarity structure – similar structures are represented by similar HRRs. The operations involved are mostly linear and thus the properties of encoding and decoding are amenable to mathematical analysis. What makes these representations particularly interesting and potentially useful is that structural operations, such as matching and transformation, can be performed on structures without unpacking their contents.

REFERENCES

[1] Chalmers, D. J. (1990). Syntactic transformations on distributed representations. *Connection Science 2*(1 & 2), 53–62.

[2] Dolan, C. P. (1989). Tensor manipulation networks: Connectionist and symbolic approaches to comprehension, learning, and planning. Computer Science Department, AI Lab. Technical Report UCLA-AI-89-06, UCLA.

[3] Gentner, D., M. J. Rattermann, and K. D. Forbus (1993). The roles of similarity in transfer: Separating retrievability from inferential soundness. *Cognitive Psychology 25*(4), 524–575.

[4] Hinton, G. E. (1990). Mapping part-whole heirarchies into connectionist networks. *Artificial Intelligence 46*(1-2), 47–76.

[5] Hummel, J. E. and I. Biederman (1992). Dynamic binding in a neural network for shape recognition. *Psychological Review 99*(3), 480–517.

[6] Hummel, J. E. and K. J. Holyoak (1992). Indirect analogical mapping. In *Proceedings of the Fourteenth Annual Cognitive Science Society Conference*, pp. 516–521.

[7] Legendre, G., Y. Miyata, and P. Smolensky (1991). Distributed recursive structure processing. In D. Touretzky and R. Lippman (Eds.), *Advances in Neural Information Processing Systems 3*, San Mateo, CA, pp. 591–597. Morgan Kaufmann.

[8] Niklasson, L. and T. van Gelder (1994). Can connectionist models exhibit non-classical structure sensitivity? In *Proceedings of the Sixteenth Annual Conference of The Cognitive Science Society*.

[9] Plate, T. A. (1994). *Distributed Representations and Nested Compositional Structure*. Ph. D. thesis, Department of Computer Science, University of Toronto. Available at http://www.cs.utoronto.ca/~tap.

[10] Plate, T. A. (1995). Holographic reduced representations. *IEEE Transactions on Neural Networks 6*(3), 623–641.

[11] Pollack, J. B. (1990). Recursive distributed representations. *Artificial Intelligence 46*(1-2), 77–105.

[12] Press, W. H., B. P. Flannery, S. A. Teukolsky, and W. T. Vetterling (1992). *Numerical Recipes in C* (Second ed.). Cambridge: Cambridge University Press.

[13] Shastri, L. and V. Ajjanagadde (1993). From simple associations to systematic reasoning: A connectionist representation of rules, variables and dynamic bindings using temporal synchrony. *Behavioral and Brain Sciences 16*(3), 417–494.

[14] Smolensky, P. (1990). Tensor product variable binding and the representation of symbolic structures in connectionist systems. *Artificial Intelligence 46*(1-2), 159–216.

[15] Sperduti, A., A. Starita, and C. Goller (1997). Distributed representations for terms in hybrid reasoning systems. Chapter 18 in this volume.

[16] Thagard, P., K. J. Holyoak, G. Nelson, and D. Gochfeld (1990). Analog Retrieval by Constraint Satisfaction. *Artificial Intelligence 46*, 259–310.

18

DISTRIBUTED REPRESENTATIONS FOR TERMS IN HYBRID REASONING SYSTEMS

Alessandro Sperduti[◇]

Antonina Starita[◇]

Christoph Goller[△]

[◇] *Computer Science Department, University of Pisa*

[△] *Institut für Informatik, Technische Universität München*

1 INTRODUCTION

Hybrid systems integrating symbolic and connectionist components should profit from the advantages and strengths of both approaches. The strength of classical symbolic AI lies in *deductive* reasoning (e.g., expert systems, planning systems, deductive data bases, theorem provers, logic programming). Symbolic systems are based on well-defined and sound logical calculi and allow deep inference chains. This seems infeasible for connectionist systems. Connectionism, on the other hand, offers very successful approaches for *inductive* learning and generalization and a well-defined concept of similarity (distance in real-valued vector spaces).

We think that deductive reasoning cannot work in a reasonable way without being complemented by inductive reasoning (and probably vice versa). One reason for this is that usually symbolic reasoning systems perform brute force search and suffer from a *combinatorial explosion* of the search space[1] or even undecidability, at least if their expressiveness is first order predicate logic or higher. Therefore *heuristics* and *strategies* are needed to guide and control the search process. Search strategies guarantee completeness,[2] a property that can be proven by meta-theoretic arguments only and not within the reasoning system. However, perfect search guidance (oracles) that always selects the cor-

---

[1]It should be noted that most of the work done in automated deduction deals with the search space problem.

[2]If there is a solution, it will be found within finite time.

rect branch in the search tree in most applications cannot exist. Heuristics do not guarantee completeness. However, they provide simple means of indicating which among several courses of action is to be preferred. They are not necessarily guaranteed to identify the most effective course of action, however, they do it sufficiently often. So in some sense they can be understood as *approximations* to complete perfect search-guiding strategies. In most cases neither strategies nor heuristics are known in advance. Heuristic knowledge is very difficult to formalize, especially because most automated reasoning systems work on a level which is quite different from that of their human counterparts. Furthermore, general heuristics cannot be as powerful as domain- or problem-specific heuristics. This leads to the demand of developing heuristics specifically for each domain or problem set. The difficulties of defining heuristics for an automated reasoning system by hand are the motivation for the application of machine learning techniques in order to extract heuristic control information from the solutions of successfully solved problems and to use this information to control the reasoning system during the solution of new problems. With this approach a reasoning system will be able to adapt automatically to a specific domain or problem set. The close relationship of the two concepts *heuristics* and *approximation* motivates the application of inductive learning techniques. Connectionist approaches seem particularly suited because of their flexible generalization abilities and their ability to deal with incomplete or even contradictory data.

An example of this approach for SETHEO (a theorem prover for first order logic, very similar to a PROLOG-system) is given in Suttner and Ertel (1990), and Goller (1994), where a feed-forward neural network is used to learn search control heuristics. The system works in two phases (see Figure 1). During the learning phase, training data about good and bad decisions (situations) are produced from successful proof searches in order to learn heuristic evaluation functions. During subsequent working-phases, these evaluation functions can be used to give heuristic guidance for solving new problems.

All the different tasks that must be performed for learning control heuristics for SETHEO, like finding a rating for the applicable rules according to the current context, selecting the next subgoal, or realizing a generalizing lemma/failure-store, can be regarded as problems of learning a classification of symbolic structures of arbitrary size. However, since neural networks have a fixed number of input units, in the current version, only very restricted information about terms can be exploited. A solution to this problem is given by the Labeling Recursive Auto-Associative Memory (LRAAM) (see Section 2 and Sperduti (1994, 1994b, 1995)), a neural network which learns fixed-width distributed representations for labeled variable-sized recursive data structures, such as graphs, lists and terms. The appropriateness of LRAAM representations for subsequent classi-

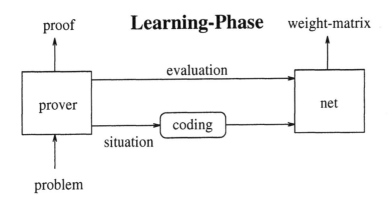

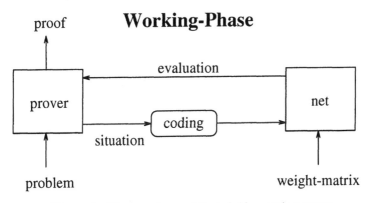

Figure 1 The two phases of the hybrid reasoning system.

fication tasks, in the context of natural language processing, has been shown, e.g., in Cadoret (1994), where the distributed representations of syntactical trees devised by an LRAAM are automatically classified according to the typology of dialogue acts. The approach described in Section 4, however, is a little bit different. The idea is to interleave the unsupervised development of representations (learning of the LRAAM) with the supervised learning of the classification task. In this way the representations are optimized with respect to the classification task. The classification becomes much easier. In Section 6, experiments with a set of term-classification problems are presented. In fact, for all these problems, an additional complex multi-layer network for classification was not needed. A single sigmoidal unit connected to the hidden layer of the LRAAM was sufficient because the representations that were devised represented the information for the classification task very directly.

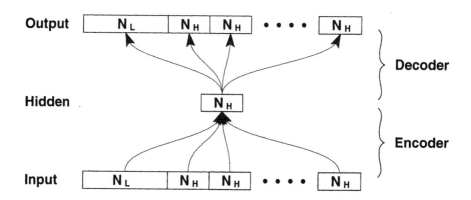

Figure 2   The network for a general Labeling RAAM.

2   LABELING RAAM

The *Labeling RAAM (LRAAM)* (Sperduti 1994, 1994b, 1995, Sperduti and Starita 1995) is an extension of the RAAM model (Pollack 1990) which allows one to encode labeled structures. The general structure of the network for an LRAAM is shown in Figure 2. The network is trained by backpropagation to learn the identity function. The idea is to obtain a compressed representation (hidden layer activation) of a node of a labeled directed graph by allocating a part of the input (output) of the network to represent the label (N_L units) and the rest to represent one or more pointers. This representation is then used as a pointer to the node. To allow the recursive use of these compressed representations, the part of the input (output) layer which represents a pointer must be of the same dimension as the hidden layer (N_H units). Thus, a general LRAAM is implemented by a $N_I - N_H - N_I$ feed-forward network, where $N_I = N_L + nN_H$, and n is the number of pointer fields.

More formally, an LRAAM network can be defined by the following equations:

$$\boldsymbol{F}_E(\vec{x}) = \boldsymbol{F}(\boldsymbol{E}\vec{x} + \vec{\theta}_H) \equiv \vec{h}, \tag{18.1}$$

$$\boldsymbol{F}_D(\vec{h}) = \boldsymbol{F}(\boldsymbol{D}\vec{h} + \vec{\theta}_O) \equiv \vec{o}, \tag{18.2}$$

where $\vec{h}, \vec{\theta}_H \in \Re^{N_H}$, $\vec{o}, \vec{x}, \vec{\theta}_O \in \Re^{N_I + nN_H}$, $\boldsymbol{F}_i(\vec{x}) = f(x_i)$, and $f()$ is a sigmoid-shaped function.

In the equations, $E \in \Re^{N_H \times N_I}$ is the encoding matrix, i.e., the weight matrix between the input layer ($N_I = N_l + nN_H$ units) and the hidden layer (N_H units); and $D \in \Re^{N_O \times N_H}$ is the decoding matrix, i.e., the weight matrix between the hidden layer and the output layer ($N_O = N_I$ units). In order to make the partition of the input and output layers explicit, E and D can be written as the composition of submatrices, one for each field in the LRAAM:

$$E = [E^{(l)}, E^{(p_1)}, \ldots, E^{(p_n)}], \tag{18.3}$$

$$D = \begin{bmatrix} D^{(l)} \\ D^{(p_1)} \\ \vdots \\ D^{(p_n)} \end{bmatrix}, \tag{18.4}$$

where $E^{(l)} \in \Re^{N_H \times N_l}$ is the weight matrix between the label field in the input layer and the hidden layer, $D^{(l)} \in \Re^{N_l \times N_H}$, is the weight matrix between the hidden layer and the label field in the output layer, $E^{(p_1)} \in \Re^{N_H \times N_H}$, is the weight matrix between the first pointer field in the input layer and the hidden layer, and so on. Following this notation, also the bias, input, and output vectors can be partitioned into subvectors:

$$\vec{\theta}_O = [\vec{\theta}_O^{(l)^t}, \vec{\theta}_O^{(p_1)^t}, \ldots, \vec{\theta}_O^{(p_n)^t}]^t, \tag{18.5}$$

$$\vec{x} = [\vec{x}^{(l)^t}, \vec{x}^{(p_1)^t}, \ldots, \vec{x}^{(p_n)^t}]^t, \tag{18.6}$$

$$\vec{o} = [\vec{o}^{(l)^t}, \vec{o}^{(p_1)^t}, \ldots, \vec{o}^{(p_n)^t}]^t, \tag{18.7}$$

where t is the transposition operator. Moreover, by definition, the dimension of each subvector referring to a pointer field must be equal to the dimension of $\vec{h}$.

Labeled directed graphs can be easily encoded using an LRAAM. Each node of the graph only needs to be represented as a record, with one field for the label and one field for each pointer to a connected node. The pointers only need to be logical pointers, since their actual values will be the patterns of hidden activation of the network. At the beginning of learning, their values are set at random. A graph is represented by a list of these records, and this list constitutes the initial training set for the LRAAM. During training, the representations of the pointers are consistently updated according to the hidden activations. Consequently, the training set is dynamic. For example, the network for the graph shown in Figure 3 can be trained as follows:

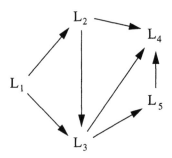

Figure 3   An example of a labeled directed graph.

input		hidden		output
$(L_1\ P_{n_2}(t)\ P_{n_3}(t))$	$\rightarrow$	$P'_{n_1}(t)$	$\rightarrow$	$(L''_1(t)\ P''_{n_2}(t)\ P''_{n_3}(t))$
$(L_2\ P_{n_3}(t)\ P_{n_4}(t))$	$\rightarrow$	$P'_{n_2}(t)$	$\rightarrow$	$(L''_2(t)\ P''_{n_3}(t)\ P''_{n_4}(t))$
$(L_3\ P_{n_4}(t)\ P_{n_5}(t))$	$\rightarrow$	$P'_{n_3}(t)$	$\rightarrow$	$(L''_3(t)\ P''_{n_4}(t)\ P''_{n_5}(t))$
$(L_4\ nil_1(t)\ nil_2(t))$	$\rightarrow$	$P'_{n_4}(t)$	$\rightarrow$	$(L''_4(t)\ nil''_1(t)\ nil''_2(t))$
$(L_5\ P_{n_4}(t)\ nil_3(t))$	$\rightarrow$	$P'_{n_5}(t)$	$\rightarrow$	$(L''_5(t)\ P''_{n_4}(t)\ nil''_3(t))$

where L_i and P_{ni} are the label of and the pointer to the ith node, respectively, and t represents the time, or epoch, of training. At the beginning of training $(t = 1)$, the representations for the non-void pointers $(P_{n_i}(1))$ and void pointers $(nil_i(1))$ in the training set are set at random. After each epoch, the representations for the non-void pointers in the training set are updated depending on the hidden activation obtained in the previous epoch for each pattern: $\forall i\ P_{n_i}(t+1) = P'_{n_i}(t)$. In order to decide whether a pointer is void or not, one bit of the label is allocated for each pointer field to represent the void condition. In principle, this convention allows us to avoid a commitment to any predefined representation for the void pointer (Sperduti 1994). However, since we are interested in performing classification tasks, it is more natural to use the null vector to represent the void pointer: the output for a new graph, i.e., a graph which is not in the training set, can be readily computed. The void representations of the output layer are, on the other hand, disregarded since the void condition bit suffices to recognize if a pointer is void or not.

If the backpropagation algorithm converges to zero error, it can be stated that:

$$L_1 = L''_1 \quad L_2 = L''_2 \quad L_3 = L''_3 \quad L_4 = L''_4 \quad L_5 = L''_5$$
$$P_{n_2} = P''_{n_2} \quad P_{n_3} = P''_{n_3} \quad P_{n_4} = P''_{n_4} \quad P_{n_5} = P''_{n_5}$$

f(a,g(X))   f(X,f(a,g(X)))

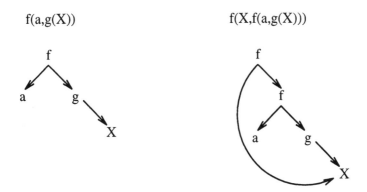

Figure 4   Example of terms represented as LDAGs.

Once the training is complete, the patterns of activation representing pointers can be used to retrieve information. Thus, for example, if the activity of the hidden units of the network is clamped to P_{n1}, the output of the network becomes (L_1, P_{n2}, P_{n3}), enabling further retrieval of information by decoding P_{n2} or P_{n3}, and so on. Note that multiple labeled directed graphs can be encoded in the same LRAAM.

3   REPRESENTATION OF LOGICAL TERMS

Logical terms are represented as labeled directed acyclic graphs (LDAGs). Function symbols are mapped to internal nodes, while constants and variables are mapped to terminal nodes. The label of each node is used to store the symbol associated to the assigned entity. Some examples of terms represented by LDAGs are given in Figure 4. The advantage of this representation consists in the possibility to uniquely represent identical subterms within a term, as shown on the right side of Figure 4, where the same variable X appears both as first argument of the function $f(,)$ and as argument of the function $g()$. This feature allows to represent terms very compactly. When considering a set of terms, the same representational strategy is used: each term (or subterm) is represented only once,[3] and repetitions of the same term are handled by resorting to point-

---

[3]Notice that the space and time complexity of the learning algorithm depends on the number of subterms in the training set.

Set of Trees   Minimal LDAG

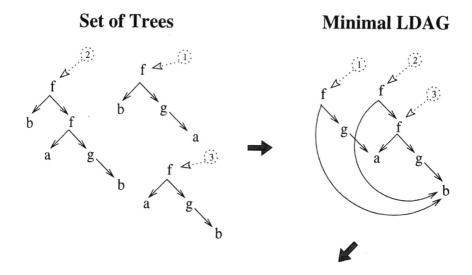

Sorted Training Set

#	label	left	right
0	b	nil	nil
1	a	nil	nil
2	g	nil	0
3	g	nil	1
4	f	1	2
5	f	0	3
6	f	0	4

Figure 5 Optimization of the training set: the set of structures (in this case, trees) is transformed into the corresponding minimal LDAG, which is then used to generate the sorted training set. The sorted training set is then transformed into a set of sorted vectors using the numeric codes for the labels and used as training set for the network.

ers. Thus, given a set of terms represented as LDAGs, the training set for the LRAAM can be constructed in two stages (see Figure 5 for an example):

1. All the LDAGs in the training set are merged into a single minimal LDAG, i.e., a LDAG with minimal number of nodes.

2. A topological sort on the nodes of the minimal LDAG is performed to determine the updating order on the nodes for the network.

Both stages can be done in linear time with respect to the original set of terms by using an efficient (linear) indexing mechanism for the identification of identical subgraphs and starting from the leaves. The advantage of having a sorted training set is that all the reduced representations (and also their derivatives with respect to the weights) can be computed by a single ordered scan of the training set. Notice that an LRAAM trained to encode a set of terms will generate a reduced representation for each intermediate term representation (pointer to a subtree) regardless of the fact that it constitutes a term we are interested in or not.

4 CLASSIFICATION OF TERMS

The main subject of this chapter is to demonstrate the feasibility of classification of terms encoded by an LRAAM. For this purpose, terms can conveniently be represented as labeled directed acyclic graphs, where function symbols are mapped to internal nodes, while constants and variables are mapped to terminal nodes. The label of each node is used to store the symbol associated to the assigned entity.

Only the representation and classification of *ground* terms, i.e., terms which do not involve variables, will be considered. However, the classification tasks that are solved involve the concept of logical variable.

The idea followed here is to classify the reduced representations devised by an LRAAM through a feed-forward neural network. Specifically, one of the network architectures shown in Figure 6 is proposed. In both of them, the first part is constituted by an LRAAM (notice the double side arrow connections) whose task is to encode the terms as discussed in the previous section. The classification task is then performed in the second part of the network through a simple sigmoidal neuron (network **A**) or a multi-layer feed-forward network with one or more hidden layers (network **B**). A very similar approach was used by Stolcke and Wu (1992). They try to learn how to unify very simple terms encoded in a RAAM.

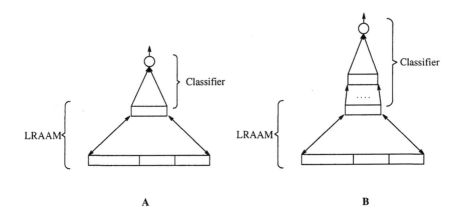

Figure 6   Two different networks for the classification of reduced descriptors devised by an LRAAM.

Assuming that the training of the system may end when the classification task is performed correctly, the different options for the training can be characterized by the proportion of the two different learning rates (for the classification error and the decoding error) and by the different degrees **x**, **y** of presence (or absence) of the following two basic features:

- the training of the classifier is not started until **x** percent of the training set is correctly encoded and successively decoded by the LRAAM;

- the error coming from the classifier is backpropagated across **y** levels of the structures encoded by the LRAAM.[4]

The reason for allowing different degrees of interaction between the classification and the representation tasks may be due to the necessity of having different degrees of adaptation of the reduced representations to the requirements of the classification task. If no interaction at all is allowed, i.e., the LRAAM is trained first and then its weights frozen (**y**= 0), the reduced representations will be such that similar representations will correspond to similar structures, while if full interaction is allowed, i.e., the LRAAM and the classifier are trained simulta-

---

[4]The backpropagation of the error across several levels of the structures can be implemented by unfolding the encoder of the LRAAM (the set of weights from the input to the hidden layer) according to the topology of the structures.

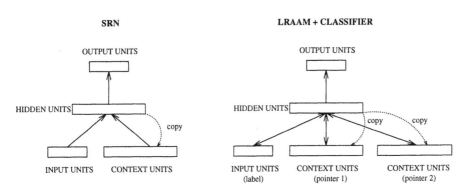

Figure 7   The network **A**, with x= 0 and y= 1 (right side), can be considered as a generalization of the Simple Recurrent Network by Elman (left side).

neously, the reduced representations will be such that structures in the same class will get very similar representations.[5]

It is interesting to note that the SRN by Elman can be obtained as a special case of network **A**, i.e., a single sigmoidal unit connected to the hidden layer of the LRAAM. In fact, when considering network **A** (with $x = 0$ and $y = 1$) for the classification of lists (sequences) the same architecture is obtained, with the difference that there are connections from the hidden layer of the LRAAM back to the input layer,[6] i.e., the decoding part of the LRAAM. Thus, when considering lists, the only difference between a SRN and network **A** is in the unsupervised learning performed by the LRAAM. However, when forcing the learning parameters for the LRAAM to be null, we obtain the same learning algorithm as in SRN. Consequently, we can claim that SRN is a special case of network **A**. This can be better understood by looking at the right side of Figure 7, where we have represented network **A** in terms of elements of a SRN. Of course, the *copy* function for network **A** is not as simple as the one used in a SRN, since the right relationships among components of the structures to be classified must be preserved.[7]

In the following, the classification capabilities of the network architecture **A** are explored. The training of the classifier is started simultaneously ($x = 0$)

---

[5]Moreover, in this case, there is no guarantee that the LRAAM will be able to encode and decode consistently all the structures in the training set, since the training is stopped when the classification task is performed correctly.

[6]The output layer of the LRAAM can be considered the same as the input layer.

[7]The *copy* function needs a stack for the memorization of compressed representations. The control signals for the stack are defined by the encoding-decoding task.

with the training of the LRAAM and the error coming from the classifier is backpropagated only to the pointers of the terms to be classified ($\mathbf{y} = 1$). It will be demonstrated that, even with this very simple architecture and learning algorithm, very good results can be obtained.

5 DESCRIPTION OF THE CLASSIFICATION PROBLEMS

In order to test the ability of the proposed architecture to deal with several classification tasks involving terms, a set of "simple" classification problems was used. These problems range from the detection of specific subterms to finding a most specific term, subsuming all terms from the positive class. While these tasks are trivially solved by ad hoc symbolic procedures once the tasks are known in advance, it is very difficult to induce the nature of the task to be performed given a set of positive and negative examples.

The characteristics of each problem are summarized in Table 1. The first row of the table reports the name of the problem, the second one the set of symbols (with associated arity) compounding the terms, and the third row shows the rule(s) used to generate the positive examples of the problem[8] with upper case letters representing all-quantified logical variables. The fourth row reports the number of terms in the training and test set respectively, the fifth row the number of subterms (subgraphs) in the training and test set (using the LDAG representation as described in Section 3), and the last row the maximum depth[9] of terms in the training and test set.

For each problem about the same number of positive and negative examples is given. Both positive and negative examples have been generated randomly. Training and test sets are disjoint and have been generated by the same algorithm.

It must be noted that the set of proposed problems range from the detection of a particular atom (label) in a term to the satisfaction of a specific unification pattern. Specifically, in the unification patterns for the problems inst1(_long) and inst7 the variable X occurs twice making these problems much more

---

[8] Remember that only ground instances are generated.

[9] We define the depth of a term as the maximum number of edges between the root and leaf nodes in the term's LDAG-representation.

Classification Problems

	lbloccl long	termoccl	inst1	inst1 long	inst4	inst4 long	inst7
Symbols	f/2 i/1 a/0 b/0 c/0	f/2 i/1 a/0 b/0 c/0	f/0 a/0 b/0 c/0	f/0 a/0 b/0 c/0	f/0 a/0 b/0 c/0	f/0 a/0 b/0 c/0	t/3 f/2 g/2 i/1 j/1 a/0 b/0 c/0 d/0
Positive Examples	no occorence of label c	the (sub)terms i(a) or f(b,c) occur somewhere	instances of f(X,X)	instances of f(X,X)	instances of f(X,f(a,Y))	instances of f(X,f(a,Y))	instances of t(i(X),g(X,b),b)
#terms (tr.,test)	(259,141)	(173,70)	(200,83)	(202,98)	(175,80)	(290,110)	(191,109)
#subterms (tr., test)	(444,301)	(179,79)	(235,118)	(403,204)	(179,97)	(499,245)	(1001,555)
depth (pos.,neg)	(5,5)	(2,2)	(3,2)	(6,6)	(3,2)	(7,6)	(6,6)

Table 1 Description of a set of classification problems.

difficult than `inst4`, because any classifier for these problems would have to compare arbitrary subterms corresponding to X.

6 RESULTS

Table 2 reports the best result obtained for each problem, described in Table 1, over 4 different network settings (both in number of hidden units for the LRAAM and learning parameters). The simulations were stopped after 30,000 epochs (except for `inst1_long` for which an upper bound of 80,000 epochs was allowed) or when the classification problem over the training set was completely solved. No extended effort for optimizing the size of the network and the learning parameters was done, thus it should be possible to improve on the reported results. The first row of the table shows the name of the problem, the second one the number of units used to represent the labels, the third the number of hidden units, the fourth the learning parameters (η is the learning parameter for the LRAAM, ϵ the learning parameter for the classifier, μ the momentum for the LRAAM), the fifth the percentage of terms in the training set which the LRAAM was able to properly encode and decode, the sixth the percentage of terms in the training set correctly classified, the seventh

Best Results

	lblocc1 long	termocc1	inst1	inst1 long	inst4	inst4 long	inst7
# Label Units	8	8	6	6	6	6	13
# Hidden Units	35	25	35	45	35	35	40
Learning Param.	$\eta = 0.2$ $\varepsilon = 0.001$ $\mu = 0.5$	$\eta = 0.1$ $\varepsilon = 0.1$ $\mu = 0.2$	$\eta = 0.2$ $\varepsilon = 0.06$ $\mu = 0.5$	$\eta = 0.2$ $\varepsilon = 0.005$ $\mu = 0.5$	$\eta = 0.2$ $\varepsilon = 0.005$ $\mu = 0.5$	$\eta = 0.2$ $\varepsilon = 0.005$ $\mu = 0.5$	$\eta = 0.1$ $\varepsilon = 0.01$ $\mu = 0.2$
% Encod. Decod.	4.25	100	100	36.14	98.86	8.97	1.05
% Training	100	98.84	97	94.55	100	100	100
% Test	98.58	94.29	93.98	90.82	100	100	100
# Epochs	11951	27796	10452	80000	1759	6993	6158

Table 2   The best results obtained for each classification problem.

the percentage of terms in the test set correctly classified, and the eighth the number of epochs the network employed to reach the reported performances.

From the results, it can be noted that some problems get a very satisfactory solution even if the LRAAM performs poorly. In this case, the reduced representations contain almost exclusively information about the classification task. An analysis for problem inst4_long shows that the first and second principal components suffice for a correct solution. For problem inst7, the second principal component alone gives enough information. Thus, it is clear that the classification of the terms is exclusively based on the encoding power of the LRAAM's encoder, which is shaped both by the LRAAM error and the classification error. However, even if the LRAAM's decoder is not directly involved in the classification task, it helps the classification process since it forces the network to generate different representations for terms in different classes.[10]

---

[10] Actually, the decoder error forces the LRAAM network to develop a different representation for each term, however, when the error coming from the classifier is very strong, it can happen that terms in the same class get almost identical representations.

7 SUMMARY

In this chapter, a neural network architecture based on the combination of an LRAAM network with an analog perceptron for the representation and classification of logical terms was presented. This architecture can be considered an extension of the SRN by Elman (1990).

Experimental results have shown that basic classification tasks on complex terms can be solved by this network. With independent test sets it has been verified that the networks really find the right generalizations. Based on these very promising results, future research can be pursued in the following two directions.

On one side, the investigation of different network architectures and learning options (see Section 4) is needed in order to achieve faster learning with smaller representations (fewer units in the hidden layer of the LRAAM). Based on the results in this chapter, it can be concluded that it pays to optimize the representations for the classification task. Therefore, the most promising option to investigate seems to be the recursive backpropagation of the classification error over the structures.

On the other side, experiments with more complex examples are due. The single basic tasks which have been solved separately in this chapter (occurrence of a specific label, occurrence of a specific subterm and the satisfaction of a specific unification pattern) have to be combined (disjunctively and conjunctively) to more complex tasks. Furthermore, the introduction of additional basic tasks can be studied: structure-sensitive tasks depending, e.g., on the number of nodes; the number of occurrences of specific subterms or the depth; the occurrence of unification patterns within a term or the recognition of simple regular languages on the paths from the top function symbol of a term to its leaves are further examples. According to our knowledge, no single symbolic learning system is able to solve all these basic learning tasks or even combinations of them. Further experiments should also be supplemented by examples coming from real applications, e.g., the hybrid reasoning system mentioned in the introduction.

Acknowledgments

This work was partially supported by the DFG, EC, DAAD and CRUI (Vigoni Project).

REFERENCES

[1] V. Cadoret, (1994). Encoding Syntactical Trees with Labelling Recursive Auto-associative Memory. In *Proceedings of the European Conference on Artificial Intelligence*, Amsterdam. pages 555–559. New York: Wiley.

[2] J. L. Elman, (1990). Finding structure in time. *Cognitive Science*, 14:179–211.

[3] C. Goller, (1994). A connectionist control component for the theorem prover setheo. ECAI94 Workshop on Combining Symbolic and Connectionist Processing.

[4] J. B. Pollack, (1990). Recursive distributed representations. *Artificial Intelligence*, 46(1-2):77–106.

[5] A. Sperduti, (1994). Encoding of Labeled Graphs by Labeling RAAM. In J. D. Cowan, G. Tesauro, and J. Alspector, editors, *Advances in Neural Information Processing Systems 6*, pages 1125–1132. San Mateo, CA: Morgan Kaufmann.

[6] A. Sperduti, (1994b). Labeling RAAM. *Connection Science*, 6(4):429–459.

[7] A. Sperduti, (1995). Stability properties of labeling recursive auto-associative memory. *IEEE Transactions on Neural Networks*, 6(6):1452–1460.

[8] A. Sperduti and A. Starita, (1993). An example of neural code: Neural trees implemented by LRAAMs. In *International Conference on Neural Networks and Genetic Algorithms*, pages 33–39. Innsbruck. Berlin: Springer-Verlarg.

[9] A. Stolcke and D. Wu, (1992). Tree matching with recursive distributed representations. Technical Report TR-92-025, International Computer Science Institute, Berkeley.

[10] C.B. Suttner and W. Ertel, (1990). Automatic Acquisition of Search Guiding Heuristics. In *Proceedings of the 10. International Conference on Automated Deduction (CADE)* (LNAI 449), pages 470–484. Berlin: Springer-Verlarg.

19

SYMBOLIC DISTRIBUTED REPRESENTATIONS

Ramon Krosley and Manavendra Misra

Department of Mathematical and Computer Sciences
Colorado School of Mines

1   INTRODUCTION

Is it possible to perform symbolic computations in a neural network? Such a capability would enable implementation of discrete logic in the massively parallel computing architecture of neural networks.

The first step toward neural symbolic computation is to implement symbols in a neural network. Later steps include the development of computing mechanisms which use these symbols in such applications as planning behavior. This paper focuses on the first step, describing a neural computing architecture which generates symbols and autonomously assigns meanings to them.

The experiments performed here examined the formation of symbolic internal representations in a simulated robot navigating among obstacles on a flat surface. The experimenter provided external signals which actuate the simulated robot's motors, causing it to move. This motion provided a flow of sensory data which the neural system used to develop symbols which are applicable to the robot's environment.

The following observations guided the design of the system.

- Humans can recall memories which correspond to single experiences. In other words, significant learning can take place during a single presentation of information.

- Humans can be reminded of particular events by similar events. That is, recognition tolerates some dissimilarity in addressing a memory which best matches experience.

- Humans can classify events, knowing that separate instances within a class are simultaneously similar and different.

The following techniques implement the functions listed above.

- Instant learning is not simply a matter of setting the learning rate parameter to a high value in a connectionist network. The learned information would be erased quickly by subsequent events if the system used this approach alone. This system uses a high learning rate, but it continually switches the structure of the network in which the learning occurs.

- This system segments its sensory environment, autonomously defining microfeatures, and recording them as symbols. The microfeatures form a distributed representation of any experience; that is, similar experiences have similar representations. Such a representation results in a graded response to experience, with the strongest response for the most similar previous experience.

- The units which symbolize each experience provide the means to represent separate instances of similar events, while the distributed representations carry the information of their similarity.

In traditional networks, learning usually occurs through an iterative process such as backpropagation which gradually develops a "subsymbolic" internal representation in the internal units of the network by accumulating many constraining facts. The starting point for learning an internal representation is a meaningless state of the internal units. The endpoint of learning is meaningful in the sense that the states of the set of internal units map reliably to states of the set of external units.

The early availability of a meaningful internal representation can facilitate learning. Transferring knowledge from a trained neural network to another network which will learn a similar task is an example of this effect (Pratt 1993). Another approach for providing such an internal representation is to learn it in an inversion of the input–output mapping through an iterative process (Hinton et al 1995).

This paper suggests an alternative method by adding a couple of modifications to the standard connectionist model. The result is a system which mixes symbolic and subsymbolic representations. The purpose of these changes is to capture events in an internal representation as they occur. Additionally, the memory of the events should be addressable as in an associative memory, with a graded response according to the degree of similarity between the memory and the stimulus.

2   UNIFYING SYMBOLIC AND DISTRIBUTED REPRESENTATIONS

The first modification added to the standard connectionist model is to provide a continually changing, focused site of learning. Instead of changing every connection in the network by a small amount at each presentation of new information, this network changes a small number of connections by a large amount at each presentation of new information.

This approach differs from the "subsymbolic" formulation of distributed representations (Hinton et al 1986; Rosenfeld & Touretzky 1988; Touretzky 1990) in which the meanings of hidden units develop as a statistical model of a population of input patterns. In a subsymbolic distributed representation of an input pattern, the meaning is a weighted sum of the estimates of the pattern in each hidden unit.

Instead, this approach immediately assigns to each hidden unit whatever meaning is at hand when it is that unit's turn for learning. As we shall describe, the meanings arise from patterns which the world external to the network provides. The important point here is that the meanings are specific fragments of experience, rather than statistics. Any hidden unit may stand alone to represent its meaning, or it may participate in a larger ensemble of units to represent a meaning which is the coincidence of the fragmentary meanings. In this sense, it is reasonable to describe this approach as a "symbolic" formulation of distributed representations.

Localized learning and using symbols for events involves the following considerations.

- There is a supply of symbols ready to acquire meanings.

■   There is an autonomous method to assign specific meanings to symbols.

Section 2.1 describes a general concept of a "symbolic" distributed representation. The following Section 2.2 describes how the system assigns primitive meanings to the microfeatures in each step of time. A recurring theme exposes the symbolic quality of these distributed representations: Attempts to achieve efficient use of representation space in the subsymbolic style find that these attempts are incompatible with this symbolic approach. Section 3 offers alternative means to use representation space efficiently in a symbolic style, enhancing the primitive symbols of Section 2.2 through additional learning which follows the initial assignment of meanings.

2.1   Distributed Representation

It is simple to imagine a neural representation for symbols. Consider an array of neural units which are all inactive. Now activate a few of these units. Call that a symbol. A different set of active units forms a different symbol. The difficult task is to structure the assignment of meanings to these symbols in order to use the neural units efficiently. That is the subject of the remainder of this section.

First, the system learns a large set of recurring parts of experiences. These parts correspond to the **microfeatures** in a distributed representation. Next, the system associates these parts to represent coincidences of microfeatures. This paper calls these assemblies of microfeatures **event symbols**. When two events share one or more parts of experience, then the units which represent these microfeatures are active in the distributed representation of both events. Other microfeatures which are active in one event but not in the other distinguish events. The result is that the representations of similar events bear similarities corresponding to the similarities in their sensory and motor patterns.

An obvious parameter of this representation is the average number of neural units, z_μ, per microfeature, and the number z_v per event symbol. The microfeatures have atomic meanings which combine to form the composite meanings of event symbols. This means that z_μ might be any integer greater than or equal to one. In a local representation, this number would be one. There are some considerations in using a larger number.

- Having more than one unit per microfeature provides redundancy that protects against failure of some of the units' hardware.

- If complete connectivity between neural units is impractical, multiple units could relay activity across a larger physical mass of neural units than is practical for complete connectivity.

These reasons for $z_\mu > 1$ relate to practical implementation.

It might be possible to allow partial overlap of the sets of units assigned to different microfeatures in order to recover the use of the memory space that is applied to redundancy, in the style of subsymbolic distributed representations. However, experimentation has shown that overlap between microfeatures is incompatible with the symbolic nature of this approach. The ambiguity resulting from overlap introduces misinterpretations, and the learning mechanisms described in Section 3 work to remove these misinterpretations. For the purpose of this paper, where simplicity and ease of experimentation are important, it is sufficient to consider $z_\mu = 1$.

In the case of event symbols, overlap is possible due to shared microfeatures representing shared parts of experience. The capacity, P, of the network for event symbols is a function of the number of internal units, N, in the network and the number of units per microfeature. There is the potential to combine the N possible microfeatures into 2^N different event symbols, if this design were to follow the subsymbolic approach. The design studied in this paper does not store such a large number of different events. This design uses a separate microfeature as a handle on each event which the system stores. For this reason, the system cannot store more events than there are internal units.

$$P < N$$

Why has this design sacrificed the enormously larger representation space which would be available if it did not use microfeatures as handles for event symbols? If the system were to store an event by increasing the weights of connections between the microfeatures which define the event then the activation of a substantial subset of an event symbol will recall the remainder of the composite symbol. This behavior is standard for an associative memory, but it tends to recall whole patterns. This behavior makes it difficult to count subsets of event symbols as separate events, and event symbols which share microfeatures could activate one another. The learning rule proposed below eliminates all associative connections between the microfeatures of an event, making it possible

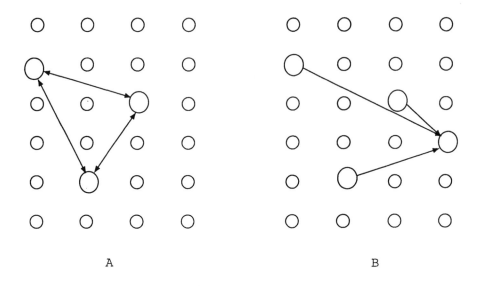

Figure 1   Compare a subsymbolic distributed representation in an associative
memory (A) with the symbolic approach used in this paper (B).

for distributed representations to describe events without interference through
shared microfeatures. The proposal also provides a mechanism to represent
multiple instances of the same event.

The system achieves this independence by learning only associations between
the many microfeatures describing an event and a single microfeature which
represents the event. Whenever a sufficient number of the microfeatures describing an event are active, then the associations activate the microfeature
which is the handle for the event. This behavior defines the meaning of the microfeature which acts as a handle. Figure 1 compares a subsymbolic associative
memory with the symbolic approach of this paper.

When the handle microfeature is active in neural computations it stands for the
event without the necessity to activate the other microfeatures which describe
the event. This design makes it possible for the network to represent two
similar events simultaneously by activating only their handles. The confusion
of overlapping descriptive microfeatures does not occur when the handles stand
for the events.

The cost of this independence is the elimination of the potential for storing a combinatorially large number of event symbols. This design can represent any part of a combinatorially large space of potential event symbols, but the storage capacity scales linearly in the number of units.

Another way to express this situation is to compare it to writing on paper. The number of strings that one can form using a given alphabet is combinatorially large, but there is only enough space on a piece of paper to write a number of strings that is proportional to the area of the page.

The next section describes the first step in the assignment of meaning to symbols.

2.2 Experiential Symbols

The preceding section established the idea of assigning a meaning to an event symbol by means of its association with other microfeatures which describe an event. That idea is incomplete without some way to assign absolute meanings to some microfeatures, referencing no other microfeatures. The most obvious way to assign this kind of meaning to microfeatures is to connect them to sensors and motors. This section describes that procedure in detail, referring to this kind of microfeature as **experiential symbols**. In Section 3.2 this paper reexamines the assignment of relative meanings to microfeatures to see a way in which more general meanings may develop from experiential symbols.

Consider the example of a robot traversing a room, using sonar for sensory input. The robot in this example has motors which cause it to roll forward, and which cause it to turn right and left. These sensory inputs and motor outputs are the external units of Figure 2.

To make use of the information in the external units, it is necessary to deliver sensory signals from them to the internal units, and to deliver motor signals in the reverse direction.

To describe the system precisely, this paper packages the activities of the internal units in a vector called $\mathbf{v}$. When referring to the activity of a particular internal unit, the notation is v_i. Similarly, the activities of external units are in the vector $\mathbf{x}$.

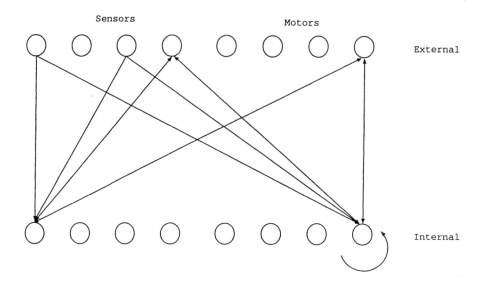

Figure 2 The experimental network.

A matrix called **C** captures the connections that deliver signals from sensory external units to internal units. To refer to the strength of the connection from external unit k to internal unit j, the notation is C_{jk}. The following equation describes the delivery of signals from external units to the internal units:

$$\mathbf{v} = \sigma(\mathbf{Cx}) \tag{19.1}$$

The function σ compresses the results of the matrix multiplication so the activities of **v** are in the range, $[0, 1]$.

To implement this range, σ is a hyperbolic tangent function. This model does not use the range of negative values of the hyperbolic tangent function. The resting state of such a unit is at zero activity, which is appropriate when a symbol is absent. Activation rises nonlinearly in response to inputs, approaching the value 1 asymptotically.

The matrix **R** defines connections from internal units to motor external units. This matrix reverses the structure defined by **C**. To refer to the strength of the connection from internal unit k to external unit j, the notation is R_{jk}. The following equation describes the delivery of signals from internal units to motor units. These signals combine with sensory inputs to determine the state of the external units.

$$\mathbf{x}_{\text{motor}} = \sigma(\mathbf{Rv}) \qquad (19.2)$$

Given the preceding definition of $\mathbf{C}$ and $\mathbf{R}$, it is possible to describe a mechanism which produces experiential symbols and assigns meanings to them:

- The system contains an internal clock which divides time into segments. Each segment defines the temporal boundaries of a symbol. A symbol which becomes active within such a segment becomes inactive at the end of the segment unless it receives stimulation from other internal or external units.

- There is a continual background of random spontaneous activations of internal units, such that about z_μ units become active near the middle of the clocking rhythm. These activations are "spontaneous" because there is no input signal from other units to cause the activations. The system recruits these units to function as new experiential symbols. This paper refers to these sets of units as **naive symbols** before their recruitment, because they do not yet have a meaning.

- Recruitment occurs when the system changes the weights of connections in $\mathbf{C}$ and in $\mathbf{R}$. If external unit k is active in the same segment of time that internal unit j becomes spontaneously active, then weight C_{jk} increases from zero to a value which is just adequate for future reactivation of internal unit j. That is, whenever the pattern of activities of external units in a time segment matches the pattern which was present during recruitment, the weights of connections from all these units to internal unit j will cause this unit to become active.

- It is necessary to focus the location of learning in just the connections between active external units and spontaneously active internal units. Otherwise, the recruitment process would include other internal units which happen to be active due to associative connections. Such unbridled recruitment would destroy microfeatures which already have meanings. This rule concentrates learning on the task of assigning meaning to a single new experiential symbol in a single instant of time.

Experimental simulations of this model set the level of spontaneous activity significantly higher than the level of associative activity determined by the range of the hyperbolic tangent activation function. This hyperactivity serves to distinguish spontaneously active units, permitting implementation by simulation algorithms local to each neural unit.

This model exploits the idea that the process of spontaneous activation differs from associative activation, in order to limit recruitment learning to spontaneously active units, excluding units which become active through associative connections. Recruitment learning occurs only in connections afferent to a spontaneously active unit, which has index i in the equation below. The explicit rule for the assignment of weights in this process has the net result that each weight is the reciprocal of the number of active external units, z_x.

$$C_{ij} = \frac{1}{z_x}$$

A plausible mechanism to implement this rule is to divide a fixed amount of weight over all connections where there is an active presynaptic unit.

The effect of these rules is to assign to the spontaneously active internal units the meaning of the pattern of activity of the external units which are active in the same segment of time.

In the example of the navigating robot, the meaning is the sonar pattern that is active at the time of learning. Any time the same set of external units become active simultaneously, the connections reactivate the recruited internal units. Any time the recruited internal units are active, they represent the pattern of activity in the external units, regardless of whether that pattern is actually active. By activating in this way, the internal units can function during computation as a symbolic internal representation of an external state.

Continuing the analogy of recording symbols on paper, one can say that this mechanism has simply drawn some pictures on the page. Each picture is an attempt to represent the experience of an instant in time. Without enhancement, this mechanism must quickly fill its page. The next section describes a set of refinements to use space more efficiently.

3   LEARNING DISTRIBUTED REPRESENTATIONS

The second modification which this paper adds to the standard connectionist model is to increase the reusability of symbolic representations. As described above, the symbolic memories are photographic reproductions of experience. Such memories will eventually exhaust the supply of symbols, so this section describes mechanisms which manage the use of representation space.

Previous discussion of the capacity of this system used the analogy of writing strings on a piece of paper. One way to increase the effective capacity of a written page is to erase some strings having specific meanings and to replace them with strings which have more general meanings. The neural architecture described here uses this same technique to increase its effective capacity by shifting the meanings of specific symbols to more general meanings.

Although the motivation for this feature is to compress more information into a limited amount of space, an important side effect is that the resulting distributed representations facilitate approximate matches when addressing associative memory. It is remarkable that the simple need to use representation space efficiently drives many of these features of the design.

- One way to store more information in a limited space is to analyze events into constituents. Instead of storing a large number of unique events which have redundant substructures, the system forms an alphabet of common components of events and uses these tokens to describe events.

- There is a mechanism to combine the alphabet of common constituents into descriptions of events.

- Another way to use a finite supply of neural units effectively is to destroy some representations and to recycle their units in new symbols.

3.1 Analysis of Experience

The simple procedure described in the preceding section for learning microfeatures does not provide an important property of a distributed representation. The symbols for similar states of external units have no mutual similarity. In order to produce truly distributed representations, it is necessary first to analyze experience into microfeatures, and then to synthesize internal representations of events from the microfeatures. This section describes a refinement of the learning rules which analyzes the states of external units to discover useful combinations of sensory or motor activities which can serve as microfeatures.

Analysis by Explanation

One attribute that indicates a useful combination is *recurrence*. The total complex combination of sensory and motor activities at any instant in time is not likely to repeat, but parts will probably appear many times. The experiential

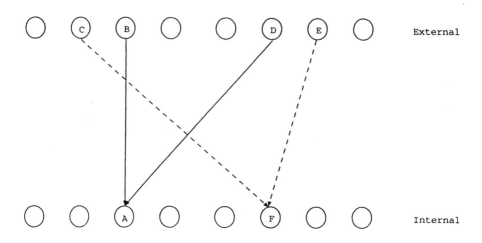

Figure 3   Segmentation of experience by "explaining".

symbols could act as handles on familiar parts of events if there were a way to segment experience.

The learning rule for C can implement this form of segmentation by detecting patterns in the external units for which the internal units already have recruited a symbol. Figure 3 illustrates this process. In this figure, internal unit A is an experiential symbol whose original meaning is the pattern where external units B and D are active. For example, units B and D might represent the sonar pattern of an object ahead of a navigating robot, which the robot has previously experienced.

Now suppose that there are two objects, one ahead and one on the right. Suppose that the object on the right activates sensory units C and E. When external units B, C, D, and E are active in the same segment of time, connections in C will deliver signals from units B and D to activate unit A. This paper describes this situation by saying that the activity of the postsynaptic unit A **explains** the activities of the presynaptic units B and D. Unit A is the experiential symbol for the sonar pattern of an object ahead. The units C and E are not yet explained, so the system should recruit a new experiential symbol to explain them.

None of the explained units should form new connections in C. Any unexplained active external units should connect immediately through C to the active units of the latest naive symbol in the internal units. This rule uses only information that is available locally at a spontaneously active postsynaptic unit in a naive symbol and its connections to unexplained presynaptic units.

A plausible mechanism for implementing this rule in hardware requires a different behavior of unexplained presynaptic units compared to those which are explained. Connections between units which have become active through associative signals provide a reverse signal to the presynaptic unit to set its state as "explained." Active units without this notification assume the default state of "unexplained" activity. Recruitment learning occurs only in connections in which the presynaptic unit has unexplained activity and the postsynaptic unit is spontaneously active. The postsynaptic unit manages the distribution of weights among its inbound connections.

The terminology of internal units explaining the activity of external units is a basic concept in this model for segmenting experience. The result of this concept is a system which can detect components of experience that first occur separately and then occur together. For example, when a navigating robot returns to a familiar place, it can detect the presence of an object which was previously absent. Separate experiential symbols represent the place and the new object because a familiar symbol explained the place, while the system recruits a new experiential symbol to explain the novel object.

Analysis by Pruning

The explanation method is unable to decompose patterns in the external units which always occur in composite form. In the example of the navigating robot, sonar detects obstacles. Small objects in the foreground may produce an echo which appears as a single active external unit. Suppose that the background always produces an echo which appears as the same set of active external units indicating a distant wall. Because the single units for small foreground objects always appear with the same large set of units representing background units, their microfeatures receive most of their activating signals from the same pattern. The wrong microfeature can easily become active along with the correct one, making it difficult for the system to distinguish a small object in front from another small object.

Figure 4 illustrates this situation. Internal unit A was previously recruited as an experiential symbol for the combination of activities of external units B, C, and D. Say that units B and C result from the background echo of a wall, while unit D results from a small feature, a door in the wall. In Figure 4 a

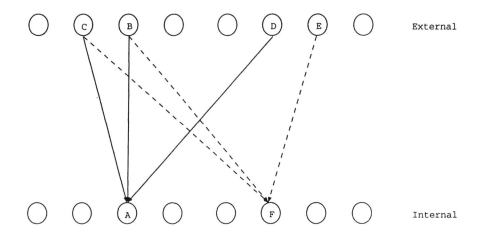

Figure 4   Generalization of experience by pruning.

new experience is occurring in which external units B, C, and E are active, but the environmental condition represented by external unit D is absent. In this example, units B and C still result from the wall, but the robot is approaching from a slightly different direction, so the sonar echo of the door activates unit E instead of unit D.

The problem is that analysis by explanation may simply learn the combinations (B, C, D) and (B, C, E) as separate microfeatures, A and F, if the system is tuned so that units B and C alone are insufficient to activate unit A. If the activation threshold is such that units B and C can activate unit A, then the system will learn unit F as representative of activity in unit E, due to explanation of units B and C. In the first case, the system fails to distinguish similar events; in the second case, the system includes too much detail in some events. In both cases, the system has failed to extract the meaning of the door in unit D.

This model uses a second method in addition to explanation to decompose composite patterns. The second method works by comparing the patterns feeding microfeatures which overlap enough to make the microfeatures become active for the wrong pattern, or which contain too much detail. When an experiential symbol becomes active incorrectly, as is unit A in Figure 4, the second method prunes away the connections which distinguish microfeature A from F. This technique seems to be striving for the wrong result when the goal is to increase the acuity of the system rather than to decrease it. However, generalizing microfeature A to represent only the pattern of concurrent activity in units B and C liberates units D and E for individual detection by later recruitment, ultimately enhancing the system's acuity.

If the connections C_{ab} and C_{ac} become stronger, and the connection C_{ad} from inactive unit D to active unit A becomes weaker, then the system can prune the external unit D from the meaning of the experiential symbol represented by unit A. By weakening the connection C_{ad} when the activities of the presynaptic and postsynaptic units differ, and strengthening the connections that agree with experience, the meaning of the original experiential symbol A shifts from its dysfunctional specific meaning to the more general meaning which overshadows the specific meaning. The reduced set of external units, (B, C), for microfeature A is more generally applicable than the initial specific meaning, (B, C, D). In this sense, the pruning rule generalizes the meanings of experiential symbols.

What becomes of the specific meanings which the pruning rule discards? Recruitment learning will assign to new naive symbols the external units representing small foreground objects. The next time that (B, C, D) appears in the external units, microfeature A will become active and will explain the activities of units B and C. Because the activity of unit D will be unexplained, recruitment will connect it to a new naive symbol.

The system forgets the unique features of the indistinct microfeatures, and it must relearn them in new microfeatures when it revisits them. In general, this mechanism progressively divides composite experiences as they contrast with similar new experiences. The result is a variety of specific and general microfeatures.

Should the pruning rule change connections as rapidly as does the explanation rule? The latter rule learns at the rate of recruitment learning, which is 1. Should pruning depend upon iterative learning which is normal for associative memory to identify what is important? This paper simply names the learning rate for pruning π, and leaves it to experimentation to determine useful values.

The following equations summarize the pruning process, as implemented in a single internal unit, v_j. This unit adjusts its inbound weights to diminish its response to omitted signals, and proportionally to enhance its response to familiar signals. The following equation holds when $x_k = 0$ and $v_j = 1$. That is, the external unit x_k was active when unit v_j was first recruited, but now it is inactive when v_j is active. The effect of this equation is to reduce the response of v_j to x_k toward zero in proportion to the learning rate for pruning, π.

$$\delta C_{jk} = -\pi C_{jk}$$

The following equation holds when $x_h = v_j = 1$. That is, the external unit x_h was active when unit v_j was first recruited, and now it is active again when v_j is active. The effect of this equation is to take all the reductions in strength of other inbound connections of v_j and to redistribute this weight equally among the inbound connections which have remained true to their original meaning.

$$\delta C_{jh} = \frac{\sum_{x_i=0} -\delta C_{ji}}{\sum_{x_i=1} 1}$$

There must be a limit to the analytic processes in this neural model; otherwise, the endpoint would consist of individual experiential symbols for each external unit, which would provide no better representation of information than the external units themselves. One possible limiting factor could be the absence of experiences which, as a group, completely divide the patterns in the external units. Another limiting factor is the learning rate for pruning, π. By making this rate a function of the number of inputs to a symbol, it should be possible to guarantee an average number of external features per internal microfeature.

Until now, this paper has concentrated on $\mathbf{C}$, the connections from sensory external units to internal units. The motor connections, $\mathbf{R}$, should behave similarly, but there is an additional consideration relating these two sets of connections. Experimental simulations suggest that behavior of a navigating robot can develop less erratically by separating sensory and motor symbols. Researchers programming robot behaviors often follow a regimen in which they test motor algorithms separately from testing perceptual algorithms. This model also separates these lessons, and it does so in the order of learning sensory patterns before learning motor patterns. The result is that the robot commits no actions without meaningful perceptions with which to associate those actions. To implement this separation between sensors and motors, this model uses the rule that changes in $\mathbf{R}$ occur only when no changes in $\mathbf{C}$ can occur.

The learning rules for $\mathbf{C}$ and for $\mathbf{R}$ provide a mechanism to assign meanings to experiential symbols by analyzing activity in external units. These experiential symbols form the microfeatures of the distributed representation described in Section 2.1. The next section describes how the complementary mechanism for synthesis establishes symbols for events which combine the microfeatures into a distributed representation.

3.2 Synthesis of Events

Section 2.2 provided a stream of naive symbols to serve as raw material for explaining experience. That section also described learning rules which change C as long as there are unexplained activities in external units. When the system has generated symbols to explain all sensory inputs of an experience, then it begins learning to explain motor outputs by making changes in **R**.

When all experiences have been explained, it seems that the system would stop learning new experiential symbols. In this jaded condition, the continual stream of naive symbols would do little more than mark time. This stream of symbols represents a resource which the system can exploit to construct the event symbols described in Section 2.1. The matrix **F** labels associative connections between internal units which can assign meanings to naive symbols, making them capable of functioning as handles on event symbols.

By applying the same learning rules to **F** as applied to **C**, the system can generate microfeatures which represent events. The same shifts in meaning, due to pruning, which generalize experiential symbols can generalize the meanings of microfeatures for events.

The connections in **F** are zero when they are presynaptic to a meaningless hidden unit. Those hidden units which acquire the meaning of events and those which acquire the meaning of experiential microfeatures may interconnect as peers so the symbols which they form can function together as peers. The microfeatures associated with an event symbol constitute a distributed representation of its meaning. These microfeatures can be experiential symbols, or they can be other event symbols.

3.3 Recovering Space

Some form of decay is needed to discard unused symbols so their connections can be recycled in new symbols. There is a natural kind of decay which must occur when the associative memory has assigned meanings to most of the units. The process of spontaneous activation which forms new symbols will begin to reuse symbols which already have meanings.

It is reasonable to assume that a different physical process occurs in spontaneously active units, compared to the process of activation via associative connections. Here is a plausible mechanism which selects neural units to be candidates for recruitment to represent new meanings in external units. There is no intent here to describe a biological process. Imagine that a substance gradually accumulates in an inactive neural unit. Normal frequencies of associative activation reset the amount of this substance to zero in a neural unit. Inactivity over a sufficiently long period of time allows the accumulation to continue until it reaches a level which triggers spontaneous activation. This mechanism of selection assures that the least useful units have a chance to acquire more useful meanings.

Experimental simulations indicate that the pruning process quickly removes the previous meaning of a spontaneously activated unit, if its new meaning is useful.

4 SUMMARY

This paper presents a neural system which produces distributed representations by rapid segmentation of patterns present in experience. The system differs from those which learn distributed representations by conducting an iterative statistical search for an efficient set of microfeatures. The system described here can produce a set of microfeatures which serves adequately for recognition of locations in experiments with a simulated navigating robot.

REFERENCES

[1] G.E. Hinton, J.L. McClelland, and D.E. Rumelhart, (1986). Distributed Representations, in D.E. Rumelhart, J.L. McClelland, and the PDP Research Group, editors, it *Parallel Distributed Processing: Explorations in the Microstructure of Cognition*, pages 77-109. The MIT Press, Cambridge, Massachusetts.

[2] G.E. Hinton, P. Dayan, B.J. Frey, and R.M. Neal, (1995). The "wake-sleep" algorithm for unsupervised neural networks, *Science*, 268:1158-1161.

[3] L.Y. Pratt, (1993). Transferring Previously Learned Back-Propagation Neural Networks to New Learning Tasks, PhD thesis, Rutgers University, Computer Science Department.

[4] R. Rosenfeld and D.S. Touretzky, (1988). Coarse-coded symbol memories and their properties, *Complex Systems*, 2(4):463-484.

[5] D.S. Touretzky, (1990). BoltzCONS: dynamic symbol structures in a connectionist network, *Artificial Intelligence*, 46:5-46.

PART V

EPILOG

20

AN ANALYSIS OF CONNECTIONIST-SYMBOLIC INTEGRATION

Frédéric Alexandre

CRIN-INRIA Nancy (France)

INTRODUCTION

Since the resurgence of interest in neural networks in the mid-80's, the possibility to profit from the respective advantages of the symbolic and neural paradigms in integrated connectionist-symbolic systems has been a persistent research goal. These systems all strive to achieve both symbolic and neural functionalities. Combining the advantages of both paradigms has a clear benefit : human cognitive capabilities are not within the reach of either symbolic or connectionist artificial intelligence because of the limitations of each approach. Combining their powerful properties could be a better way to model these fundamental capabilities.

Two major trends can be identified in the state of the art: these are what we call unified and hybrid approaches to connectionist-symbolic integration (CSI). Whereas the unified or "connectionist-to-the-top" or "connectionist symbol processing" approach claims that complex symbol processing functionalities can be achieved via neural networks alone, the hybrid approach is premised on the complementarity of the two paradigms and aims to combine them synergistically in systems comprising both neural and symbolic components.

These two trends have developed in peaceful coexistence over the past decade, sometimes without a full awareness of their own specific objectives and implications. This awareness has emerged recently as a result of workshops and books (Sun and Bookman 1995) whose main goal is to gather the CSI community and discuss these topics.

Such was the goal of the IJCAI Workshop on Connectionist Symbolic Integration: From Unified to Hybrid Approaches, which was held in August 1995 with the aim of clarifying and comparing the assumptions, mechanisms and the cognitive and computational implications of these two approaches. It is now possible to try to analyze more deeply the ideas that were exchanged during this meeting and to draw some perspectives for the future.

1   ANALYSIS

It is clear that the work reported here is far from an exhaustive account of the state of the art in connectionist symbolic integration. Work in this area is increasingly intensive and certainly represents hundreds of researchers. We can argue that this field is very active because there is a need to cope with problems integrating symbolic and connectionist aspects. In fact, this need is twofold. First, we are now at the point that if we want to improve the capabilities of our cognitive artificial systems, we have to mix symbolic and connectionist properties. Second, progress in this domain is such that we now consider it more feasible to try to understand relations between the symbolic and the numeric worlds.

These different motivations, added to the always increasing size of this domain, raise the threat of the expansion of CSI without any control of its aims. That is the reason why we judge it fundamental for this community to meet and analyze the evolution of its work. Even if nonexhaustive, we think that the experiences gathered here are representative of this evolution and are therefore a good basis for such an analysis: we analyze more deeply both the potential and the foundations of CSI.

1.1   Potential of CSI

Most of the experiences reported here correspond to the CSI implementation of human cognitive capabilities. Natural language processing is clearly the most frequently investigated domain (cf. for parsing, chapter 12; for word sense disambiguation, chapter 13; see also a good review in (Dyer 1995)), but other cognitive aspects (cf. abductive reasoning, chapter 6) are also represented. Concerning natural language processing, this domain is also deeply investigated in classical Artificial Intelligence, but is still far from being solved. It is thus interesting to note that CSI is rapidly being adapted as an alternative solution and being extensively explored accordingly.

From a more global point of view, the analysis of all these experiments also gives a good idea of the advancement of the CSI domain. First, it is sometimes said that CSI is an empty nutshell, without a common fundation and that, in fact, CSI models are purely empirical, ad hoc models, only designed as needed to solve one precise symbolic or connectionist limitation. We admit that the criticism is possible for some of the earliest CSI models proposed.

Nevertheless, the recent work, presented here, cannot clearly be reduced to simple implementations of a given ad hoc mechanism. One of the most interesting common aspects of the work is that it looks for a generic aspect of human intelligence, tries to relate its assumptions to other CSI or cognitive work, and discusses its plausibility and its situation with regard to other AI paradigms. More generally, it can be reasonably said that the same is true for most of the work regarding CSI today.

Chapter 3 (and also (Khosla and Dillon 1994)) is a good example of this kind of work. Here, the task structure and the computational level architecture of symbolic and connectionist models are deeply studied and allow for the definition of computational phases. This architectural analysis then leads to a generic approach of CSI that has been successfully applied to an alarm processing application.

Chapter 10 is also an important contribution toward the generality of CSI. It describes an open platform, based on distributed artificial intelligence, for an easy and efficient implementation of CSI models. The design of this tool, as a result of the European ESPRIT MIX project, also required a strict and general analysis of CSI principles to define the necessary and sufficient properties of such a platform. This tool is currently validated on a variety of real-world applications.

This kind of work shows that generality is now a need and can be seriously considered as feasible. This is undoubtedly a sign that CSI is beginning to mature.

This remark can also be extended to another classical criticism to CSI. It is often said that CSI is only applied to elementary toy problems and cannot deal with real-world applications that include perceptual or behavioral components. It is increasingly evident that CSI models can also be applied to (and are even sometimes specially designed for) this kind of real-world problem. Here, chapters 7, 9 and 15 report models whose goal is to be applied to autonomous robots.

To conclude with this section, we emphasize that all the models presented here respect the definition reported above: they all choose a human cognitive capability whose functionalities are difficult to capture with pure symbolic or connectionist models, and they show that a CSI model leads to a better implementation of these functionalities.

1.2   Foundations of CSI

Beyond these experiments, all these chapters can also be read as an attempt to better understand CSI and also human cognitive capabilities. This aspect is certainly closer to the core of CSI than the particular experiments which are, most of the time, only a way to assess the plausibility of these more fundamental ideas.

For example, we can read these papers as attempts to propose efficient data representation and manipulation for cognitive tasks. The (nonexhaustive) list would correspond to a correlation matrix, a tensor product, or a holographic memory with distributed or localist representation.

Such a taxonomic approach can be found in chapter 2. There, the classification of a number of CSI papers leads to the extraction of fundamental properties of CSI techniques. It is surprising to note that many papers can be related to relatively few principles that are undoubtedly the underlying logic of CSI.

Another important aspect of this latter work is that it can lead to the definition of a common vocabulary. One of the most important weaknesses of CSI is certainly that many researchers define new terms that were already employed by other authors. It is thus often difficult to make a fruitful cross correlation between related work. Overviews such as Hilario's could thus be a solid foundation to stabilize this essential common lexicon.

The cognitive dimension of CSI is also an important issue in this debate. This aspect was intensively treated in the past (see for example (Sun *et al.* 1992)), but remains a central aspect in this field, as we can see throughout this book. Chapter 4 is centered around this topic and proposes a relation (and even an isomorphism) between CSI models, ranging over a numeric/symbolic spectrum, and cognitive capabilities, ranging over a synthetic/analytic spectrum.

It is worth noticing that other authors in this book explicitly refer to the use of this relation as a justification of their choice of CSI for a particular cognitive aspect. We give here some clear examples. In chapter 6, which proposes a hybrid model of abductive reasoning, justification of the use of CSI techniques is provided by the explicit nature of rules and the implicit nature of explanatory strengths. In chapter 7, the need for both procedural and declarative knowledge justifies the balance of the two for complex cognitive agents and thus the two-level integrated connectionist architecture. The same can be said about chapter 11, where the need for discrete and continuous descriptions leads to the use of symbolic and connectionist formalisms.

2 CONCLUSION

It seems now clear that CSI begins to be a mature domain of Artificial Intelligence. It has been shown many times that CSI models are able to perform tasks out of the reach of purely symbolic or connectionist approaches. More importantly, the correct analysis is, in fact, to understand that CSI can be a better approach for entire domains of Artificial Intelligence. A good example has been given above with natural language processing. When important problems arise, CSI is now naturally considered as an alternative to classical artificial intelligence.

This maturity aspect can also be seen with regard to the funding of research projects. For example, during the IJCAI workshop, it appeared that the Office of Naval Research, the European Communities (with the ESPRIT MIX project), and also Swiss and Italian grants supported some of the presented work. Even if not yet sufficient, as mentioned during the roundtable discussion of this workshop, this funding shows that CSI is now recognized as a serious candidate to handle difficult problems and can now reasonably consider as its next step the development of pre-commercial products.

Not only mature, CSI is also a very active field. Apart from workshops or special issues in journals, many books have also been published in this domain (see for example (Hinton 1990; Sun and Bookman 1995; Kandel and Langholz 1992; Goonatilake and Khebbal 1995; Dinsmore 1992; Honavar and Uhr 1994)) and give a good idea of the state of the art together with more fundamental theoretical aspects. This activity also has another important aspect that can be easily seen during these workshops: researchers in CSI come from very different domains and not necessarily from artificial intelligence. Beyond the richness of the mixture of these different skills and experiences, this is also a good proof that CSI appears as a need in many domains. This intensive activity also means that the near future of CSI will certainly be a crucial step toward its success.

3   FUTURE DIRECTIONS

Now, what is the future for CSI? It is quite usual to say that the hybrid approach is a short-term, technical way to get efficient but not generic systems, whereas the unified approach, although still in its infancy, is potentially more powerful. We can now seriously wonder if this analysis is valid.

On the one hand, we have emphasized that the hybrid approaches are less and less limited to ad hoc models and are now slanted toward generality. We can thus think that the essential role of the hybrid approach is to show the necessity of modular capabilities for most kinds of information processing (including perceptual, spatial, temporal, causal) (Hilario et al. 1994; Gallant 1988; Hendler 1990). On the other hand, the unified approach has recently made important progress (see for example (Edelman 1992; Alexandre and Guyot 1995)) and can now be seriously considered.

In fact, the recent state of the art of CSI also shows that the hybrid and unified approaches are not opposite solutions, as has often been said, perhaps in relation to a classical (and also false) view of connectionist and symbolic artificial intelligence. Rather, as with connectionist and symbolic artificial intelligence, the hybrid and unified approaches are complementary. More precisely, the role of the unified approach is not the same as the role of the hybrid approach summarized above. It rather corresponds to explaining the meeting of symbols with an unified substratum and thus the meeting of the mind with the brain (Dreyfus and Dreyfus 1988).

These unified and hybrid approaches are also not opposite because there are no clear boundaries between these two domains. For example, it is proposed (see chapter 2) to call translational hybrids this intermediate class between unified and hybrid models, compiling or extracting symbolic structures for connectionist processors. Another interesting example is given by the DUAL model (see chapter 11). This model cannot clearly be labeled as unified or hybrid. Both aspects are present in the vertical and horizontal integrations, respectively giving discrete (symbolic) and continuous (neuronal) descriptions. We thus obtain an unified model of hybrid micro-agents clearly showing the complementary properties of both.

Understanding that hybrid and unified approaches are not opposite could avoid a pointless war between the two approaches, as was the case between symbolic and connectionist domains before their complementarity was understood. In any case, this possible war is all the more useless as much needs to be done in the future. Even if CSI results are already impressive at the moment, we must not forget that CSI is potentially useful for most of artificial intelligence domains, thus offering opportunities for numerous unsolved AI problems.

CSI not only has to address difficult classical AI issues increasingly well. It also has to solve internal CSI problems that arose during the genesis of the CSI domain. Among them, learning is a good example, but also one of the most important topics. It is not clear yet that the claim of CSI (combining the advantages of both symbolic and connectionist paradigms) is achieved, as far as learning is concerned. One of the most important steps in the near future will certainly be to explain how learning techniques could be mutually exploited by both kinds of modules.

SUMMARY

This recent work, together with discussions in specialized meetings such as the IJCAI workshop, shows an undeniable progress of maturity and seriousness in the world of CSI. Recent advancements correspond to making more efficient cognitive systems as well as trying to understand connectionist-symbolic integration. They try to solve precise, realistic artificial intelligence problems and to have a lucid view on the status of the CSI domain. This gives an increasingly coherent domain, with a deep consciousness of its very powerful properties but also of all the work that needs to be done in the future to fulfill its tacit contract, to model and understand human cognitive capabilities.

REFERENCES

[Alexandre and Guyot, 1995] F. Alexandre and F. Guyot. Neurobiological inspiration for the architecture and functioning of cooperating neural networks. In *Proceedings of Int. Workshop on ANNs*, pages 24–30, Malaga, Spain, June 1995.

[Dinsmore, 1992] J. Dinsmore, editor. *The Symbolic and connectionist paradigms: Closing the Gap*. Northvale, NJ: Lawrence Erlbaum Associates, Inc., 1992.

[Dreyfus and Dreyfus, 1988] H. Dreyfus and S. Dreyfus. Making a mind versus modeling the brain: Artificial intelligence at a branchpoint. *Daedalus*, Winter:15–44, 1988.

[Dyer, 1995] M. Dyer. Connectionist natural language processing: A status report. In Sun and Bookman [1995], pages 389–429.

[Edelman, 1992] G. Edelman. *Bright air, brillant fire. On the matter of the mind*. Basic Books, 1992.

[Gallant, 1988] S. I. Gallant. Connectionist expert systems. *Communications of the ACM*, 31(2):152–169, February 1988.

[Goonatilake and Khebbal, 1995] S. Goonatilake and S. Khebbal, editors. *Intelligent hybrid systems*. New York: J. Wiley and Sons, 1995.

[Hendler, 1990] J. Hendler. Developing hybrid symbolic connectionist models. In J. A. Barnden and J. B. Pollack, editors, *Advances in Connectionist and Neural Computation Theory: High-Level Connectionist Models*, pages 363–416, Norwood, New Jersey, 1990. Ablex Publishing Corporation.

[Hilario et al., 1994] M. Hilario, C. Pellegrini, and F. Alexandre. Modular Integration of Connectionist and Symbolic Processing in Knowledge-Based Systems. In *Proceedings International Symposium on Integrating Knowledge and Neural Heuristics*, pages 123–132, Pensacola Beach (Florida, USA), May 1994.

[Hinton, 1990] G. E. Hinton, editor. *Artificial Intelligence: Special issue on connectionist symbol processing*, volume 46(1-2). North-Holland, Amsterdam, November 1990.

[Honavar and Uhr, 1994] V. Honavar and L. Uhr, editors. *Artificial intelligence and neural networks : Steps toward principled integration*. Academic Press, 1994.

[Kandel and Langholz, 1992] A. Kandel and G. Langholz, editors. *Hybrid architectures for intelligent systems.* CRC Press, Boca Raton, Florida, 1992.

[Khosla and Dillon, 1994] R. Khosla and T. Dillon. Learning Knowledge and Strategy of a Generic Neuro-Expert System Model. In *Proceedings International Symposium on Integrating Knowledge and Neural Heuristics,* pages 103–112, Pensacola Beach, Florida, May 1994.

[Sun and Bookman, 1995] R. Sun and L. A. Bookman, editors. *Computational architectures integrating neural and symbolic processes : A perspective on the state of the art.* Kluwer academic publishers, Norwell, Massachussetts, 1995.

[Sun et al., 1992] R. Sun, L. Bookman, and S. Shekhar (editors). *Proceedings of the AAAI Workshop: Integrating Neural and Symbolic Processes: the Cognitive Dimension.* AAAI Press, San-Jose, California, July 1992.

ABOUT THE EDITORS

Ron Sun is currently an assistant professor of computer science at the University of Alabama. He received his Ph.D. in computer science from Brandeis University in 1991. Dr. Sun's research interest centers around the studies of intellegence and cognition, especially in the areas of reasoning, learning and connectionist models. He is the author of over 50 papers, and has written, edited or contributed to 8 books, including his recent monograph: *Integrating Rules and Connectionism for Robust Commonsense Reasoning*, published by John Wiley and Sons. He organized and co-chaired the AAAI Workshop on Integrating Neural and Symbolic Processes in 1992 and the IJCAI Workshop on the same topic in 1995. He was the guest editor of the special issue of *Connection Science* on architectures for integrating neural and symbolic processes and the special issue of *IEEE Transaction on Neural Networks* on hybrid models. For his paper on integerating rule-based reasoning and connectionist models, he received the 1991 David Marr Award from Cognitive Science Society.

Frederic Alexandre is a senior research scientist at INRIA-Lorraine/CRIN-CNRS in Nancy, France. He holds a PhD in Computer Science from the University Henri Poincare, Nancy. His dissertation is entitled "A functional modelization of the cortex: the cortical column". He also has one Master's degree in Psychology, one in Physiology and another one in Mechanics. His current research interests concern neurosymbolic integration with a special focus on unified models with biologically inspired architectures and learning rules for network design with application to associative learning, vision, language and reasoning. As a leader of the CORTEX group, Dr. Alexandre is the author of more than 30 papers and has co-chaired the IJCAI Workshop on Connectionist-Symbolic Integration, 1995.

INDEX

Printed and bound by CPI Group (UK) Ltd, Croydon, CR0 4YY

17/10/2024

01775656-0002